CELEBRATING GREATER
KANSAS CITY

BY ARTHUR S. BRISBANE, LAURA MAXWELL SHULTZ,
AND SUZANNE ROBINSON

PROFILES IN EXCELLENCE AND CAPTIONS BY
MICHAEL J. FLYNN AND LINDA KEPHART FLYNN

ART DIRECTION BY
JIL FOUTCH

SPONSORED BY THE GREATER KANSAS CITY CHAMBER OF COMMERCE
AND THE KANSAS CITY AREA DEVELOPMENT COUNCIL

© LAURA MAXWELL SHULTZ

LIBRARY OF CONGRESS CATALOGING-IN-PUBLICATION DATA

Brisbane, Arthur S., 1950- .
    Celebrating greater Kansas City / by Arthur S. Brisbane, Laura
Maxwell Shultz, and Suzanne Robinson ; profiles in excellence and
captions by Michael J. Flynn and Linda Kephart Flynn.
        p. cm. —(Urban tapestry series)
    Includes index.
    ISBN 1-881096-61-0 (alk. paper)
    1. Kansas City Region (Mo.)—Civilization. 2. Kansas City Region
(Mo.)—Pictorial works. 3. Business enterprises—Missouri—Kansas
City Region. 4. Kansas City Region (Mo.)—Economic conditions.
I. Shultz, Laura Maxwell, 1943- . II. Robinson, Suzanne, 1943-
. III. Title. IV. Series.
F474.K25B75 1998
977.8'411—dc21   98-30775

Towery Publishing, Inc., The Towery Building,
1835 Union Avenue, Memphis, TN 38104

PUBLISHER: J. Robert Towery
EXECUTIVE PUBLISHER: Jenny McDowell
ASSOCIATE PUBLISHER: Michael C. James
NATIONAL SALES MANAGER: Stephen Hung
MARKETING DIRECTOR: Carol Culpepper
PROJECT DIRECTORS: Dawn Park-Donegan, Jim Tomlinson,
Glenda Van Meter, Jewell West

EXECUTIVE EDITOR: David B. Dawson
MANAGING EDITOR: Lynn Conlee
SENIOR EDITOR: Carlisle Hacker
EDITOR/PROFILE MANAGER: Susan Hesson
EDITORS: Mary Jane Adams, Lori Bond, Jana Files,
Brian Johnston
ASSISTANT EDITOR: Rebecca Green
EDITORIAL ASSISTANT: Sunni Thompson

CREATIVE DIRECTOR: Brian Groppe
PROFILE DESIGNERS: Laurie Beck, Kelley Pratt, Ann Ward
DIGITAL COLOR SUPERVISOR: Darin Ipema
DIGITAL COLOR TECHNICIANS: John Brantley, Eric Friedl
PRODUCTION RESOURCES MANAGER: Dave Dunlap Jr.
PRODUCTION ASSISTANT: Robin McGehee
PRINT COORDINATOR: Tonda Thomas

CONTENTS

KANSAS CITY IS A CITY WITH A STORY TO TELL. The question is how to tell it. ■ Back in my days as a columnist for *The Kansas City Star*, I realized that storytelling has to reach people where they live. You can't deal with the esoteric. You have to go straight for the jugular. ■ In Kansas City, though, a wise fellow by the name of Jimmy Green once said, "It's so nice to be nice," which is the way his statement is rendered, now that the words are printed on a sign in his front yard at 27th and Benton. Jimmy also had a Tahitian hut in his living room, but I digress . . .

"Being nice," I am trying to say, is part of the Kansas City credo. So you can't really tell stories here by going for the jugular. It's better to begin with the stomach.

I suppose the whole sweep of Kansas City's tale could be seen as stomach-driven. You know, a wretched frontier town lies mired in mud going nowhere, when suddenly the railroad comes along; next thing you know, millions of head of cattle swarm the stockyards, hamburger results, America pays Kansas City money, people move here by the thousands, sophisticates start the opera, and town burghers prep for the 21st century.

That kind of thing. ▶

Each year from Thanksgiving through the holiday season, the **Country Club Plaza** is decorated with more than 175,000 colored lights—60 miles of Santa reds, toy soldier blues, and fire-flame yellows. But Kansas City jazz shines throughout the year, at myriad nightspots like the **Phoenix**, a downtown music club.

BY ARTHUR S. BRISBANE

But the story is better told (and at much greater length) through the lives of the people who have made their mark here. Fortunately, some of them made their mark with food. So we will, after all, begin there.

Once upon a time in Kansas City, there was a boy named Larry "Fats" Goldberg, who loved his milk shakes and a lot of other foodstuffs. As a lad in a midwestern city where gravy means hogfat with flour in it, Fats absorbed much of what the town had to offer and yet yearned for more.

So he went to New York City. Yes, I *am* beginning my story with a fellow who grew up here and left town the first chance he got. But I *do* have a purpose, so stick with me.

In New York in the 1970s, Fats founded a chain of pizza parlors and grew rich beyond his dreams. He also grew heftier and, being an entrepreneur, capitalized on that, too. He wrote a diet book called *Controlled Cheating*.

The whole premise of Fats' book was that you could lose weight and still binge on food. Fats was a genius. He was a Kansas Citian who could beat New Yorkers at their own game, then sell them the game, then sell them the instructions to the game. Having achieved all

a person could, Fats returned to Kansas City in the 1980s, triumphant, and resides here once more.

We are still waiting, though, for the return of Calvin Trillin, which we consider inevitable and, frankly, overdue. Like Fats, Calvin grew up here in the 1940s and 1950s and went east to take advantage of the gullible people in New York.

Calvin went to work for the *New Yorker*, apparently hoping that the magazine title would help his friends remember where he had moved. As a writer for that publication, Calvin achieved fame and fortune. But though he dealt with many of the great issues of his time, he often returned to his favorite subject: Kansas City's food, specifically barbecue.

Calvin, it should be understood, started the world-wide publicity campaign on behalf of Kansas City barbecue. He did it—somehow—by foisting on the sophisticated readership of the *New Yorker* a surprising number of references to barbecue joints he had visited when he was too young to worry about the effects of hogfat.

But those New Yorkers bought it and Calvin got rich. Plus, everyone now knows about Kansas City barbecue and, finally, we have a tourist attraction. ▶

Kansas City took root just south of the Missouri River, giving rise to City Market, which still flourishes today for both produce vendors and enthusiastic customers.

The first sign, in my experience, that Kansas City barbecue was going to be a major tourist attraction appeared in 1979 when the president of the United States dropped by Arthur Bryant's.

Mr. Bryant was still alive back then, and the place was clearly the barbecue capital of Kansas City. That was before Calvin's campaign fueled the massive barbecue expansion that produced many, many pretenders to Mr. Bryant's throne.

Mr. Bryant used to say that the key to barbecue was the grease. And, when visiting his place, you could see that he really lived his philosophy. Not only did the french fries soak through multiple layers of butcher paper, but a patron's trip from register to table was extremely perilous because of Mr. Bryant's apparent belief in the efficacy of hogfat as a floor wax.

At any rate, it was to this shrine that Jimmy Carter made his pilgrimage in 1979, accompanied by a phalanx of Secret Service and media. The president offered

deferential comments to Mr. Bryant and sat down to a plate, as I recall it, of beef.

Beef. Well, there it is. Beef is a topic you really need to deal with if you are going to tell the story of Kansas City.

Richard Rhodes, the Kansas Citian who won the Pulitzer Prize for his book *The Making of the Atomic Bomb*, completely overlooked beef when he wrote his scathing *Harper's* magazine essay on Kansas City called "Cupcake Land," a reference to the suburban homogeneity that has grown all around Kansas City. And Richard paid the price for the oversight.

So powerful was the response to his analysis of Kansas City's 1980s suburbia that Richard was forced to move to New England. His thesis—that Kansas Citians had grown bland in their sleepy subdivisions—failed to account for the rawboned, beefy qualities that marble the character of this great city.

It's a mistake I don't plan to make. ▶

You might call it "Barbecue City," considering the popularity of the smoked meat in these parts. In 1979, President Jimmy Carter devoured his share at Arthur Bryant's (ABOVE), one of the city's nearly 100 barbecue restaurants. Connoisseurs can also chow down at a host of barbecue contests, fairs, festivals, and other special events.

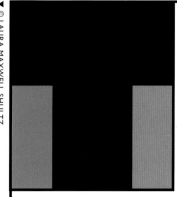

O GIVE BEEF ITS DUE, YOU NEED TO GO BACK, WAY back, to the origins of Kansas City. In 1838, a man known as One-Eyed Ellis presided over a meeting of 14 members of a new town company that had acquired more than 250 acres on the south shore of the Missouri River near its confluence with the Kansas River. ■ Old One-Eyed was the closest thing to a notary in these parts back then. And he was said to be a reliable witness if you caught him early enough in the morning.

With One-Eyed keeping close watch on things, the group set to the task of naming the new town. A member of the company, Abraham Fonda, argued vociferously for Port Fonda, but was shouted down. Another company man suggested Rabbitville, but, fatefully, he too was shouted down. Another—it might have been the famous mountain man Captain William L. Sublette—proffered Possum Trot, and, yes, was also shouted down.

In the end, the group settled on Town of Kansas, after the nearby river and Indian tribe.

It was a miserable decision. Some 160 years later, we have two Kansas Citys (one in Kansas and another in Missouri), and there isn't a visiting celebrity who fails to say while on stage in Missouri that it's "certainly a pleasure to be here in Kansas."

I'm blaming old One-Eyed. Even at the time, the town company members had a bad feeling. John C. McCoy was quite pessimistic about the town he had just founded and dismissed the idea that it would amount to anything more than "the idle vaporings of a demented intellect." ▶

Locals continue to debate about whether today's Kansas City isn't still a cow town after all. The evidence often speaks for itself, in the area's steak houses, rodeo events, and annual cattle drives (albeit dramatically smaller than in the olden days).

But McCoy, you see, also had failed to reckon with beef. You can't blame him though. Back then, all you could see were shacks, forests, and thousands and thousands of beaver pelts.

The truth is, the Town of Kansas (later commissioned Kansas City) didn't amount to much before the cattle came. It wasn't until the Hannibal bridge was built in 1869 that the railroad network could make Kansas City America's gateway to the hamburger.

Boston money men financed the founding of the cattle yards. Then the cowboys, the Armours, and the Swifts turned the old bottomlands not far from One-Eyed's shack into a sprawling marketplace unmatched west of Chicago.

Thus, the city's first really big business had started, and everything else flowed from there. The railroads and packing houses brought thousands of jobs and money for magnates.

While the aristocratic likes of Kersey Coates built mansions on the high ground overlooking the rivers, the

CELEBRATING GREATER KANSAS CITY

broad-shouldered Pendergast brothers, Jim and Tom, began their people's empire down in the flats where the Irish, Italian, Mexican, and Slavic immigrants got their start.

Beef, as things would turn out, begat much of what we think of as Kansas City today—a lot of business, a lot of politics, a lot of fine art (I'll explain this connection later), and a whole lot of chicken. People, you see, needed a respite from beef, and so Kansas City became a chicken capital, too.

Panfried purveyors, like Chicken Betty Lucas and Kansas City's two extremely popular Stroud's restaurants, grew famous on their chicken delicacies, thanks in no small part to Calvin Trillin, who touted fried chicken when he wasn't touting other fatty foods.

John Agnos also made his mark with chicken, albeit indirectly, by creating the link between Kansas City's meat industry and Kansas City's jazz.

Agnos was a Greek immigrant who owned horse-drawn buckboard wagons that plied the busy streets of Kansas

The *Bull Mountain* sculpture (OPPOSITE TOP) and the *Bull Wall* (BELOW) both stand sentinel near Kemper Arena, where the Kansas City stockyards once processed the most beef of any U.S. market. By the 1990s, however, the last of the stockyards were closed, marking the end of an era for this midwestern crossroads.

BIRD
CHARLES
PARKER
AUGUST 29, 1920
MARCH 12, 1955

City during the jazz heyday here in the 1920s and 1930s. Agnos offered his customers a diverse menu that included pork tenderloins, fish, pig snoots, hot dogs, brain sandwiches, and Limburger cheese.

Agnos also sold chicken. And, legend has it that a young saxophonist named Charlie Parker ate so much of it that his friends started calling him Bird. The rest, as they say, is history.

Parker would go on to worldwide fame, along with many other Kansas City jazz greats—names like Count Basie, Jay McShann, Big Joe Turner, Lester Young, and many others. Agnos did not, but his chicken helped nurture a talent that solidified Kansas City as a jazz capital. You can look it up at the Jazz Museum at 18th and Vine—the new shrine to Kansas City's greatest contribution to American culture. ▶

How influential was Charlie "Bird" Parker? Jazz aficionados continue to visit his Kansas City grave to pay tribute to one of music's great innovators, who died in 1955 (OPPOSITE). The city's jazz creativity lives on today through musicians like Queen Bey, who frequently shares her talent in venues all over town (ABOVE).

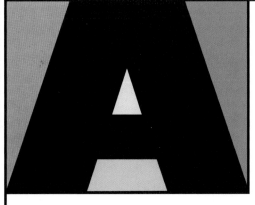

AS IMPORTANT AS CHICKEN WOULD BECOME in the story of Kansas City (not to mention jazz), it was probably not the most significant outgrowth of the city's early beginnings in beef. ■ Beef set the stage for a lot of things in Kansas City, giving rise eventually to a remarkably broad and stable local economy. The gross regional non-beef product (GRNBP) today includes huge contributions from the telecommunications, transportation, greeting card, automotive, financial services, engineering, pharmaceutical, and printing industries, not to speak of the very large federal government presence here that employs nearly 30,000 people.

In fact, Kansas City's economy has evolved so nicely that we've gotten a bit cocky about it. We've branded ourselves the Heart of America. Our economic development experts market us as the Smart Cities. We tell people we have the nicest and hardest-working people in the entire country. We tend to go on and

In its early days, Kansas City huddled close to the Missouri River, slowly creating a vibrant downtown just south of the tributary fondly called the Muddy Mo (BELOW). Today, the metropolitan area crosses a state line and encompasses 11 counties and more than 140 municipalities. Still, all roads lead to downtown Kansas City, Missouri (OPPOSITE).

on about the great qualities of Kansas City.

And then the NFL play-off season begins, and we have to regroup.

In the 1990s in Kansas City, you have to understand, the Chiefs are the man. Wherever the national anthem is sung in Kansas City, it always ends with the crowd proclaiming this as "the land of the free and the home of the CHIEFS!"

While earlier generations of Kansas Citians struggled to tame the land, fight the great wars, overcome economic privation, and build a strong economy, residents today struggle to reach the Super Bowl. Fortunately, we needn't lose sleep over the Chiefs' annual play-off collapse. There are other things to do.

Such as, watching the Kansas City Royals. After the long spell of no football, the opening of the Major League Baseball season is traditionally a time of optimism and renewal for Kansas City fans.

Our town also offers a growing menu of cultural and entertainment amenities, including new-in-the-1990s riverboat gaming casinos that have made Kansas City something its forebears never envisioned—a regional gambling center.

The community's "winning" alternatives (or losing, depending on how the slots treat you) are too numerous to list, but a few warrant special mention.

Kansas City's unique shopping district, the Country Club Plaza, is an architectural delight that envelops shoppers, diners, and browsers in a Spanish Revival atmosphere created by developer J.C. Nichols in the 1920s.

The metro area's green spaces are so extensive that we are sometimes called a "city within a park." These greenways weave a healthy proportion of nature into the urban settlement that has spread far from its origins near old One-Eyed Ellis' shack.

The arts are strikingly alive, and they are found everywhere in Kansas City. Indigenous jazz and blues live on in clubs all over town. The Kansas City Symphony, the Lyric Opera, the Kansas City Camerata, and other wonderful musical organizations cater to audiences that hunger for classical forms.

And Kansas City is a regional capital of the visual arts. The Kansas City Art Institute, a noted four-year college of art, has peppered the city with creative alumni who produce provocative works for the growing list of galleries around town. The largest of these, the Nelson-Atkins Museum of Art, draws visitors from all over the world—some of them to see the enormous shuttlecocks arrayed on the Nelson's grounds by sculptors Claes Oldenburg and Coosje van Bruggen.

Arguably the cultural center of Kansas City, the Nelson sits atop a promontory once occupied by Oak Hall, the mansion built by William Rockhill Nelson with the proceeds from his most successful enterprise, *The Kansas City Star.* ▶

© SUSAN PFANNMULLER

Never let it be said that Kansas Citians are a placid lot. Come late summer, the Kansas City Chiefs rev up the masses in the area's annual bid for the Super Bowl (OPPOSITE). Kindred in spirit if not in costume, frenzied medievalists dodge and parry every year at the colorful Renaissance Festival in Bonner Springs (LEFT).

Nelson, perhaps more than anyone else, acted on the vision of Kansas City as more than . . . well, more than beef. Arriving in town in 1880, he agitated for civic improvements and galvanized citizens to diversify and modernize a town that was just beginning to emerge from the bottomlands and muddy bluffs.

Time magazine described Nelson as "a volcanic autocrat whose No. 1 tenet was to lead the people. Nelson told the citizens how to build their houses, what to put in their gardens, how to feed their babies, how to cultivate a pleasant voice. He also fought corruption and was Kansas City's greatest booster."

Nelson and his newspaper helped define the politics and conflicts that forged the Kansas City of the future. On one side were moneyed interests that focused their energies on business development in a city that was positioning itself as gateway to the West and Southwest.

On the other side were political factions representing the laboring classes that manned the slaughterhouses, railroad yards, road building crews, and smelting operations of the city. Atop the factions were the Pendergast brothers, whose political machine set the racy tone for Kansas City's jazz age. ▶

Believe it or not, only Rome boasts more fountains per capita than Kansas City. And when it comes to artistic ornamentation, a masterpiece like the Ritz-Carlton fountain in the Country Club Plaza rivals even its Italian counterparts (BELOW). But beauty comes in all forms, as demonstrated by the world-renowned Nelson-Atkins Museum of Art (OPPOSITE), home to one of the most impressive collections of Oriental, European, and American works in the nation.

Ultimately, Nelson's newspaper would align with the moneyed interests against the Pendergast organization. But before that happened, Kansas City enjoyed decades of growth, first fueled by business expansions and then, in the 1930s, by New Deal money from Washington.

The essential character of the community was clearly established by this time. But when native son Harry S. Truman, himself a Pendergast protégé, took the reins of national power toward the end of World War II, Kansas City's idealized image of itself took a clearer shape.

Earthy, self-reliant, plainspoken, hardworking—Truman embodied Kansas City's infatuation with the self-made person.

© DALE MONAGHEN

© WILBORN & ASSOC. PHOTOGRAPHERS

Whether it's Ewing Kauffman, who built a billion-dollar pharmaceuticals business from scratch, or Joyce Hall, who turned his salesman's skills into Hallmark, or John "Buck" O'Neil, the Negro Leagues baseball player who provided the voice of common wisdom for Ken Burns' baseball documentary—whoever it is, Kansas Citians seem to love those who rise from the rank and file.

And Truman certainly was that. As a result, Kansas Citians reflect nostalgically on

the Truman presidency, remembering the entire period through rose-colored glasses. It is recalled as a time when good old midwestern sense ruled the country and, indeed, reached across a world that was busy rebuilding after war. ▶

© HARRY BARTH

Famous Kansas Citians have included everyone from jazz great Count Basie, whose big band was one of the finest of the swing era (OPPOSITE TOP), to baseball legend Satchel Paige of the Kansas City Monarchs (BOTTOM, SECOND FROM LEFT), to Harry S. Truman, the plain-speaking politician from Independence who became the 33rd U.S. president in 1945 (LEFT).

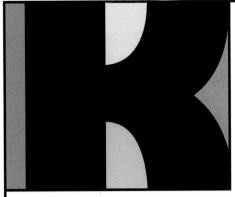

KANSAS CITIANS ARE APT TO FORGET THE GREAT and symbolic event that just preceded Truman's retirement from the scene. I am speaking of the great flood of 1951 that devastated the stock-yards and packing houses—all but wiping beef from Kansas City's economy. ■ The post-beef, post-Truman era has been somewhat more complex than what preceded it. And great questions linger in the air. Are we a cow town? Are we one community or a complex of communities spread over multiple counties and two states? Should we eat less beef and more chicken?

Slowly, we are resolving these matters. We aren't really a cow town anymore, but rather an agribusiness capital and a well-diversified regional center. We should not eat less beef, just more chicken and considerable amounts of pork—or at least enough to maintain our barbecue infrastructure.

And, yes, we are one community. Though Kansas City has spread out into what Richard Rhodes lamentably named Cupcake Land, it has in recent years regrouped as a single, more-or-less-unified entity. Kansas Citians' desire to stand as one was clearly revealed in 1996 when voters approved a bistate cultural tax to fund the reconstruction of Kansas City's greatest physical structure, the Union Station train depot. Taxpayers on both sides of the state line agreed that we share mutual interests and that we are all willing to reach into our pocketbooks to defend them.

The train station will become home to Science City, an interactive science museum, when construction is completed at the turn of the century. It's also likely to become a transportation hub that will knit together the far-flung community that started so many years ago at old One-Eyed Ellis' shack.

This seems fitting—that a railroad depot should, once again, be a symbol of where Kansas City is heading. A century and a quarter ago, the trains signaled the beginning of Kansas City's first great economic enterprise in beef. Now Union Station is slated to become a center for the scientific education of future generations.

Which is yet another indication, I guess you could say, that we've come a long way. But one thing hasn't changed—we're still eating barbecue. ■

The Country Club Plaza's tallest tower is a 130-foot replica of the famous Giralda in Seville, Spain (OPPOSITE). In fact, the structure overlooks a virtual outdoor museum, which includes monumental fountains, statues, and tile murals representing more than $1 million in artwork. The plaza was developed in 1922, eight years after the opening of Union Station (BELOW).

CELEBRATING GREATER KANSAS CITY

CELEBRATING GREATER KANSAS CITY

KANSAS CITY'S MAJESTIC Union Station was once the quintessential gathering place, both for travelers crisscrossing the country and for locals who came to dine in its restaurants and soak up its at- mosphere. Opened in 1914, the station was designed by re- nowned Chicago architect Jarvis Hunt in a classical Beaux Arts style and has been listed on the National Register of Historic Places since 1972.

CELEBRATING GREATER KANSAS CITY

CLOSED TO PASSENGER traffic in 1983, a newly revitalized Union Station is scheduled to open in late 1999, welcoming generations of new visitors to its historic halls. Under the watchful eye of the non-profit Union Station Assistance Corp., this architectural treasure will become Science City, an activity-based museum featuring some 40 exhibits.

CELEBRATING GREATER KANSAS CITY

O VER THE YEARS, KANSAS City's rivers have been critical to the region's growth and success. The Missouri River Queen (OPPOSITE) offered dinner and dancing with a skyline view until it was sold in late 1997, leaving the area without an excursion boat for the first time since 1947. The waters still run deep, however, for the solitary barge captains who ferry their craft up and down the Mighty Mo.

DURING THE SUMMER months, the colors change rapidly at City Market, depending upon what's in season (PAGES 38-41). Farmers bring in the freshest crops—from oranges to onions, peppers to watermelon—for display and hopeful sale to eager buyers from around the region.

THE CITY MARKET HAS BEEN bustling since its earliest days, when pioneers arrived on steamships to purchase supplies for the long journey west. Today, the market is an urban gathering place, complete with shops, restaurants, and the Arabia Steamboat Museum.

A collection of perfectly preserved frontier supplies from the steamship *Arabia* that sank in the Missouri River in 1856, the popular tourist site is operated by Bob Hawley and his sons David and Greg, three of the steamboat's discoverers (ABOVE).

KANSAS CITY ARCHITECTURE is some of the most engaging in the country, as seen in the neo-Palladian Folly Theater, originally a burlesque house (TOP), and Union Station, once the third-largest rail station in the country (BOTTOM LEFT). Another local treasure, the former New York Life Building (BOTTOM RIGHT), was at one time Kansas City's tallest skyscraper. Today, the structure's two-ton bronze eagle, with its impressive, 12-foot wingspan, still holds court from atop the main entrance (OPPOSITE).

I N 1927, LOEW'S BUILT THE elegantly ornate Midland Theatre for $4 million, marking a new, more modern day for moving pictures in the city. No longer a venue for film, the 2,800-seat facility, which is listed on the National Register of Historic Places, is home to several performing arts groups. The Midland today stands in the shadow of the skyline's tallest monument to contemporary architecture, the 42-story One Kansas City Place.

AMONG THE METRO AREA'S artistic riches are the bas-reliefs of Liberty Memorial (OPPOSITE). In 1919, Kansas Citians raised more than $2 million in 10 days to pay for the structure, which honors those who fought and died in World War I. City Hall, built during the Great Depression, offers its own collection of art deco details, including this portrayal of the solid work ethic that still influences the community today (ABOVE).

ALTHOUGH POLITICIAN Thomas J. "Boss Tom" Pendergast had questionable ethics, Kansas City owes a debt of gratitude to the former leader of the Jackson County Democratic Club. Amid the Great Depression, Pendergast managed to acquire funds to construct public buildings that are true art deco treasures. Among his contributions are City Hall (OPPOSITE) and the ornate Municipal Auditorium (ABOVE).

AN ART DECO SENSATION, the Kansas City Power & Light Company Building, completed in 1931, puts on its finest show at night, when floodlights draw the eye toward the tower's six-story crown (OPPOSITE). More recent signage has contin- ued the art deco call, from the Main Street entrance of the 96,000-square-foot Town Pavilion shopping complex (LEFT) to the recently renovated Fine Arts Theatre in nearby Mission (RIGHT).

IT WAS A CONTROVERSIAL move when, in 1994, a $130 million expansion of H. Roe Bartle Hall incorporated four, 200-foot-tall concrete pylons topped with artist R.M. Fischer's distinctive sculptures. The pylons support a series of cables that suspend the convention center's ceiling, allowing for an unusually wide expanse of columnless meeting and event space.

CELEBRATING GREATER KANSAS CITY

HOME OF
AMERICAN ROYAL

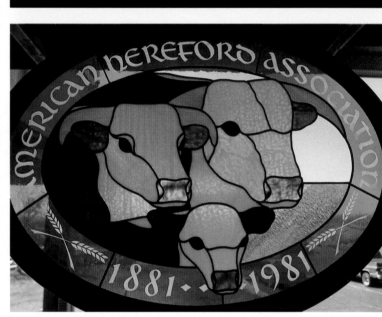

MERICAN HEREFORD ASSOCIATION
1881 · 1981

NO MATTER HOW SOPHISTI-cated it becomes, Kansas City retains its cow town past, and nowhere is that more evident than in the former American Hereford Association Building—where the tenants may change, but the massive bovine on top stays put (LEFT). Further proof of the city's stockyard past lives on in the West Bottoms, once home to a thriving beef industry. Today, American Royal, promoter of an annual livestock exhibition, horse show, and rodeo, maintains a strong presence in the area (TOP RIGHT).

ALTHOUGH MUCH OF THE West Bottoms today has deteriorated into piles of old brick, some of the finer crafts like saddle making still thrive. Jay B. Dillingham, legendary veteran of the Kansas City Livestock Exchange, still maintains a careful watch over the area's activities (BOTTOM LEFT).

E ach fall, the American Royal Livestock, Horse Show & Rodeo takes over in Kansas City, showcasing the town's historic past as a crossroads of the cattle industry. In addition to bronco bustin' and cattle ropin', the event includes the American Royal Barbecue Contest, which attracts competitors from across the country; a parade that travels through downtown; world-class horse shows and livestock judging; and musical entertainment.

Celebrating Greater Kansas City

SINCE ITS OPENING IN THE West Bottoms in 1974, the Helmut Jahn-designed Kemper Arena has attracted a variety of concert and sporting events, including University of Kansas basketball and the women's NCAA Final Four.

WITH BASKETBALL TEAMS from several area colleges to emulate, kids all across the city fly to the goal, hoping to hear the sweet swooshing sound of ball meeting net.

CELEBRATING GREATER KANSAS CITY

W E LIKE TO PLAY, WE LIKE to win, and we like to have fun in the process. At least that's the spirit in Kansas City, from football players at Blue Valley North High School (OPPO- SITE TOP) to a trio of women boxers (OPPOSITE BOTTOM) to these suds-oriented hops—er hoops—players on the streets of downtown (ABOVE).

Kansas City's Latino community has its roots in the opening of the Santa Fe Trail. Now concentrated in the West Side neighborhood, local Hispanic culture comes alive through area shops and building murals, and in more official ways, as well.

DIEGO RIVERA
"Dia de muertos"

FRIDA KAHLO
"Autoretrato"

CELEBRATING GREATER KANSAS CITY

Celebrating Greater Kansas City

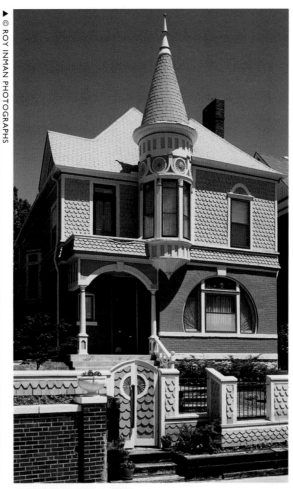

HOUSING CHOICES ABOUND in Greater Kansas City, from the large, upscale homes of Briarcliff West (OPPOSITE TOP) and Mission Hills (OPPOSITE BOTTOM), to row houses on Quality Hill (TOP LEFT), "painted ladies" in the Northeast district (TOP RIGHT), and early-20th-century homes in Westport (BOTTOM).

THE FACES OF KANSAS CITY reflect a melting pot of traditions and cultures that give the area its cosmopolitan air, with wide-ranging influences from Asia, India, the Pacific Islands, Europe, and the Americas.

CELEBRATING GREATER KANSAS CITY

THROUGHOUT THE METRO-
politan area, ethnic festivals
provide opportunities galore to
celebrate cultures from around
the world. The demure move-
ments of a group of young
señoritas at a local Cinco de
Mayo festival (OPPOSITE) stand in
contrast to the buoyant bell
ringing of this German-inspired
lad at the annual Lee's Summit
Oktoberfest.

Celebrating Greater Kansas City

RADITIONAL CELEBRATIONS give Kansas Citians a chance to kick up their heels. Dancers at the Lee's Summit Oktoberfest (OPPOSITE TOP), maidens at the Renaissance Festival in Bonner Springs (OPPOSITE BOTTOM), and students at Pembroke Hill School's May Day festivities (LEFT) all enjoy the thrill of a moment spent in another place and time.

CELEBRATING GREATER KANSAS CITY

'LORDS AND M'LADIES, 'tis time for Kansas City's annual Renaissance Festival, where you'll have the chance to brandish a lance, sing with roving minstrels, and catch the eye of a dashing, armor-clad knight.

IN 1925, THE DIVISION commanders of the Union and the Confederacy came together to honor the 61st anniversary of the Battle of Westport, which was fought in October 1864 (RIGHT). While the real heroes of the Civil War are long gone, reenactments of the conflict's major battles are still popular in the region.

From another front and a different century, the returning throng of World War I veterans was feted by a lavish parade up Grand Avenue in 1919 (PAGES 80 AND 81). City fathers installed a temporary arch for the occasion, and decorated the Emery Bird Thayer Dry Goods building with a giant flag.

"Union of the Blue and the Gray."
Division Commanders
Alfred Zartman   A. A. Pearson.

DEDICATION OF THE LIBERTY MEMORIAL
KANSAS CITY, MO.   NOV. 11TH, 1926
ARMISTICE DAY

I T WAS A PROUD DAY WHEN President Calvin Coolidge came to Kansas City in 1926 to dedicate the Liberty Memorial, which features a museum at its base to house World War I memorabilia (PAGES 82-85). Today, the structure is slated for refurbishing, and Kansas City's two oldest WWI veterans, Wil Vrana and Elmer Rasch (OPPOSITE BOTTOM), are among the many supporters who have emphasized the importance of the monument.

IN HO

F THOSE WHO SERVED IN THE WORLD WAR
ENSE OF LIBERTY AND OUR COUNTRY

DEDICATED · NOVEMBER · 1 · 1921
IN THE PRESENCE OF
MARSHAL FOCH · ADMIRAL BEATTY · GENERAL PERSHING
GENERAL DIAZ · GENERAL JACQUES
VICE PRESIDENT CALVIN COOLIDGE
ROBERT ALEXANDER LONG
PRESIDENT OF THE LIBERTY MEMORIAL ASSOCIATION
GUESTS OF THE AMERICAN LEGION

TRIBUTES TO VETERANS OF both foreign and domestic conflicts abound in Kansas City, home to the VFW national headquarters since the late 1920s. Also honored are the Buffalo Soldiers (RIGHT), members of an African-American regiment that helped tame the West. A monument to their service is located in nearby Leavenworth.

Celebrating Greater Kansas City

ET IN THE CENTER OF THE nation, Kansas City attracts bigwigs looking for votes and influence. During his long tenure in the U.S. Senate, Kansan Bob Dole often called on his local constituents (OPPOSITE TOP), and President Ronald Reagan was another popular visitor (OPPOSITE BOTTOM). South African Bishop Desmond Tutu brought his anti-apartheid message—which won him a Nobel Peace Prize in 1984—to the University of Missouri-Kansas City (TOP), and Bill Clinton—seen here with Kansas City, Missouri, Mayor Emanuel Cleaver and his wife, Dianne—has been a frequent caller throughout his presidency.

LOCAL POLITICIANS FIND plenty of ways to make their mark on the metropolitan area. On the Kansas side, Carol Marinovich was the first woman elected mayor of the Wyandotte County seat (TOP). Her counterpart on the Missouri side is Mayor Emanuel Cleaver, a Methodist minister and the first African-American to assume the post (OPPOSITE). Cleaver was voted in after former Mayor Richard L. "Dick" Berkley stepped aside following 12 years in office (BOTTOM).

CELEBRATING GREATER KANSAS CITY

COOLING OFF YOUR DOGS is often a necessity on those festival-rich last days of summer, which count among their numbers the annual Kansas City Spirit Fest in Penn Valley Park. Following an almost guaranteed day of scorching temperatures, the night sky plays a black velvet canvas to exploding sprays of fireworks magic as the annual celebration draws to a close.

THE DAYS MAY BE HOT FROM June through August, but that never slows these girls of summer. Kids can enjoy the area's many public lakes, cool down in the municipal pools, or hit the garage-sale circuit, which runs Thursdays through Sundays each week.

CELEBRATING GREATER KANSAS CITY

THE BLAZING SUN AND HIGH humidity of Kansas City summers can drive heat indexes into the triple digits, but locals— both man and beast—long ago discovered ways to adapt.

ANSAS CITY'S WATERY reputation flows beyond the Missouri and Kansas rivers and its hundreds of public fountains. Sometimes residents take matters into their own hands, whether at the 60-acre Oceans of Fun water park (OPPOSITE) or at a summertime car wash to raise funds for a worthy cause (ABOVE).

PUBLIC AND PRIVATE LAKES keep Kansas Citians watered, recreated, and refreshed from early spring through late fall.

ARKS AND LAVISHLY LAND-scaped boulevards have long been Kansas City trademarks, prompting some to call us a city within a park. Residents frequent the abundant green spaces for a mixture of frolic, fitness, and good old-fashioned family time.

WHETHER THEY'RE CHAS-ing bubbles in the park or blowing their own in a contest at the Lenexa Spinach Festival, Kansas City kids float on fun. The YMCA's Linwood facility is just one of many local spots where organized activities are sure to turn frowns into glowing smiles (OPPOSITE BOTTOM).

CELEBRATING GREATER KANSAS CITY

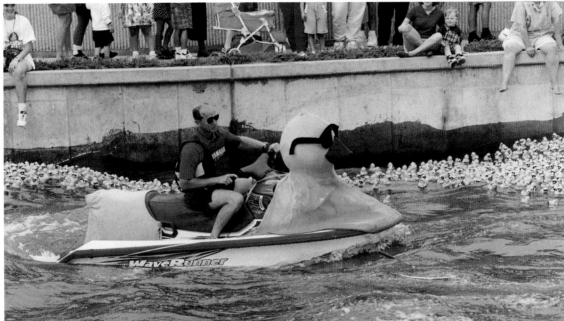

THE AMERICAN CENTURY Duck Derby splashes down the Country Club Plaza's Brush Creek each year to raise funds for a number of charities. Thousands of participants "sponsor" the rubber duckies, which form a flocking flotilla en route to the finish line.

APPARENTLY INTENT ON bringing the kids up properly, portions of Kansas City's duck population seek the spiritual confines of Village Presbyterian Church for a hatching site each spring (RIGHT). A little closer to the heavens, a rooftop at the Burr Oak Woods Nature Center provides these baby birds a lofty haven from their four-legged foes (OPPOSITE).

KANSAS CITY PRESENTS A
wealth of opportunities
for mothers and their children
to learn and play together, from
the annual Take Our Daughters
to Work Day to a training-wheel
spin in the park or a slide across
Crown Center's outdoor Ice
Terrace.

THE HECTIC HOLIDAYS LIGHT up Kansas City, where Crown Center (TOP) welcomes the Mayor's Christmas Tree—among the tallest decorated pines in the nation—and the Country Club Plaza becomes a fairy-tale gingerbread village, iced with more than 175,000 colored lights (BOTTOM). Other twinkling treasures include the glittering tree that rises behind the trademark eagle of downtown's former New York Life Building (OPPOSITE BOTTOM).

KRIS KRINGLE MAY NOT BE listed in the local telephone directory, but come November and December, the bearded bagman pops up all over town. Even longtime restaurant owner Maxine Byrd (TOP) likes to get in on the act, despite stiff competition from Kansas City's official Santa, Dick Conklin (OPPOSITE), and a host of other Saint Nicks-in-training (BOTTOM).

SNOW BURIES KANSAS CITY on occasion, and the usual dump-freeze-thaw-slush sequence keeps residents loaded with conversation starters throughout the winter months. But the season brings plenty of beauty, as well, in a snow-covered bridge at the Kansas City Zoo, a cardinal's flight in Fleming Park, or a smiling snowman in Loose Park.

ⓞNE OF THESE THINGS IS not (quite) like the other at the recently renovated and expanded Kansas City Zoo, home to some 1,500 animals and at least one unexpected hybrid (PAGES 118 AND 119).

CELEBRATING GREATER KANSAS CIT

A COMMUNITY ASSET SINCE 1909, the 200-acre-plus Kansas City Zoo today includes the Okavango Elephant Sanctuary, opened in 1994 and modeled after Botswana's Okavango Delta (OPPOSITE). Not far away, graceful flamingos wade through a natural pool of their own (LEFT).

WILDLIFE TAKES ON YET another meaning aboard Kansas City's multiple gambling boats, first approved in 1993. Grand and garish, delightful and draining, these popular riverboats include the Flamingo Hilton Casino (OPPOSITE TOP) and Station Casino (LEFT).

CELEBRATING GREATER KANSAS CITY

Celebrating Greater Kansas City

RELIGIOUS EXPRESSION RUNS the gamut in the metro area, where such familiar services as baptism and confirmation remain an important part of traditional Christian worship. In nearby Olathe, East meets West as Thai Buddhist monks find serenity in their trailer/shrine.

SIMILARITIES ABOUND, EVEN in our differences: As they mark the end of Ramadan, a Muslim mother and daughter mirror the Christian image of Mary and the Christ child from a stained-glass panel at St. Marks Lutheran Church.

MPRESSIVE ARCHITECTURE recognizes few religious boundaries: Kansas City's Temple B'nai Jehuda and its spiraling glass canopy merit attention, (OPPOSITE) as does the striking RLDS world headquarters, home to the Reorganized Church of Jesus Christ of Latter Day Saints (LEFT).

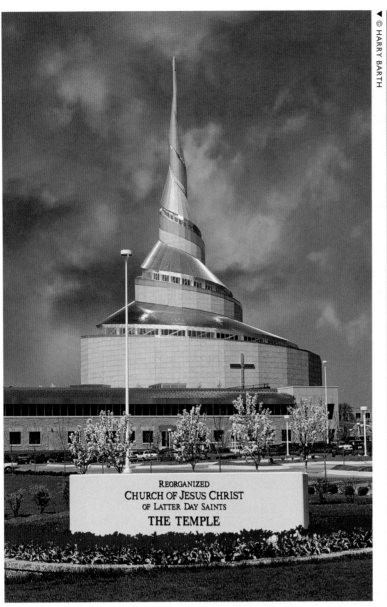

REORGANIZED
CHURCH OF JESUS CHRIST
OF LATTER DAY SAINTS
THE TEMPLE

SINCE 1920, THE RLDS world headquarters has been located in nearby Independence. The church's modern-day facilities include the architectur- ally captivating Temple, inspired by the shape of the nautilus shell, and the 5,800-seat auditorium, which features a 6,334-pipe Aeolian-Skinner organ.

A MULTITUDE OF SPIRES thrust heavenward throughout Greater Kansas City. The illustrious gold-leaf cupola atop the Cathedral of the Immaculate Conception rises along West 11th Street downtown (OPPOSITE). Golden in years if not in patina, the pinnacle of Guardian Angels Church stands watch over the night sky. And from the traditional to the artful, the bell tower of Our Lady of Sorrows Church (BOTTOM LEFT) keeps company with the moon, which is getting a little competition these days from the steeple of light atop Community Christian Church, visible for miles around (BOTTOM).

SIGNS OF THE TIMES CONVEY
a plethora of messages—
both earthly and ethereal.

© DALE MONAGHEN

HEAVENLY SPECTACLES FILL the wide prairie skies over Kansas City. Whether it's lightning bolts snaking across the landscape, the Comet Hale-Bopp shooting over Powell Gardens, or an eclipse glimpsed from the University of Missouri-Kansas City observatory, something sensational is always up.

THE CELESTIAL VERSION CER-
tainly has merit as an item
of natural beauty, but from
ground level, it's hard to beat a
field of golden sun—flowers,
that is (PAGES 140 AND 141).

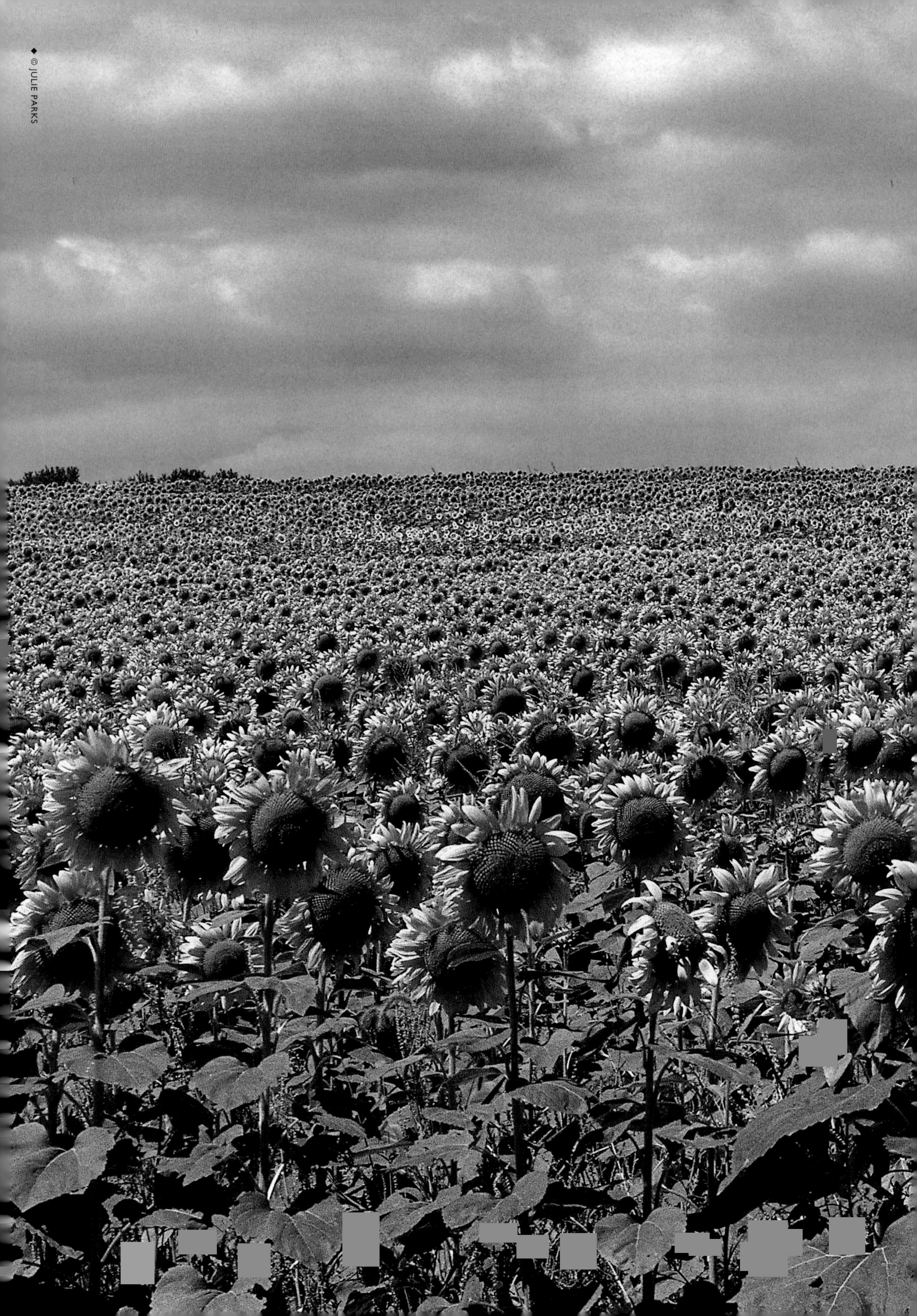

◆ © JULIE PARKS

■N THE LATE 1830S, SETTLERS from Kentucky, Virginia, and Tennessee began planting tobacco in Weston, Missouri, just 40 miles northwest of Kansas City. Though no longer the big business it once was, tobacco farming continues in this one-time agricultural hotbed, where tradition (and tourism) thrive, thanks to the town's 100 antebellum buildings and homes.

ALTHOUGH IT'S GROWN INTO a sophisticated metropolis, Kansas City still nurtures the relationship with its agricultural past, as farms throughout the bi-state area produce everything from soybeans to sorghum.

Even today, ripe wheat is an enduring image of the Midwest, born of decades of sweat, struggle, and hard work by some of the country's most prolific farmers (PAGES 146 AND 147).

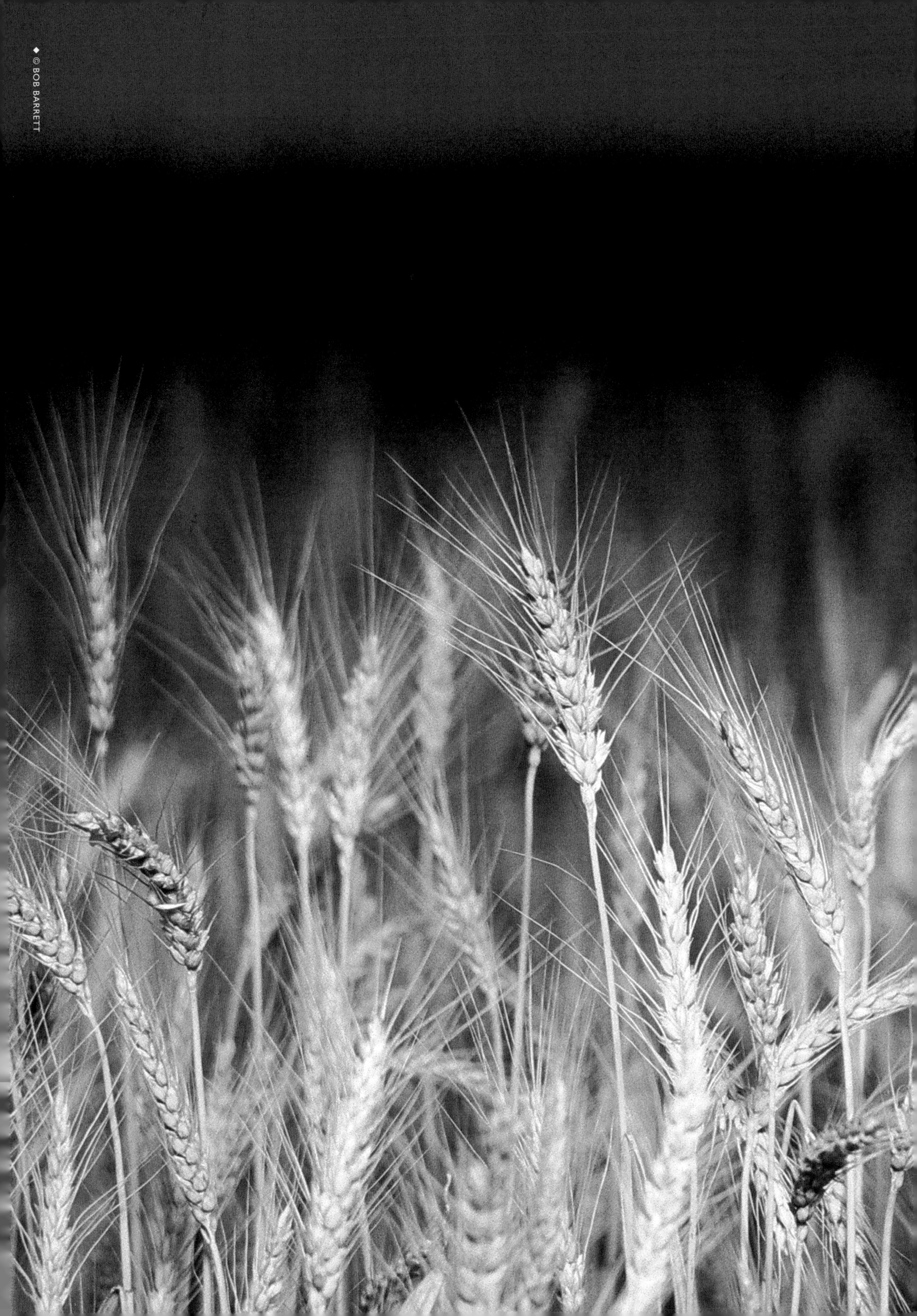

THROUGHOUT THE REGION, evidence of a rural past abounds. Nostalgia buffs can embrace that history through surrey rides at Longview Horse Park (TOP), or a visit to Missouri Town 1855 (BOTTOM), a 30-acre site where period buildings depict life more than a century ago.

GREATER KANSAS CITY CELE-brates its rich cultural heritage in a variety of modern-day museums. The Strawberry Hill Museum and Cultural Center in Kansas City, Kansas, details the lives and history of the Slavic people who immigrated to the area (OPPOSITE). In nearby Fairway, Kansas, the Shawnee Indian Mission State Historic Site highlights the Methodist-sponsored educational services provided to Native American children from 1839 to 1862 (ABOVE).

Names visible on memorial wall:

JOE...
ROBERT S. G...
STEVEN J. GROSSMAN...
ALBERT L. GROSSER...
LARRY X. GUYE...
ROBERT B. HADDEN
JOHN D. HADDEN
BERT A. HALE
MICHAEL E. HAMILTON
GARY L. HAMILTON JR.
MICHAEL L. HANLIN
PATRICK S. HARRIS
DONALD K. HARRIS
JA...

...HIX
...VE D. HIX
...MES M. HOBB...
...L. HODGE...
...HOLROYD
...OLSWOR...
...NCE R...
...ARD E. HO...ER
...HEN J. HONN...R
...EL E. HOPPERS
...S L. HORN
...L. HOSKINS
...HOUSH
...TON
...PETH

Since the first explorers discovered this bend in the Missouri River, people of every sort have joined forces to create today's midwestern metropolis. In downtown Kansas City, Kansas, some 400 members of the Huron tribe lie in peaceful repose at the Huron Indian Cemetery (OPPOSITE TOP). Many of the region's earliest pioneers are buried in historic Union Hill Cemetery (OPPOSITE BOTTOM), while the area's more recent military casualties are commemorated at the Vietnam Veterans Memorial (LEFT).

S THE 33RD PRESIDENT OF the United States, Harry S. Truman has long been Kansas City's favorite son. In 1956, he and other local luminaries broke ground for the Truman Library and Museum (BOTTOM), which stands today as his burial site and a proud monument to his presidency (TOP). Truman's inspiring story was given a Hollywood twist in 1996, when actor Gary Sinise brought the former commander in chief to life in an award-winning TV drama (OPPOSITE RIGHT). Today, Truman mania continues in nearby Independence, where history buffs can view the revered politician's desk and papers at the former Jackson County Courthouse (OPPOSITE LEFT).

Located just east of Kansas City, Independence boasts several historic mansions, including the Victorian-style Truman Home on North Delaware Street (OPPOSITE). Known as the Summer White House during Truman's presidency, the historic abode was occupied by Harry and Bess from the time they married in 1919 until their deaths. The 31-room Vaile Mansion-Dewitt Museum (ABOVE), built by entrepreneur Harvey Vaile in 1881, is considered one of the area's finest examples of the Second Empire Victorian style. The elegant estate is scheduled to be featured in a 1999 edition of A&E's well-known TV program *America's Castles*.

THE GROWTH AND EVOLU-
tion of Greater Kansas City
can be traced, in part, by the
area's architecturally diverse
public buildings. In 1920, for
example, the Jackson County
government operated from this
brick Victorian structure, originally built in Independence in
1836 and expanded five times
during the 19th century (ABOVE).
A modern tribute to the region's
bright future, downtown Kansas
City's newest courthouse was
opened by the federal government in 1998 (OPPOSITE).

THE KANSAS CITY SKYLINE grows more impressive with the years, as new architecture continues to spring up downtown and in the area's once-sleepy suburbs. Although it's all in a day's work, window washers can't help but enjoy the view, whether they're flying high in the city's heart (OPPOSITE AND TOP) or hanging out above Overland Park's College Boulevard.

TALK ABOUT YOUR BIRD'S-
eye view: Kansas City's
working-class daredevils show
no fear in reaching the heights
of their profession.

CELEBRATING GREATER KANSAS CIT

KANSAS CITIANS LOVE THEIR public art, from sculpture in silhouette to fountains before fiery skies. From its perch in Penn Valley Park, the *Pioneer Mother Memorial* honors the spirit of the women who crossed the Great Plains (OPPOSITE, BOTTOM RIGHT), while its neighbor *The Scout* reigns as one of the area's most famous outdoor works (OPPOSITE TOP). In Barney Allis Plaza, a cowboy in the Remington style cracks his whip (OPPOSITE, BOTTOM LEFT), as the *St. Martin of Tours* sculpture atop *William Volker Memorial Fountain* takes its place along Brush Creek at the south end of Theis Mall (LEFT).

CELEBRATING GREATER KANSAS CIT

EVERY COMMUNITY HAS ITS heroes, and Kansas City is no exception. On October 6, 1991, the *Firefighters Fountain* in Penn Valley Park was dedicated in honor of local firefighters who have lost their lives in the line of duty (ABOVE).

FALL INSP.
KANSAS CITY P
OCT. 30, /

RTMENT

A GATHERING OF TODAY'S Kansas City Police Department—some 1,200 strong—would no doubt outnumber this force from 1927, looking shipshape for its fall inspection on the grounds of the Liberty Memorial.

CHILDREN WILL PLAY NO matter what elements await them outside, an axiom that holds true both for little girls and the statues they inspire. Whether experiencing the cold splash of a sprinkler to quell the summer's heat or freezing in youthful repose atop *Children's Fountain*, Kansas City's younger generation finds a way to cope.

KNOWN AS THE CITY OF Fountains, the area counts among its collection the Wheeler Williams-designed *Muse of the Missouri*, who casts her net from the Mighty Mo southward (OP-POSITE), and the Country Club Plaza's *Fountain of Bacchus*, created in 1911 and brought to the city from Worcestershire, England (ABOVE).

SCULPTURE INFUSES THE Country Club Plaza with an aura of gentility. Brought from England in 1911, the Fountain of Neptune, an 8,000-pound, cast-lead rendition of the Roman god of the sea, rises from the waters of an oval pool (OPPOSITE). First cast in 1857 by the Italian artist Benelli, Kansas City's Bronze Boar is one of three reproductions of the piece by the Marinelli Studios of Florence, Italy (TOP). A life-size sculpture of Ben Franklin was donated in 1990 by the Miller Nichols family, developers of the plaza, and is the work of George Lundeen of Loveland, Colorado (BOTTOM).

S ORNATE AND LAVISH as its fountains may be, Kansas City's architectural details show yet another side of the city's face.

CELEBRATING GREATER KANSAS CITY

CELEBRATING GREATER KANSAS CIT

A VISION OF FARSIGHTED entrepreneur J.C. Nichols, the Country Club Plaza took shape as a shopping center before such a thing was even heard of. Designed in the architectural spirit of Seville, Spain, its Moorish influences are reflected in the imported tile and terra-cotta features of the old Plaza Bank Building (OPPOSITE TOP). Opened in 1928, the Plaza Theater (LEFT) drew a packed, predominantly female crowd of more than 2,000 to a meat-cutting demonstration hosted by the Kroger Co., a plaza supermarket resident, in 1948 (OPPOSITE BOTTOM).

Today, new and old mingle harmoniously in the heart of Kansas City as the Country Club Plaza provides a stunning foreground to the twin American Century Towers (PAGES 180 AND 181).

I N KANSAS CITY, ART DOESN'T exist as mere history. Each fall since 1932, the three-day-long Plaza Art Fair has dominated the Country Club Plaza district with juried works from more than 200 artists covering 40 states (OPPOSITE AND TOP). The annual Westport Art Fair attracts its share of autumn crowds with booths set up along Pennsylvania Avenue (BOTTOM).

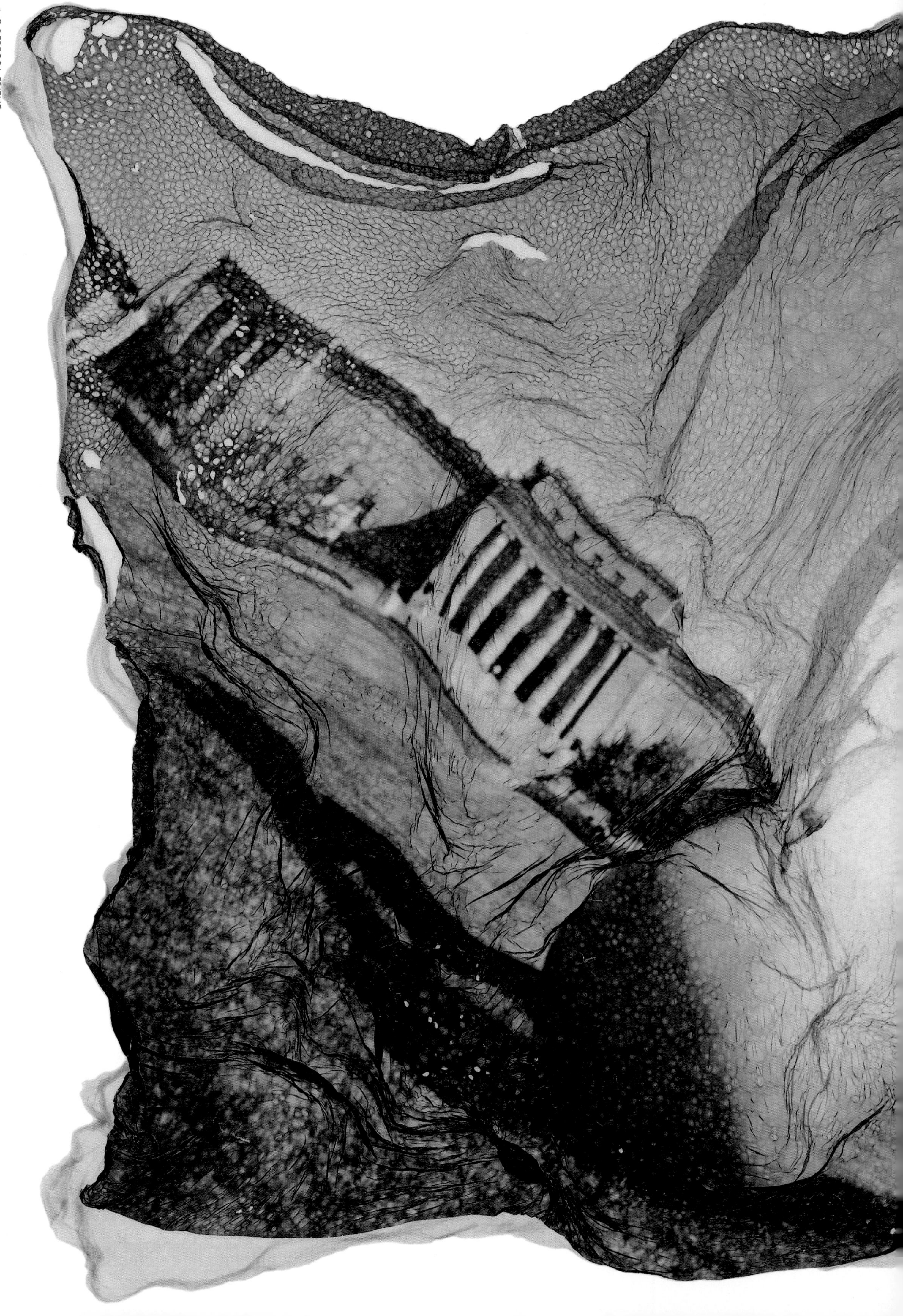

▲ © REBECCA FRIEND

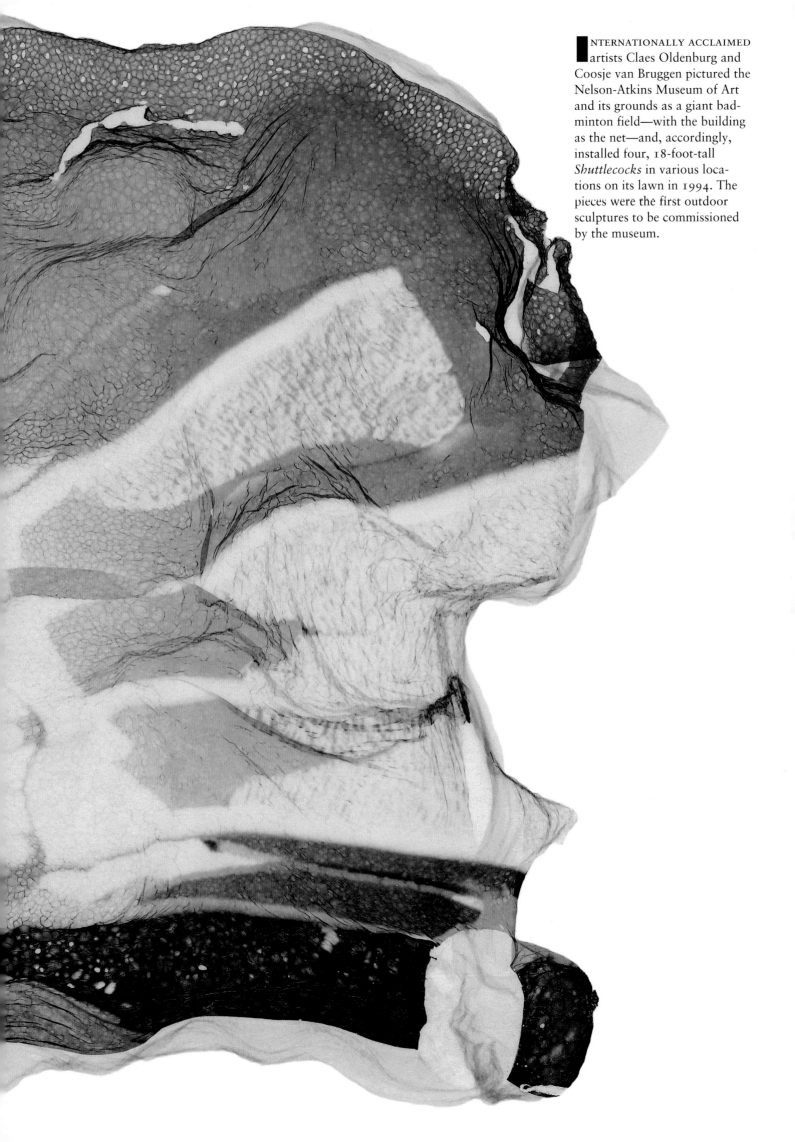

INTERNATIONALLY ACCLAIMED artists Claes Oldenburg and Coosje van Bruggen pictured the Nelson-Atkins Museum of Art and its grounds as a giant badminton field—with the building as the net—and, accordingly, installed four, 18-foot-tall *Shuttlecocks* in various locations on its lawn in 1994. The pieces were the first outdoor sculptures to be commissioned by the museum.

CELEBRATING GREATER KANSAS CITY

THE NELSON HOUSES SOME of the finest works in the nation. Its Henry Moore Sculpture Garden, opened in June 1989, features 13 monumental outdoor pieces by the distinguished British artist, including *Sheep Piece* (PAGE 186, TOP). Inside the facility, Rozzelle Court offers café hospitality in a romantic setting (PAGE 187). Director Marc Wilson presides over it all (PAGE 186, BOTTOM).

ONE OF KANSAS CITY'S most famous and beloved artists was Thomas Hart Benton, whose body of work is represented at the Nelson through such pieces as *Persephone* (OPPOSITE). Benton lived and worked at his Kansas City home and studio from 1939 until his death in 1975.

CELEBRATING GREATER KANSAS CIT

⬤ PENED IN 1994, THE Kemper Museum of Contemporary Art displays permanent and rotating exhibits by internationally acclaimed artists such as Jasper Johns, David Hockney, Robert Motherwell, William Wegman, Georgia O'Keeffe, Willem de Kooning, and Robert Mapplethorpe.

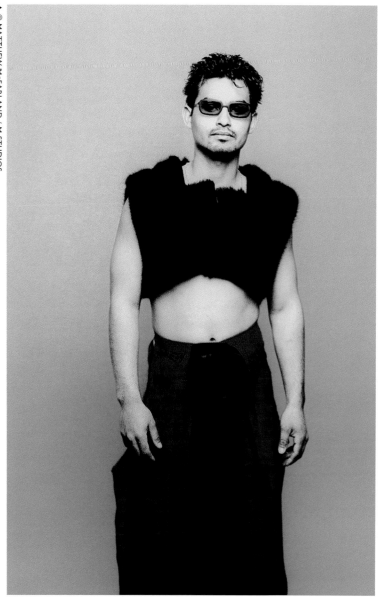

Since its founding in 1885, the Kansas City Art Institute (KCAI) has been a hotbed for emerging painters, sculptors, and other creative types.

Each year, a group of these enterprising virtuosos hold the Beaux Arts festival to model their own aesthetic creations.

CELEBRATING GREATER KANSAS CIT

FROM STUDENT WORKS USING fiber as a medium (OPPO-SITE) to the rounded creations in a circularity workshop (BOTTOM), KCAI's doors constantly open to reveal stunning originality.

IN KANSAS CITY, ART HAS
exceeded the bounds of cultural and educational pursuits
to become an international
business—Hallmark Cards. The
homegrown company employs
the largest creative staff in the
country to produce its greeting
cards, gifts, and other products
(OPPOSITE). Founded in 1910,
Hallmark is today headquartered in Crown Center, an 85-
acre complex filled with two
hotels, 20 restaurants, more
than 70 retail shops, the company's Visitors Center (TOP),
and an outdoor ice-skating
rink (BOTTOM).

CELEBRATING GREATER KANSAS CIT

FALL FOLIAGE PROMISES riotous color across the metropolitan region, from the wide-open spaces of Johnson County, Kansas, to the tree-lined streets of the area's urban neighborhoods.

AUTUMN BRINGS CRISP DAYS
and reasons to play, especially when Halloween rolls around. The annual Boo at the Zoo may lay claim to the season's largest pumpkin (OPPOSITE), but the prize for the most haunting lineup belongs elsewhere (ABOVE).

CELEBRATING GREATER KANSAS CITY

KANSAS CITY IS A PERFORMing arts mecca, counting among its multitude of professional companies the Lyric Opera, which celebrated its 40th season in 1998 (OPPOSITE); the State Ballet of Missouri and its annual presentation of *The Nutcracker* (CENTER); and the Missouri Repertory Theatre, promoting the dramatic arts since 1964 (ABOVE).

THE COMPETITION IS IN-tense, the dancers lithe and graceful, as students at the State Ballet School execute perfect pirouettes and elegant entrechats. Begun in 1981, the Kansas City-based school trains its young charges in the studios of the State Ballet of Missouri, where they can experience firsthand the life of professional dance.

CELEBRATING GREATER KANSAS CITY

I N KANSAS CITY, YOUNGSTERS often find creative expression through movement. While some prefer the more solitary pursuit of classical ballet, others opt for the boisterous camaraderie of the Marching Cobras. Established some 30 years ago, the 180-member drill team is still going strong, as its talented drummers and dancers entertain local, national, and international audiences.

CELEBRATING GREATER KANSAS CIT

KANSAS CITIANS LOVE TO get dressed up, whether it's cotillion time, hosted by the alumnae chapter of Delta Sigma Theta sorority (OPPOSITE TOP), or prom night, celebrated across town at the Country Club Plaza (OPPOSITE BOTTOM). And while the annual Jewel Ball may be one of Kansas City's better known debutante events (TOP), the more mature set finds its own excitement at the John Knox Village retirement community (BOTTOM).

NIGHTLIFE TAKES ON MANY forms in Kansas City. The 18,200-seat Kemper Arena hosts a variety of touring acts each year, among them rapper LL Cool J (TOP). At the Hurricane, a popular nightspot in historic Westport, acts range from alternative rock to solo acoustic guitarists (BOTTOM).

THERE'S PLENTY OF MUSI-cal—not to mention physical—activity on tap at the area's outdoor performance venues. The annual Spirit Fest, held on the grounds of the Liberty Memorial, attracts thousands of enthusiastic revelers each fall (TOP). Some Kansas Citians, however, prefer to get their kicks on the twangy side at such country-and-western hot spots as Westport's Beaumont Club (BOTTOM).

The area is a haven for autograph hounds, thanks to a steady stream of internationally acclaimed performers who always include Kansas City on their itinerary (PAGES 212 AND 213). Over the years, audiences have welcomed (CLOCKWISE FROM TOP LEFT) B.B. King, Tina Turner, Paul Stanley and Kiss, Paul McCartney, Vince Gill, Ray Charles, Buddy Guy, Elton John, and Garth Brooks.

CELEBRATING GREATER KANSAS CIT

CELEBRATING GREATER KANSAS CIT

Duke Ellington wrote an astonishing array of music. Drawing inspiration from African American music, as well as music from Europe, South America, Asia, and Africa, he wrote symphonies, suites, comic operas, and tone poems. He scored films, plays, and ballets. He also composed sacred music. Ellington is credited with over 2,000 compositions.

WHETHER THEY'RE JOINING together in song at Pembroke Hill School (OPPOSITE TOP) or discovering the nuances of stringed and other instruments in the classroom (OPPO- SITE BOTTOM), kids learn that music isn't just for the big names in Kansas City. Area youngsters can also explore local ties to music history at the newly opened Kansas City Jazz Museum, which shares a 55,000-square-foot facility with the Negro Leagues Baseball Museum in the 18th & Vine Historic District (ABOVE).

HOW COMPELLING IS KANSAS City's colorful past? In 1996, director Robert Altman, a local native, took audiences back to 1934 in his epic *Kansas City*.

Filmed on location in the 18th & Vine Historic District, the international release showcased the area's rich jazz heritage and criminal past.

ALTHOUGH COUNT BASIE was modest about his accomplishments, the acclaimed pianist and bandleader helped refine the distinctive swing style that is most often associated with Kansas City music. In 1979, Basie played a crowd-pleasing concert on his 75th birthday in celebration of his long and illustrious career (OPPOSITE). Other local jazz influences include legends Jay McShann, a renowned band-leader since the 1930s, and Claude "Fiddler" Williams, who has played his unique brand of jazz violin for seven decades (ABOVE).

HERE'S JUST SOMETHING so "saxy" about the Kansas City sound, thanks in part to musician Eddie Saunders. One of the area's elder statesmen of jazz, Saunders keeps his cool outside the Mutual Musician's Foundation, a union hall and concert venue that reached its zenith in the jazz heydays of the 1930s and still stands watch over the 18th & Vine Historic District today.

A MURAL IN THE RECENTLY rejuvenated 18th & Vine Historic District pays tribute to Count Basie, who found his footing in the landmark musical neighborhood (TOP). Just as the city's sound has done for years, the riffs of Stan Hegeman's sultry saxophone seemingly stir the beasts to rise (BOTTOM).

© ELI REICHMAN

© DALE MONAGHEN

WHEN IT COMES TO JAZZ, Kansas City still draws the musicians and the crowds with events like the Corporate Woods Jazz Festival, set amid a mixture of trees and office buildings in Overland Park (OPPOSITE). Local favorites, including vocalist Ida McBeth (LEFT), enliven stages across the metro area, from concerts at the Nelson-Atkins Museum of Art (TOP) to the Kansas City Blues & Jazz Festival in Penn Valley Park (BOTTOM).

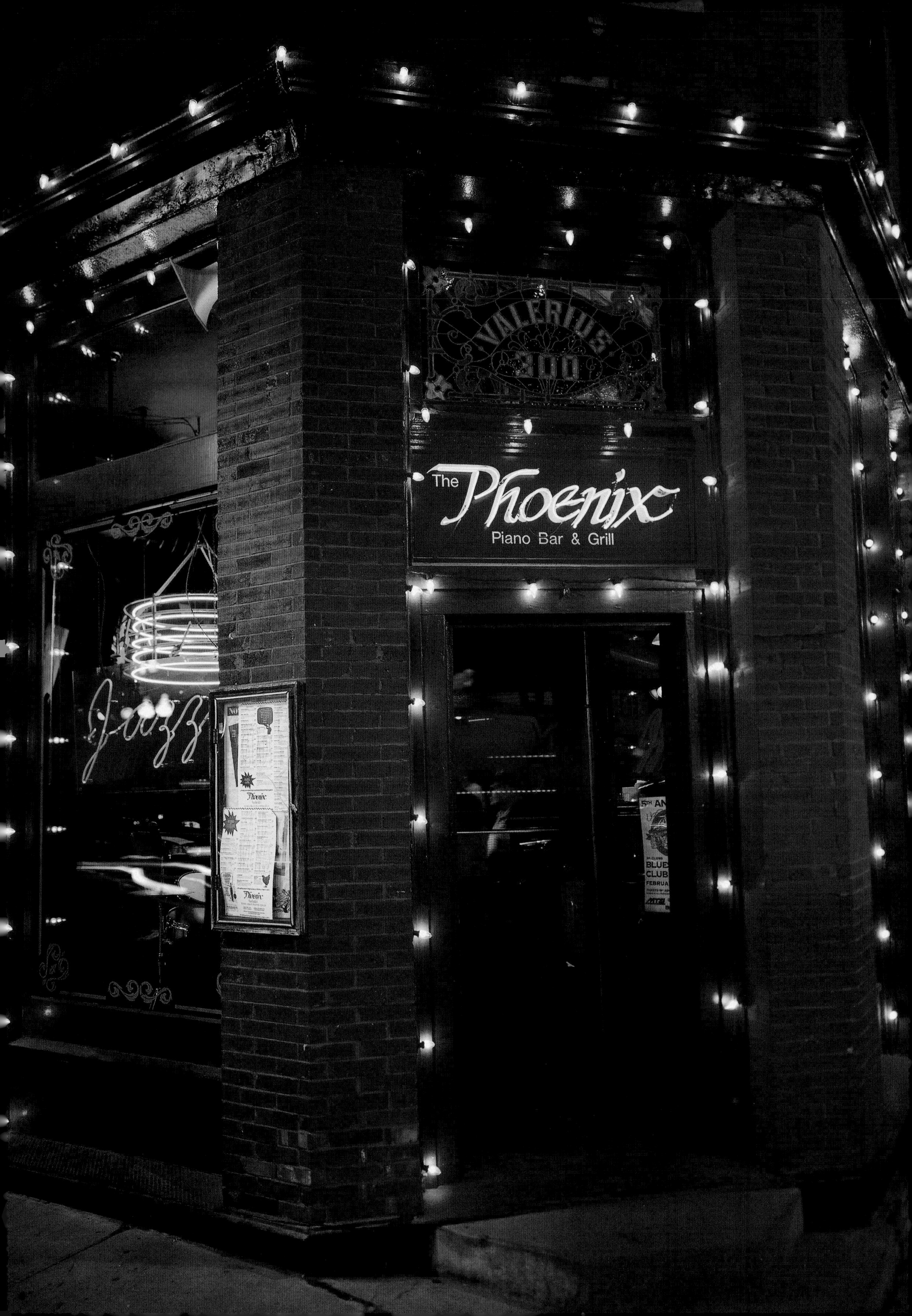
VALERIUS
300
The Phoenix
Piano Bar & Grill
Jazz

THE PHOENIX PIANO BAR &
Grill is a permanent fixture
in downtown Kansas City, successfully drawing top local musical talent and the crowds to
match. Its intimate, old-jazz-club
atmosphere provides the perfect
setting for such performers as
pianist extraordinaire Tim
Whitmer and his K.C. Express.

CELEBRATING GREATER KANSAS CIT

AMODERN-DAY FIXTURE IN the 18th & Vine Historic District, the remodeled and revitalized Gem Theater originally opened in 1912 as a movie house. The storied venue got a hand from local celebrities Queen Bey, Pat Jordan, and Lenny Williams to launch the building's renovation in 1993 (OPPOSITE). During a recent festival, musician Sonny Kenner held court in front of the landmark's gleaming new doors.

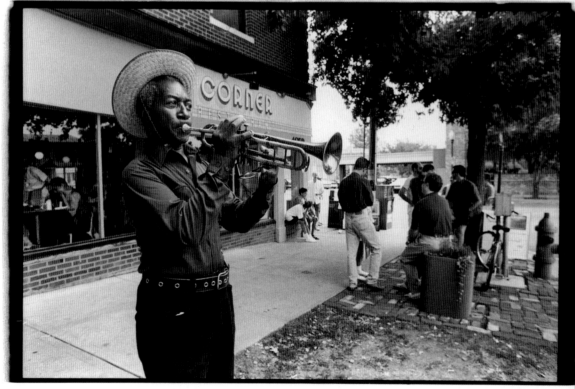

JAZZ GREATS—FROM SAX man Art Jackson (OPPOSITE TOP) to piano man Elbert "Coots" Dye (TOP)—have helpd to keep Kansas City jumpin' no matter how cosmopolitan it gets. Trumpeter Bernard "Step-Buddy" Anderson jammed with the likes of Charlie Parker and Dizzy Gillespie before a bout with tuberculosis in 1944 forced him to the sidelines (OPPOSITE BOTTOM). Determined to keep the beat alive, bassist Milt Abel insisted that his children, Milton Jr. and Chloe, begin learning the trade formally through piano lessons. With that solid foundation in place, the two have moved on to play flute and upright bass—often with their famous father (BOTTOM).

O NE OF KANSAS CITY'S
premier blues clubs,
midtown's Grand Emporium
has hosted everyone from blues
diva Anetta "Cotton Candy"
Washington to harmonica
prodigy Brody Buster.

CELEBRATING GREATER KANSAS CITY

NIGHT AFTER NIGHT, THEY play the clubs, nightspots, and jazz haunts hidden throughout the city. Whether it's a perennial pianist like Oliver Todd (OPPOSITE) or a gregarious guitarist like Gerald Scott (ABOVE), they're Kansas City's working musicians, and the show can't go on without them.

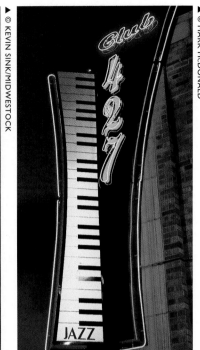

ALL THAT JAZZ: JUST ABOUT any hankering for the sultry sound can be assuaged at nightspots across the city, including Westport's Jazz: A Louisiana Kitchen (OPPOSITE); The Majestic, located downtown (LEFT); the City Market's Club 427 (TOP CENTER); or 18th & Vine's Blue Room (TOP RIGHT).

Whatever message they impart, the bright lights of Kansas City reflect the vibrant nightlife that always keeps your toes tapping and your fingers snapping (PAGES 236 AND 237).

CELEBRATING GREATER KANSAS CIT

CHALK IT UP TO A STRONG working class, early Irish immigrants, or a work-hard/ play-hard mentality, but Kansas City has long loved its pubs, taverns, and other assorted watering holes. Today, downtown's comforting Quaff continues old traditions, rooted in an earlier day when WHB radio announcer Lew Brock (ABOVE, WITH MICROPHONE) broadcast live from another popular drinking establishment.

THE BUILDING THAT HAS housed Kelly's Westport Inn since 1947 is purported to be Kansas City's oldest. Dating to 1837, the neighborhood fixture has operated as a pub for so long now that most locals know it as nothing else. Over the years, business leaders, politicians, and artists—most notably painter Thomas Hart Benton—have all bellied up to the bar, occasionally enjoying impromptu entertainment with an old-world twist.

IRISH IMMIGRANTS CAME to town as laborers, and the city has never forgotten them. Sentiments run so strong, in fact, that St. Patrick's Day is practically an official holiday for many residents. For more than 25 years, the city has hosted what is among the country's largest St. Paddy's parades, drawing close to 200,000 revelers along the two-mile route. The partying inevitably spills over into nearby taverns, like O'Dowd's Little Dublin in the Country Club Plaza.

E LVIS MAY HAVE LEFT THE
building, but he's never
quite left Kansas City. Thanks
to a local radio station, the annual KY Elvis Parade (TOP AND
BOTTOM) has graced downtown's
Barney Allis Plaza for more than
a decade. And with no formal
prompting, the occasional shrine
to the King pops up every now
and then in the city's storefront
windows (OPPOSITE).

LOCAL RESIDENTS MAY NOT have invented doughnuts, coffee, or bagels, but they've certainly made an art form of the tasty treats. Ray LaMar's pastries (RIGHT) have held their own since 1933 against a host of outside competitors, while 1993 marked the beginning of Danny O'Neill's Roasterie, a local business that aims to produce "the best specialty coffee in the world" (OPPOSITE TOP). Bagel & Bagel, now known nationally as Einstein Bros Bagels, also got its start right here in 1983 (OPPOSITE BOTTOM).

CELEBRATING GREATER KANSAS CIT

PLEASE...
ONLY ONE DESSERT
PER PERSON.
Thank "U"

WITH APOLOGIES TO WILL Rogers, few Kansas Citians have ever met a dessert they didn't like. Competitors at a local pie-eating contest prepare to dig in, while one frustrated cafeteria owner, fearing the worst, finally had to draw the line.

CELEBRATING GREATER KANSAS CITY

GOOD FOOD ABOUNDS IN Kansas City, a testament in many cases to the hardworking proprietors behind the counter or in the kitchen. Ruby McIntyre works her culinary magic at Ruby's Cafe and Ruby's Soul Food & Catering, located east of downtown (OPPOSITE). Patrick Weber presides over Westport's trendy new bistro, The Stolen Grill, as chef (TOP). And Mimi Perkins and her son, Victor, make Vietnamese cuisine a family affair at Saigon 39, near the University of Kansas Medical Center.

ARTISTIC EXPRESSION TAKES on many forms in the city's public spaces, with colorful outdoor murals cropping up everywhere, from a city bus (TOP) to downtown's Phoenix Piano Bar & Grill (OPPOSITE TOP). Always eye-catching, their messages range from the informative (BOTTOM) to the declarative (OPPOSITE BOTTOM).

KANSAS CITY
1998 NCAA WOMEN'S
FINAL FOUR

CELEBRATING GREATER KANSAS CITY

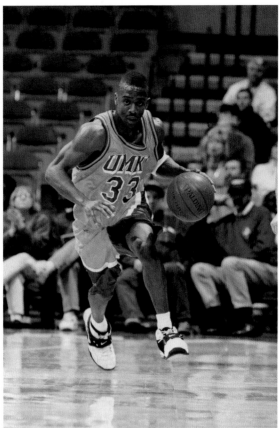

IN KANSAS CITY, THE plethora of professional and collegiate sports teams guarantees something to cheer about year-round. A fixture on the scene since 1996, the Wizards draw legions of loyal Major League Soccer fans to their games in Arrowhead Stadium (OPPOSITE TOP). Indoor soccer made its local debut in 1991 with the Kansas City Attack, members of the National Professional Soccer League (TOP LEFT). Pro golf also puts on a show for links addicts, especially when native Tom Watson comes to town (OPPOSITE BOTTOM). The University of Missouri-Kansas City is just one of the college teams to satiate the city's hoop dreamers (TOP RIGHT). And for fans of the ice, the International Hockey League's Kansas City Blades have been slapping their pucks since 1990 (BOTTOM).

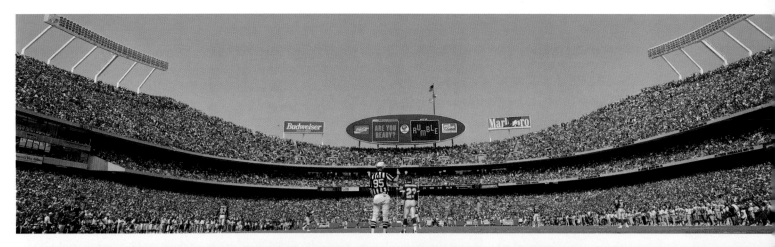

CHIEFS FEVER TAKES OVER Kansas City from late summer to early January. Under the direction of Head Coach Marty Schottenheimer since 1989, the team draws thousands to Arrowhead Stadium on its annual march to victory in the NFL. Many football greats have donned pads for the Chiefs, among them running back Marcus Allen, who was one of the team's most popular players before retiring after the 1997 season (TOP LEFT).

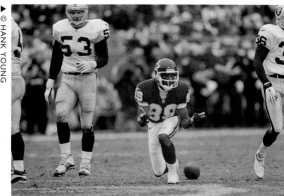

CELEBRATING GREATER KANSAS CIT

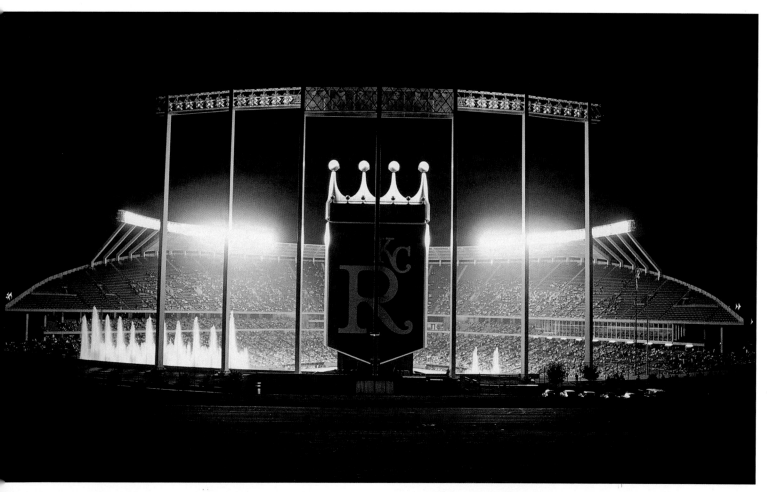

S INCE 1973, THE KANSAS City Royals have been keeping America's pastime alive. With help from players such as Frank White (OPPOSITE, TOP LEFT), currently the team's first base coach, and George Brett (OPPOSITE, TOP RIGHT), the Royals have notched numerous records in baseball history, celebrating in true Kansas City style when they won the World Series in 1985 (OPPOSITE, BOTTOM LEFT). Among the participants in the city's post-series parade were beloved Royals Manager Dick Howser and his wife, Nancy (OPPOSITE, BOTTOM RIGHT). Howser, who managed the team from 1981 through the 1986 season, died of cancer in 1987.

CELEBRATING GREATER KANSAS CIT

© SUSAN PFANNMULLER

EXCEPTIONAL HORSEMAN- ship is alive and well in Kansas City, even though the last real cowboy hung up his spurs decades ago. Today, equestrian excellence is more likely to be seen on the polo field or during fox hunts held by the Fort Leavenworth Hunt Club, which dates from 1835. Whatever the occasion, English riders come in all shapes and sizes.

Celebrating Greater Kansas City

OMPETITION TAKES ON
diverse forms in Greater
Kansas City. From the annual
Head of the Kaw Regatta to
the lively Soap Box Derby All-
American Race, the finish line is
always in sight.

GOOD SCHOOLS, LOW crime rates, and an affordable cost of living have helped give Kansas City a kid-friendly reputation. That standing is sup-ported throughout the year by such activities as the Kid's Run through Brookside (OPPOSITE), a hug from Woodsy the owl, or a thrilling caterpillar ride.

EDUCATION REMAINS A HIGH priority for area students, although learning sometimes takes a backseat to the thrill of summer vacation or the excitement of high school graduation.

All told, Greater Kansas City contains 72 school districts, with more than 20,000 faculty members in 600 schools serving nearly 300,000 students.

ANSAS CITY IS A HAT-
wearin' kind of town,
where tastes can range from the
more traditional at a late fall
Oktoberfest (OPPOSITE TOP) to
the dragon-inspired delights at
the annual Renaissance Festival
in Bonner Springs (OPPOSITE
BOTTOM). Others need only look
to the hometown team for inspiration (LEFT).

THE COLORFUL CURVES OF
a balloon hat make for a
unique sight at Flamingo Hilton
Casino (OPPOSITE), while in the
city's Crossroads district, artist
Stephanie Leedy—the Queen of
Neon—offers unusual twists of
her own at the aptly named
Downtown Neon and Gallery
(ABOVE).

Celebrating Greater Kansas City

THE OPEN SPACES SURROUNDING Kansas City provide plenty of opportunities for locals to exercise their daredevilry. Fortunately for one young practitioner, his preferred instrument of flight was merely a kite.

CELEBRATING GREATER KANSAS CIT

BOOKS AREN'T THE ONLY educational tools at Lee's Summit Public Library, where learning the strategies of chess can take your concentration— not to mention your spirits—on a roller coaster ride.

Celebrating Greater Kansas Cit

E THNIC IDENTITY IS VALUED
and fostered throughout
Kansas City, from celebrations
of Martin Luther King Jr. Day
(OPPOSITE) to events that expose
area youngsters to traditional
African dance (LEFT).

GREATER KANSAS CITY'S African-American community boasts a rich history, which is being celebrated and preserved through a number of local institutions. Former Monarchs player and coach John "Buck" O'Neil delights in his work as founder of the Negro Leagues Baseball Museum (TOP). Dr. William E. Robertson, through his accomplishments as director of the Bruce R. Watkins Cultural Center, helps honor the ongoing contributions of Kansas City's African-American residents (BOTTOM). And although she's reached her 80s, Lucile Bluford never tires of her work as editor and publisher of *The Kansas City Call* newspaper (OPPOSITE).

CELEBRATING GREATER KANSAS CITY

When it comes to innovation and artistry, Kansas Citians really know how to put the wheels in motion.

KANSAS CITY SPREADS FROM
its downtown center, be-
yond its urban neighborhoods
and into the suburbs that reach
in all directions. Today's metropolitan area crosses a state line
and covers more than 6,000
square miles in 13 counties.

Celebrating Greater Kansas City

GETTING FROM HERE TO there has lots of meanings in Greater Kansas City, whether you're harvesting a golden crop of wheat, transporting goods by rail, or negotiating a busy interchange. In fact, the metropolitan area has more highway miles per capita than any other major U.S. city.

CELEBRATING GREATER KANSAS CITY

THE VIEWS—AS WELL AS THE
vehicles—may have changed
over the years, but the quintessential Sunday afternoon ride
has never lost its charm.

CELEBRATING GREATER KANSAS CITY

WITH DARING DISPOSITIONS and a penchant for radical recreation, rollerbladers have forged their trails all over town. The activity has become so popular, in fact, that officials are considering a plan that would provide a city-sanctioned skate park for practitioners of the sport.

LOCAL TRANSPORTATION options sometimes involve a clever combination of legs and wheels. That's certainly the case with the die-hard rollerbladers who attend a regular sunrise training session at Kansas City's downtown airport (ABOVE). For a more relaxed tour of the urban landscape, popular horse-drawn carriages course the streets at the Country Club Plaza during the warm-weather months (OPPOSITE).

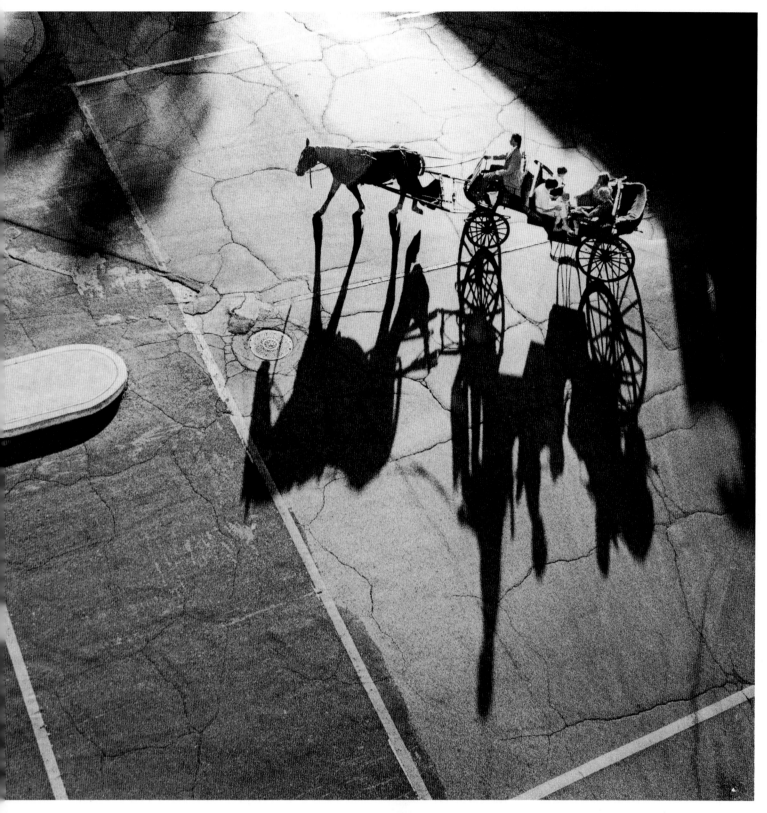

N O MATTER HOW KANSAS Citians choose to get around, and no matter where they may go, a common thread runs throughout the metro area: From its famous sculptures and fountains to the quiet streets of its Missouri and Kansas suburbs to the golden wheat fields of the surrounding plains, there is always cause for celebration (PAGES 292 AND 293).

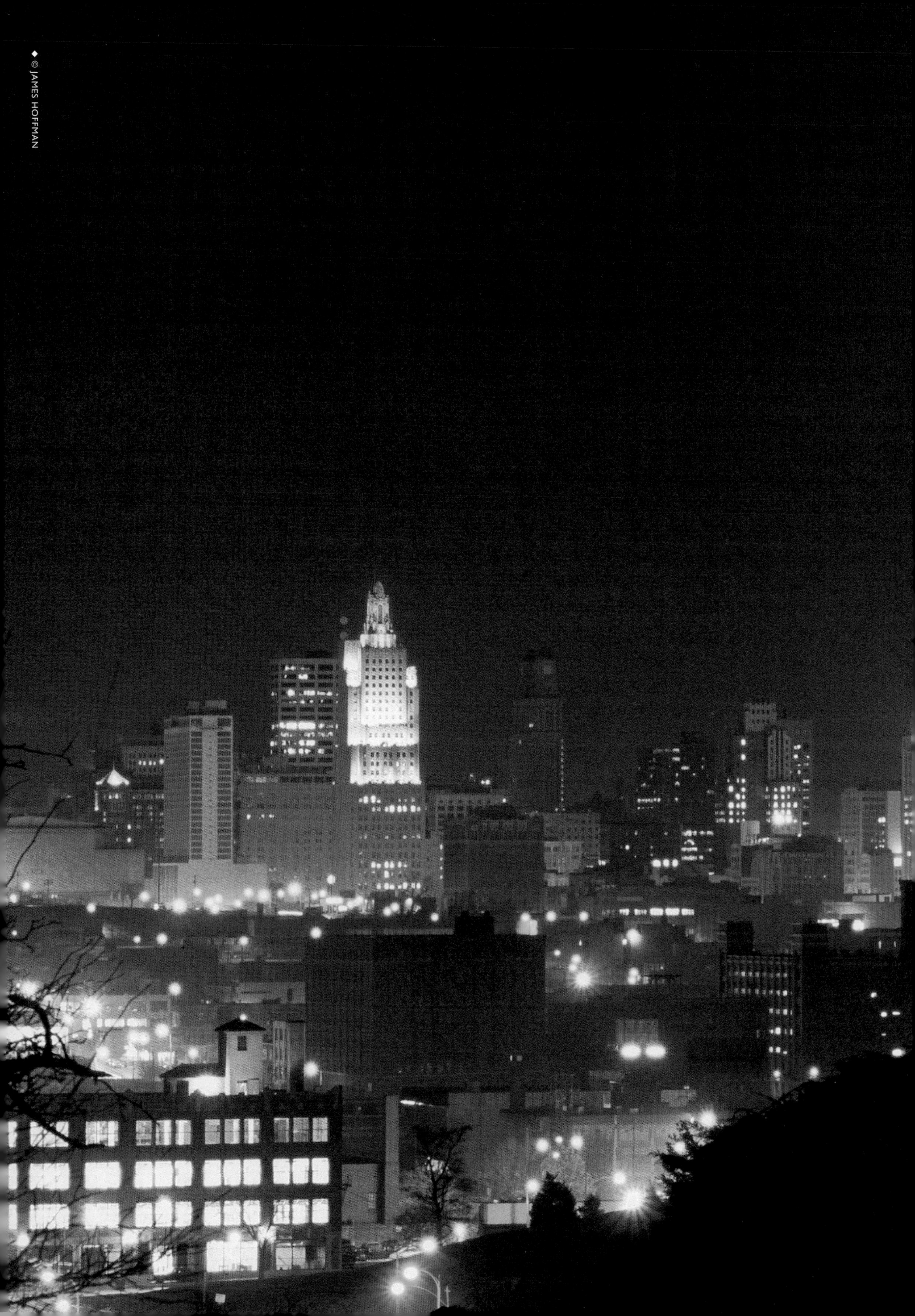

PROFILES IN EXCELLENCE

A LOOK AT THE CORPORATIONS, BUSINESSES, PROFESSIONAL GROUPS, AND COMMUNITY SERVICE ORGANIZATIONS THAT HAVE MADE THIS BOOK POSSIBLE. THEIR STORIES—OFFERING AN INFORMAL CHRONICLE OF THE LOCAL BUSINESS COMMUNITY—ARE ARRANGED ACCORDING TO THE DATE THEY WERE ESTABLISHED IN GREATER KANSAS CITY.

ACCOMMODATIONS BY APPLE ■ ADVANTAGE HEALTH SYSTEMS ■ AlliedSignal FEDERAL MANUFACTURING & TECHNOLOGIES ■ AMC ENTERTAINMENT INC. ■ AMERICAN CENTURY INVESTMENTS ■ ANDERSEN CONSULTING ■ APPLEBEE'S INTERNATIONAL ■ ASAI ARCHITECTURE ■ AUTOMOBILE DEALERS ASSOCIATION OF GREATER KANSAS CITY ■ BEST COMPUTER CONSULTANTS, INC. ■ BETHANY MEDICAL CENTER ■ BIOFF SINGER AND FINUCANE ■ BLACK & VEATCH ■ BLACKWELL SANDERS PEPER MARTIN LLP ■ BOARD OF PUBLIC UTILITIES ■ BURNS & MCDONNELL ■ BUTLER MANUFACTURING ■ CAMP FIRE BOYS AND GIRLS ■ CARONDELET HEALTH ■ CCP ■ CLINICAL REFERENCE LABORATORY ■ CORPORATE WOODS ■ CROWN CENTER ■ CyDEX, INC. ■ DEVINE deFLON YAEGER ARCHITECTS, INC. ■ DiCARLO CONSTRUCTION COMPANY ■ DODSON GROUP ■ DOUBLETREE HOTEL KANSAS CITY ■ ENTERCOM ■ ERNST & YOUNG LLP ■ ESOT RESOURCES, INC. ■ EVEANS, BASH, MAGRINO & KLEIN, INC. ■ EXECUTIVE BEECHCRAFT, INC. ■ EXECUTIVE TELECONFERENCING SERVICES ■ FARMLAND INDUSTRIES, INC. ■ FAULTLESS STARCH/BON AMI COMPANY ■ FIKE CORPORATION ■ FOGEL ANDERSON CONSTRUCTION CO. ■ FORD MOTOR COMPANY ■ FORT DODGE ANIMAL HEALTH ■ FORTIS BENEFITS INSURANCE COMPANY ■ GATEWAY ■ GENERAL MOTORS CORP./MLCG FAIRFAX ASSEMBLY PLANT ■ GOULD EVANS GOODMAN ASSOCIATES ■ GREATER KANSAS CITY CHAMBER OF COMMERCE ■ GREATER KANSAS CITY COMMUNITY FOUNDATION ■ GST STEEL COMPANY ■ HALDEX BRAKE PRODUCTS CORP. ■ HALLMARK CARDS, INC. ■ H&R BLOCK, INC. ■ HARMON INDUSTRIES, INC. ■ HAVENS STEEL ■ HEALTH MIDWEST ■ HELZBERG DIAMONDS ■ HISTORIC SUITES OF AMERICA ■ HNTB ARCHITECTS ENGINEERS PLANNERS ■ HOECHST MARION ROUSSEL, INC. ■ HOTZ BUSINESS SYSTEMS ■ IBM CORP. ■ IBT, INC. ■ IKON TECHNOLOGY SERVICES KANSAS CITY ■ INDEPENDENCE REGIONAL HEALTH CENTER ■ INGRAM'S MAGAZINE ■ ITRAVEL ■ JAMES B. NUTTER & CO. ■ J.E. DUNN CONSTRUCTION COMPANY ■ JOHN DEERE COMPANY ■ KANSAS CITY AREA DEVELOPMENT COUNCIL ■ KANSAS CITY BUSINESS JOURNAL ■ KANSAS CITY KANSAS AREA CHAMBER OF COMMERCE ■ KANSAS CITY LIFE INSURANCE COMPANY ■ KANSAS CITY MARRIOTT DOWNTOWN ■ THE KANSAS CITY STAR ■ KANSAS CITY WATER SERVICES DEPARTMENT ■ KCTV5 ■ KPMG PEAT MARWICK LLP ■ LA PETITE ACADEMY ■ LabOne, INC. ■ THE LARKIN GROUP, INC. ■ LATHROP & GAGE L.C. ■ LEWIS, RICE & FINGERSH, L.C. ■ MANPOWER, INC. ■ MARK ONE ELECTRIC CO., INC. ■ MARLEY COOLING TOWER COMPANY ■ NATIONSBANK ■ NORTH KANSAS CITY HOSPITAL ■ OVERLAND PARK REGIONAL MEDICAL CENTER ■ PERIPHERAL VISION INFOSYSTEMS, INC. ■ PFIZER ANIMAL HEALTH GROUP ■ POLSINELLI, WHITE, VARDEMAN & SHALTON, P.C. ■ PRIMEDIA INTERTEC ■ REALTY EXECUTIVES/METRO ONE ■ RIGHT MANAGEMENT CONSULTANTS ■ THE RIVAL® COMPANY ■ ROCKHURST COLLEGE ■ ROCKHURST HIGH SCHOOL ■ SAINT LUKE'S-SHAWNEE MISSION HEALTH SYSTEM ■ ST. TERESA'S ACADEMY ■ THE SALVAJOR COMPANY ■ SOUTHWESTERN BELL ■ SPENCER FANE BRITT & BROWNE LLP ■ SPENCER REED GROUP ■ SPRINT CORPORATION ■ STEWART TITLE OF KANSAS CITY ■ THOMAS MCGEE, L.C. ■ TRANSAMERICA LIFE COMPANIES ■ TranSYSTEMS CORPORATION ■ TURNER CONSTRUCTION COMPANY ■ UNION BANK ■ UNION SECURITIES ■ UNITOG COMPANY ■ THE UNIVERSITY OF HEALTH SCIENCES ■ THE UNIVERSITY OF KANSAS MEDICAL CENTER ■ UNIVERSITY OF MISSOURI-KANSAS CITY ■ UTILICORP UNITED ■ VARIFORM, INC. ■ VETERANS OF FOREIGN WARS ■ WALTON CONSTRUCTION COMPANY INC. ■ WORLDS OF FUN AND OCEANS OF FUN ■ YELLOW CORPORATION ■ THE ZIMMER COMPANIES

CELEBRATING GREATER KANSAS CITY

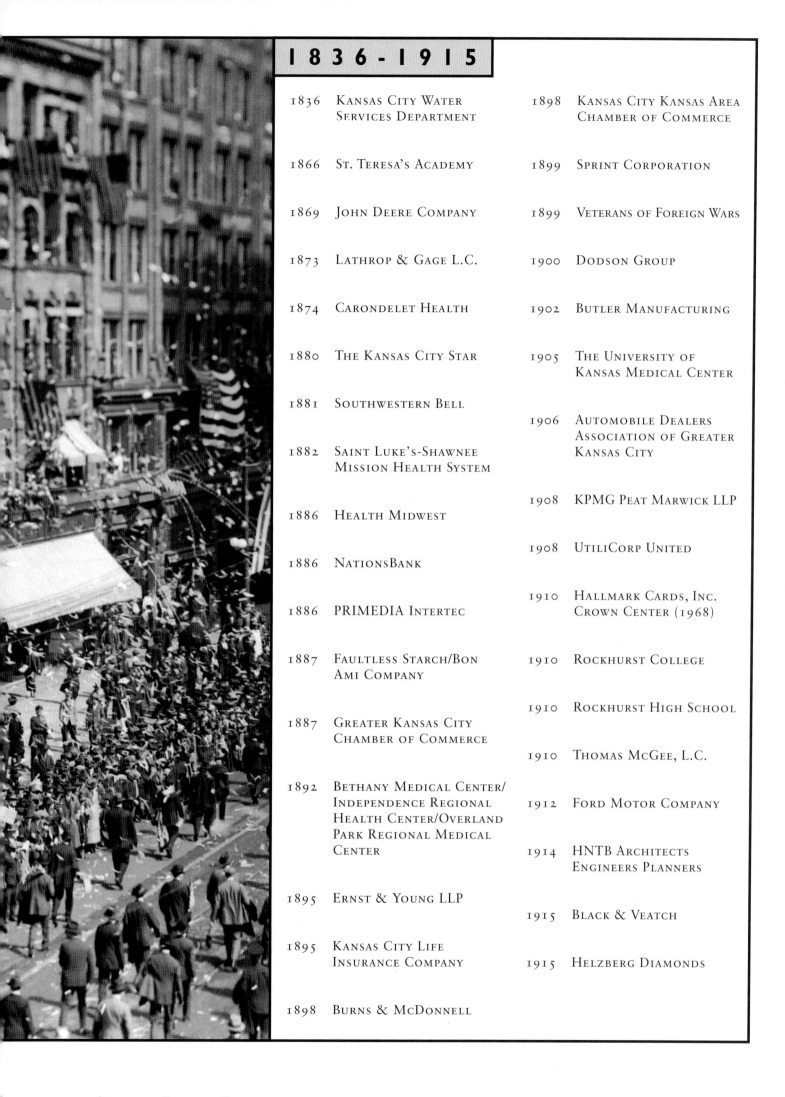

1836-1915

1836	KANSAS CITY WATER SERVICES DEPARTMENT	1898	KANSAS CITY KANSAS AREA CHAMBER OF COMMERCE
1866	ST. TERESA'S ACADEMY	1899	SPRINT CORPORATION
1869	JOHN DEERE COMPANY	1899	VETERANS OF FOREIGN WARS
1873	LATHROP & GAGE L.C.	1900	DODSON GROUP
1874	CARONDELET HEALTH	1902	BUTLER MANUFACTURING
1880	THE KANSAS CITY STAR	1905	THE UNIVERSITY OF KANSAS MEDICAL CENTER
1881	SOUTHWESTERN BELL		
1882	SAINT LUKE'S-SHAWNEE MISSION HEALTH SYSTEM	1906	AUTOMOBILE DEALERS ASSOCIATION OF GREATER KANSAS CITY
1886	HEALTH MIDWEST	1908	KPMG PEAT MARWICK LLP
1886	NATIONSBANK	1908	UTILICORP UNITED
1886	PRIMEDIA INTERTEC	1910	HALLMARK CARDS, INC. CROWN CENTER (1968)
1887	FAULTLESS STARCH/BON AMI COMPANY	1910	ROCKHURST COLLEGE
1887	GREATER KANSAS CITY CHAMBER OF COMMERCE	1910	ROCKHURST HIGH SCHOOL
		1910	THOMAS MCGEE, L.C.
1892	BETHANY MEDICAL CENTER/ INDEPENDENCE REGIONAL HEALTH CENTER/OVERLAND PARK REGIONAL MEDICAL CENTER	1912	FORD MOTOR COMPANY
		1914	HNTB ARCHITECTS ENGINEERS PLANNERS
1895	ERNST & YOUNG LLP	1915	BLACK & VEATCH
1895	KANSAS CITY LIFE INSURANCE COMPANY	1915	HELZBERG DIAMONDS
1898	BURNS & MCDONNELL		

BEFORE SETTLERS, BEFORE STEAMSHIPS, BEFORE CITIES, THERE was the Missouri River. Sometimes more than a mile wide, the waterway curls for thousands of miles through America's rich heartland before joining the Mississippi River near St. Louis. A ready-made trade route, the river spawned an abundance of

settlements along its bluffs and floodplains. Beautiful but treacherous—it was a graveyard for early riverboats loaded with cargo for settlers bent on taming the vast reaches between the river and the Colorado Rocky Mountains.

Now the Missouri runs narrower, faster, and somewhat more subdued through the help of human engineering. The river can still rage from its banks, as it did during the massive flooding in 1993, but these occasions are more rare than in days gone by. Still, residents of river communities keep a wary eye on the Big Muddy, and swap tales of past floods that wiped out entire towns in mere moments.

The river now remains a vital shipping route, but just as im-

portant, it is the water source for more than 450,000 residents in Kansas City, Missouri, and 24 communities in the Greater Kansas City area. In total, the Missouri is the water supply for more than 1 million people in the Kansas City metropolitan area.

Building a Service

During Kansas City's infancy, most residents drew water from cisterns and hand-dug wells. Waterborne illnesses were rampant, and fire protection was nearly nonexistent. Concerned by the disastrous situation created by an unclean and unreliable water source, the city commissioners took action, selecting the National Water Works Company of New York to build and operate the city's first waterworks

in 1874. Within a year, Kansas City operations were under way with 12 miles of water mains and a capacity of 5 million gallons per day. By 1887, the Missouri River had become the prime water source for the new community.

During the following decade, the city took control of its water supply by buying out the National Water Works Company and forming what is today the Kansas City, Missouri, Water Services Department. In a major expansion, the department began to lay down a network of new water lines, and in 1925, it began construction of a three-mile-long tunnel beneath the river to transport water to residents south of the city. By 1930, the Kansas City North Water Treatment Plant was completed and able to provide the city with as many as 100 million gallons of water per day.

"The department has never rested on its laurels," says Gurni Gunter, director of the Water Services Department. "We have always striven to provide water of the highest quality—and always better than state and federal standards have mandated."

Always Improving

To accomplish this, major treatment and system improvements have been ongoing. Water softening was introduced in the 1940s, and major filter and plant expansions were completed in 1958, 1975, and 1980.

By 1997, the department was producing an average of 115 million gallons of safe drinking water each day, transforming the Big Muddy's flow into potable water to serve the vital needs of the surrounding communities.

Today, the Kansas City Water Services Department manages a

The Kansas City Water Treatment Plant (top), operated by the Kansas City Water Services Department, was completed in 1930, and today provides the city with as many as 240 million gallons of water per day. Construction began on the plant in 1924 (bottom).

LIGHTFOOT PHOTOGRAPHY

improvements to the Water Treatment Plant and a major two-inch-main replacement program that will enhance water pressure and fire protection for a number of customers.

Committed to Quality

So what drives the associates of the Kansas City Water Services Department toward excellence? Gunter sums it up by quoting the department's mission statement: "To be the finest water supply, wastewater treatment, and storm water management utility, while maintaining excellent customer service and product quality at a reasonable price in an environmentally responsible manner."

That goal is also mirrored in the department's ongoing commitment to responsible stewardship of Missouri River resources. The department oper-

ates eight wastewater treatment facilities to ensure that effluent released into the river meets all guidelines. In addition, the department carefully manages Kansas City's storm water system to ensure that runoff from city streets does not create pollution problems in streams that empty into the river.

The Missouri River remains at the center of life in Kansas City. Everyone within the Water Services Department realizes that both the present and the future depend on the continuing health of the river, and that the Missouri is not a renewable resource, but a precious commodity to be treated with great care. "The river was here before all else, and will remain when all else vanishes," says Gunter. "It demands, and receives, complete admiration and absolute respect from all of us."

ast water distribution network hat includes more than 2,300 niles of water mains, and the department oversees a series of major improvements funded by a $150 million bond program approved by voters in 1996. Among pending projects are

The construction of the Trans-Missouri River Tunnel Project, completed in 1993, was an integral part of improvements that, by 1997, helped the department produce an average of 115 million gallons of safe drinking water each day.

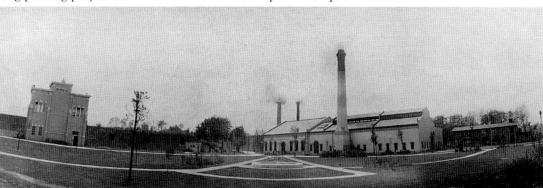

The Kansas City Water Services Department built the Quindaro Water Treatment Plant in 1914 to transform water from the Missouri River into potable drinking water.

N 1869, ILLINOIS-BASED DEERE & COMPANY CHOSE KANSAS CITY AS its first branch distributor. For the agricultural machinery manufacturer, Kansas City was the gateway to the most rapidly developing farming section of the country, which would help position it as an integral part of this emerging Bread Basket of the World. Kansas City was then a

growing railroad hub, and its first bridge spanning the Missouri River gave it a connection to booming agricultural points in the South. This was the start of a long and prosperous relationship between Kansas City and one of its leading businesses.

Today, Deere & Company is a Fortune 200 company with more than $11 billion in annual sales, more than 34,000 employees worldwide, and business in more than 160 countries. The company and its subsidiaries manufacture, distribute, and finance a full range of agriculture, construction, forestry, lawn and grounds care, and recreational equipment. In addition, Deere & Company is heavily involved in equipment financing, commercial property-casualty and life insurance coverage, and health care benefit management services.

"Throughout its long history, Deere & Company has always kept its customers at the forefront of what we do," says Charles

Kansas City was chosen by the Illinois-based John Deere Company as its first branch distributor in 1869. Today, the facility employs more than 200 people (top).

The 9610 Combine is marketed and serviced by the Kansas City facility (bottom).

Gause, general manager of John Deere Company, Kansas City. "That has helped us grow into the nation's leading farm equipment manufacturer and an important part of the world's agricultural production."

Be the Best

Deere & Company had its beginnings in 1837, after blacksmith John Deere invented the self-scouring steel plow to break the stubborn prairie sod. When he began producing the plow for others, Deere demanded that the invention carrying his name be of the highest quality. That tradition has held through the years.

"As farmers testify, the quality and dependability of Deere products still best describes the company," says Gause. "Since John Deere himself, the company's standards have been 'nothing but the best for our customers.'"

John Deere Company, Kansas City is a division of Deere & Company, headquartered in Moline. Initially located in the West Bottoms, the local branch has occupied a 16-acre site on East 85th Street since 1950, where its familiar leaping deer logo is easily visible from U.S. Highway 71. Approximately 200 employees work at the location, while another 100 work in Davenport and Wichita training centers, and at a parts depot in Denver. One of six North American sales branches, the Kansas City division markets and services agricultural products and lawn- and grounds-care equipment and parts through

individually owned and operated John Deere dealerships in six midwestern states.

The Kansas City branch represents a corporate citizen that has lent strength, stability, and steady employment as well as tax dollars to the community. Beyond its business roots, John Deere and its employees are actively involved with a wide range of community, government, and service organizations, from neighborhood associations to the chamber of commerce, and from boys' homes to agricultural organizations for school-age kids.

"The fact that John Deere has operated in Kansas City for nearly 130 years speaks well for the stability of the community and its economy," says Gause. "I don't see that changing, even though we are constantly changing to meet our customers' needs."

Leadership Qualities

The Kansas City division is part of a company that is the world's largest producer of agriculture equipment. John Deere is also a leading producer of construction and forestry equipment, and markets North America's broadest line of lawn- and grounds-care equipment. Deere's parts division promotes parts sales to owners of other brands as well as its own, and coordinates the international distribution and management of inventory and materials.

The company is also a leader in new products to improve farmers' capabilities and profit. Seeding equipment, such as the 750 No-Till Grain Drill, for example, was designed to plant seeds in high-residue fields or in soil lacking seed-bed preparation, thus saving trips through the field to prepare it for planting.

A new-products innovator, John Deere invests more than $200 million annually in research and development. Engineers, customers, unions, staffs, and outside suppliers all are involved in the product development process concurrently.

"John Deere products are designed to add genuine value and save time and money for our customers," says Gause. "We know that satisfied customers mean repeat customers."

Going Further

In addition to quality, safety is also a company hallmark. For example, John Deere engineers developed a rollover protective structure (Roll-Gard) and a power takeoff safety guard for its farm machinery in response to agricultural safety concerns. Both products were made available to other manufacturers for farmer protection.

John Deere also has been quick to respond to the environmental concerns of its communities and customers by initiating recycling. The Kansas City branch was one of the first of the company's nonmanufacturing units to have a recycling process in its facility.

Moreover, the company is proud of its education partnership programs with colleges and state governments. Currently, John Deere offers agricultural technology programs in 21 colleges across the United States and Canada, providing two-year associate degrees in agriculture to high school graduates. In addition, a mentor program at universities in Missouri, Illinois, Kansas, and Nebraska helps students prepare for management positions in John Deere dealerships.

In fact, one of John Deere's visions for the future is to expand its education and business partnerships as model training programs that develop skills needed for the 21st century. "Such programs have long-term benefits for the communities in which most of us live, and certainly for all of the Midwest," says Gause. "With them, we'll see continued growth and opportunity."

The 9400 four-wheel-drive tractor provides modern technology for pulling heavy draft loads.

The 8000T-Tracks tractor provides farmers an alternative for traction and flotation.

ATHROP & GAGE L.C. HAS BEEN A PROMINENT KANSAS CITY law firm for more than 125 years. Resulting from the merger of two distinguished firms—Lathrop & Norquist and Gage & Tucker—the firm has played an ongoing role in Kansas City's evolution from frontier outpost to commercial hub.

Gardiner Lathrop launched his Kansas City law career in the 1870s with a major early client being the Atchison, Topeka & Santa Fe railroad company. Lathrop's practice grew to represent different industries over the years, but the firm's relationships with railroad companies endure to this day.

John B. Gage started his law career in 1912 and founded his own law firm in 1930. In the 1940s, Gage served as mayor of Kansas City. He is credited with many of the reforms that improved the city's financial condition and with ousting the

Pendergast political machine. The Gage firm counted Hall Brothers, later Hallmark Cards, among its earliest clients and handled the city's second urban renewal project.

Today, Lathrop & Gage is the third-largest law firm in the Kansas City area, numbering nearly 200 attorneys. In addition to its main office in downtown Kansas City, the firm maintains offices in Overland Park, Jefferson City, Springfield, and St. Louis, as well as in Washington, D.C. The firm acts as general counsel to international businesses based in the Midwest and provides

regional counsel for many national companies. Lathrop & Gage also represents numerous governmental entities, schools and universities, and civic and charitable institutions.

By emphasizing existing specialty areas from environmental and media law to health care and technology, the firm has expanded its already formidable local, regional, and national client base. "We're focusing on our strengths and adding on in other areas," says Tom Stewart, managing partner of Lathrop & Gage. "We're also opening offices in new marketplaces, all with an eye to serving clients on a broader basis."

Size Counts

We've won a lot of business by virtue of our size—business that neither of our previously separate firms would have gotten," says Stewart. "Because we're a large firm, we're able to draw on expertise in many areas of the law whenever a particular matter calls for it."

Lathrop & Gage has grown its practice by recruiting experienced lawyers and developing associates in legal areas that emerged in the 1990s. "We are already leading the way in intellectual property law and telecommunications law," says Stewart. "Those are the hotbeds these days, and we're well established in both. Listening to and responding to our clients' needs has helped us stay ahead of the competition. I fully expect that to continue."

In January 1998, the firm added lawyers from the distinguished law firm Bennett, Lytle, Wetzler, Martin & Pishny to its Kansas office and opened an office in Jefferson City. In

PAUL CHILDRESS

Lathrop & Gage has a well-established regulatory and public law practice. (From left) David Shorr, of the firm's Jefferson City office; Terry Satterlee; and Bert Bates frequently represent clients at the state capitol.

March, an office in Springfield was opened. Stewart takes an aggressive approach toward growth, but strives to maintain a small firm culture. "Growing our numbers allows us to efficiently handle matters whose sheer mass makes them unmanageable for smaller firms. Our challenge is to keep everyone involved and engaged, to hold on to the sense of cohesion that's made this firm strong for so many years."

Getting Involved

From the firm's earliest days, service to the community has been a hallmark of the Lathrop & Gage practice. Firm members, past and present, have included a U.S. senator, three mayors of Kansas City, governors of Missouri and Kansas, a U.S. commissioner, federal and state judges, members of the City Council of Kansas City, and a police commissioner. The firm's lawyers have also provided professional and civic leadership as president of the Missouri Bar, the Kansas Bar Association, various local bar associations, and the University of Missouri Board of Curators. Lawyers with Lathrop & Gage currently serve on or chair the boards of more than 50 local and regional charitable or civic organizations.

"Our first and foremost concern is for our clients, but we're also committed to enhancing the community. And when it comes to that, all our people pitch in," says Stewart. "We recognize our part in Kansas City's culture and tradition, and we strive to continue making contributions by finding new roles for ourselves and striking out in new directions."

On a Mission

Despite the firm's strong and loyal commitment to its hometown, attorneys at Lathrop & Gage find their clients have expanded their interests nationally and internationally. That growth has already taken Lathrop & Gage to all corners of the earth, a trend Stewart expects will continue.

"We strive to know our clients and their business. We want to be able to represent them whatever direction they go," says Stewart. "This is a global economy, and many Kansas City companies are going regional, national, and international today. Our mission is to be prepared to go with them."

Never content to dwell on its past, Lathrop & Gage continues to set the highest professional standards, to grow and innovate, and to represent excellence in serving its clients and community.

Lathrop & Gage attorneys have played an integral role in the redevelopment of Kansas City's historic Union Station. (From left) Firm attorneys Terry Brady, Ann Mesle, Jerry Riffel, Tom Stewart, John Eckels, and Judith Weaver are well known for their involvement in community and charitable projects.

Attorneys from the Bennett Lytle law firm joined Lathrop & Gage's Corporate Woods office in 1998. Bob Lytle and former Kansas Governor Bob Bennett join John Vratil and Harry Wigner (back row), and Janice Martin, Scott Beeler, and Jeff Ellis (front row) at the site of firm client Aldi's regional distribution center at the K-10 corridor.

ALTHOUGH FORMALLY ESTABLISHED IN 1997, CARONDELET Health has a long tradition of providing quality health care to Kansas Citians. Saint Joseph Health Center—a division of Carondelet—was the first private hospital in Kansas City, having been established by the Sisters of St. Joseph of

Caysondelet in 1874. At that time, the facility consisted of only 10 rooms in downtown Kansas City.

Today, not-for-profit Carondelet Health incorporates the Saint Joseph Health System and St. Mary's Hospital of Blue Springs under the sponsorship of the Sisters of St. Joseph of Carondelet. Saint Joseph Health Center now includes a 300-bed, acute care hospital and the Medical Mall, added in 1995. The Medical Mall houses all outpatient-related departments, including rehabilitation therapy and outpatient surgery, and also contains physician offices, a retail pharmacy, a food court, and a gift shop.

A younger facility, St. Mary's Hospital of Blue Springs opened in 1981 under the auspices of the Sisters of St. Mary Healthcare System. Today, the hospital is a 119-bed, acute care facility with

a variety of health care services, including radiology, nuclear medicine, magnetic resonance imaging (MRI), ultrasound, and radiation therapy.

Skilled Nursing Care

In addition to its hospitals, Carondelet offers long-term skilled nursing care at three facilities. Villa Saint Joseph in Overland Park was the first unit of its kind owned by the system in the Kansas City area. The facility boasts 120 beds and offers physical, occupational, and speech therapies.

Carondelet Manor, located on the Saint Joseph Health Center campus, is the largest of the three long-term-care facilities, with 180 beds. It provides a subacute unit, hospice care, and short- and long-term care. Carondelet Manor is Medicare and Medicaid certified, and offers rehabilitative services.

St. Mary's Manor, adjacent to St. Mary's Hospital of Blue Springs, includes 132 skilled nursing beds. In addition, residential care units are available, allowing independence for residents while offering the security of on-site medical care.

A Mission from God

Carondelet Health is more than just health care. Both staff and patients point to the system's mission statement as a unique part of what it offers. "The mission and its components are not simply words on paper," says CEO Mike Abell. "We are in the health care business, the business of healing, and that includes all aspects of a person's health—physical and spiritual."

At Carondelet Health, everyone is united by its mission. Abell continues, "Carondelet Health consists of Catholic organizations dedicated to the healing ministry of Jesus Christ. Our commitment to human dignity compels us to provide compassionate, quality health care for body, mind, and spirit, with a special concern for the poor. We are responsible stewards serving the needs of all people from conception to death."

Additional services provided under Carondelet Health include Carondelet Care Resources, Carondelet HomeCare Services, Carondelet Hospice, St. Mary's Home Health Services, Carondelet Infusion Services, Carondelet Medical Equipment Services, Carondelet Pharmacy, Saint Joseph Health Center Foundation, and Saint Mary's Hospital of Blue Springs Development. Also affiliated with Carondelet Health are Carondelet Family Medical Care and Carondelet Internal Medicine.

Carondelet Health, a not-for-profit organization, incorporates the Saint Joseph Health System and St. Mary's Hospital of Blue Springs under the sponsorship of the Sisters of St. Joseph of Carondelet. Saint Joseph Health Center includes a 300-bed, acute care hospital and the Medical Mall, which was added in 1995 (top).

St. Mary's Hospital in Blue Springs opened in 1981 under the auspices of the Sisters of St. Mary Healthcare System. Today, the hospital, part of Carondelet Health, is a 119-bed, acute care facility with a variety of health care services (bottom).

SINCE 1892, BETHANY MEDICAL CENTER HAS BEEN KNOWN FOR ITS high-quality medical care and important innovations. In 1961, for example, Dr. Hughes Day established the world's first Coronary Intensive Care Unit at Bethany, initiating procedures and standards for coronary care that are still used today. Day coined the term

"code blue," invented the crash cart, and revolutionized intensive care nursing by integrating nurses into the critical care team.

Recently, Bethany became a sister hospital to Independence Regional Health Center and Overland Park Regional Medical Center. Located in the heart of Kansas City, Kansas, Bethany today is a 300-bed, acute care facility with 200 physicians and 1,000 employees.

Serving primarily Wyandotte, Leavenworth, and northern Johnson counties, Bethany offers comprehensive inpatient and outpatient services. The hospital's specialized programs include wound care, home care, sleep disorders, rehabilitation, pain clinic, obstetrics and gynecology, and geriatrics.

Healing Independence

When established in 1909, Independence Regional Health Center was known as the Independence Sanitarium and Hospital. Founded by the Reorganized Church of Jesus Christ of Latter-day Saints, the facility was planned as a convalescent home. During its first week, however, a railroad accident necessitated the amputation of a man's leg. That man became the hospital's first patient—just five days after it opened. Since then, the hospital has grown

from its original 11 beds to its present 366-bed capacity, and is one of the largest employers in the eastern metro area, having a staff of more than 1,300 employees, 330 physicians, and 400 active volunteers.

Centrally located for Independence residents, the center offers comprehensive health care services that include its 24-hour trauma center; a full range of cardiac services; the Santa Fe Trail Senior Health Center; the National Association of Senior Friends; cancer services; diabetes resource center; and HealthLine, an 11,000-square-foot exercise facility open to the public.

Johnson County Care

Overland Park Regional Medical Center is the youngest of the three Kansas City-area sister facilities. Established in 1978, the hospital is a 400-bed, acute care facility originally called Suburban Medical Center. Conveniently located near Overland Park's thriving business and residential communities, the hospital offers a full range of diagnostic, therapeutic, emergency, and surgical services. Overland Park Regional Medical Center has the only Level III neonatal intensive care unit and the only trauma service in Johnson County.

The organization's Heart Center includes open-heart sur-

gery, cardiac rehabilitation, a cardiac catheterization laboratory, and 24-hour emergency cardiac care. The hospital also features the Diabetes Wellness Center, a stroke program, seniors programs, and a burn unit. Its Women's Center offers services in advanced infertility treatment, perinatology, obstetrics, gynecological oncology, urology, and surgery. The medical center employs one of the largest workforces in Overland Park, with more than 1,000 employees. The medical staff features more than 700 physicians.

Together, these three sister hospitals are as committed to wellness and good health as they are to medical excellence and community leadership.

Clockwise from top: Serving primarily Wyandotte, Leavenworth, and northern Johnson counties, Bethany Medical Center is situated on 12th Street in Kansas City, Kansas.

The Independence Regional Health Center, off Truman Road in Independence, offers comprehensive health care services that include its 24-hour trauma center and cardiac services.

Overland Park Regional Medical Center, on Quivira Road in Overland Park, is the youngest of the three Kansas City-area sister facilities.

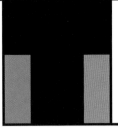

HE STORY OF *The Kansas City Star* IS CLOSELY INTERTWINED WITH the story of Kansas City itself. A 118-year chronicle of Kansas City, the paper has not only reflected the change and growth of the city, but it's been a community leader as well. ■ Founded as *The Star* on September 18, 1880, the newspaper's first visionary was William

Rockhill Nelson, an Indiana native who had run a construction business and owned the *Fort Wayne Sentinel*. Back then, Kansas City had dirt roads and few sidewalks, which contrasted with Nelson's sense of civility. A public works contractor for part of his career in Indiana, Nelson used *The Star* to campaign for paved streets and crusade for improved sidewalks and sewers, decent public buildings, better streetlights, and more fire and police protection. But Nelson's most enduring legacy was the city's parks and boulevard system, which he began promoting in 1881.

"I think the history of *The Kansas City Star* and the Kansas City community are just two chapters in the same book," says Arthur Brisbane, publisher. "That gives us a great stake in our community, a lot of pride in what our paper has meant to the community, and a sense of pride in what Kansas City has become."

All the News

The *Kansas City Star* serves more than 660,000 daily readers and more than 860,000

Sunday readers, providing in-depth coverage of local, national, and international news. With more than 390 staff journalists, *The Star* is the largest news gathering source in the region.

Touted as a news industry innovator, the newspaper has received numerous accolades. Since 1931, *The Star* has won eight Pulitzer Prizes, including one for national reporting. Among its other honors are two George Polk awards, two National Headliner awards, two Sigma Delta Chi awards, and the 1996 James K. Batten Award for Excellence in Civic Journalism. *The Star* has also been recognized for having one of the best newspaper Web sites worldwide and has received the Digital Edge Award for its classified advertising application on the Internet.

The Kansas City Star offers readers more than daily news. In recent years, the company has diversified to include an increasing number of community-specific, zoned publications; StarTouch, a telephone information service; and kansascity.com, a community-based Web site.

"It is our goal to make our readers well informed about matters that are close to home—in their neighborhoods, in their

counties, and in the metro area as a whole—and also to give them a good digest of national and world news," says Brisbane, who praises the efforts of all 1,900 *Star* employees.

Says Editor Mark Zieman, "We've been an advocate for a better community in the pages of our newspaper since we were founded. I think it is a function of our paper to work with the community to build a better Kansas City."

Making Connections

Back at the turn of the century, *Star* founder Nelson made a name for himself with

Clockwise from top:
The Star has four news bureaus throughout Kansas City and the surrounding areas, including this bureau located on College Street.

Arthur Brisbane has been publisher of *The Kansas City Star* since 1997.

Built in 1893-94, the newspaper's fifth plant location stood at the corner of 11th and Grand.

the nation's political thinkers. Dignitaries such as William Jennings Bryan, Lincoln Steffens, and William Howard Taft regularly passed through Nelson's offices. Theodore Roosevelt became a personal friend and came to Kansas City to seek Nelson's advice.

In 1891, Nelson wanted to extend his reach, and launched *The Weekly Kansas City Star*, which went to farmers and country towns in Kansas, Missouri, Nebraska, Colorado, and the Indian Territory (later Oklahoma). In 1894, *The Star* published its first Sunday edition. And in 1901, Nelson bought *The Kansas City Times*, a Democratic-leaning daily.

When Nelson died in April 1915, his daughter, Laura Nelson Kirkwood, ran *The Star* with her husband, Irwin. During this period, Ernest Hemingway worked as a *Star* reporter. When Laura Kirkwood died in 1926, 30 employees bought *The Star*.

The employee-owned *Star* was so successful that the group decided to buy a Wisconsin paper mill after paper shortage worries that began during World War II. But the mill was a heavy polluter, and in the 1970s, the cost of cleaning it up contributed to the decision by employee owners to sell *The Star*.

Bigger and Better

Trapped with the high cost of the paper mill cleanup, as well as outdated equipment and poor sales of stock to employees, the newspaper was sold to Capital Cities Communica-

tions, Inc. in January 1977. This proved to be a wise decision, as the new publisher, James Hale, overhauled every newspaper department, cut costs, and made numerous improvements. During Hale's 15-year tenure, *The Star* won three Pulitzer Prizes, expanded its zoned operations, extended coverage of business and regional news, boosted its ability to print color, and set record profits.

Like many newspapers in recent years, *The Star*'s operating company consolidated its two daily papers in 1990, ceasing publication of the afternoon edition. The new morning newspaper, which combined features of the afternoon *Star* and the morning *Times*, was named *The Kansas City Star* and first appeared March 1, 1990.

In 1992, Hale retired and Robert Woodworth was named publisher. Capital Cities merged with Disney in 1996, and in 1997, *The Star* was sold to Knight-

Ridder, one of the largest newspaper organizations worldwide.

"No matter who has owned *The Star*, there has always been a commitment to the community we serve," says Brisbane, who succeeded Woodworth as publisher in 1997. "We're very closely connected with the people of Kansas City, and that will continue to be our greatest strength in the future."

Clockwise from top left:
The Star has grown over the years to include a variety of sections and community newspapers.

The newspaper's presses run around the clock.

The Star moved into its current plant at 18th and Grand in 1911.

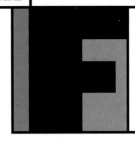

OR MORE THAN 100 YEARS, SOUTHWESTERN BELL HAS BEEN building a legacy of customer service in Kansas City. And when it comes to serving customers, the company's 3,500 metro-area employees live up to that legacy in a big way. In fact, every business day in Kansas City and its surrounding communities,

Southwestern Bell handles in excess of 17 million telephone calls from local customers relying on one of the most powerful networks in the world.

Today's Southwestern Bell is a wholly owned subsidiary of SBC Communications, Inc., ranked number one on *Fortune* magazine's list of the world's most-admired telecommunications companies.

Reaching Out to Customers

Southwestern Bell, together with sister companies Pacific Bell, Nevada Bell, and Cellular One, has 32 million access lines and more than 5 million wire-

less customers across the United States, as well as investments in telecommunications businesses in 10 foreign countries. Southwestern Bell Wireless has the highest market penetration of all wireless providers, and together with SBC's other wireless affiliates, serves customers in 78 markets nationwide.

But Southwestern Bell's legacy of service goes beyond the big numbers. "We believe it's the little things we do each day that make the difference to customers," says Van Taylor, regional president of network operations for Southwestern Bell in Kansas, Missouri, Oklahoma, and Arkansas. "That's why we're striving to give customers the services they want, when they want them. We're also making it easier for customers to do business with us. And we're empowering communities for the future through innovative partnerships."

For example, the four new Southwestern Bell Tele*Community* Centers, located on campuses of the Metropolitan Community Colleges, have helped taxi thousands of users to the information superhighway. Every day, these "town halls of technology" offer

a growing number of people the opportunity to experience firsthand the tools of the 21st century—at no charge to the user. Each facility features videoconferencing capabilities for large and small groups; a large, state-of-the-art Internet/computer learning lab that is accessible to the physically challenged; and all the free training users need.

Throughout the metropolitan area, Southwestern Bell FiberParks have given commercial real estate developers a cost-efficient and effective way to recruit new tenants and retain current companies. Now, tech-savvy tenants in some of Kansas City's premier

Clockwise from top right: Van Taylor is the regional president of network operations for Southwestern Bell.

Users in Southwestern Bell's Tele*Community* Center's learning lab take their first step onto the information superhighway as they participate in a training session about the Internet.

Penn Valley Community College is one of the three sites for the Southwestern Bell Tele*Community* Centers at the Metropolitan Community Colleges of Kansas City.

Fiber-optic cable has been one of the major innovations in the telecommunications industry in the last 25 years.

locations, including Crown Center, Southlake Technology Park, and Marion Park, can take advantage of the practical capabilities of state-of-the-art technology.

Specialized Services

Both business and residential consumers are embracing new services provided by Southwestern Bell—including money-saving packages that appeal to the budget conscious. Calling plans like 1+SAVER Direct and Metro Plus have been especially popular with customers wanting to reduce expenses for nearby long-distance calls. CallNotes® voice mail is fast becoming the formidable replacement of the answering machine. And bundled services like The WORKS® and The BASICS℠ offer packaged convenience, real value, and increased functionality of the telephone.

For today's fast lives, Southwestern Bell's integrated services digital network (ISDN) finds steady demand in Kansas City. In 1995, the area became one of the first major markets in the nation to be equipped with metro-wide service. ISDN—which allows voice, video, and high-speed data to be transmitted simultaneously through a single phone line—benefits residential customers and businesses alike. For example, ISDN makes it easy for telecommuters to tie into the office computer, for retail stores to speed up credit authorizations, and for doctors to make video consultations or transmit X rays. Throughout the metro area, Southwestern Bell has helped bring the cutting-edge capabilities of ISDN to a wide range of users—from law enforcement agencies, now saving time and taxpayers' money via video arraignments, to a unique desktop videoconferencing network that connects a group of Kansas City's top business and civic leaders.

Southwestern Bell also plays a key role in the Kansas City Area Development Council's SmartCities program, an initiative to advance the region's reputation as the best place to do business electronically. With enhancements in telecommunications technology and the power of one of the strongest networks in the world, Southwestern Bell is a leading force for economic development in the area.

Since its market entry in the early 1980s as Kansas City's first wireless provider, Southwestern Bell Wireless has been catering to the needs of busy professionals and families. Today, Southwestern Bell Wireless continues to keep Kansas Citians in contact—whether in the car, at the grocery store, or on the way to just about anywhere—with innovative wireless products and services, such as a unique phone that doubles as a wireless and cordless phone, and prepaid cellular and paging services.

Southwestern Bell Wireless is also moving schools and neighborhoods into the 21st century. Through programs like ClassLink, the company has introduced wireless technology as an effective tool in the classroom, and the Communities on Phone Patrol (COPP) program has linked neighborhood watch associations throughout the metro area with police via wireless phone service at no charge.

Telecommunications is a global growth industry that is changing at lightning speed. As voice, video, data, and computer technologies continue to merge, endless opportunities exist to enrich consumers' lives through instant access to information, entertainment, and personal and business communication. As for Southwestern Bell, the traditional telephone company image is evolving with the times, but its commitment remains the same. The company believes the future holds great promise, and promises to continue serving customers in the way it knows best—with new services, new products, and new possibilities. Day in and day out, Southwestern Bell demonstrates its commitment to being a friendly neighborhood global communications company.

Physicians and patients rely on Southwestern Bell's telemedicine services for conferencing and second opinions (top).

Southwestern Bell line crews work around the clock to maintain the utility's vast communications network and provide reliable service (bottom).

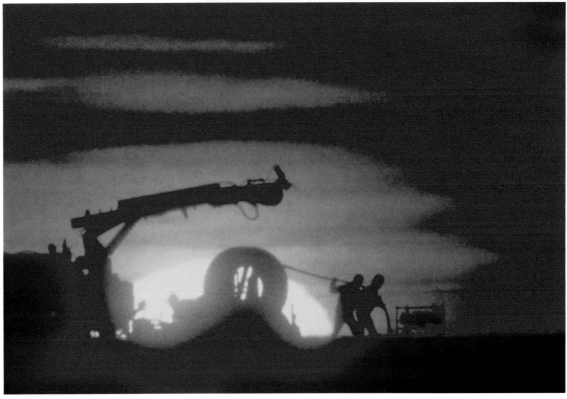

GOOD HEALTH IS A BIT LIKE CLEAN AIR—PEOPLE WHO HAVE AN abundance of it rarely reflect upon its importance, while those who don't are left gasping for more. That's why the more than 5,000 employees of Saint Luke's-Shawnee Mission Health System want to ensure that Greater Kansas City breathes easily by providing a

full range of health care services. From its renowned Mid America Heart Institute to its women's care, cancer, behavioral health, primary care, and prevention services, Saint Luke's-Shawnee Mission Health System supplies the metropolitan area with quality health care services.

Now operating from eight hospital facilities and numerous affiliated physician practices, Saint Luke's-Shawnee Mission Health System treats approximately 50,000 inpatients and more than 500,000 outpatients each year from Kansas City and the surrounding midwestern region. The Ask-A-Nurse Resource Center provides physician referrals and medical information through a 24-hour access line. Staffed by registered nurses, Ask-A-Nurse has served more than 1 million callers since it was launched in 1986.

Although many of its principal facilities have a longer history, Saint Luke's-Shawnee Mission Health System began with the decision in 1989 to build a Saint Luke's facility at Interstate 29 and Barry Road. The expand-

Saint Luke's-Shawnee Mission Health System's Ask-A-Nurse Resource Center enables callers to make a doctor's appointment, register for a health event, or ask a nurse about a medical condition (top).

A commitment to education and research is a fundamental element of the mission to provide outstanding patient care (bottom).

ing health system then added Crittenton, Wright Memorial, and Anderson County hospitals. When Saint Luke's and Shawnee Mission Medical Center merged in 1996, the system was formed.

"We are committed to bringing the quality and experience of our health system to as many people as possible," says Robert H. West, chairman of the system's board of trustees. "We now have the ability to handle nearly every kind of primary, acute, tertiary, and chronic health care service at multiple locations throughout the region. We've done that by

looking realistically at the future and by expanding community access to our system."

Tradition of Caring

Saint Luke's Hospital got its start in 1885 when All Saints' Episcopal Church recognized a need for medical assistance in Kansas City's early years. Religious leaders formed the Church Charity Association, and built a hospital to serve the emerging community.

As a tertiary care hospital, Saint Luke's houses some 650 beds. Its network of 550 physicians represents more than 356 medical specialties. Within its midtown Kansas City facility, the hospital's special strengths include the highest standard of trauma and neonatal care in the state at its Level I trauma center and Level II intensive care nursery; comprehensive cardiac care in the Mid America Heart Institute; the regional Center for High Risk Maternity Care; the Ambulatory Surgery Center; the Cancer Center; the 15-bed, dedicated Stroke Center; the Sexual Assault Treatment Center; and the Kidney Dialysis-Transplant Center.

In addition, Saint Luke's is a focal point for medical education, including a physician resi-

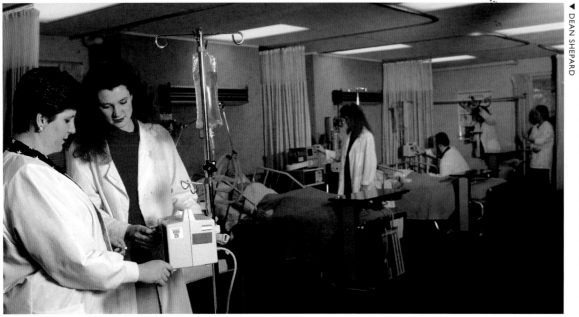

DEAN SHEPARD

dency program and a College of Nursing program. The hospital is a primary teaching hospital for the University of Missouri-Kansas City School of Medicine.

Kansas Anchor

The next largest component of the Saint Luke's-Shawnee Mission Health System is Shawnee Mission Medical Center. Opened in 1962, the 383-bed, acute care facility located in Merriam, Kansas, is a Seventh-day Adventist community service. Within its 54-acre campus, the medical center houses an outpatient surgery facility, a community health education facility, five medical office buildings, and a community fitness course.

Shawnee Mission Medical Center distinguishes itself through its specialties in cardiovascular services, behavioral health, outpatient care, and the Center for Women's Health.

Covering the Region

North of the Missouri River, Saint Luke's Northland Hospital at Smithville opened in 1938. It offers a 92-bed hospital with skilled nursing care, inpatient rehabilitation services, mental health care for adults and seniors, home care, transportation services, emergency care, and urgent care services.

Saint Luke's Northland Hospital on Barry Road is a 55-bed facility providing medical/surgical care, intensive care, comprehensive outpatient services, 24-hour emergency care, radiology services, surgical services, maternity care with a Level II nursery, and cardiac catheterization services.

The reach of Saint Luke's-Shawnee Mission Health System extends farther still. Crittenton, with roots back to 1896, offers behavioral care for children and their families on its 156-acre campus in south Kansas City, as well as through clinics in four metropolitan locations. At Crittenton, children receive dedicated care at the psychiatric hospital, in a residential program, or through a combination of partial hospital care and day school.

CLINT GILLESPIE

Anderson County Hospital in Garnett, Kansas, and Wright Memorial Hospital in Trenton, Missouri, are part of the Saint Luke's-Shawnee Mission Health System. At Wright Memorial Hospital, patients find specialty clinics for cardiology, gastroenterology, and pulmonary medicine. Anderson County Hospital, 75 miles southwest of Kansas City, offers acute care, long-term care, a geriatric psychiatric unit, and an on-site outreach cardiology clinic.

Quality in Action

Saint Luke's-Shawnee Mission Health System prides itself on quality care and patient satisfaction. The organization has received local, state, and national citations for the quality care delivered. Saint Luke's Hospital of Kansas City received the 1997 National Quality Health Care Award, the highest honor given to a hospital. In 1996, the Voluntary Hospitals of America (VHA) bestowed the Quality Leadership Award in Clinical Effectiveness, and in 1995, Saint Luke's Hospital received the Missouri Quality Award, becoming the first health care organization ever to receive this honor. In 1997, Shawnee Mission Medical Center was selected by *Self* magazine as one of the top 10 women's centers in the nation. These achievements reflect the emphasis placed on quality throughout the system.

DEAN SHEPARD

DEAN SHEPARD

Mid America Heart Institute

The Mid America Heart Institute is recognized as one of the finest cardiac facilities in the world, serving as a major referral center for cardiac patients. The Women's Cardiac Center was among the first programs in the nation to address specific cardiac health issues faced by women, and the Cardiovascular Clinical Research Center conducts landmark research into equipment, drugs, and new techniques.

Women and Children

Saint Luke's-Shawnee Mission Health System meets the special needs of women with high-risk pregnancies. An experienced staff specializing in high-risk maternal/fetal care provides prenatal diagnostic testing and treatment, and intensive care nurseries provide the best care

Clockwise from top left: Volunteers at Saint Luke's-Shawnee Mission Health System give the gift of time to patients and their families.

Committed to children for more than 100 years, Crittenton offers comprehensive behavioral health care through a variety of inpatient and outpatient programs.

The National Quality Health Care Award, presented by the National Committee for Quality Health Care (NCQHC), is the highest honor bestowed on a hospital.

possible for high-risk newborns. The system offers the area's only hospital-based certified nurse midwife program.

The Center for Women's Health addresses health issues unique to women, educates women about risk factors and the importance of early detection, and encourages healthy lifestyles. Saint Luke's-Shawnee Mission Health System delivers more than 6,000 babies annually.

Behavioral Health

Saint Luke's-Shawnee Mission Health System offers comprehensive mental health and substance abuse programs. The system covers all levels of care, including inpatient, outpatient, employee assistance, partial hospitalization, intensive outpatient, and in-home services. The region's leading psychiatrists, psychologists, clinical social workers, and

nursing professionals are affiliated with the network.

Health and Wellness

Saint Luke's-Shawnee Mission Health System provides a full range of health and wellness programming. Community programs include screenings and fitness classes, as well as smoking cessation, weight management, and complete health management programs. The It's Time to Feel Good membership program provides a variety of health and wellness information, including a bimonthly publication offering updates on fitness and educational programs, and general health information, as well as health benefit connections to area businesses.

Saint Luke's Stroke Center

Saint Luke's is the only hospital in Kansas City offering a specialized center for the

treatment of strokes. Trained to provide quick response, the multidisciplinary care team provides an aggressive treatment plan using the latest advances in stroke care. Aggressive treatment reduces a stroke patient's length of stay in a hospital by more than 25 percent and can significantly reduce or reverse the effects of the stroke.

Primary Care

Saint Luke's-Shawnee Mission Health System has more than 30 primary care practices throughout the Kansas City region. Specialties include family practice, internal medicine, pediatrics, and obstetrics and gynecology. In addition, Saint Luke's-Shawnee Mission Health System provides occupational health services through its CorporateCare clinics.

◄ Older Adult Services

The Older Adult Services program complements the Saint Luke's-Shawnee Mission Health System mission by providing care and patient support services to meet the growing needs of older adults. A comprehensive program of established services promotes healthy, more independent lifestyles. Health insurance assistance, medication counseling, and access to health education programs, as well as information about community services and programs, are available through the Older Adult Services program. In addition,

Clockwise from top:
The Level II intensive care nursery provides special care for high-risk newborns.

When moments count, Saint Luke's-Shawnee Mission Health System has the resources available for a quick response.

Health screening programs like Healthy Breaks offer valuable health and wellness information at convenient community and workplace locations.

DEAN SHEPARD

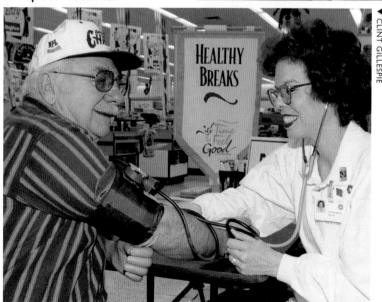
CLINT GILLESPIE

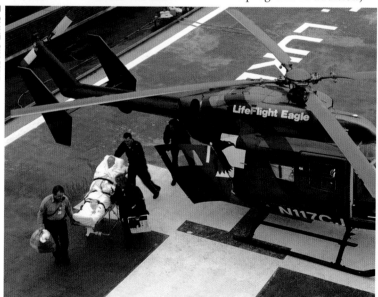

CELEBRATING GREATER KANSAS CITY

both outpatient and inpatient behavioral health care are available to help older adults maximize their quality of life.

Emergency Services

Saint Luke's Hospital received national verification by the American College of Surgeon's Committee on Trauma, placing Saint Luke's Trauma Center among a leading group of trauma centers across the country. As a Level I trauma center, Saint Luke's Hospital cares for the most critically injured adult and pediatric trauma patients.

Shawnee Mission Medical Center's emergency department is one of the busiest in Johnson County, treating more than 50,000 patients a year. Saint Luke's Northland Hospital provides 24-hour emergency care at both its Barry Road and its Smithville campuses.

LifeFlight Eagle air ambulance service, operating within a 150-mile radius of Kansas City, is staffed and equipped to treat and transport victims of life-threatening illnesses and injuries.

Telemedicine

Combining the latest in communications technology with the finest in medical care, the Saint Luke's-Shawnee Mission Health System has introduced telemedicine, providing physicians, nurses, and administrators access to a full complement of patient information from multiple locations throughout Greater Kansas City and the Midwest. Patients in rural locations can now consult directly with physicians in Kansas City without the expense and time involved in travel.

Community Commitment

In addition to its fundamental connections with the University of Missouri-Kansas City, Saint Luke's-Shawnee Mission Health System emphasizes its commitment to the community through school partnerships and a rape crisis center. The system has also established an affiliation with the Cabot Westside Clinic, a provider of bilingual primary health care.

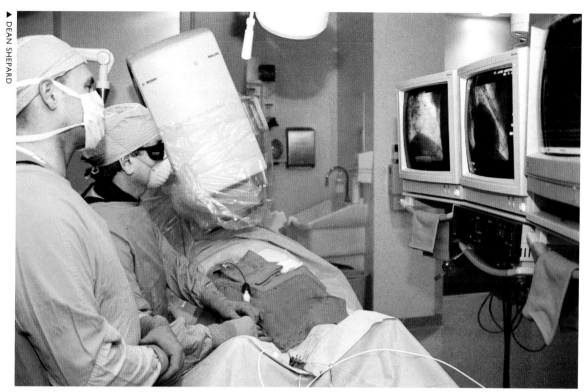

Advances in medical care are an integral part of the tradition of excellence in patient care (top).

In partnership with Saint Luke's-Shawnee Mission Health System, the Cabot Westside Clinic provides services to Kansas City's West Side and Hispanic communities (bottom).

Senior PGA Tour Event

For more than eight years, Crittenton has been the beneficiary of an annual Senior PGA Tour event sponsored by Saint Luke's-Shawnee Mission Health System. Top Senior PGA Tour players compete in this event held at Loch Lloyd Country Club.

Caring and Curing

As the 21st century approaches, Saint Luke's-Shawnee Mission Health System continues to focus on providing comprehensive health care to the communities it serves. In addition to its hands-on and call-in services, the system's Web site (www.saint-lukes.org) keeps patients and others informed about new developments within its many facilities.

"When I look to the future, I see a health system based on ideas, as well as bricks and mortar," says G. Richard Hastings, Saint Luke's-Shawnee Mission Health System president and CEO. "Saint Luke's-Shawnee Mission Health System is committed to enhancing the physical, mental, and spiritual health of the communities we serve. That means cutting-edge research and community education. That means matching our quality with our compassion.

"I am proud of our state-of-the-art facilities, but I am prouder still of the people who staff our facilities," Hastings continues, "for it is they who create a place of caring and curing."

HESE DAYS, HEALTH CARE INVOLVES MORE THAN TAKING TWO aspirin and calling the doctor in the morning. Increasingly high tech and high touch, today's state-of-the-art health care entities have forged new paths toward better patient care and education. In the Kansas City region, Health Midwest has led the way.

Health Midwest's story dates to the late 1970s, when leaders of what would eventually become Health Midwest had a vision: a system in which patients could move from one health care delivery point to another within a single system—conveniently, efficiently, and cost effectively. "While that vision is still a work in progress," says Tom Cranshaw, senior vice president of strategic planning, "Health Midwest continues to be the Kansas City health care leader in achieving dramatic and innovative changes in the way health care is delivered to area residents."

A Star Is Born

Although the visionaries discussed ideas more than 20 years ago, the Health Midwest name is fairly new to Kansas City. In 1991, Research Health Services (which dates to 1886, when Kansas City's German Hospital, the predecessor of Research Medical Center, was founded) and Baptist Health Systems merged to form a new entity under a new name—Health Midwest. Since then, Health Midwest has grown to reflect its advertising and promotional efforts: "Health Midwest: Leading the way to better health."

The Health Midwest of today is Kansas City's leading not-for-profit health delivery system, encompassing 14 general acute care, rehabilitation, and behavioral health centers; 2,300 physicians; numerous outpatient facilities and medical office buildings; and a broad spectrum of other health-related services. With 12,000 employees, Health Midwest is also Kansas City's second-largest nongovernmental employer.

Through the Physician Services and Office Facilities corporations, Health Midwest ensures that an adequate supply of well-trained physicians is always available to urban, suburban, and rural communities that might otherwise be underserved. Also, family practice residency programs at Health Midwest's Baptist Medical Center, Park Lane Medical Center (in cooperation with the University of Health Sciences College of Osteopathic Medicine), and Trinity Lutheran Hospital provide the area with an ample supply of well-trained family care physicians. "Health Midwest recognized the importance of primary care physicians long before it became fashionable to trumpet their importance in a reforming health care system," says Cranshaw.

Clockwise from top:
When it opened in October 1996, Health Midwest's new Menorah Medical Center became the finest acute care hospital available to Johnson County, Kansas, residents.

Each year the maternity units at seven Health Midwest hospitals deliver more than 5,000 babies.

Health Midwest's Employer Health Services helps area companies keep their employees—and ultimately their businesses—well.

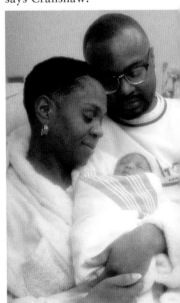

Acute Care Services

Health Midwest's urban-suburban-rural network of 12 general acute care facilities demonstrates the advantages of a system approach to health care delivery. "Health Midwest has responded to declining inpatient utilization by strategically real-locating scarce resources within our system," says Cranshaw. Health Midwest's four tertiary care hospitals are located in the more densely populated areas of Kansas City, while secondary care facilities are found in out-lying or rural regions.

A network of physician offices and clinical outreach services gives rural and suburban areas access to medical and surgical specialties, while the LifeFlight Eagle air ambulance, a joint venture between Health Midwest and several other health care organizations in Kansas City, also extends tertiary care to outlying areas.

Health Midwest's 12 general acute care hospitals include urban facilities Research Medical Center, Baptist Medical Center, Trinity Lutheran Hospital, and Park Lane Medical Center. Suburban hospitals include Menorah Medical Center, Medical Center of Independence, Lee's Summit Hospital, and Research Belton Hospital. Rural facilities are Cass Medical Center, Lafayette Regional Health Center, Allen County Hospital, and Hedrick Medical Center. In all, these Health Midwest acute care fa-

cilities, along with the system's two specialty care hospitals—Research Psychiatric Center and The Rehabilitation Institute—total more than 2,500 licensed beds.

Health Midwest offers a full array of general acute care services, including heart, lung, brain, kidney, cancer, diabetes, infectious disease, joint, eye, ear, urinary tract, geriatric, rehabili-tation, behavioral health, and women's health, as well as clinical outreach services to more than 30 rural hospitals in Missouri and Kansas. Patients have access to senior adult programs, health and wellness services, and com-munity health screenings. Health Midwest also has the region's only Gamma Knife technology that treats tumors and blood vessel abnormalities of the brain.

Changing Lives

The Rehabilitation Institute is a prime example of Health Midwest's ability to concentrate specialized expertise and services in a single area. The institute strives to restore disabled pa-tients to their highest physical, social, and vocational potential. Health Midwest supplements specialized care at The Rehabili-tation Institute with inpatient and outpatient rehabilitation services throughout the community.

Clockwise from top:
Health Midwest is Kansas City's leading provider of home health and hospice care services.

The Midwest Gamma Knife Cen-ter, based on the campus of Re-search Medical Center, offers the most advanced means avail-able for treating difficult tumors and blood vessel abnormalities of the brain.

LifeFlight Eagle, the premier air ambulance service in the Greater Kansas City area, has logged some 20 years of service in the community. It is a joint venture of Kansas City's leading medical institutions, including Health Midwest hospitals, and is the area's only air ambulance ser-vice that is locally owned and has local hospital affiliation.

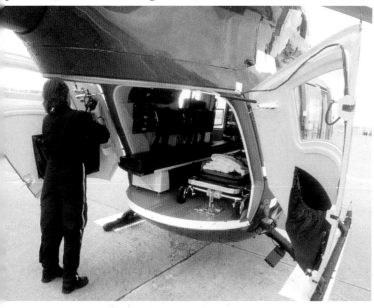

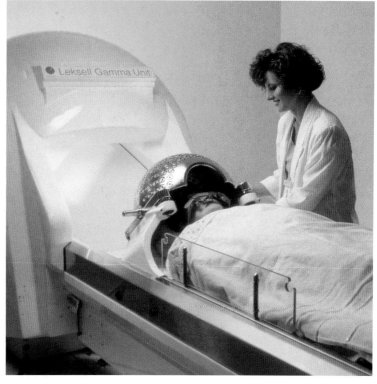

Health Midwest's behavioral care services treat those who confront mental, substance abuse, or obsessive-compulsive disorders. Research Psychiatric Center provides a spectrum of inpatient and partial hospitalization behavioral health care services; Research Mental Health Services offers behavioral health and substance abuse services at four locations in Kansas City; and a variety of programs and services at Trinity North, Baptist Medical Center, Menorah Medical Center, and other Health Midwest hospitals help change lives as well. Also, Health Midwest, Blue Cross/Blue Shield of Kansas City, and Menninger are partners in New Directions Behavioral

Health, Kansas City's leading behavioral health managed care organization.

Home and Away

Health Midwest's health care services don't end with a hospital stay. The system is also Kansas City's leading provider of home health and hospice care services.

Through the Visiting Nurse Association and several hospital-based home health agencies, Health Midwest is dedicated to providing area residents with professional, educational, and supportive health care services in the comfort and familiarity of home. Services include nursing; physical, occupational, and speech therapies; social work; dietitians; aides; volunteers; and home medical equipment.

Kansas City Hospice provides a wide range of services, too, in the home or in a homelike setting (such as a nursing home), for terminally ill patients and their families. Under the guidance of the patient's physician and the hospice medical director, Kansas City Hospice coordinates a team of trained professionals, including nurses, home health aides, therapists, social workers, chaplains, bereavement counselors, and volunteers. Hospice strives

to provide comfort for the patient, a semblance of control, and support for the family.

Older patients also find what they need through Health Midwest. Many system hospitals sponsor senior adult membership programs with social activities, timely health information and screenings, counseling on health-related financial information, and other services. Several Health Midwest hospitals operate skilled nursing units; the system also owns Trinity Lutheran Manor, a 120-bed nursing home. "Comprehensive older adult services have become increasingly important as the mix of senior adults in the American population increases," says Cranshaw.

Staying Well

Health Midwest's Employer Health Services (EHS) helps area companies keep their personnel—and ultimately their businesses—well. EHS works with area businesses through five divisions: Health Promotion, Employee Assistance, Occupational Medicine, Rehabilitation, and Hearing Conservation to improve and protect the physical, emotional, and psychological health of employees. "Employers soon realize that healthy employees, fewer work site injuries, reduced absenteeism, and higher productivity lead to a healthier bottom line," says Cranshaw.

Health Midwest sponsors a variety of family practice, nursing, allied health, and continuing medical education programs. The Bixby Institute for Continuing Education, the Orear Institute for Continuing Medical Education, and the Shirley Fearon Training Institute keep practicing physicians and other health care professionals tuned to new developments.

In addition to family practice residency programs, the Research College of Nursing, in partnership with Rockhurst College, offers a broad-based liberal arts education with clinical course work at Research Medical Center. By providing trained nurses for the region, the college further extends quality health care into the community. "Our system

Health Midwest's Trinity Lutheran Hospital is the title sponsor of the Hospital Hill Run, the premier running event in Kansas City. Health Midwest organizations sponsor a wide variety of athletic events designed to promote healthy lifestyles among area residents (top).

Health Midwest's Partnership for Change program strives to revitalize the major urban core business district and provide one of Kansas City's most extensive neighborhood revitalization programs (bottom).

has a strong belief that its excellence is directly tied to a commitment to teaching and learning," Cranshaw says.

Community Services

Health Midwest takes its commitment to the community seriously. One example of that responsibility is The Professionals® of Health Midwest, which provides callers with health information and physician referral services 24 hours a day. The service is staffed with local registered nurses who can answer virtually any health information question or guide callers to physicians who meet their needs.

Another is The Cancer Institute of Health Midwest, which is dedicated to improving the quality of life for residents throughout the Kansas City area. From prevention and early detection to advanced treatment and extended care, the institute fights cancer with an unmatched array of outreach programs, educational resources, and screening services, all backed by the latest in medical technology. "In fact," Cranshaw says, "Health Midwest providers diagnose and treat more than twice as many cancer cases as anyone else in the Kansas City area." The Cancer Institute offers free or reduced-price screening programs for colorectal, prostate, breast, and skin cancer to community residents. These programs have resulted in the early detection of cancer—drastically improving the prognosis—for hundreds of Kansas City-area residents.

"A key value at Health Midwest is the responsibility to serve our cities and our neighborhoods even beyond our role as a health care provider," says Cranshaw. "We define 'health' more broadly than the mere absence of disease. We extend it to encompass the total environment of our neighborhoods and our communities." One of the system's more visible community initiatives is its Partnership for Change program, an ambitious undertaking designed to revitalize Kansas City's urban core business district and neighborhoods.

In addition, Health Midwest provides the area's only family bereavement camp, creating opportunities for sharing and healing for families that have recently experienced the loss of a parent, child, or grandparent. Health Midwest also provides educational programs for expectant parents designed to help ensure a healthy baby, and offers treatment and rehabilitation services for mothers and babies addicted to crack, cocaine, or other drugs.

Health Midwest also offers in-home services for severely

emotionally disturbed children; sexual abuse prevention and safety programs for children; programs that provide free health screenings to area elementary schoolchildren, preventing health problems that could interfere with learning and the potential for success; and programs to prevent alcohol-related car accidents during the holidays.

Moreover, Health Midwest board members, physicians, and employees give time and talents to numerous civic and neighborhood groups. The system's efforts to strengthen families and neighborhoods encompass involvement in the United Way, the Neighborhood Family Project, the Main Street Corridor Redevelopment Corp., the East Meyer Community Association, the Southtown Council, and a variety of school partnership programs.

"The bottom line is, we care deeply about helping to make the Kansas City area the best possible place to live," Cranshaw says. "We'll continue to work with everyone to make this the 'healthiest' community, in the broadest sense of the word, in the entire country."

Family practice residency programs at Health Midwest's Baptist Medical Center, Park Lane Medical Center, and Trinity Lutheran Hospital provide the Kansas City area with an ample supply of well-trained family care physicians (top).

More than 2,300 of the Kansas City area's finest physicians are on the medical staffs of the 14 Health Midwest hospitals (bottom).

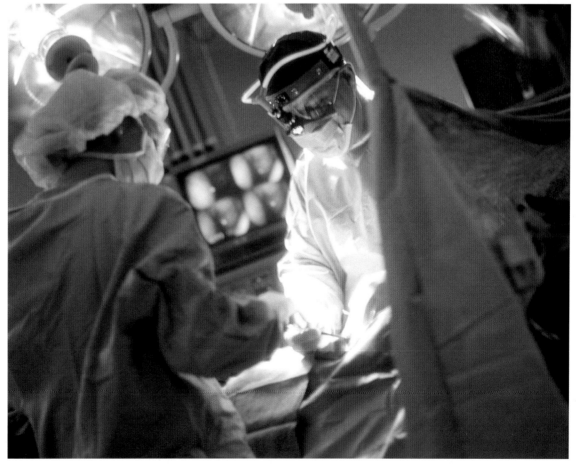

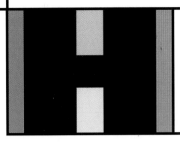

ENRY STEIN WOULD BE AMAZED AT JUST HOW FAR HIS company has come. Since he launched his *Kansas City Implement and Farm Journal* in 1886, the newsman's publishing empire has exploded. Now one of the largest trade magazine publishers in the world, PRIMEDIA

Intertec has grown to include more than 90 trade magazines and newsletters serving a host of industries from agriculture to real estate, from communications and entertainment to construction and automotives. These days, more than 3.8 million readers around the world regularly turn to PRIMEDIA Intertec publications for information needed to do their jobs better.

In addition, PRIMEDIA Intertec does much more than publish magazines. Supplementary products include buyers' guides, directories, trade show dailies, postcard decks, market research, and more than 350 technical books and pricing guides. More than 30 trade shows and conferences connect exhibitors and attendees as well as educators and conference participants in interactive forums. The development of Internet sites,

including the corporate site at www.intertec.com, and CD-ROM products that complement PRIMEDIA Intertec's trade publications, illustrate the company's commitment to the future of electronic media.

"Our growth at PRIMEDIA Intertec has certainly been phenomenal," says Raymond E. Maloney, president and CEO. "In the 30 years I've been with the company, I've been very proud of the company's dramatic growth—both in the number of quality magazines we publish and the revenues they generate. In the 10 years between 1987 and 1997, for example, our annual revenues have increased from $39.2 million to $233.6 million."

Filling a Need

For 112 years, PRIMEDIA Intertec's continuing growth and success have developed from

its ability to find an information need and fill it. Stein's *Kansas City Implement and Farm Journal* targeted the needs of the thriving farm machinery wholesale distribution industry of the Kansas City area. Eleven years later, the company was incorporated as the Implement Trade Journal Company and, by 1952, it evolved into Implement & Tractor Publications Inc.

Branching into book publishing in 1948, the Technical Publications Division, now known as the Book Division, was founded with the launch of the first universal, flat-rate, and repair manual for farm tractors. This initial thrust into technical book publishing proved so successful that a wide range of technical manuals were introduced as repair and trade-in guides for farm, marine, and industrial equipment and recreational vehicles.

Through the years, expanding product lines offered readers international marketing and technical information. Thus, in 1967 the name Intertec Publishing Corp. was established under the ownership of International Telephone & Telegraph (ITT). The company remained an ITT subsidiary until 1985, when the publisher was acquired by Macmillan Inc. When English media baron Robert Maxwell bought Macmillan in 1988, the publisher was spun off as a freestanding company owned by Rothchild Inc., a New York City-based investment-banking firm. Then, in 1989, former Macmillan executives William Reilly, Charles McCurdy, and Beverly Chell took an interest in the company. Backed by equity financing from Kohlberg Kravis & Roberts Company, the trio formed K-III Communications

PRIMEDIA Intertec supports the needs of 3.8 million subscribers who rely on 90 publications to help them work smarter and to help their businesses profit and grow.

Corp., which purchased Intertec and several other companies. After nine years, K-III, now PRIMEDIA Inc., has grown to be a $1.4 billion information enterprise with magazines that include *Seventeen, New York, Weekly Reader,* and *Modern Bride.* To better reflect the parent company's brand name, Intertec Publishing was changed to PRIMEDIA Intertec in 1998.

Trade Powerhouse

A subsidiary of PRIMEDIA, PRIMEDIA Intertec has its corporate headquarters in Overland Park, with divisional offices in Atlanta; Chicago; Denver; Detroit; Houston; Minneapolis; New York City; Stamford; Irvine; Clarksdale, Mississippi; Indianapolis; and London.

One of the largest trade magazine operations in the United States, PRIMEDIA Intertec employs more than 1,500 people, 400 of whom are located in Overland Park. There, employees carry out the company's display and classified advertising sales, editorial and art, marketing and promotions, credit services, accounting, human resources, circulation, corporate communications, information services, new media, planning and research, travel, and print production functions. Many of these functions are also performed in the company's 22 divisional offices.

PRIMEDIA Intertec employees pride themselves on producing

magazines that rank among the leading business-to-business publications in the world. The editors are in constant contact with their industry's professionals; most have worked in the field their publications serve and often hold advanced academic degrees in their areas of expertise. That knowledge is appreciated by PRIMEDIA Intertec's qualified readers, who turn to the company's many publications for essential statistics, informative news features, how-to articles, and updated technical advice. Readers are the top decision-makers who are able to respond to product introductions and advertising for their companies' purchasing needs.

The company's work pays off in a variety of ways. For example, each year the American Business Press, an association of trade publishers, recognizes editorial excellence in business publications. PRIMEDIA Intertec's editors have been recognized with numerous Jesse H. Neal Certificates of Merit and several coveted Jesse H. Neal Editorial Achievement Awards, trade publishing's equivalent to the Pulitzer Prize.

Most recently honored for individual achievement, David Smith, one of Intertec's many talented editorial directors, was recognized for his long-term contributions to editorial excellence as the 1996 recipient of the prestigious American Business Press Crain Award.

What's Ahead

Since its acquisition in 1989 by PRIMEDIA, PRIMEDIA Intertec has experienced tremendous growth through the acquisition of more than 75 magazines and related properties. In addition, PRIMEDIA Intertec and PRIMEDIA nurture organic growth through the development and launch of new magazines that reach underserved or newly energized niche markets. The company also strives to implement strategies to expand its product lines to meet the information needs of audiences in China, Latin America, and Europe.

"We've earned a position as a leader in the business-to-business publishing arena," says Maloney, "and we expect that growth to continue far into the future."

PRIMEDIA Intertec's 90 trade magazines serve the communications and entertainment, technology and transportation, marketing and professional services, agribusiness, and industrial industries (top).

PRIMEDIA Intertec employs more than 1,500 people, 400 of whom are located at its corporate headquarters in Overland Park (bottom).

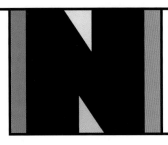

ATIONSBANK IS THE FINANCIAL SERVICES MARKET LEADER in Kansas City, offering a wide range of financial products and services nationally and internationally to individuals, businesses, corporations, institutional investors, and government agencies. ■ NationsBank's predecessor, First

National Bank, was chartered in Kansas City in 1886. At the end of its first day of business, the bank's total resources were more than $760,000. By attracting an impressive list of customers across the franchise and serving them well, NationsBank Corporation today, with $315 billion in total assets, is the nation's third-largest bank with full-service operations in 16 states and the District of Columbia.

NationsBank offers banking centers throughout Kansas City, with many featuring 24-hour banking.

On April 13, 1998, Bank-America Corporation and NationsBank Corporation announced a merger agreement that created the first truly national U.S. banking franchise. The merger established the company with $570 billion in assets, $45 billion in shareholders' equity, and a market capitalization of $133 billion. Following the merger, the company will have relationships with 29 million households in 22 states across the nation and serve 2 million businesses in the U.S. and 38 other countries.

Customers will have access to more than 14,700 ATMs and 4,800 banking centers. Today in Kansas City, NationsBank customers have access to 58 banking centers and more than 200 ATMs.

Customer Service Focused

Despite its size, Nations-Bank has always focused on customer service and on providing solutions to customers' concerns–before they even realize they have them.

MARK MCDONALD PHOTOGRAPHY

NationsBank's historic main lobby at 10th Street and Baltimore Avenue is a downtown landmark.

"What we have in Kansas City is the best of both worlds," says William C. Nelson, chairman, NationsBank Midwest and president, NationsBank Kansas City Region. "Consumers come to us because of the incredible convenience of our banking centers both in Kansas City and nationwide. From a corporate standpoint, we have the capabilities of a global bank delivered through a personal, hometown community network of banking professionals who have operated here for years. Big is only bad if it's impersonal, but big is good if it's backed by well-trained, personable, caring people who can deliver extra capabilities."

In fact, NationsBank has initiated a program called Model Banking. This brings to the market standard customer-focused products, computer systems, processes, and services in every banking center throughout the franchise. It allows NationsBank to capitalize on its size by linking locations, products, and services while retaining a local flavor.

Extensive Range of Services

The complete range of NationsBank banking services includes corporate finance, consumer banking, small business lending, international services, asset management, food and agribusiness financing, and residential and commercial real estate lending. Additionally, NationsBanc Investments, Inc., a brokerage affiliate, offers investors their choice of personal investment consulting services or discount brokerage services.

With a legal lending limit of nearly $3.3 billion, the highest among Kansas City area banks, NationsBank is the bank of choice for corporations both large and small.

The acquisition of NationsBanc Montgomery Securities has enabled NationsBank to provide clients true one-stop shopping capabilities. Clients have access to financial products and services from bank loans and bridge financings to debt and equity underwriting and risk management.

NationsBank Private Client Group manages $60 billion in assets and is the second-largest investment money manager for the affluent market in the country.

Building Communities

NationsBank builds upon its commitment to the Kansas City community by providing generous corporate contributions, as well as donating thousands of volunteer hours. In May 1998, NationsBank and BankAmerica unveiled a $350 billion, 10-year national commitment to community development lending and investment. "This commitment, which underscores our investment in the future of the communities we serve, roughly equals the combined total of all community lending goals made by the rest of the banking industry since the Community Reinvestment Act became law in 1977," says Nelson.

In fact, Nelson himself has been a dedicated civic volunteer. Since moving to Kansas City in 1988, he has served as chairman of the Civic Council, the Area Development Council, and the Partnership for Children. He has championed community policing, immunization, and low-income mortgage lending. Also, Nelson has supported the Muehlebach Hotel renovation, has led the drive for a new down-

town arena, and has served as chairman of the Business Partners/ Kansas City Symphony and as honorary chairman of the State Ballet of Missouri. In addition to directing the 1995 Heart of America United Way Campaign, Nelson is vice chairman of the Greater Kansas City Chamber of Commerce and the Greater Kansas City Community Foundation.

NationsBank embraces its commitment to the communities it serves. NationsBank associates are given two hours of paid time off every week to volunteer in public or private schools. A staunch supporter of Kansas City's Promise campaign, NationsBank has promised to recruit at least 10 percent of its 2,100 Kansas City associates to serve as YouthFriends volunteers and to serve in a leadership and financial partnership role with YouthNet to open 88 after-school Safe Place venues. NationsBank has also committed to establishing 25 Make a Difference Centers—including one in Kansas City—which will provide after-school education programs and activities for as many as 260,000 youth across the nation.

Managers throughout the company are encouraged to work out flexible schedules so that associates can participate in commu-

nity activities or continue their education. That combination of people and progress will be the mark for NationsBank in the future. As the company continues to install increasingly complex technology, it remains committed to serving people first.

"You've got to manage technology through people," says Nelson. "A lot of bank customers still want services they can only get through their neighborhood branch, but more and more people want automation. One of our biggest challenges is training our people to handle customers in whatever way that customer is most comfortable in dealing with his or her finances. Either way, the key is people."

NationsBank is committed to convenience, featuring in-store banking centers and more than 200 ATMs in the Kansas City metropolitan area (top).

NationsBank consumer bankers provide professional service to customers (bottom).

OR MORE THAN A CENTURY, KANSAS CITY'S OWN FAULTLESS Starch/Bon Ami Company and its wonderful employees have been making people look good. From the original corn starch ("No cooking—just add water!") to aerosol spray starches of several varieties, the Faultless Starch/Bon Ami Company has made a

name for itself with folks who want their clothing to look snappy, even brand new. More than that, Faultless has maintained its position in the market with unique products that are simple to use.

Through the years, Faultless has added other products—from the Bon Ami and Kleen King lines of cleansers to yard and garden care products such as the Garden-Weasel® and the Garden Claw®. The Laundry Products Group markets a line of specialized products to commercial laundries and dry cleaners. The International Department

markets many of these products to other companies around the world, who then market the products in their own country. The newest product line to be marketed is Trapp's® Private Garden® line of specially fragranced ambience aroma candles and aerosol room fragrances. Conceived and created by Kansas City interior decorator Bob Trapp, of Trapp & Company—a Kansas City landmark enterprise itself—these products are distributed nationwide through gift store channels. The other products are distributed nationwide through supermarkets, hardware stores,

drug stores, home centers, department stores, and mail order catalogs.

Faultless Starch/Bon Ami products have found a wide appeal for many generations. "With our Faultless line of fabric care products, we're basically in the appearance business," says Gordon T. Beaham III, the company's president and chairman, and the fourth generation of the Beaham family to lead the company. "It's a fact that when two strangers meet, first impressions are made at once. Right after the face, the next things noticed are the clothes each have on. And first impressions are difficult to change, so it's important. When a person looks good, that individual is proud of his or her appearance—and that makes us happy."

Family Affair

Faultless Starch's long history includes a succession of Beahams at the helm. Major Thomas G. Beaham, the current president's great-grandfather, launched the company in 1887. The major purchased the Faultless Starch formula from Bosworth Manufacturing Company after he moved to Kansas City from his native Zanesville, Ohio, the year before. His son, Gordon T. Beaham, joined his father in 1901 and continued at Faultless until his retirement as CEO in 1951.

Gordon T. Beaham Jr. also went to work in the family business, beginning in 1931. He retired in 1986, handing the reins to his son, who had started working at Faultless in 1960. Gordon Beaham III's wife, Nancy, also works at the company as director of consumer relations. They have four children, Cathy, Carolyn Beaham West, Bob, and David.

Faultless Starch/Bon Ami Company has been in the business of making people look good for more than a century.

The Faultless/Bon Ami family of products includes spray starch, glass cleaners, and cleansers. The company's International Division distributes several of its specialty cleaning and laundry care products to overseas markets (top).

Faultless acquired Bon Ami cleanser in 1971. First manufactured in Connecticut by the J.T. Robertson Soap Company, Bon Ami's signature label with a little yellow chick and tagline "Hasn't Scratched Yet!" is an early American trademark, and touts the cleanser's gentle abrasive (bottom).

Bob and David work for the company now.

With such enduring ties, it's only natural that Faultless products have such wide appeal. From the company's earliest days, Faultless Starch became an extended family affair, as housewives found many uses for the product other than starching clothes. They used it as an elegant finish to embroidery and lace, as a treatment for skin irritations, and as both a baby powder and a bath powder.

Faultless' popularity was further enhanced among families when salesman John Nesbitt took wagon loads of storybooks into Texas and the Indian Territory in the 1890s, attaching them to Faultless Starch boxes with rubber bands. Designed as a supplement or substitute for school primers, the 36 Faultless Starch books published from the 1890s to the 1930s actually taught many children in Texas, Oklahoma, and the rest of the Midwest and Southwest how to read. "That was an early marketing plus for the company," says Beaham. "Kids wanted to collect all 36 books, so many families became loyal Faultless Starch users."

Buying Bon Ami

Kleen King® was acquired in 1968. And although Bon Ami® wasn't acquired by Faultless Starch until 1971, the original Bon Ami Company could also trace its roots into the last century. Founded in Manchester, Connecticut, in 1886, Bon Ami was first manufactured by the J.T. Robertson Soap Company. Its signature red and yellow label with a little yellow chick and the tag line "Hasn't Scratched Yet!" is an example of an early American trademark, devised from the fact that newly hatched chicks don't scratch the ground for food until a few days after they emerge from their shells. It also differentiates Bon Ami, which had—and still has—a mild abrasive, from the abrasive cleansers that were all harsher.

Several years after it purchased Bon Ami cleanser, Faultless added the Bon Ami name to its own to emphasize the return of a product that had very nearly disappeared. The Bon Ami reintroduction was heralded in a letter Gordon Beaham III wrote for the product in the September 1974 *Whole Earth (Catalog) Epilog.* "We live in a time, I believe, when many 'old fashioned'

reliable products are about to become new products and products of the future," he wrote, pointing out that Bon Ami could be considered less harmful to the environment than other cleaners because it didn't use phosphates, chlorine, perfume, or dyes.

Faultless beefed up Bon Ami sales by launching an advertising campaign that played on the product's original affiliation with baby birds. "Never Underestimate the Cleaning Power of a 94-Year-Old Chick with a French Name" read the slogan that helped sales rise 12 percent in the first six months of the campaign. Today, Bon Ami maintains a good share

of the cleanser market, ranking as the third-best-selling powdered cleanser in the United States.

Listening to Consumers

For nearly three-quarters of a century, Faultless concerned itself with only one line of business: packing and selling dry laundry starch. But by 1960, times were changing, and the company realized that housewives were looking for greater convenience.

"We went to Arthur D. Little, Inc., and they created a unique formula for us that was head and shoulders above anything else available," says Beaham, who started his career at Faultless the same year the company was introducing its new landmark product, aerosol starch. "A lot can go wrong when spraying starch on clothing. For example, if the spray isn't right, it can stick to the iron or wet the fabric too much. They were really chemical magicians in coming up with this high-quality aerosol starch."

Soon after introducing its Faultless Spray-On Starch, the

company unveiled other new products. Its Faultless Fabric Finish debuted in 1964, its Faultless Hot Iron Cleaner in 1965. And for three years in the decade of the 1960s, the total aerosol starch category was among the top 10 fastest-growing categories in U.S. supermarkets, due in part to the company's pioneering of the 22-

ounce size aerosol starch can. This was when supermarkets were carrying between 12,000 and 15,000 products.

In the 1970s, the starch and fabric-finish market declined sharply for Faultless and others, as permanent press and synthetic fabrics became the new darlings of the fashion world. The trend was to be short-lived, however. When the price of synthetic, petroleum-based fabrics rose and the synthetics were found to be less comfortable than cotton clothes, people returned to cotton. "In hot environments, people wore a lot of cotton, because it is so comfortable, more so than any other fabric, so southern areas have always been good markets for us," says Beaham. "And in the state of Texas, you can wear starched jeans with creases in them to everything but black tie affairs. Many people wear starched jeans almost all the time."

More recently, expansion has meant new products altogether. The Faultless Laundry Products Group now offers more than 75 different starches, chemicals, and specialty products to commercial laundries and dry cleaners. In 1976, the company acquired the exclusive U.S. sales rights to the Garden-Weasel, a German garden tool that the company still sells through hardware channels. In the 1990s, Faultless increased its home and garden tool line by

The Kleen King line of cleansers was added in 1968 (top).

In 1976, Faultless acquired the exclusive U.S. sales rights to the Garden-Weasel, a German garden tool that the company still sells through hardware channels. During the 1990s, the company expanded its home and garden tool line by adding the WeedPopper®, the Hoe-Down®, and the Garden Claw® (bottom).

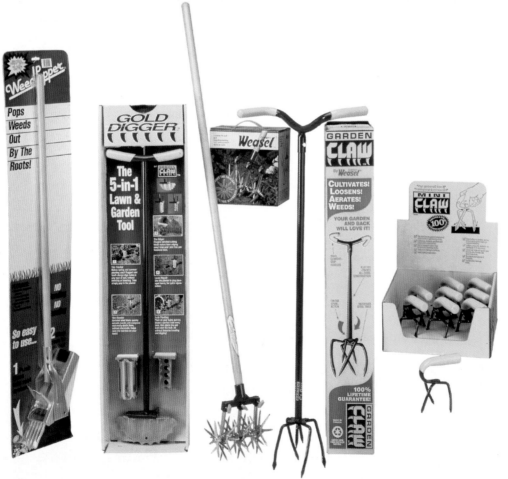

adding other products that included the RuXXac® Fold-Flat® Cart, the WeedPopper®, the Hoe-Down®, and the Garden Claw®.

The company acquired the Magic® line of aerosol sizing and fabric finishes in 1997.

Going Global

Although people use its products close to their own homes, Faultless itself has done anything but stay domestic. The company has been selling its products worldwide since 1962 through U.S. military commissaries and exchanges. In addition, Faultless Starch/Bon Ami created an International Division that has exported several of the company's specialty cleaning and laundry care products to overseas markets for years.

"We're in 30 or 40 different countries now," says Beaham. "We opened Mexico about four years ago. In Mexico, a person's appearance is important, and the appearance of a family's children is especially important to their parents."

Faultless has formed such partnerships with businesses that range from the Blattmann Company in Switzerland (1962), to Hoffman's Starkefabriken AG, and the Gebr. vom Braucke Company, inventors of the Garden-Weasel and the RuXxac Cart in West Germany (1964-1985), and to Mexican Company Industrias H-24, S.A. De C.V. (1997). Faultless products have been sold in Europe, Central and South America, the Caribbean, and the Near and Far East.

Although Faultless Starch/Bon Ami now spans the globe with its wide variety of products, the company has maintained its headquarters in Kansas City, moving only from the West Bottoms to downtown to the River Market district, where the headquarters now resides. The company maintains two other Kansas City sites, housing a laboratory and a distribution center. Faultless' manufacturing plants are located in Kansas City and Humansville, Missouri.

In the Future

A company that's survived for more than 100 years has a good chance of being around for another century. Through its history, Faultless Starch/Bon Ami has relied on a winning combination of conservative management strategy and focused innovations. The company's next generation of associates—the fifth—will, no doubt, carry on.

In addition to pursuing new markets and new ways of selling select products—most notably the home and garden tool line—the Faultless family has believed since early on that all their consumer product packages, including aerosols, should be recycled. "We would hope that 100 percent of all consumer packages worldwide can eventually be recycled," says Beaham.

The Trapp Private Garden line of candles in more than six different fragrances is the company's newest venture. It's the first time Faultless has pursued the gift store market, but it won't be the last time they try totally new ideas. "We're always looking for new opportunities," says Beaham. "Who knows what might be next?"

Clockwise from top left: Faultless acquired Magic Sizing in 1997.

Faultless has formed similar partnerships with the Gebr. vom Braucke Company, inventors of the Garden-Weasel and the RuXXac Cart in West Germany.

The Trapp Private Garden line of candles in more than six different fragrances is Faultless/Bon Ami's newest venture.

N 1997, THE GREATER KANSAS CITY CHAMBER OF COMMERCE DECIDED to make some changes as it celebrated 110 years of community service. To underscore the anniversary, the group streamlined its management operations, introduced a new logo that better declares its focus, and developed a personality statement that clearly proclaims its goals. Then

the Chamber announced its 1998 theme as Greater Together, which sums up the enterprising association's newly energized philosophy.

Greater Together is more than just a motto. For the Chamber, it is a mission—to seek out ways that the Greater Kansas City region can unite toward building a greater metropolitan region for all businesses and citizens. After all, the Chamber believes, the region truly is greater when it stands together.

The opportunity to create this unity presents itself in a host of ways—government arenas, business networking and education, and international circles. Relying on a strong foundation as a community leader, the Chamber has positioned itself to be the catalyst that will make those things happen.

The new logo is the visible sign of changes. Its interlocking rings symbolize the unity between Kansas and Missouri business communities, and the subtle image of a heart signifies the heart of the nation. Additionally, the organization has become known as the Chamber, and is now the metro's oldest and largest business organization covering the entire region.

"We are changing because business is changing and facing new challenges," says Pete Levi, president of the Chamber. "We are a different organization from the stereotypical chamber of commerce. We aren't afraid to get involved in difficult issues, whether it's transit initiatives, building metrowide partnerships, or pushing those business concerns that used to fall only in the social

realm. It's the Chamber's mission to strive for continuous improvement of Greater Kansas City's business environment, and, in doing so, we're always at the forefront of community development."

Enhancing Existing Businesses

Among its many members, the Chamber counts local giants, as well as smaller firms. Together, Chamber members establish strong support systems that help local companies do their business better.

One example is the Chamber's fight against the local labor shortage. Each year, Kansas City area companies recruit eager job applicants at job fairs sponsored by the Chamber, along with other local chambers. Moreover, the Chamber's Drugs Don't Work

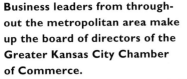

Business leaders from throughout the metropolitan area make up the board of directors of the Greater Kansas City Chamber of Commerce.

The 1997-1998 Chamber Chairman Wynn Presson (left), of Health Midwest, and Chamber President Pete Levi surround the Chamber's new logo, introduced early in Presson's term.

program also assists existing companies by signing up drug-free workplace subscriber businesses. This initiative has reached more than 50,000 individuals throughout the area.

In addition, the Chamber has begun to tackle social issues, such as child care, school-to-career development, and welfare-to-work transitions. "These three specific focuses will target the expansion of our local workforce, an urgent need in our tight labor market," says E. Wynn Presson, 1997-1998 Chamber chairman and vice chairman of the board for local health care corporation Health Midwest. "Whether it is helping employers deal with drugs in the workplace, championing small-business development and recognition, or leading the focus on solutions to major metrowide issues—such as public transportation—the Chamber is about making Greater Kansas City a greater place in which to live and work."

Working with Government

Throughout all of its activities, the Chamber maintains a strong connection to governmental allies in order to foster a business-friendly political environment. The Chamber realizes that these relationships are key to a strong economy and continues to promote business concerns at all levels—local, state, and federal.

Perhaps the Chamber's most important work in Washington, D.C., came when it formed the Mo-Kan Washington Forum in cooperation with Farmland Industries. Through the forum, Washington-based lobbyists from local companies meet regularly to discuss area issues and protect the region's best interests. In addition, the Chamber formed the Washington Scholars Program that allows five business executives to spend four days in the nation's capital to get an insider's view of national politics.

"It's absolutely essential that business have a representative at the table at the local, state, and national levels," says Dell Godbold, the Chamber's former small-business vice chair and president of his own company, the Godbold Group. "No one is going to take care of us better than one of our own. The Chamber is the best suited and most quali-

fied organization to do that for businesses both large and small."

Going Global

Kansas City area businesses have worked to expand their global opportunities, and the Chamber is helping to make it happen. In 1997, the Chamber launched a plan to help establish the Kansas City area as a premier international business community. Twelve companies have signed on as International Investors for these international activities. Among the initiatives has been an increased effort to bring international leaders to the area. In 1997, for example, the Midwest-U.S. Japan Conference was a resounding success, attended by more than 530 business leaders, including 140 from Japan.

The Chamber also has been instrumental in creating a business-friendly environment between Mexico and Kansas City since the North American Free Trade Agreement (NAFTA) became effective in 1994 and opened countless trading opportunities. In 1997, more than 100 North American mayors gathered in Kansas City to promote trade along the Interstate 35 corridor, a follow-up to the first Mayor Summit in Monterrey. The Chamber was Kansas City's original supporter in developing trade along the corridor and helped initiate the summits to thrust the Kansas City area and its partners into the international arena.

"Every Chamber member should consciously remind people that the Kansas City area and its business community are aware of the globalization taking place within our economy, and that we recognize and support the importance of international business opportunities that can be developed for Midwest-based businesses," says Harry Cleberg, 1996-1997 Chamber chairman and CEO of Farmland Industries. "As deepwater ports become increasingly crowded, greater opportunities can exist for communities that didn't historically perceive themselves as ideally located for active involvement in international commerce."

The Inner Workings

Another of the Chamber's priorities is a dedication to improving and promoting the transportation, infrastructure, and environmental needs of

Greater Kansas City. For example, thanks to the organization's efforts, as well as the efforts of others, the Kansas City area received $500,000 in federal money for a feasibility study for an international freight processing center at Richards-Gebaur Airport. If the study determines that such a center would be valuable, it could create as many as 40,000 jobs.

A crucial element to creating a united Kansas City metro area is a seamless public transportation system that crosses state and county lines, and that would replace current systems that are separately maintained by each

city. The Chamber has worked to make that system a reality by forming the Metro Transit Steering Committee with the Mid-America Regional Council. The group immediately began studying current transit services and developing a business plan for an integrated metrowide system. In addition, it closely examined various alternative modes of travel. The Chamber asked for participation from every other chamber and city in the area and met with a strong response.

"The quality of life in our community is impacted positively through the strong and

The annual dinner of the Greater Kansas City Chamber of Commerce, traditionally held in late November, is one of the area's most prestigious business events. It sells out with more than 1,500 guests and a large waiting list.

The Chamber's Kansas Citian of the Year is the highest honor presented by the business community. Each year, an individual is singled out for contributions to the betterment of the entire region. The award recipient is honored at the organization's annual dinner, and past honorees traditionally pose for a group photograph.

Mitch Wheeler shows off the Mr. K trophy at the Chamber's Small Business Celebration on May 15 after his company, Marketing Associates International (MAI), was named the Chamber's 1998 Small Business of the Year. Congratulating Wheeler are (from left) Deb Turpin of River City Studio, chair of the Chamber's Metropolitan Entrepreneurs Council; Chamber Vice Chair of Small Business Michael Carter of Carter Broadcast Group; Chamber Chair Wynn Presson of Health Midwest; Chamber President Pete Levi; and MAI's Don Schmidt and Harry Campbell.

effective Chamber of Commerce that we enjoy," says Peter Lemke, president and CEO of EFL Associates and the Chamber's 1997-1998 chair. "Frankly, the Chamber represents not just member organizations but the entire business community, as well as the community at large. Virtually all of our initiatives today are bistate in nature and run the gamut from legislative affairs through transportation initiatives and various workforce issues that affect all Kansas Citians."

Staying Strong for Members

In addition to at-large community outreach, the Chamber wants to keep its members actively interested and participating in every aspect of the organization. One way it has accomplished this is through Kansas City's first on-line business resource, www.kcchamber.com. The immensely popular Web site offers such features as the Small Business Starting Point, an excellent source for questions about starting and running a business. Additionally, the Chamber provides free Web pages to each member, enabling them to more effectively reach local, regional, national,

and international markets, and links them back to the Chamber's own site.

The Chamber also publishes directories and resources for guiding members in making better business decisions. Among the publications produced are the *MBE/WBE Directory*, which lists minority- and women-owned businesses; the *Membership Directory and Buyers Guide*; various editions of economic data; the *Greater Kansas City International Business Directory*; and the *Heartland Freight Coalition Update*. Members also receive business news through Chamber publications such as the *Kansas Citian*, *Weekly Wrap-up*, and *Growth*.

Another membership benefit comes to those who have shown exemplary business and civic leadership. Each year, the Chamber gives its Kansas Citian of the Year award to the individual who is most involved in improving the business and social fabric of the Kansas City area. The award, presented at the Chamber's annual dinner, is the highest honor presented by the local business community. For example, R. Crosby Kemper, chairman and CEO of UMB Financial Corp.,

received the award for his commitment to providing financial products and services through UMB Banks and his involvement with cultural and philanthropic activities, which included his $6.6 million gift to found the Kemper Museum of Contemporary Art and Design. In previous years, honorees have included civic leaders Adele Hall and Anita Gorman, Ollie Gates (owner of Gates & Sons Bar-B-Q), Richard C. Green Jr. (chairman and CEO of UtiliCorp United), Dick Berkley (former mayor of Kansas City, Missouri), and Lamar Hunt (Kansas City Chiefs owner).

This honor sums up the Chamber's mission to create cohesion in the community through volunteer efforts that focus on unity. "We have to bring people from different communities and different interests together," says Levi. "We're all about partnerships. Our new logo, for example, with its curves and lines, appears in motion because we are a dynamic Chamber, a cutting-edge Chamber moving full-force into the future."

Indeed, the Chamber is the place where businesses come together to create a greater Kansas City.

WHEN ARTHUR YOUNG ARRIVED IN KANSAS CITY, IT was a dusty cattle town where agriculture and commerce met in a noisy allegiance to progress. The young Scotsman, who hailed from the first country to recognize accounting as a profession, traveled to America

Arthur Young, together with his younger brother Stanley, established the firm of Arthur Young & Co. in 1906 in the New York Life Building. This firm has evolved into Ernst & Young LLP.

Ernst & Young is involved in the March of Dimes Walk-a-Thon, as well as Christmas in October, Kansas City Spirit Festival, American Cancer Society, Big Brothers/Big Sisters, and many other interests.

to look after the investments of various English companies and found very little competition in his chosen line of work. He opened his own accounting firm in Chicago in 1893 and, in 1895, landed in Kansas City with orders to liquidate the failing Phillips Investment Company for several British financiers.

What was supposed to be a temporary assignment, however, turned into a permanent one, when Young instead decided to take over Phillips. The same year, he and partner Charles Stuart, sufficiently impressed with the growth prospects of their burgeoning midwestern discovery, opened a branch of their Stuart & Young accounting firm in downtown Kansas City.

In 1906, Young and Stuart dissolved their original partnership. Together with his younger brother Stanley, Young then

established the firm of Arthur Young & Co.

Competition grew quickly in the accounting field, as businessmen came to realize the value of bookkeeping, auditing, and tax-related services. One competitor, Ernst & Ernst, opened a Kansas City office in 1919 during an expansion plan that

placed the firm in some 16 cities at the time. Founded in Cleveland, Ohio, in 1903, the company was known later as Ernst & Whinney. In 1989, a merger with Arthur Young & Co. created the accounting powerhouse Ernst & Young LLP.

Covering the Globe

Today, more than a century after Arthur Young first planted his standard in Kansas City, the firm now boasts a stunning roster of industry achievements. For example, Ernst & Young has offices in some 650 locations in more than 130 countries, including 316 in Europe, 175 in the Americas, more than 100 in Asia and the Pacific Rim, and 67 in the Middle East and Africa. It is the second-largest management consulting practice among the major professional services firms, with nearly 10,500 consultants worldwide. With global revenues in excess of $7.8 billion, Ernst & Young is the leader in serving the manufacturing, financial services, and consumer products industries worldwide.

In addition, the firm has the largest international tax practice in terms of revenues. "Ernst & Young has developed so that we offer far more than tax and auditing services," says Mike Morrissey, managing partner of the Kansas City office. "We try to give our clients the absolute best solution to solve their business issues. We have a fanatical desire to serve our clients."

Closer to Home

On a national scale, Ernst & Young audits more Fortune 500 companies than any other firm, and leads the pack in industries such as manufacturing, consumer products, real estate,

health care, and construction. In Kansas City, the firm reflects the concerns of area businesses, tending to specialize in providing ideas, solutions, results, and value building for companies in telecommunications, financial services, insurance, and health care. The local practice also includes a considerable emphasis on entrepreneurial businesses.

In order to serve its clients, Ernst & Young has long emphasized hiring top-notch accountants and business consultants—from management experts to health care consultants, financial advisers to information technology specialists. Such broad coverage allows the firm to provide a virtual one-stop shop for corporations, organizations, and small businesses to find the help they need.

"Our ability to attract and retain the best and brightest people we possibly can has been a key to our success," says Morrissey. "We think we demonstrate industry-based credentials and industry-relevant experience to do whatever work our clients need."

Community Involvement

The day-to-day operations of the early Kansas City office were managed by Stanley Young. As a native Scotsman, one of Stanley's most enduring legacies came from his lament that golf was unknown in the Midwest. As a result, he set about introducing locals to the game, then gathered like-minded duffers to lease Seth Ward's cow pasture, now Jacob L. Loose Park, for a proper links. By 1897, the Kansas City Country Club had opened a nine-hole course, clubhouse, and tennis courts on the site. A year later, the club inaugurated its second nine holes.

Today, Ernst & Young exposes Kansas Citians and the world to causes it believes are important. The firm sponsors its National Entrepreneur of the Year program each June in 45

cities, including Kansas City, and then recognizes the award recipients during an awards ceremony broadcast by CNBC. Locally, the firm sponsors the Midwest Venture Capital Conference twice each year, as well as the State & Local Tax Quarterly Breakfast, Corporate and Insurance Year-End Updates, and Spring Government Forum. Civically, Ernst & Young is involved in Christmas in October, Kansas City Spirit Festival, American Cancer Society, March of Dimes Walk-a-Thon, and Big Brothers/Big Sisters, among many other interests.

"The Kansas City metro area is a fabulous place to live," says Morrissey. "The future is bright for the entire region, and it's very bright for Ernst & Young here, too. Our solid, steady rate of growth will do well by Kansas City, and it will reflect positively on Ernst & Young as well."

In 1989, Ernst & Ernst merged with Arthur Young & Co., creating the accounting powerhouse Ernst & Young LLP.

The firm sponsors its National Entrepreneur of the Year program each June in 45 cities, including Kansas City, and then recognizes the award recipients during an awards ceremony broadcast by CNBC.

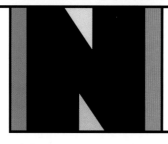

OW WELL INTO ITS SECOND CENTURY, KANSAS CITY LIFE Insurance Company can look back proudly on a history that began in 1895 in a three-person office. Through years of astute planning and management, Kansas City Life has grown into a highly respected family of companies.

While many businesses have come and gone, Kansas City Life has prevailed.

A Centennial of Safety, Security, and Stability

Kansas City Life President and Chief Executive Officer R. Philip Bixby says, "The honesty and integrity of all our people, from our agents to home office associates, is unmatched. And we have a quality product. When you have good people selling quality products, it allows you to endure for more than a hundred years."

Kansas City Life has done more than just endure. By 1998, the group of companies had $3.5 billion in assets, with more than $26 billion in life insurance in force. Kansas City Life itself is ranked by A.M Best among the top 10 percent of all stock life insurance companies in statutory assets. Ward's Financial, a nationally prominent, independent management consulting firm, regularly places Kansas City Life on the Ward's 50 list of selected companies it considers to exhibit the highest safety, consistency, and performance for five consecutive years.

"Our very conservative and prudent fiscal policies have allowed us to take good care of the funds entrusted to us," Bixby states. "That lets us fulfill our promise to our customers, and what we sell is that promise—to deliver when the money is needed. We strive to give individuals and families a quality of life that they would not otherwise be able to afford."

Building on a Firm Foundation

Kansas City Life has come a long way since its founding, surviving wars, epidemics, the Great Depression, and various other ups and downs in the national economy. More recently, dramatic changes in the insurance industry have challenged the company. "The sophistication of our business has been dramatic. We've invested heavily in technology and personnel to maintain a competitive level," says Bixby.

With a field force of more than 1,100 agents, Kansas City Life serves in excess of a half million policyowners with individual and group life insurance, annuities, and variable products available through approximately 125 career general agencies in 48 states. Two subsidiaries— Old American Insurance Company and Sunset Life Insurance Company of America—add another 430,000 customers.

Recognizing the growing importance of investments to individual retirement planning, Kansas City Life added Sunset Financial Services, Inc. This wholly owned broker/dealer supports Kansas City Life's own Century II variable product line, and serves the field force of both the parent company and Sunset Life with a wide array of mutual funds, unit investment trusts, limited partnerships, and general securities. According to Bixby, "Our cutting-edge abilities have enabled us to offer variable insurance that fits individual customers like never before."

Throughout the years, one element that hasn't changed is Kansas City Life's commitment to the community it calls home. The company is a major contributor to Children's Mercy Hospital, the Nelson-Atkins Museum of Art, Ronald McDonald House, and Kansas City, Missouri, Police Department, among others.

"You'd be hard pressed to look at any facet of life in our community that Kansas City Life hasn't appreciably touched," Bixby states. "From education to outdoor activities to enhancing efforts in community policing, we've assisted the entire metropolitan area. That's been an important part of our past and it will continue to be an important part of our future."

In summing up the Kansas City Life story, Bixby says, "While all companies must make changes to meet new challenges, in one way we'll stay the same—safe, stable, and committed to our agents, policyowners, and community." This promise is a sure sign Kansas City Life will remain true to its motto, "We'll be with you. We're Kansas City Life."

Bubbling water supports a 2,155-pound, floating granite Kugel ball, the centerpiece of Kansas City Life Insurance Company's 100th Anniversary Commemorative Plaza (top).

With twin lionesses flanking the entrance, Kansas City Life's home office complex has been a local landmark since 1924 (below).

have contributed to Burns & McDonnell's success.

A century ago, two young men stood on a street corner in Kansas City, watching troops parade by on their way to the Spanish-American War. Like many other young men of the time, both had seriously considered joining the fight. But they decided to stay behind to fulfill their own mission.

Robert McDonnell and Clinton Burns had arrived in Kansas City just a few months earlier. When their train rolled into town in the early morning darkness of April 1, 1898, it was the first time either man had seen the city.

Despite their lack of firsthand knowledge of the city, the two Stanford University graduates knew it was a land of opportunity for consulting engineers like themselves. Having studied the area in detail, they knew the region surrounding Kansas City needed more basic infrastructure projects than any other metropolitan area.

And time has proved them right. From humble beginnings in a one-room office, offering power generation, water, and wastewater engineering to municipalities within an overnight train ride of Kansas City, Burns & McDonnell has grown into an internationally known, full-service firm with offices around the world.

Heading into the Future

As proud as Burns & McDonnell is of past accomplishments, its focus is on tomorrow. "We've accomplished a lot in the first 100 years," says Dave G. Ruf Jr., chairman and chief executive officer. "And there are no limits to what we can achieve in our second century."

Ruf says Burns & McDonnell will continue as a leader in the

movement toward strategic alliances. "We establish true partnerships with our clients, working with them to provide services they need to compete successfully."

Because Burns & McDonnell is employee owned, everyone working at the company is motivated to excellence. This company structure generates high performance standards—and a 75 percent repeat client base. The firm works for large and small corporations, institutions, and government agencies. At any one time, Burns & McDonnell is working on hundreds of projects for clients around the world.

The Burns & McDonnell Team

The 1,300-person Burns & McDonnell staff includes engineers of every discipline, architects, planners, economists, environmental scientists, and computer experts. This professional team applies multifaceted expertise to projects that include airports and aviation facilities; air pollution control facilities; architecture and interior design; civil and transportation infrastructure; construction services; defense facilities; electric power generation and transmission; electric substations, transmission,

and distribution substations; environmental and permitting studies; food and food ingredient processing; industrial facilities; petroleum and chemical processing; waste management and environmental services; water resources; and wastewater management.

"Our ability to provide such a broad range of services means Burns & McDonnell has few limitations in creating solutions for clients' needs," Ruf says. "For a century we've provided superior service, technical expertise, and innovative solutions. We know that by staying true to these cornerstones, our next 100 years will be even better."

Burns & McDonnell used its engineering expertise on the Bartle Hall expansion.

The bridge over Brush Creek is both functional and attractive, adding to the overall ambience of the Country Club Plaza.

UCH HAS CHANGED SINCE THE KANSAS CITY KANSAS Area Chamber of Commerce was founded 100 years ago. The Chamber has attracted dozens of companies to locate within its domain; Kansas City has become an industrial powerhouse in the state; and the local

administration is now called the Unified Government of Wyandotte County and Kansas City, Kansas.

Yet, much has stayed the same in this peaceful community that rises from the bluffs at the mouth of the Kansas River. A classic melting pot of various cultures, Kansas City, Kansas, has interesting, historic neighborhoods; a devotedly loyal citizenry; and a small-town feel despite the large companies that call it home. In addition, the Chamber has remained dedicated to helping its members and the community thrive throughout the group's century-long history.

"We've demonstrated for the past 100 years that we're a viable force for political, social, cultural, and business progress," says Dan Schenkein, president and CEO of the Chamber. "As our community continues to prosper, so will our members, the businesses working here."

From the Ground Floor

Back in 1898, a group of businessmen met to organize the Kansas City Kansas Mercantile Club, the Chamber's forerunner. According to the original charter, the purpose of the newly founded corporation was for "social enjoyment, promoting the commercial and industrial advancement of Kansas City, Kansas, enhancing the city's credit, and making it a better place to live in." Eleven people were elected to the board that first year, charged to oversee an estimated value of goods, chattels, lands, rights, and credits worth $250 and a capital stock value of $1,000, which they divided into 200 shares of $5 each.

Nearly 20 years later, the Mercantile Club changed its name to the Kansas City Kansas Area Chamber of Commerce and filed new articles of incorporation with the state. The Chamber board hired a manager to oversee the organization's daily activities and policies. For years, the Chamber had been located in the Elks Building at 727 Minnesota Avenue. After a fire destroyed the building in 1917, the Elks sold what remained to the Chamber. With $75,000 in bonds, the Chamber remodeled the building, which gave the business group ample room to expand.

"It's amazing when you take a look at members' names from the earliest days," says Schenkein. "Many of their descendants are still involved. Our earliest lead-

The Soldiers and Sailors Memorial (left) and the Vietnam and Korean Wars Memorial in Kansas City, Kansas, pay tribute to those citizens of Wyandotte County who served their country in the armed forces.

The Kansas City, Kansas Fire Department participates in the annual Polski Days Parade, one of the many festivals that take place in the city each year (right).

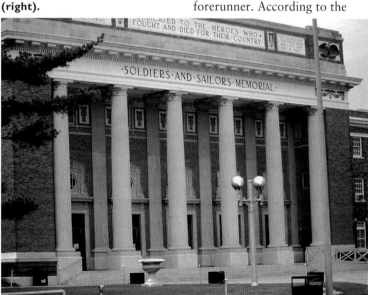

ership made a commitment to the area and successive membership has maintained it."

Today and Tomorrow

Today, the county's largest chamber, the Kansas City Kansas Area Chamber of Commerce boasts close to 700 members. They range from the largest employers—the University of Kansas City Medical Center and General Motors—to one-person and home-based businesses. Membership also includes CertainTeed Corporation; Owens-Corning Fiberglas; Sunshine Biscuits, Inc.; Lady Baltimore Foods; and other Kansas City, Kansas, plants. Hospitals account for significant employment in the area: Providence Medical Center and Bethany Medical Center staff about 1,000 people each. Colgate-Palmolive Company and Procter & Gamble also number among the Chamber members.

Over the years, the Chamber has played an important role in the economic development of the Kansas City and Wyandotte County environment. In 1997, for example, the group helped attract NASCAR and the International Speedway Corporation to the city. In the western portion of the county, International Speedway plans to build a $200 million, 1.5-mile track that will open by 2000. Initially, according to the company, three major races a year would draw some 200,000 overnight visitors and add as much as $118 million to the economy.

In addition, the Chamber was instrumental in the 1997 combination of the Kansas City and Wyandotte County governments. "Back in 1993, the Chamber began to look at the high tax levy here, and wanted to see how we could become more effective," says Schenkein. "Com-

bining the city and county governments was one of the ideas. The governor created a committee to study the issue, and the Chamber played a key role in the process. In April 1997, the residents voted to consolidate."

The Chamber also has its sights set on the future with programs such as the Business/ Education Coalition. Through the activities of about 200 of its members, the Chamber uses the Business/Education Coalition's Reality 101 program to help prepare school-age children for the world of work through visiting speakers, workshops, and career fairs.

"Our greatest strength is in our membership and the volunteerism and benefits they can provide the community," says Schenkein. "We've had 100 years of continuous service, and we expect to have another 100 years of helping the community grow."

Clockwise from top: Wyandotte High School, an architectural masterpiece, was constructed in 1934.

The residents of Kansas City, Kansas, enjoy frequent street fairs and festivals throughout the spring, summer, and fall months.

The National Agricultural Hall of Fame, honoring innovations in agricultural technology, has been located in Wyandotte County since 1962.

SPRINT CORPORATION

MONG KANSAS CITY-BASED COMPANIES, SPRINT CORPO-
ration is an obvious leader. Its $15 billion in annual
revenues make it, by far, the largest company in the area,
while its more than 9,600 local employees (out of more
than 50,000 worldwide) make Sprint one of the largest

local employers, second only to the federal government.

But the telecommunications company is a giant in the national and global arena, too. One of only three nationally known telecommunications service brands, Sprint is one of the fastest-growing major telecommunications companies, operating the only nationwide, all-digital, fiber-optic network in the United States. The company recently formed a valuable alliance with Deutsche Telekom and France Telecom, creating an international powerhouse called Global One. Sprint also ushered in a new era of wireless service with its Sprint PCS venture, and entered the Internet services market through its EarthLink alliance.

"Our goal is to provide a complete package of communication services," says Bill Esrey, Sprint chairman and CEO, "including not only long-distance, local, and wireless services, but also data, international, paging, and Internet access services. The

more sophisticated our customers become, the more they recognize the value of what Sprint has to offer."

Nearly 100 Years of Leadership

Sprint has always been a leader in technology, dating back to its inauguration in Abilene as the Brown Telephone Company in 1899. Founder Cleyson L. Brown quickly began an ambitious expansion program that, by the late 1920s, had established operations in Kansas, Pennsylvania, Indiana, Ohio, and Illinois.

Following the Great Depression, the business reorganized as United Utilities and in 1959, moved its headquarters from Abilene to Kansas City. In the 1960s, the company embarked on the Growth Through Additions program, which nearly doubled its size. But it wasn't until 1984 that the Sprint name burst onto the national scene when the company announced plans to install the first nationwide, all-digital, fiber-optic network and enter the deregulated long-distance market. Five years later, Sprint conducted the first transatlantic fiber-optic phone

call, a powerful symbol of the remarkable technological capabilities emerging worldwide.

"The technological advances have been astounding," says Esrey. "But telecommunications technology will continue to evolve at an even more rapid pace, and the impact on our lives will be even more profound. The advent of highly reliable, cost-effective, high bandwidth will happen within the next decade. If genuine competition in local markets is achieved, we can bring this technology into local homes and businesses, and begin to change how our economy and society works."

Rapid Expansion

Sprint serves the growing telecommunications market through several divisions and business units. The long-distance division serves nearly 11 million customers in the United States and provides voice, video, and data communications worldwide. Through nearly 7.5 million customer lines, the local telecommunications division supplies local telephone service in 19 states. In addition, Sprint/North Supply is one of the nation's largest wholesale distributors

Clockwise from bottom left: Sprint Corporation's new corporate campus will feature visually pleasing, low-rise buildings on a 260-acre site at 119th Street and Nall. Occupation is scheduled to begin in late 1999.

Sprint is at the forefront in integrating long-distance, local, and wireless telecommunications services.

Kansas City is home to Sprint's world headquarters.

Who will deliver?
WHEN THE BOUNDARIES ARE GONE...

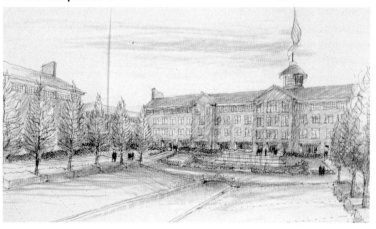

of voice, data, and teleconferencing equipment, as well as security and alarm systems. Sprint Publishing & Advertising, the 10th-largest yellow pages publisher in the United States, produces some 320 telephone directories with an annual circulation of more than 20 million across 20 states.

Sprint PCS, a powerful joint venture with three major cable TV companies, is building a nationwide network to provide wireless personal communications service. Global One offers a comprehensive array of advanced voice and data services with 1,200 switching centers in more than 65 countries around the world. Internationally, Sprint has also established relationships with telecom providers in Canada and Mexico.

Winning New Customers

Since the days of long-distance deregulation, major U.S. telephone companies have engaged in a vast array of promotions to increase their market share. Sprint's marketing savvy—from number-one ranked spokesperson, Candice Bergen, to such initiatives as Fridays Free and the flat-rate, dime-a-minute Sprint Sense—has helped to secure its leadership position.

More recently, the company became the official telecommunications provider to the National Football League and its member teams, unleashing the season-long Sprint Sense Dime Blitz in 1996. In addition, the company cosponsored the massive NFL Experience Exhibit during the 1997 Super Bowl. In the latter part of 1997, Sprint

became the name sponsor for the Rolling Stones' *Bridges to Babylon* tour, further enforcing its brand in a creative and high-profile manner.

Also in 1997, the company launched an alliance with RadioShack™ to create nationwide stores within stores for Sprint-brand pagers, Internet and long-distance service, wireless products, and more. Through this marketing partnership, Sprint equipment and service are now within a short drive from home or work for nearly 95 percent of the U.S. population.

"Sprint is leading the way in leveraging innovative sponsorships, marketing strategies, and distribution channels," says Esrey. "All of these tactics have communicated, sustained, and extended the Sprint-brand image to millions of new and existing customers, which is critical in our business."

The changes will continue as the company remains committed to its mission to provide high-quality telecommunications services to customers around the globe. "Sprint is uniquely positioned as one of the few companies with a robust international alliance, a nationwide long-distance network, a nationwide wireless franchise and strategy, and local telephone expertise," says Esrey. "Our challenge is to utilize our capabilities to provide the communications services that customers in the next century will want."

**Clockwise from top:
Traffic on Sprint's nationwide, all-digital, fiber-optic network is monitored at various facilities in metropolitan Kansas City.**

Sprint is fully engaged globally, with multifaceted strategies aimed at rapidly growing markets worldwide.

This Sprint PCS store in the Country Club Plaza offers digital PCS wireless services and phones.

T THE VETERANS OF FOREIGN WARS (VFW) NATIONAL headquarters, on the southwest corner of Broadway and Linwood in Kansas City, an outdoor monument contains soil from overseas battlefields on which Americans have fought and died. Decorated with three flagpoles and

a sweeping wall, the monument is a symbolic part of the VFW's patriotic legacy.

The headquarters is the nerve center of a worldwide organization with 10,000 posts and 2 million members. The VFW celebrates its centennial anniversary in 1999, making it the oldest major veterans organization in America.

Rooted in the Pride of Veterans

Founded in September 1899 in Columbus, Ohio, by veterans of the Spanish-American War, the organization grew quickly as it addressed the needs of that era's veterans, who came home victorious, but received no medical care for battle wounds they had incurred in Cuba and the Philippines. Following the example of the Columbus group, other veterans formed organizations in Denver and in Altoona, Pennsylvania. With growing numbers and a common purpose, the three groups joined forces and in 1914, adopted the name Veterans of Foreign Wars of the United States.

As a national organization, the VFW carried the voice of the veteran into the halls of Congress and the White House. Those who had served at the behest of

the government were now seeking compensation, rehabilitation, and pensions for that same military service. Years later, a historian would say that the efforts of the VFW at that time set the course that veterans affairs would follow to this day. *Fortune* magazine, in its December 8, 1997, issue, ranked the VFW 16th in its listing of the 25 most effective lobbying groups in Washington, D.C.

Joe L. Ridgley, VFW chief financial officer and chairman of the 100th anniversary committee, attributes VFW success to "the grassroots efforts of our 2 million members. The strength,

power, and influence we have in Washington, D.C., is based on what we do out here. That sends a message of commitment to Washington and allows us to be successful in protecting and extending veterans' entitlements, and in having an influence on national defense and foreign policy."

Serving America

At the local level, VFW members, along with the Ladies Auxiliary to the VFW, support a wide range of programs and projects designed to build better communities and a stronger nation. Much of their work

Clockwise from top:
VFW national headquarters in Kansas City has undergone major improvements, including installation of a state-of-the-art fire alarm system.

The VFW and its Ladies Auxiliary direct much of their work toward young people. The VFW's premier youth program, the Voice of Democracy scholarship program, annually grants more than $2.7 million in college scholarships to high school students.

Miss Kansas waves to a crowd of nearly 75,000 spectators at the Heart of America Rally for veterans of the Persian Gulf War in June 1991, sponsored by the Veterans of Foreign Wars.

ROBERT WIDENER

JERRY HIRT

is directed toward young people—from sports to citizenship education to the VFW's premier youth program, the Voice of Democracy (VOD) scholarship program. VOD annually grants more than $2.7 million in college scholarships to high school students. The organization sees today's youth as tomorrow's leaders.

Through its National Disaster Relief Fund, the VFW has provided more than $1 million to victims of floods, hurricanes, and earthquakes. Annually, its Buddy Poppy program receives more than $15 million in contributions, which support its veterans service programs and its VFW National Home at Eaton Rapids, Michigan, where needy children receive care and attention in a familylike atmosphere.

The 750,000-member Ladies Auxiliary has its own charitable programs. Of these, Cancer Aid and Research has raised $47 million over the past four decades. Its Junior Girls program offers girls aged six to 16 the opportunity to take part in many volunteer projects, which develop pride and a sense of accomplishment.

Kansas Citians have seen the VFW in action on many occasions during its history. In recent years, they saw the organization welcome home Persian Gulf War veterans with a rally that drew 75,000 people.

In 1995, the VFW became a sponsor of the VFW Senior Championship, a PGA Seniors event. Proceeds from the tournament benefit the Saint Luke's Hospital Health System Crittenton program, which provides emotional, behavioral, and chemical dependency care for children.

Service people stationed overseas in wartime have always received letters, cards, and gifts from the VFW. Today, the VFW reaches out to thousands of U.S. active duty personnel stationed around the world through its Operation Uplink free phone card program and its support of troop entertainment programs like the USO.

Kansas City Roots

Early in its development, the VFW sought a geographically neutral location for its headquarters that would be easily accessible to all members. It chose Kansas City, Kansas, in 1924, renting space in the American Legion Memorial Building. On January 1, 1930, the VFW moved to its present location.

Today, with a staff of 172 and an annual payroll of $6.3 million, the headquarters manages and coordinates the activities of the organization in 50 states, the District of Columbia, and three overseas departments. It is also home to the VFW Insurance Department, which offers a wide range of coverages to members, and to the VFW Emblem & Supply Department, which is one of the largest mail-order operations in the area. In keeping with the VFW's patriotic legacy, it is one of the largest American flag distributors in the nation.

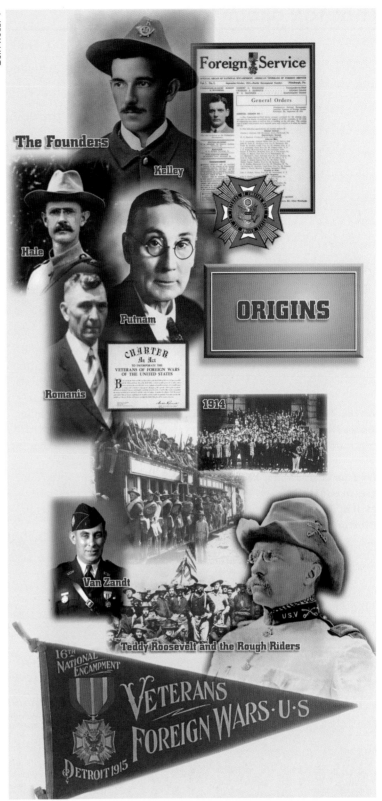

Foreign Service

General Orders

The Founders

Kelley

Hale

Putnam

Romanis

CHARTER
An Act
TO INCORPORATE THE
VETERANS OF FOREIGN WARS
OF THE UNITED STATES

ORIGINS

1914

Van Zandt

Teddy Roosevelt and the Rough Riders

16TH NATIONAL ENCAMPMENT

VETERANS FOREIGN WARS · U·S

DETROIT 1915

Looking Ahead

The challenge facing us today," Ridgley says, "is to do as good a job in laying the groundwork for our next 100 years as our founders did in their time. Everything we do here and in our Capitol Hill office in Washington, D.C., is dedicated to serving our members and our communities, and in turn all of America's 26 million veterans."

Senator John Glenn (D-Ohio) addressed Voice of Democracy winners as they toured the U.S. Capitol in 1997 (left).

Founded in 1899 in Columbus, Ohio, by veterans of the Spanish-American War, the VFW grew quickly as it addressed the needs of that era's veterans. Today, it is ranked as one of the 25 most effective lobbying groups in the nation (right).

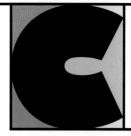

CATHLEEN DODSON MACAULEY LITERALLY GREW UP IN THE insurance firm her great-grandfather founded in 1900, but the fourth-generation owner of Dodson Group never expected to run the company. After all, insurance was a male-dominated field, and in 1983, when she was named chairman, no woman could even contemplate commanding the helm of such a large enterprise.

Today, however, Macauley is CEO of the Kansas City-based commercial lines insurance company, which reported a total income in 1997 of $87.4 million. Moreover, she heads the largest woman-owned business in town, according to the *Kansas City Business Journal*, and she's one of the few female CEOs in the entire insurance industry nationwide. All in all, it's quite an accomplishment for the woman who got her start posting bills and proofing accounting records during summer breaks in high school.

"About five years into running the company, I realized just what an odd bird I was in the flock," says Macauley. "My approach has always seemed simple enough to me: I think about how I want to be treated and work to offer that to our customers. Initially, it was difficult to remain confident in what I believed, but I'm now beginning to see some payoff."

Strong Foundation

Macauley was not the first in her family to have innovative ideas about how a company should be run. As the 20th century dawned, her great-grandfather, Bruce Dodson, decided he wanted to start a business that would concentrate on a novel idea in the insurance industry. He founded Brewers' Exchange to provide protection against losses from fire to 12 subscribing breweries in Missouri, Nebraska, and Illinois. According to this new insurance vehicle, each brewery owner could save money by buying insurance based on the cost of paying each other's losses. Within three years, Dodson had signed on 110 companies and, soon after, he expanded to include other industries.

In 1905, Dodson changed the company's name to Reciprocal Exchange, reflecting his ability to handle the insurance needs of a variety of qualified industries across the country, including bakeries, carbonated beverage bottlers, dairy products concerns, and printing exchanges. Although united within Reciprocal Exchange, each specialty retained its own separate exchange under the umbrella organization.

A year later in 1906, Dodson faced a test that would prove to be the downfall of many other insurance companies. An earthquake and fire in San Francisco resulted in such an avalanche of claims that many insurers were unable to fulfill their commitments. Dodson, however, satisfied every account and was noted publicly by insurance authority A.M. Best for its "entirely satisfactory" customer courtesy.

When Dodson died in 1926, the company's leadership passed

As the 20th century dawned, Bruce Dodson entered the insurance industry (top).

Dodson Group's first headquarters overlooked Liberty Memorial Mall in downtown Kansas City (bottom).

to his son, Bruce Dodson Jr. The second generation led the insurance concern through the stock market crash and the Great Depression, retaining his entire staff and payroll despite the crisis. In addition to the company's growing workers' compensation line, the younger Dodson began offering personal insurance lines through independent agencies, and coverage for privately owned cars and long-haul trucking concerns. In 1963, Dodson moved the company to its current location on State Line Road, and renamed it Dodson Insurance Group. He passed away in 1977. "Still today, I meet people whose grandfathers worked at Dodson," says Macauley. "They recognize my name and recall the stories they heard. Apparently, my grandfather's foresight, and his response to people's problems, made quite an impression."

Business for the Future

Today, Dodson Group is one of the largest privately held companies in Missouri and employs approximately 300 people. Casualty Reciprocal Exchange and Equity Mutual Insurance Company form the organization's foundation. ASPECT, Inc. offers actuarial and economic consulting services to insurance companies. Dodson General Agency, Inc. is a full-service insurance agency and brokerage that provides insurance products and services to agents and bro-

kers. Together, Dodson Group is licensed to write policies and conduct business in 38 states and the District of Columbia.

Macauley has poised her company for the future, when "business will be something other than 'we have this product and we'll sell it to you,'" she says. In addition, part of Macauley's strategy of progress includes the active involvement of her son Hale Johnston, vice president of group operations. Johnston begins the fifth generation of Dodsons to work at the company.

"We've remained entrepreneurial during growth phases that most companies find lead to greater complexity," says Macauley. "Our focus is clear and constant. In growth modes, we look for clients with an interest that is not being served well. That's been our history and will continue to be so in our future. We're constantly niching our business so that we can have good client relationships that serve our customers in the best possible ways."

Dodson Group remains family-owned and -operated. Cathleen Dodson Macauley, the founder's great-granddaughter, is chairman of the board and CEO (top).

Dodson Group is headquartered in south Kansas City, just minutes from the downtown area (bottom).

ANY COMPANY THAT STAYS IN BUSINESS AS LONG AS BUTLER Manufacturing will certainly experience its share of challenges. From the 1903 West Bottoms flood, which devastated Butler's facilities only two years after its inauguration, to the early deaths of its two founders, and from two World

Wars to inevitable slumps in the construction industry, Butler Manufacturing has prevailed.

Today, Butler is an international leader in the marketing, design, and production of systems and components for nonresidential structures, including everything from factories to shopping centers to office buildings. Butler operates manufacturing, engineering, and service centers throughout the United States and in 16 foreign countries, handling sales, installation, and service through approximately 4,000 independent dealers. The company also provides complete design-and-build construction services directly to larger companies with multiple sites or projects of unusual size or complexity.

"Butler has stayed on top through persistence and by honing our core strengths," says Robert West, Butler's chairman and CEO. "When the economic cycle goes down, everyone's affected. The test, however, is who comes out a better company when business goes up again. That attitude has made us a leader."

Combining the best-performing products with the best distribution networks has helped make Butler an industry leader (top).

Butler is an international leader in the marketing, design, and production of systems and components for nonresidential structures (bottom).

Idea and Execution

Butler Manufacturing was founded in 1901 by Emanuel Norquist, a hardworking, quiet young man in Clay Center, Kansas. Norquist constructed livestock watering tanks from copper-bearing galvanized steel, which wouldn't rust or leak. His colleague, Charles Butler, was a natural-born traveling salesman with grand ideas on how the pair could build a business. Together, they crafted a company that, by 1997, would bring in some $925 million in annual revenues.

The company is divided into Building Systems, Roof Systems, Real Estate Development, Construction Services, Vistawall Architectural Products, and International Operations groups.

International Growth

Butler's international business has grown dramatically, as the company has expanded beyond U.S. borders during the 1990s. In 1997, Butler's international business accounted for about 20 percent of its annual revenues, compared with 8 percent only five years earlier. Butler's international operations serve five geographical areas—Mexico, Central America, and the Caribbean; Central and Eastern Europe; Asia; South America; and the Middle East.

"The big future at the moment is the development of our international capability so that it's every bit as good as our domestic performance," says West. "We have the best-performing product and the best distribution through our independent dealers in various markets, and we want to expand that throughout the world. In addition, we have a culture of selflessness. Our employees have a willingness to share recognition and success, and we have the same orientation in serving our customers."

Throughout Butler's long history, however, an additional attribute necessary for survival and prosperity has surfaced. "We have a willingness to take intelligent risks," says West, "and the flexibility to change, adapt, and respond to differences in the marketplace. That has made us a leader in our industry and will continue to keep us at the top."

OME COMPANIES CELEBRATE THEIR ANNIVERSARIES WITH ELABORATE parties or expensive getaways. KPMG Peat Marwick LLP, however, chose another route in September 1997, when the world's largest professional services firm marked its centennial with a day of community service. KPMG's 22,000 U.S. employees celebrated by giving

back to the communities that support them by contributing more than 176,000 hours of community service.

"The community provides us our paychecks," says Charles Peffer, managing partner for KPMG's Kansas City office. "Without a strong community, there would be no need for so many of us. For a number of years, we've made both monetary contributions and time for our own people to volunteer. Our anniversary celebration, which we called World of Spirit Day, was a way to show our appreciation in an even bigger way."

Auspicious Beginnings

Peat Marwick was founded in New York in 1897 by two Scottish immigrants, James Marwick and S. Roger Mitchell. Slightly more than a decade later, the company expanded to Kansas City, opening an office downtown in 1908. In 1924, the company merged with William Peat's British accounting firm, which established it as an international partnership. Finally, in 1987, Peat Marwick International merged with Klynveld Main Goerdeler to form Klynveld Peat Marwick Goerdeler (KPMG) to further expand its international presence.

Today, KPMG boasts annual revenues of more than $9.1 billion. The firm does business in 145 countries, with 830 offices and 83,000 people. The largest portion of its business has been, and continues to be, attesting to the fair representation of its clients' financial statements. But accounting has traveled far from its turn-of-the-century origins. Modern businesses require intelligent and innovative business consulting skills from specialists in a wide variety of fields.

In Kansas City, for example, KPMG serves a variety of clients, primarily in the areas of financial services; manufacturing, retailing, and distribution; health care; public service; personal financial planning; international tax; and information, communications, and entertainment. Clients include everyone from banks to government agencies to research institutions, all of which need well-rounded and informed business assistance.

"We try to offer customers valuable ideas and valuable assistance in a prompt and most effective manner," says Peffer. "We want to go beyond their immediate needs and anticipate what they'll need in the near and far future."

People as Resources

Part of KPMG's success with its client-based orientation comes from its 190 Kansas City-based employees—and its 83,000 employees worldwide. That's why the firm constantly looks for the best and brightest individuals. Once they're hired, KPMG's professional development program keeps staffers on the cutting edge of client needs and motivates them as they advance in their careers.

"All of our assets get on the elevator to go home every night," says Peffer. "The value of this business is our people. Quality client service is, and will continue to be, the primary focus at KPMG. We believe such quality is delivered by our team of professionals working closely together in an atmosphere of goodwill and camaraderie."

Clockwise from top:
KPMG serves a variety of clients, primarily in the areas of financial services; manufacturing, retailing, and distribution; health care; public service; personal financial planning; international tax; and information, communications, and entertainment.

Part of KPMG's success with clients comes from its 190 Kansas City-based employees. A professional development program keeps staffers on the cutting edge of client needs.

KPMG's 22,000 U.S. employees celebrated the company's 100th anniversary with a World of Spirit Day, contributing more than 176,000 hours of service to the communities in which the company has offices.

SINCE IT OPENED IN 1905, THE UNIVERSITY OF KANSAS (KU) MEDICAL Center has consistently set records. It has led the nation in the past few years in the treatment of such illnesses as Parkinson's disease and cytomegalovirus. KU Hospital was the nation's first to perform a procedure on previously inoperable brain aneurysms, and the

nation's first to develop a way to accurately predict seizures in epilepsy patients. The hospital's Comprehensive Epilepsy Center and Center on Aging are virtually unique in the region, providing a full continuum of services under one roof. These examples represent a mere fraction of the efforts that have consistently set the facility apart.

A powerful combination of patient care services, education, and research, KU Medical Center comprises the 459-bed KU Hospital; the KU Schools of Medicine, Allied Health, and Nursing; the Research Institute; and the Center for Continuing Education. Although any of KU Medical Center's functions could stand alone, the close association among hospital, schools, and research has created a facility that is hailed by medical professionals and patients alike. In fact, health care accreditation officials have rated the KU Hospital among the nation's best.

"Our mission combines a dedication to health education, research, and patient care," says KU Hospital CEO Irene Cumming. "Virtually all of our profession-

als care for patients, teach the next generation of professionals, and conduct research. As a result, we bring the latest knowledge and the most recent technology and expertise to the care of our patients."

Patient Care at KU Hospital

The University of Kansas Hospital was established—and continues to operate—as Kansas' premier, primary through tertiary care hospital. From immunizations to complex organ transplants, the KU Hospital provides the full continuum of service for patients throughout the Midwest. The hospital's clinics and multidisciplinary centers treat everything from minor ear infections to trauma, and from difficult births to burn care.

Patients who need transplants—whether liver, kidney, cornea, bone marrow, skin, or tissue—find hope for their future at the KU Hospital. Others who are living with cancer receive much of their care as outpatients in the highly regarded KU Cancer Center. With an emphasis on convenience for patients, the oncology facility offers 24-hour-a-day outpatient care.

In addition, cancer patients can receive cutting-edge diagnostic and screening services, risk assessment, treatment, and information at the KU Comprehensive Breast Center. Diagnostic services include the latest equipment in breast ultrasound and stereotaxic biopsy.

A recently approved, $3.93 million federal grant has dramatically enhanced the KU Center on Aging elder care program. The funding will establish the KU Center for Health in Aging, which will bring cutting-edge, comprehensive geriatric care to Kansas. Designed to serve as a model practice for urban and

Clockwise from top:
A powerful combination of patient care services, education, and research, the University of Kansas (KU) Medical Center comprises the 459-bed KU Hospital; the KU Schools of Medicine, Allied Health, and Nursing; the Research Institute; and the Center for Continuing Education.

KU Children's Center provides comprehensive primary through tertiary care.

The Eugene D. Burnett Burn Center treats all phases of burn care, from trauma to rehabilitation and follow-up outpatient services.

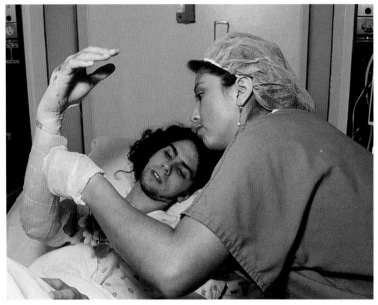

rural health care providers, the program will provide single-entry service for geriatric assessment, primary and specialty geriatric care, mental health services, health education, and community-based restorative services. An additional $8 million grant will establish the Kansas Claude D. Pepper Older Americans Independence Center, a community-based partnership striving to improve the care and quality of life for stroke survivors and their families. The center's focus will be on stroke rehabilitation research.

KU Hospital draws neurology patients from across the country who need specialized treatments in conditions ranging from Parkinson's disease to Alzheimer's disease to epilepsy. Among the treatments that are virtually unique to this area are the pallidal brain stimulation technique pioneered at KU Hospital, surgical relief of seizures unresponsive to medication, and comprehensive diagnostic and treatment approaches to Alzheimer's disease.

Another specialty area, the Eugene D. Burnett Burn Center, is the region's only extensive burn clinic and serves patients who have suffered minor to severe injuries. The Hyperbaric Medicine Center is dedicated to improving the healing of wounds that have failed to respond to standard treatment; the center provides immediate treatment for carbon monoxide poisoning due to smoke inhalation or other causes.

In addition, KU Hospital is recognized nationally for serving people who have complicated, chronic conditions. The Comprehensive Epilepsy Center, for example, uses state-of-the-art technology to detect, analyze, and treat seizures, as part of the center's comprehensive care for patients. The Cray Diabetes Management Center presents free educational programs for patients and families, in addition to providing medical, nursing, social, and dietetic management techniques. The Hearing and Speech Department's Family Center provides parent educa-

tion, as well as social and educational development for deaf infants and toddlers.

At KU Hospital, patient care extends into the community. Primary care centers throughout the metropolitan area provide convenient, accessible service to people in need of family physicians, obstetrics-gynecology specialists, and pediatric specialists. In the winter of 1998, KU Medical Center opened KU MedWest, a state-of-the-art, primary and multispecialty care and ambulatory surgery center in Shawnee, Kansas.

"As a member of the Greater Kansas City and Kansas communities, we'll continue to reach out to those who are seeking the highest-quality health care and the best in health education," says Cumming. "And we'll continue to provide these services with genuine concern for each patient and each student."

Teaching the Future

At KU Medical Center, patient care goes hand in hand with teaching health care professionals for the future. More than 700 students attend KU

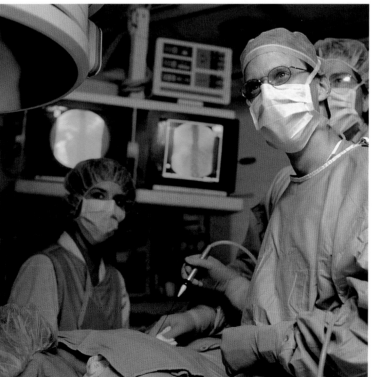

Clockwise from top:
KU Medical Center pioneered the development and use of telemedicine and is among the top 10 telemedicine centers in the nation.

More than 140 graduate students in basic sciences prepare for careers in pathology, cytology, genetics, immunology, and serology at KU Medical Center's School of Allied Health.

As an academic health center, KU Medical Center provides state-of-the-art technology and procedures to patients.

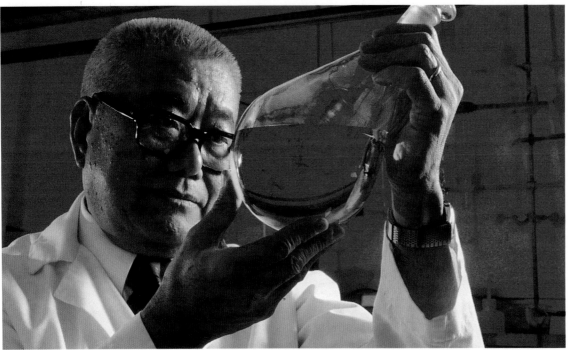

Clockwise from top:
**Basic medical research is a
cornerstone of KU Medical
Center's mission.**

**KU Medical Center's main campus and satellite facilities provide easily accessible primary
health care services.**

**KU Mobile Medical Unit provides diagnostic tests, physical
examinations, and industrial
hygiene services throughout
Kansas.**

School of Medicine campuses in Kansas City and Wichita, where the curricula emphasize both current scientific knowledge and the art of medicine. Under the leadership of Deborah Powell, M.D., recently appointed executive dean of the School of Medicine, KU Medical Center will reemphasize its focus on finding a cure for breast cancer, as well as gynecological and ovarian pathologies.

KU Medical Center's School of Nursing undergraduate and master's degree programs prepare nurses for careers as primary care nurse practitioners, nursing administrators, or clinical nurse specialists. In addition, the school offers the only nursing doctoral program in Kansas.

KU Medical Center's School of Allied Health, among the country's largest, prepares students in occupational, physical, and respiratory therapy; dietetics and nutrition; nurse anesthesiology; medical technology; health information management; hearing and speech; biometry; and cytotechnology.

Commitment to Research

With more than $47 million each year in outside grants from the National Institutes of Health, private foundations, and other sources, KU Medical Center boasts nationally and internationally renowned researchers in cancer treatment, neurology, and infectious diseases. Many of these researchers work at the new Lied Biomedical Research facility, a $14 million structure that houses some 35 laboratories with the sophisticated laboratory support needed for complex scientific studies.

Neurologists at KU Hospital have blazed new trails in the treatment of several disorders. KU researchers were the first to treat Parkinson's disease by conducting the nation's first thalmic brain stimulation, covered on ABC's television program 20/20. In addition, researchers at KU Alzheimer's Disease Center are advancing knowledge of the degenerative disease. And having successfully identified a mechanism to predict the onset of seizures, physicians at KU Com-

prehensive Epilepsy Center are developing tools that someday will prevent seizures.

KU Medical Center researchers also have made breakthroughs in AIDS treatment; kidney disease; and breast, prostate, and lung cancers. In fact, the development of an HIV-type virus in monkeys that allows for the testing of AIDS vaccines and treatment procedures was so important that news coverage was broadcast on more than 75 television stations nationwide.

As a result of KU Hospital's innovative use of telemedicine and telepsychiatry, patients in rural areas now receive treatment without driving hundreds of miles for care. Physicians across the Midwest can consult with KU Medical Center faculty about the most recent diagnostic and treatment options for their patients.

One of only two such centers funded by the National Institutes of Health, KU School of Nursing's Center for Biobehavioral Studies of Fatigue Management has developed a strong reputation for research into lifestyle behaviors

as well as social, financial, and psychological factors that affect health.

Research at KU Medical Center's School of Allied Health has also gained international visibility. For example, the Hearing and Speech Department has contributed significantly to modern-day procedures for identifying and treating speech, language, and hearing disorders with its studies in hearing status assessment of newborns, and its research in regaining language skills among older stroke patients.

"We take pride in delivering patient-centered care in one of the nation's best academic environments, which also stands at the forefront of health care research," says Cumming.

Providing Physician Services

The doctors who practice at KU Hospital are members of Kansas University Physicians, Inc. (KUPI), the largest multi-specialty group practice in the state. The formation of KUPI—with 280 physicians in fields from anesthesiology to cardiovascular medicine to ophthalmology—represents the culmination of an important and exciting process that will position the clinical faculty to succeed in the 21st century.

KUPI has state-of-the-art administrative systems resulting in enhanced patient access to primary care and multispecialty physicians. This new system provides convenience and continuity for patients and their families; simple billing procedures; and direct, timely communication with referring physicians.

In addition, KU Hospital's health care professionals work to assure the health of families and workers throughout the area. KU Center for Environmental and Occupational Health

maintains a fully equipped mobile medical unit that provides audiometry, chest X rays, history and physical examination, mammography, phlebotomy, and pulmonary function tests. In addition, the center's Field Service Division provides industrial hygiene services, operates a CDC-certified lead laboratory, and provides patient and professional education services.

"KU Physicians, Inc. is the state's largest medical practice group, whose members provide primary and preventive care and the most highly specialized care available in the metropolitan area," says Cumming. "As a result, KU Hospital provides a seamless system of care, affording patients all the health services they need within the same institution."

Mission of Excellence

At the University of Kansas Medical Center, excellence has become the facility's mission. Whether it's concentrating on patient care, teaching new health care professionals, or conducting important research, KU Medical Center staff emphasize trust, respect, learning, and innovation.

That dedication pays off in a variety of ways. Recently, for

example, 39 KU Hospital physicians were ranked among the nation's finest in the book *The Best Doctors in America: Central Region*. Frequent news reports about landmark discoveries and developments have also become regular occurrences at KU Medical Center. But the most important mission at KU Hospital comes down to taking responsibility for the health of the community that surrounds it. "We focus on ensuring that everyone who walks through our doors receives the best care, regardless of where they live or their economic status," says Cumming. "That is an integral part of our mission—equal to education and research."

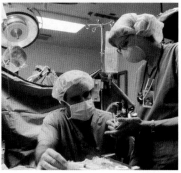

Clockwise from top: KU Medical Center faculty have gained a national reputation for the high quality of education they provide.

Each year, more than 2,500 medical, nursing, and allied health students learn their profession in KU Medical Center's technologically superior educational environment.

Already known for its leadership in regional health care, KU Medical Center is recognized as one of the best health care educational facilities in the nation.

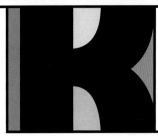

ANSAS CITY COULD RIGHTLY BE CALLED "CAR CENTRAL." With the General Motors and Ford assembly plants, regional parts distribution centers, and numerous finance and marketing offices, the area claims wide-ranging automotive expertise. In addition, 100 franchised new-vehicle dealers

The Automobile Dealers Association of Greater Kansas City produces its annual International Auto Show, featuring the latest innovations in automobile design.

and the nationally recognized Greater Kansas City International Auto Show—displaying more than $35 million of the latest in automotive technology—combine to make Kansas City "a major automotive capital of the world," according to the executive vice president of the Automobile Dealers Association of Greater

Kansas City, Bill Morrison.

Since 1981, Morrison has led the active Automobile Dealers Association of Greater Kansas City, which includes all franchised new-vehicle dealers within the metropolitan area.

The association, established in 1906 as the Motor Car Dealers Association, has gone beyond its

initial goals. These days, it does much more than provide support to the retail automobile industry, promote sound and ethical business practices, and provide programs that benefit auto dealership employees. In addition, it now produces the annual Greater Kansas City International Auto Show.

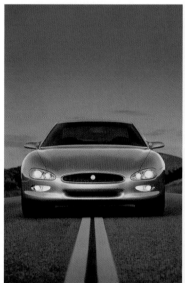

Auto Showplace

In 1993, the board of directors named Morrison producer and director of the annual Greater Kansas City International Auto Show. Since then, this worldwide, professionally produced, five-day event has received national recognition as one of the finest auto shows in North America.

In fact, the Greater Kansas City International Auto Show is of such importance that automobile manufacturers from all over the world make it a point to supply a wealth of futuristic concept vehicles, advanced interactive engineering displays, and the best new-car exhibit properties available. It makes for an exciting event, one that looks into the future of the automotive industry.

"Kansas City is blessed with a newly expanded exposition facility in the H. Roe Bartle Hall," says Morrison, "and that makes it the ideal place to see a first-class auto show." Billed as The Place to Go! each year during the first week in March, Kansas City's auto show commands Bartle Hall's 400,000 square feet of column-free space, providing show attendees more than eight football fields of new cars, trucks, sport utility vehicles, and vans in a lavishly decorated and brightly lit atmosphere. It is designed to provide people both in Kansas City and the Midwest with outstanding entertainment and a forum for obtaining valuable information about new vehicles.

HALL OF FAME
Presidents of the Automobile Dealers Association of Greater Kansas City.
Many have served as chairmen of Greater Kansas City International Auto Shows.

YEAR	NAME	FRANCHISE	YEAR	NAME	FRANCHISE
1906-07	Committee		1956	Don Armacost	Studebaker
1908	H. E. Rookledge	White Steamer	1957	Jerry Smith	Buick
1909-11	J. Frank Witwer	Reo	1958	Jerry Scott, Jr.	Lincoln - Mercury
1912	E. P. Moriarty	Durea - Packard	1959	R. S. Armacost, Jr.	Pontiac
1913	J. E. Martin	Buick (Br. Mgr.)	1960	R. S. O'Neill	Oldsmobile
1914	Estel Scott	GMC Truck	1961	H. W. Ireland	Chevrolet
1915	W. J. Brace	Hudson	1962	Dick Smith	Ford
1916-17	A. T. Clark	Detroit-Electric	1963	Bud Brown	Chrysler - Plymouth
1918	R. C. Greenlease	Cadillac	1964	Bill Sight	Chevrolet
1919	H. M. Genung	Stutz	1965	Bud Laner	Pontiac
1920	J. A. Butler	Dodge	1966	F. Lee Major, Jr.	Cadillac
1921-22	Estel Scott	GMC Truck	1967	Galen Boyer, Sr.	Pontiac
1923	Nelson S. Riley	Studebaker	1968	Leon Faddis	Chrysler - Plymouth
1924	A. P. Ten Brook	Oakland - Br. Mgr.	1969	Bill Hicks	Chevrolet
1925	S. W. Ramsey	Oldsmobile	1970-71	Sherrill Minter	Ford
1926	W. J. Brace	Hudson	1972-73	Don Stein	Buick
1927	Estel Scott	GMC Truck	1974	Gene Cable	Chevrolet
1928	W. P. Hemphill	Willys	1975	Jay Wolfe	Pontiac
1929	R. P. Rice	Chrysler	1976	Bob Murray	VW
1930-31	Hal Brace	Hudson	1977	R. C. Cunningham	Oldsmobile
1932	E. F. Walsh, Jr.	Dodge - Plymouth	1978	Bill George	Chrysler - Plymouth
1933-34	R. M. Armacost	Studebaker	1979	Thomas P. Klein	Pontiac
1935	D. E. Williams	Ford	1980	William J. Stoffle	Ford
1936	Sam C. Clasen	Chevrolet	1981-82	John Caster	VW
1937	Roland H. Record	Dodge - Plymouth	1983	Tom Sight	Lincoln - Mercury
1938	Carl L. Shaw	Packard	1984	Hal Quinn	Buick
1939	John Cunningham	Hudson	1985	Bill Mansfield	Nissan
1940	E. H. Norrington	Chevrolet	1986	Jack Miller	Chrysler - Plymouth
1941	Harry F. Rice	Buick	1987	Frank Thompson	Jeep - Eagle
1942	N. S. O'Neill	Oldsmobile	1988	Chuck Fisher	Buick
1943	Kenneth V. Bostian	Chevrolet	1989	Mark Smith	Ford - Suzuki
1944	Don E. Fitzgerald	Pontiac	1990	Lee Major III	Cadillac - Pontiac
1945	Ralph Knight	Hudson	1991	Scott Adams	Toyota - Ford
1946	Earl N. McClure	Chevrolet	1992	Bob Balderston	Ford - Nissan
1947	Keith V. Ware	Chrysler	1993	John McCarthy	Chevrolet Nissan
1948	Rudy M. Fick	Ford	1994	Phil Brown	Chrysler - Plymouth
1949-50	Herbert Kincaid	Studebaker	1995	Randy Reed	Pontiac - Buick - GMC
1951	Ralph Perry	Pontiac	1996	Robin Cunningham	Chev-Olds-Audi-VW
1952	J. H. Scott, Sr.	Desoto	1997	Rich Ellison	Honda-Nissan
1953	R. G. Bentrup	Ford	1998	Stan Michaels	Chevrolet-Oldsmobile
1954	Ray Faddis	Chrysler	1999	Diane Woods	Ford
1955	Ervin Feld	Dodge	2000	Paul Broome	Oldsmobile-Cadillac

Since the association's founding in 1906, a number of prominent Kansas Citians have served as chairman of the annual auto show.

Focused on Growth

The Automobile Dealers Association of Greater Kansas City goes beyond producing the annual auto show and promoting its own member concerns. The group has long been involved in the economic progress of the area. Through the years, the Automobile Dealers Association has created a viable partnership with other local businesses to concentrate on innovative, metrowide growth and development. Actively supporting the Kansas City Area Development Council's objectives to attract new business and jobs to the region, the association

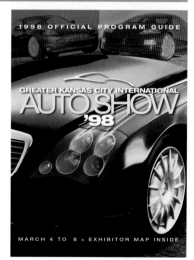

supplies two new automobiles each year to aid in recruiting new companies by enhancing the council's image.

All in all, the Automobile Dealers Association takes pride in progressive advancements within the automotive industry and in partnering with others in the growth of the greater metropolitan area.

HEN THEY THINK OF UTILITIES, MANY PEOPLE ENVISION conservative, slow-moving companies that rarely take risks. Kansas City's UtiliCorp United, however, provides a startling contrast to that image. With annual revenues of nearly $9 billion in 1997, UtiliCorp has

Since its first move into Canada in 1987, UtiliCorp United has also entered markets overseas (left).

UtiliCorp began as a Missouri electric utility. Today, it is also a top U.S. marketer of gas and power (right).

experienced explosive growth, with sales more than doubling from only a year before. In addition, earnings per share have increased by an average of nearly 11 percent a year since current Chairman and CEO Richard C. "Rick" Green Jr. took the helm in 1985.

This growth has been largely due to aggressive expansion, both in acquisitions and in territory. Nearby companies such as

Kansas Public Service and distant ones such as West Kootenay Power in British Columbia became part of UtiliCorp's growth plans as the company extended its electric and gas distribution network to include eight North American utilities and various operations in Australia, New Zealand, and Britain. In addition, UtiliCorp has diversified into nonregulated energy businesses such as marketing of natural gas and electricity, as well as gas pipelines and processing.

"UtiliCorp's evolving strategy is designed to enable us to become a major multinational provider of energy products and services," says Green. "We continue to fine-tune our structure and focus as we move deeper into the execution phase of the plan we launched in 1995 with the introduction of the EnergyOne[SM] brand. Both in North America and overseas, our energies are devoted to deepening and enlarging market share in our businesses."

Natural Past

One could say that Green was born to his job. His great-grandfather Lemuel founded the company in 1908, but sold it in 1927 to move west. Lemuel's son returned to Kansas City in 1940 to buy the company, then called Missouri Public Service, out of bankruptcy. Green and his brother, Robert—who is president of the company—are now the fourth generation to run the show.

It was Rick who changed the company's name to the more globally focused UtiliCorp United and began its far-reaching expansion program. The CEO hired on with the company in 1975 just out of college and joined the board in 1983. It was early in the era of deregulation, when utility executives were suddenly forced into thinking differently about their industry. Green was more than up to the task.

"We had to take a close and introspective look at who we

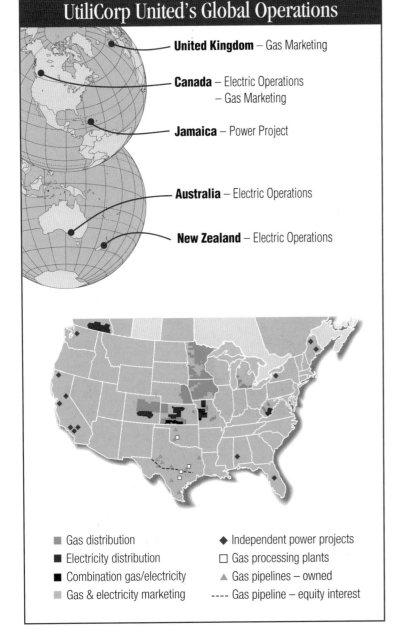

UtiliCorp United's Global Operations

United Kingdom – Gas Marketing

Canada – Electric Operations
– Gas Marketing

Jamaica – Power Project

Australia – Electric Operations

New Zealand – Electric Operations

- ▪ Gas distribution
- ▪ Electricity distribution
- ■ Combination gas/electricity
- ▪ Gas & electricity marketing
- ◆ Independent power projects
- ☐ Gas processing plants
- ▲ Gas pipelines – owned
- ---- Gas pipeline – equity interest

were and what we do," says Green. "What we discovered was that we had to make radical changes, and that was the road we began traveling. Our corporate idols became McDonald's, Southwest Airlines, and Wal-Mart, because they are fun, convenient, and low-cost companies. They know how to compete, and that's what our new goal had to become, too."

Historic Connection

UtiliCorp United also felt a strong sense of place and connection to Kansas City. That's partly why, in 1994, the company decided to renovate the former New York Life Building, which had been standing empty for nearly eight years. Built in 1888 by the renowned architectural firm of McKim, Mead & White, the 10-story, brick, Italianate structure was erected at a time of great promise in Kansas City. It was, by far, the tallest building in town and one of the most important in the region. William W. Howard wrote in *Harper's Weekly* in 1888 that the edifice "conveys as forcible impression of ultimate height and breadth as any building in the West."

But UtiliCorp didn't just spruce up the facade and polish the imposing bronze eagle over the building's main entrance. The company undertook a complete, $30 million renovation of the brownstone blocks, terra-cotta tiles, marble floors, vaulted ceilings, intricate ironwork, and bronze light fixtures. More impressively, UtiliCorp retrofitted the building it would use for its world headquarters—renaming it 20 West Ninth—with state-of-the-art fiber-optic communications technology, energy-efficient electric sensors for lighting and thermostatic control, and an environmentally friendly interior, from paints to carpeting to recycling capabilities.

"We discovered that preservation and environmentally sensitive design complement each other very well," says Green. "We now have a modern headquarters in a stunningly reno-

vated historical building in the heart of downtown Kansas City."

Growth Curve

From that base, UtiliCorp United will continue to explore opportunities in new geographic regions, as well as new business partnerships and brand alliances. The company's Aquila Energy subsidiary, which specializes in gas and electricity for wholesale markets, has moved forward to rank among the top five U.S. wholesale energy marketers in the decade since it was founded. Aquila Gas Pipeline Corporation, 82 percent owned by the company, has established a major presence in natural gas and gas liquids markets in Texas and Oklahoma.

UtiliCorp will also continue to extend its reach into global markets. The company manages United Energy, the first Australian electric distribution utility to be privatized, as 34 percent partner. United Energy serves more than 500,000 customers in metropolitan Melbourne. In New Zealand,

UtiliCorp has interests in utilities serving another 250,000 electric customers.

"Networks for electric and gas distribution, wholesale energy, and retail businesses are our three key focus areas," says Green. "No matter what we do specifically, UtiliCorp will continue fine-tuning the strategies that will enable us to gain size, market share, and earnings in those businesses."

Clockwise from top left: UtiliCorp energy traders work from centers in Kansas City, Omaha, and Calgary.

The company's meticulous restoration of 20 West Ninth Street earned national awards.

UtiliCorp launched the utility industry's first national brand, EnergyOne℠, in 1995.

"OOD LUCK . . . AND MAY SUCCESS FOLLOW YOU LIKE YOUR ALUMNI newsletter!" Millions of Americans bought the greeting card with those words because it expressed their thoughts in a comical and unexpected way. That sentiment represents only one of some 40,000 different cards and personal expression products created

by Hallmark each year. This Kansas City company covers the whole range of personal communications, from the sassy Shoebox Greetings line to the Impromptu line of alternative cards, the distinctive Hallmark Keepsake Ornaments series, and the award-winning *Hallmark Hall of Fame* television specials.

"I am thankful that we are in this kind of business," says Hallmark Chairman Don Hall, who grew up in the company founded by his father, Joyce C. "J.C." Hall. "This business allows us to make a meaningful contribution to the lives of people who use our products," he says.

Hallmark cards are published in more than 30 languages and distributed in more than 100 countries. In addition to roughly 20,000 new greeting cards developed each year, the company sells albums, calendars, gift wrap, party goods, personal expression software, and related products in more than 40,000 retail outlets. Hallmark's $3.7 billion in

Today, Hallmark cards are published in more than 30 languages and distributed in more than 100 countries. The company also sells albums, calendars, gift wrap, party goods, personal expression software, and related products in more than 40,000 retail outlets (top).

Hallmark's Kansas City world headquarters was developed in 1968 and encompasses Crown Center, which is home to an office compex, an apartment and condominium community, two hotels, a shopping center, the Hallmark Visitors Center, and more (bottom left and right).

annual revenues makes it the largest player in the $6 billion greeting card industry.

A Determined Beginning

In 1910, shortly after arriving in Kansas City from his native Nebraska, 18-year-old J.C. Hall launched what would become Hallmark Cards. He brought with him a shoe box full of postcard packs, which he mailed to midwestern merchants from his room at the Kansas City YMCA. The merchants bought his packs, and Hallmark was in business.

Hall was always interested in advertising. In 1928, he published the company's first national ad in *Ladies' Home Journal*. In

the 1930s, Hall had the idea of selling greeting cards under a brand name. To promote the idea, he found an advertising agency that would link his company with a radio program as a sponsor. This was an early precursor to the company's *Hallmark Hall of Fame* series.

Under Hall's leadership, the company contracted with artists such as Norman Rockwell, Georgia O'Keeffe, Salvador Dalí, and Pablo Picasso to reproduce original artwork for card designs.

Don Hall succeeded his father as CEO from 1966 until 1986, when he presided over a period of explosive growth. Don Hall guided the company's transition

to a multifaceted, global enterprise through Hallmark International. In 1984, he expanded Hallmark's personal development business with the acquisition of Binney & Smith, makers of Crayola crayons. Under his leadership, the company introduced the collectible Hallmark Keepsake Ornaments and Shoebox Greetings, the industry's most successful alternative humor line. In 1986, Don Hall appointed a new chief executive officer, but he continues to influence and shape the company as chairman of the board.

Over the years, Hallmark also developed the world's largest creative team, which now includes some 740 artists, designers, photographers, writers, editors, and lettering artists who create sentiments that speak to the human relationship. The company employs more than 20,000 full-time workers worldwide.

A World-Class Brand

Hallmark consistently is rated by consumers among the world's leading brands. In a 1997 Equitrend survey of leading brands rated for quality, Hallmark ranked fourth among the top 10 World-Class Brands.

In 1951, the company introduced *Hallmark Hall of Fame* to enhance awareness of the Hallmark name. Following the initial TV broadcast—Gian Carlo Menotti's opera *Amahl and the Night Visitors*—the company has continued to air classic programs ranging from *Hamlet* in 1953 to *Old Man* in 1997. In all, more than 70 *Hallmark Hall of Fame* productions have won Emmy awards, making it television's most honored and enduring dramatic series.

Beyond Greeting Cards

While best known for helping people express their emotions and touch the lives of others, Hallmark also owns and operates thriving businesses in personal development and family entertainment.

In addition to Crayola, Hallmark's Binney & Smith personal development subsidiary mar-

kets familiar products branded Liquitex, Magic Marker, Revell-Monogram, and Silly Putty.

In 1994, Hallmark created Hallmark Entertainment—the world's leading producer of family-oriented network movies and miniseries. The following year, the company formed Hallmark Entertainment Network to initiate several 24-hour, premium cable channels worldwide.

Community Involvement

In 1968, Hallmark began the redevelopment of 85 acres of once-blighted property near downtown Kansas City. Surrounding the company's world headquarters, the complex was renamed Crown Center after Hallmark's distinctive trademark. Today, the center features an office complex, an apartment and condominium community, two hotels, an enclosed shopping center, restaurants, two live professional theaters, a six-screen cinema, and the fascinating Hallmark Visitors Center.

Opened in 1985, the Hallmark Visitors Center tells the company's nearly 90-year story through more than a dozen exhibits, and shows how Hallmark writers and artisans develop their products. Next door, a creative art exhibit called *Kaleidoscope* en-

courages children aged five to 12 to experiment with paints and pastels. Crown Center also hosts summertime outdoor programs for the public, and its wintertime ice-skating rink is open daily to the public.

Hallmark's community connection extends to its own employees, too. The company consistently earns high ratings from a variety of organizations and publications. Voted in the top 10 of the 100 Best Companies to Work for in America in 1984 and 1993, Hallmark also won *Personnel Journal*'s Optimas Award in 1996 for its commitment to the quality of life of individual employees. The company was included from 1985 to 1998 on *Working Mother* magazine's 100 Best Companies for Working Mothers list, and was awarded Columbia University's Lawrence A. Wien Prize in Social Responsibility in 1995.

At Hallmark, quality is critical, and that shows in the company's products, work environment, and people. "It is impossible to place a monetary value on our reputation for quality," says Don Hall. "It is an intangible that must be protected. It has a direct and important impact on our success as a company, both now and in the future."

Hallmark employs the world's largest creative team, which now includes some 740 artists, designers, photographers, writers, editors, and lettering artists who create sentiments that speak to the human relationship. The company has more than 20,000 full-time workers worldwide (top).

Kaleidoscope, **a creative art exhibit that is part of Hallmark's Crown Center, encourages children aged five to 12 to experiment with paints and pastels (bottom).**

ROUND THE WORLD, HALLMARK CARDS' SLOGAN HAS BEcome instantly recognizable: "When you care enough to send the very best." Within the privately held corporation, however, another slogan has held true through its history: When you care enough to *create* the very best. That's certainly been

The Link, Crown Center's elevated pedestrian walkway, offers enclosed, climate-controlled access from the Hyatt Regency Crown Center hotel to the Westin Crown Center hotel. The Link also provides access to Crown Center's shops, restaurants, theaters, and other entertainment activities.

the case with Crown Center, the 85-acre redevelopment project that has become to Kansas City what Rockefeller Center is to New York or the Embarcadero Center is to San Francisco.

"Crown Center's mix of office, residential, retail, and entertainment is unmatched in the region," says Bill Lucas, president of Crown Center. "Owned and operated by Hallmark Cards, which has a fierce dedication to quality and a commitment to community and its own long-term projects, Crown Center is nationally renowned."

Something from Nothing

Crown Center was the dream of Hallmark founder J.C. Hall and his son, Hallmark chairman Donald Hall. In the 1960s, the Halls surveyed the blighted area surrounding their Kansas City headquarters and decided they would transform it into an urban oasis. They broke ground on the project's first phase in 1968, and completed Crown Center's first five-building, seven-story complex in 1971. That initial 660,000 square feet of office space was joined by the Crown Center shopping center, which opened in 1973, featuring

national retailers, small specialty chains, and the 100,000-square-foot specialty department store, Halls Crown Center.

Other office buildings followed, including 2405 Grand, a 245,000-square-foot, 14-story building completed in 1987, and 2600 Grand, a 279,000-square-foot tower completed in 1991. In addition, a new, 230,000-square-foot building is under construction, soon to be the headquarters for the National Association of Insurance Commissioners. In the next 20 years, Crown Center expects to add office space, as well as additional retail and residential units to the complex.

Entertainment Venue

In addition to entertainment attractions, Crown Center boasts a variety of dining options, from the acclaimed Mobil four-star American Restaurant to Japanese and Italian cuisine. Entertainment choices include a 450-seat, Broadway-style theater, the American Heartland Theatre; the Coterie Theatre for families and young audiences; and Kansas City's only public outdoor ice skating rink, the Ice Terrace. Two Hallmark facilities

also are popular free attractions Kaleidoscope, a creative art workshop for kids ages five to 12, and the Hallmark Visitors Center. At Christmastime, Crown Center is home to the nation's tallest Christmas tree on Crown Center Square. In the summer, free Friday Funfests in July offer evenings of fun and music for the entire family.

Crown Center Hospitality

Two world-class hotels, the Westin Crown Center and the Hyatt Regency Crown Center also highlight the development's reputation as a major convention and tourist destination. Crown Center's six-acre urban residential neighborhood includes 110 garden apartments and 135 high rise condo units, as well as a social clubhouse, tennis courts, a swimming pool, and landscaped garden areas.

"Our position in the marketplace is that we're a family, cultural, and entertainment center," says Lucas. "We're going to continue to evolve as a place where families can come together for high-quality, shared experiences. We've created a unique experience, and we expect to continue that philosophy far into the future."

The Christmas season begins in Kansas City with the lighting ceremony of the 100-foot Mayor's Christmas Tree on Crown Center Square, marking the start of the annual citywide holiday charity drive.

EARLY 90 YEARS AFTER ITS FOUNDING IN 1910, THOMAS McGee, L.C. continues its quest to be the best insurance broker in the country. Located only two blocks from its original downtown Kansas City office, today Thomas McGee is the oldest privately held insurance brokerage firm in the area,

and one of the largest full-service, independent insurance agencies in Kansas City to be locally owned and operated. The company provides commercial property and casualty insurance, surety bonds, employee benefits programs, claims management, risk management services, loss control, and personal lines to satisfied clients nationwide.

What has set Thomas McGee apart over the years has been its long tradition of excellence and its ability to adapt. Although the insurance industry has changed dramatically over the decades, Thomas McGee's commitment to determining client needs has not.

In analyzing the specific risks clients face, Thomas McGee personnel take the time to familiarize themselves with clients' entire operations. "It's important that we understand our clients' business and needs," says Eugene A. Klein, Thomas McGee's administrative member. "We work to know our clients, then design our services around what they need."

Independent Agents

From its office in Kansas City, Thomas McGee represents the country's major insurance companies and specialty markets, which allows it to tailor insurance for every customer. Among commercial lines, the firm focuses on clients in fields such as contracting, communications, institutions, sports, retail and wholesale, and manufacturing. For companies that need employee benefits plans, Thomas McGee can help devise corporate stock redemption funding, key man insurance, estate planning, 401(k) profit sharing plans, disability or group health, and life insurance. When it comes to surety bonds, Thomas McGee's combination of experience and service has gained it recognition as one of the premier surety bond experts.

In fact, Thomas McGee has made a name for itself as an insurance authority, partly through its active memberships in professional organizations. Staff members are not only knowledgeable about the insurance industry, but they play an active role in industry developments. "We're very keen on insurance company relationships," says Klein. "By leveraging our relationship with the industry, we're able to communicate with the insurance industry in ways that a typical agent can't touch."

That connection has only added to Thomas McGee's standing in the insurance community, which has translated to healthy client-company relationships. "We bring a value-added aspect to the process instead of just offering off-the-shelf insurance," says Klein. "We want to be the preferred provider of cost-effective, timely brokerage and risk management services that consistently exceed the expectations of our clients."

The Broadway office of Thomas McGee, L.C. overlooks the downtown airport.

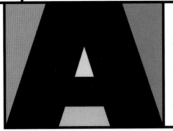

ALL TOO OFTEN, YOUNG SCHOLARS ARE STEERED INTO memorizing facts and figures, rather than learning how to ask the right questions. But at Kansas City's Rockhurst College, one of 28 Jesuit colleges and universities in the United States, the cornerstone of its long history has been

to nurture and encourage the free exchange of opinions and ideas throughout its numerous and diverse degree programs.

At Rockhurst, everyone realizes that one of the most valuable skills students can take away from college is the ability to think for themselves. That attitude, combined with a wide range of academic programs, a full complement of cocurricular activities, and an impressive 14-to-1 student-faculty ratio, consistently ranks Rockhurst as one of the best educational buys in the Midwest, according to *U.S. News & World Report*. With bachelor's and master's degrees in everything from biology, computer information systems, and psychology to theater arts, human resources, and physical therapy, Rockhurst provides its 3,000 students with a well-rounded education on a 35-acre campus just south of Kansas City's Country Club Plaza.

"Rockhurst's emphasis on values and lifelong learning leads students to new definitions of success," says the Reverend E. Edward Kinerk, S.J., who took over as the 13th president of his alma mater in June 1998. The

Clockwise from top right: Each fall, students relax and take advantage of studying outdoors on the beautiful Rockhurst College campus.

Sedgwick Hall, on the Rockhurst College campus, housed both the high school and the college until the early 1960s.

While academic pursuits are strongly encouraged at Rockhurst, students find plenty of opportunities for less scholarly endeavors.

ability to be successful in the world has been mastered by many famous Rocks, as Rockhurst alumni are known. Rockhurst graduates have become space scientists, entrepreneurs, founders of clinics for crack babies, and college presidents. Famous Rocks are found in nearly every state, making a difference in their fields and in their communities.

Firm Foundation

Rockhurst College was founded in 1910 when the state of Missouri granted the Jesuits a charter to offer high school and college classes. But the Jesuits date much further back in history. The Society of Jesus was founded by Saint Ignatius Loyola in 1534. Loyola and his followers were ordained priests who took vows of poverty and chastity and gave their allegiance to Pope Paul III. The order grew so rapidly that when Loyola died in 1556, the small seed had flowered to nearly 1,000 members. Today, the Jesuits are the largest Roman Catholic religious order.

The Jesuits have become renowned during more than four centuries of history for providing service to others though a liberal education. In addition to

Rockhurst College, Georgetown University, Fordham University, Boston College, and Marquette University are among the 28 well-respected colleges and universities run by the Jesuits nationwide.

"Rockhurst has a fine educational tradition that combines solid academics with a welcoming environment," says Kinerk. "In the coming years, we will further develop the academic facilities at the college, continue to take advantage of Rockhurst's urban location, and strengthen the institution's Jesuit mission. I cannot think of a better way of being a priest and a Jesuit than in serving as president of Rockhurst College."

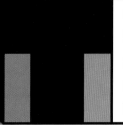

HE TEEN YEARS ARE A CRITICAL TIME FOR CHILDREN, WHICH is why Rockhurst High School has played such an important role in the formation of local youth. For nearly a century, the educational institution, one of only 47 Jesuit high schools in the United States, has shaped more than 12,000 local young men

as leaders of the future.

Located at 93rd Street and State Line Road in Kansas City, Rockhurst takes seriously its calling to educate young men to be academically excellent. But the school's mission goes much further. Rockhurst wants its graduates to embrace an active philosophy of service to others, maintain a religious and loving attitude, and always stay open to personal growth. In a nutshell, Rockhurst helps its students adhere to the ideals of Saint Ignatius Loyola, embodied in the school's creed, "Men for Others."

"Our education stresses precision of thought, clarity of expression, and the translation of ideas into action," says the Reverend Thomas A. Pesci, S.J., president of Rockhurst High School. "In an unwavering pursuit of excellence in education, the Jesuits can point to more than 450 years of experience in shaping the minds and hearts of 'Men for Others.' A Jesuit high school graduate becomes part of an international brotherhood of men distinguished by their competence, conscience, and compassion."

Growth Curve

Rockhurst was officially chartered in 1910 as the Rockhurst Academy. Although it took four years to build the first academic structure, some 42 students enrolled in the high school's first freshman and sophomore classes in 1914. In 1917, nine men received degrees as the first graduating class of Rockhurst.

Rockhurst High School established its own separate campus away from Rockhurst College in 1962. Since that time, more than 5,000 young men have enrolled and consequently graduated from Rockhurst's Greenlease Memorial Campus. The school's leadership continues to strive to improve the quality of life for each of its students through regular enhancements to academic, spiritual, and extracurricular programs. The landmark Defining Moment capital project recently established a full-service Student Commons; a multilevel Student Services Core with state-of-the-art science laboratories, seminar classrooms, and administrative offices; a freestanding chapel; an upgraded technological system; modern fine arts and journalism centers; a refurbished, 860-seat Rose Theatre; a performance gymnasium and expanded multicourt annex; a combination baseball/soccer complex; an enlarged football stadium; and enhanced endowment for the institution.

Cocurricular activities represent an important part of Rockhurst's well-rounded education. Interscholastic sports range from baseball, basketball, soccer, wrestling, and football to golf, lacrosse, tennis, track, cross-country, and swimming. In the late 1980s and early 1990s, the athletic program claimed eight Missouri state titles and 36 district championships, while competing with the state's largest schools and schools across the Midwest. Other popular cocurricular activities at Rockhurst include the Eilert Ecology Club, Student Government, and National Forensic League Speech and Debate.

"More than 95 percent of Rockhurst graduates continue their education at prestigious four-year colleges throughout the country," says Pesci. "When they leave here, our graduates are accomplished young men who have been involved in academics and activities, who have given of themselves to their communities and their colleagues. All in all, our students are pretty impressive when they graduate from Rockhurst High School."

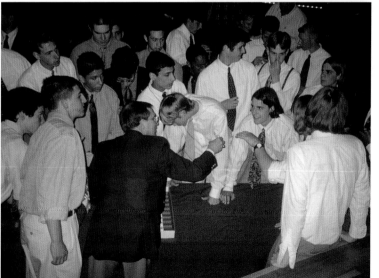

Located at 93rd Street and State Line Road, Rockhurst takes seriously its calling to educate young men to be academically excellent. Rockhurst wants its graduates to embrace an active philosophy of service to others, maintain a religious and loving attitude, and always stay open to personal growth (top).

Students participate in the "Junior Ring Ceremony" at Rockhurst High School (bottom).

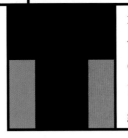

HE OLDEST SCHOOL IN KANSAS CITY, ST. TERESA'S ACADEMY was founded in 1866 when six Sisters of St. Joseph came to Kansas City at the request of Father Bernard Donnelly. Established one year before the Kansas City Public Schools system, the school is distinguished as the oldest educational institution in Kansas City.

Originally located in an area called Quality Hill near 12th and Washington streets, the all-girl school received hundreds of day students and boarders, and became a center of cultural life to which early Kansas Citians pointed with pride.

St. Teresa's Academy grew in enrollment and prestige, but gradually the city moved to the south and the Sisters decided to relocate. In 1908, the Mother Superior, Sister Evelyn O'Neill, undertook the almost impossible task of relocating and building a new facility. Sister Evelyn purchased 20 acres at 5600 Main Street, south of Country Club Plaza. St. Teresa's has grown in enrollment and prestige in some 130 years, and now boasts a three-building campus with nearly 500 students enrolled in grades nine through 12, having come from 70 different middle schools and grade schools.

Although the academy is more than 130 years old, the administration has been proactive in the development of up-to-date programs that ensure educational excellence. The campus has undergone progressive change, as evidenced by the addition of both intranet and Internet connections in each classroom. The network-

ing of the three buildings puts St. Teresa's on the cutting edge technologically among the Catholic schools in Kansas City. St. Teresa's students excel in math, science, computer programming, literature, art, drama, journalism, and athletics. The success of the academy can be measured by the acceptance of 100 percent of its graduates at excellent colleges and universities throughout the country. More than half of the young women graduating each year enter college with academic or special merit scholarships.

"Our only reason for being here is to educate young women and ensure their success in the future," says Dr. Faith Wilson, president. "Everything we do must contribute to that goal. At

St. Teresa's, the mission is alive and well, and it's working."

Philosophy

St. Teresa's Academy, an independent, Catholic, college preparatory school, sponsored by the Sisters of St. Joseph of Carondelet, commits itself to the education of the total young woman. The school promotes excellence in education through a college preparatory curriculum, a single-sex environment, a diverse student body, Christian values, and a balance of freedom and responsibility.

Aware of the academic advantages of single-sex education, St. Teresa's encourages participation in math, science, and technology, areas that women have been traditionally discouraged from exploring. This female environment enhances leadership, self-confidence, and the development of a positive self-image.

Mutual respect, support, trust, and concern are among the Christian values that provide a basis for the St. Teresa's school community. Understanding the school's heritage and gifts, students realize the corresponding duty to make a contribution to society. The academy strives to raise consciousness concerning local and global responsibilities as reflected in the gospel.

Clockwise from top:
St. Teresa's Academy has grown in enrollment and prestige at its 20-acre location at 5600 Main Street, and now boasts a three-building campus with nearly 500 students.

Mutual respect, support, trust, and concern are among the Christian values that provide a basis for the St. Teresa's school community. A statue of Saint Joseph greets students and guests at the main entrance.

St. Teresa's students excel in math, science, computer programming, literature, art, drama, journalism, and athletics. Donnelly Hall is one of the three buildings comprising St. Teresa's.

CASUAL EXAMINATION OF A BLACK & VEATCH PROJECT list reveals the firm's extensive presence around the world. From an airport in the Philippines to an electrical facility in Australia, from a hydroelectric plant in Pakistan to a treatment facility upgrade in England, Black & Veatch

covers the globe with its quality-oriented, customer-driven engineering and construction work. With 7,000 professionals in more than 90 offices worldwide—including Egypt, Indonesia, Chile, and the Czech Republic—this Kansas City-based partnership has grown substantially during its 83-year history.

"Until about seven years ago, we were primarily a domestic services firm," says John Robinson Jr., Black & Veatch's chief development officer. "But now, we're a global design and building firm. We've located new markets around the world through a very clearly defined and strategically planned effort."

The company's success can be measured partly in its growing revenues. Black & Veatch grossed some $2 billion during 1997, with about 65 percent from international markets. Recent projects include the largest ozone disinfection project in North America, located in Canada; the first modern coal-fired power plant in Central America; and the reconstruction and renovation of a 15th-century building to a five-star, 72-room U Sixtu Hotel in the heart of Prague's Old Town Square. "We've been landing projects internationally since the 1960s, but our current growth has been much more rapid," says Robinson.

Specialty Areas

Black & Veatch has built its award-winning reputation on the work performed by its three major sectors: Power, Infrastructure, and Process. Through these divisions, the partnership has perfected services that include engineering, procurement, construction, telecommunications, architectural, financial, informa-tion, and management consulting for utilities, commerce, industry, and government agencies.

Such work has garnered countless kudos for Black & Veatch. *Network World Magazine* recognized the company as one of the best and brightest around the globe in innovative networking technology. *Engineering News-Record* has named Black & Veatch first among the top 200 international design firms in power, third among the top 200 in water supply, and third among the top 200 in sewerage, along with many other rankings.

The quality of Black & Veatch's corporate culture has put the company at the top in engineering and construction work. "Tom Veatch was a classic gentleman," says Robinson, referring to one of the company's original partners. "He created the integrity that's the basis of all we do."

The quality of Black & Veatch's corporate culture has put the company at the top in engineering and construction work. One example of the company's high-quality work is the Cedar Bay Generation Plant in Jacksonville, Florida (left).

Engineering News-Record **has named Black & Veatch third among the top 200 in water supply. The Modesto Water Treatment Plant exemplifies the company's quality work (right).**

Y THE TIME HENRY FORD ANNOUNCED HIS PLAN TO BUILD
a Kansas City manufacturing facility, Ford Motor Company
had already had a local sales office for three years. Since 1906,
Ford's salesmen had taken orders for Model Ks, Model Fs, and
Model Ns from their downtown Kansas City location. But

Henry Ford's decision to make
cars in Kansas City was of major importance to the town set
along the Missouri River: The
Kansas City factory would be
the world's first automotive assembly plant outside the Detroit
area.

In fact, Kansas City's central
location made it an ideal spot both
for selling and for manufacturing
Ford's new models. The company
also believed that the midwestern
workforce would benefit from
its productivity efforts, giving
it an edge over growing competition. Henry Ford's hunch seemed
accurate from the beginning:
When Model T production began
at the 1025 Winchester Avenue
plant in 1912, local media reported that employees there
would build "as many as seven
cars a day."

After operating on Winchester
Avenue for 45 years, Ford moved
its assembly plant operation to
its current Claycomo, Missouri,
location in 1957. The company
had actually started construction
six years earlier, but was inter-
rupted when the outbreak of the
Korean War diverted employees
from building cars to producing
wings for the B-47 Stratojet

Clockwise from top:
**Since 1906, Ford salesmen had
sold Model Ks, Model Fs, and
Model Ns from their downtown
Kansas City location. But Henry
Ford's decision to make cars
in Kansas City established the
world's first automotive assembly plant outside the Detroit
area.**

**The Ford assembly plant located
on Winchester Avenue was built
in 1912 to produce Model Ts.**

**From left, Salvation Army
Colonel Theodore Dahlberg,
restauranteur Carl DiCapo, and
Ford Plant Manager Gerry Minor
discuss holiday activities at the
Claycomo, Missouri, assembly
plant.**

bomber. Finally, on January 7,
1957, the Claycomo factory's
first car—a Ford Country Squire
station wagon—rolled off the
assembly line. Since then, the
plant has also made Fairmonts,
Zephyrs, Falcons, Ranch Wagons,
Fairlanes, Comets, Rancheros,
Meteors, Mavericks, Tempos,
and Topazes.

A Production Leader

F ord's Kansas City plant has
come a long way since its
opening. Today, the operation
produces more than 770 F-150
pickups and another 880 Ford
Contour and Mercury Mystiques
daily. Its more than 5,000 employees work two eight-hour shifts
at Ford's facility in Claycomo,
an enormous, 3.7 million-square-
foot plant set on more than 339
acres. One of Ford's largest assembly plants in North America—
the Kansas City facility ships
vehicles to all 50 states, Canada,
Mexico, and a number of overseas locations, including Saudi
Arabia, Kuwait, and China. In
fact, from 1912 through 1996,
Kansas City Ford workers pumped
out some 13,508 cars and trucks.

And Ford has even bigger
plans for the future. "Following
our Ford 2000 plans, this plant
has the ultimate objective to be
one of the leading auto produc-

ers in the world," says Gerry
Minor, Ford's plant manager
in Kansas City. "We're building
world-class quality out here. Customer satisfaction is the driver
of everything we do."

One way that Ford has opti-
mized its focus on customer satisfaction is by making sure its
own operations run smoothly.
In the past several years, the
company has worked to reduce
costs and remove profitability
constraints. Interactive leadership and teamwork have been
reemphasized to improve job
satisfaction and productivity.
"What separates us from other
plants is the mutual respect we
all have for one another," says

Minor. "When workers see management walking the walk, it returns manyfold. That's not just a philosophy, but the way we really try to operate our facility."

Employee Satisfaction, Too

Knowing that happy employees are productive employees, Ford has adopted innovative technologies to make the job run more smoothly. Constructing cars and trucks can be very physically demanding work, and one way Ford has enhanced its operations has been through the use of robotics. Kansas City, in fact, was one of the first plants to install a robot in the plant; now, there are more than 300 of them.

In addition, the company orients employees toward change; whenever a car line changes, which occurs regularly, assembly plant staff must quickly make internal adaptations to systems and processes. In addition, cross training has become a critical factor at Ford's Kansas City plant, since it is the only remaining Ford plant that makes both cars and trucks.

Focusing on satisfied and well-trained employees has paid off at Ford Kansas City. In 1997 alone, the company experienced a phenomenal 35 to 45 percent improvement in quality. "Japan became the quality benchmark for many years, but not any more," says Minor, a 30-year Ford veteran who has been at the Kansas City assembly plant since early 1997. "If everyone is all going in the same direction, then you're virtually unstoppable."

Essential in the Community

Despite Ford's long history in Kansas City, many residents still don't understand the impact the plant has on the community. The operation's annual payroll amounts to nearly $300 million, and the company spends some $680 million a year just to run the Claycomo assembly plant. That represents a significant investment, one that Ford likes Kansas Citians to learn more about by taking one of its free Friday tours.

The plant's employees also like to give to the community. "Workers in Kansas City are probably the most giving people I've worked with around the country," says Minor. "They've given between $470,000 and $480,000 to United Way, $80,000 to $90,000 to the Salvation Army around the holidays, and another several hundred thousand to other charities. It's a midwestern spirit, a unified feeling here. They truly believe that this is their plant and they're proud of it."

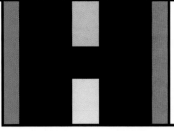

NTB's PROJECT ROSTER READS LIKE A WHO'S WHO OF architectural, engineering, and planning achievements. Local landmarks designed by the firm include the Truman Sports Complex, Kansas City International (KCI) Airport, Bartle Hall, the Town Pavilion, the National Collegiate

Athletic Association's headquarters, and all the area bridges across the Missouri River. And these are only a few of the firm's achievements.

Throughout the metropolitan area, HNTB's presence is visible and noteworthy. Among the ongoing projects in which the firm is playing a leading role are Science City at Union Station, the new Kansas International

Speedway, development of the Power & Light District, planning and design of new facilities at the Pembroke Hill School, terminal renovations at KCI, Bruce R. Watkins Drive, improvement of the Grandview Triangle, and the multistate I-35 Trade Corridor study.

"Our reputation for innovative design, quality services, and leading-edge management has given us a solid foundation to grow from," says Robert Coma, HNTB chairman. "People wonder 'How does HNTB do it?' We have always had an impressive group of people dedicated to the concept of helping our clients find solutions to their problems. Our people are the secret of our success."

Bridge to the Future

HNTB was founded in 1914 as a small, Kansas City-based bridge design firm. As the firm matured and the country's

need for improved transportation systems exploded, HNTB added specialists in highway, railroad, transit, and airport design. Today, HNTB ranks among the top five transportation engineering firms in the United States.

In 1975, HNTB acquired the prestigious Kansas City architectural firm of Kivett & Myers,

HNTB's impact extends well beyond Kansas City's boundaries. Recent architectural projects range from new passenger terminals at major airports around the country to arenas and stadiums for NBA, NFL, and major-league baseball teams, and office buildings for corporate and government clients.

launching an architectural practice that is now one of the largest in the nation. In the spring of 1998, HNTB added to its outstanding portfolio of architectural and urban design services by acquiring the highly regarded Kansas City architectural firm of Mackey Mitchell Zahner Associates.

HNTB's impact extends well beyond Kansas City's boundaries. Today, the firm has more than 40 offices nationwide, employing 2,000 people. Recent architectural projects range from new passenger terminals at major airports around the country to arenas and stadiums for NBA, NFL, and major-league baseball teams, and office buildings for corporate and government clients. Engineering projects include new and innovative transportation systems throughout the country; highway and railroad bridges across the nation's major rivers; and transit systems in America's leading cities.

Positioned for Change

There's just an unbelievable amount of change in our industry right now," says Coma. "But, HNTB has always been at the forefront in using new approaches to meet our clients' needs. For example, the firm's experience with delivery systems, such as design-build, and innovative financing strategies, such as tolls and public-private funding partnerships, can help our clients advance their projects to completion much more quickly than traditional methods," he says.

"As we approach the next century, we know that we will continue to be one of the leading firms in the United States and we also will increase our global presence. We've responded to the impact of technology and changing U.S. business philosophies, and are positioned to help our clients meet the challenges of their ever changing marketplaces in newly creative ways," says Coma.

Kansas City Commitment

HNTB's commitment to Kansas City has been apparent since its earliest days. In addition to the projects that have shaped Kansas City's skyline and byways, HNTB has provided extensive civic and charitable support throughout the area. It's just part of the firm's ongoing belief in the place it has called home for more than 80 years. "Although we have offices and projects in locations around the country, our heart is in Kansas City," says Coma. "It's important that we show how connected we are to Kansas City by supporting the community that's supported us for so long."

HNTB's engineering projects include new and innovative transportation systems throughout the country; highway and railroad bridges across the nation's major rivers; and transit systems in America's leading cities.

N 1915, THE HELZBERG FAMILY BEGAN BUILDING ITS BUSINESS IN the heart of America. Since then, Helzberg Diamonds has focused on providing exceptional jewelry and personalized customer service, helping each and every customer select a true gift from the heart. ■ Still headquartered in Kansas City, the company has grown into a national

jeweler with an average store sales performance of more than double the industry average. The company operates more than 200 stores in 28 states and plans for continued expansion.

Helzberg Diamonds has two highly successful store formats—as a traditional mall jeweler with a reputation for quality, style, convenience, and service; and as a freestanding jewelry store in power strip centers, combining outstanding selection with additional services such as an on-site jeweler and convenient parking.

A Legacy of Success

The company was founded by the Helzberg family, and built by three successive generations—each a leader in the industry and the Kansas City community. This midwestern success story caught the attention of Warren Buffett, and the company was acquired by his holding company, Berkshire Hathaway, in 1995.

Morris Helzberg opened the original Helzberg Diamonds store at 529 Minnesota Avenue in Kansas City, Kansas. The shop was a small force in its day, but was established with high principles that would predicate phenomenal growth. After a few

short years in business, Morris suffered a stroke and his young son, Barnett, took over the operation. Barnett was determined to build the business and sell diamonds and jewelry in stores across the Midwest. It wasn't long before his dreams began to come true.

By 1929, Barnett had added stores in Topeka, Wichita, and in downtown Kansas City, Missouri. The Helzberg Diamonds shops were a highly respected business that gave time and money back to the community. Barnett was so confident as an entrepreneur, he even denied the miserable economy of the Great Depression. The *Kansas City Star* reported, "When he doubled the size of the Eleventh and Walnut store in 1932, Barnett Helzberg became a symbol of courage to Kansas City."

Always on the leading edge and concerned about the comfort of customers, Helzberg was one of the first to offer customers "cooling by refrigeration" (air-conditioning). As World War II ended, Barnett expanded to the growing suburbs, providing jobs for returning servicemen. By 1947, Helzberg operated eight stores in Missouri, Kansas, and Iowa, and was known as the Middle West's Largest Jeweler.

In 1950, Helzberg Diamonds showcased the legendary Hope

Diamond at its elegant Country Club Plaza store in Kansas City, Missouri, donating all proceeds to the campaign to fight polio.

I AM LOVED®

Barnett Helzberg Jr. became the third-generation leader of the family firm in 1963, taking command of 39 stores. Barnett Jr. created a name for himself with his leadership and management abilities, and it was his modest promotional idea that created a national name for Helzberg Diamonds.

In 1967, Barnett proposed marriage to a young lady and in his euphoria, he developed a small red lapel button with the words I AM LOVED®. He knew firsthand that love was a great feeling. The slogan was intended to be a two-week marketing campaign, but it evolved into a timeless, worldwide goodwill effort.

Diamonds and diamond jewelry fashions have always been the focal point of Helzberg Diamonds' merchandising position (center).

Helzberg Diamonds has a reputation for providing quality, style convenience and service in regional shopping malls (bottom) and power strip (top right) centers across the nation.

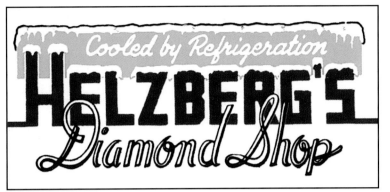

Since its conception, Helzberg Diamonds has given away millions of buttons in five languages.

It was also in the late 1960s that the company opened its first corner store in a shopping mall. Success in the mall was immediate, and Barnett Jr. decided the best future for the company would be long-term leases in regional shopping malls. The company began an aggressive expansion plan, opening an average of three new mall stores per year.

By 1980, Helzberg had adopted a merchandise position that focused on diamonds. Fine quality had always been a prerequisite, but it was in this decade that fashion and style became equally important.

By the mid-1980s, Helzberg had become one of the most productive jewelers in the country and rapid growth continued. In 1988, Barnett Jr. brought retail leader Jeffrey W. Comment in as president of his family's firm. Seven years later, Berkshire Hathaway acquired the company—a move that positioned Helzberg Diamonds for continued growth and strength in the 21st century.

A Culture of Customer Service

Throughout its history, Helzberg Diamonds has excelled at keeping clients happy by offering an exceptional array of fashionable, fine jewelry and emphasizing top quality and personalized service. Backed by a longstanding heritage and impeccable reputation, the company's basic philosophies center on ethics, integrity, and courtesy.

Says Comment, the company's current CEO, "Our mission statement is to serve each and every customer in a very special way, and we really take that to heart. If you're going to work with us, you'll build relationships with the customers; that's a given. We have a reputation of being one of the most service-oriented establishments in the retail industry. When you're selling a product like ours, people have to come in and have a good experience."

While the company's mission statement draws its strength from a heritage of service, Helzberg Diamonds' vision statement charts the future for the Kansas City company: Helzberg Diamonds will be known for fine jewelry gifts that express the heartfelt emotion of the giver.

As with the I AM LOVED® promotion, a recent advertising theme, "If it comes from the heart, shouldn't it come from Helzberg Diamonds?" has moved beyond marketing and become part of the company's culture—illustrating the company's commitment to making each customer interaction meaningful. Helzberg Diamonds is in the business of helping real people express their love—and the company seeks daily to prove that if a gift comes from the heart, it should come from Helzberg Diamonds.

Clockwise from top: Helzberg was one of the first stores to offer customers "cooling by refrigeration" (air-conditioning).

An advertisement in 1967 announced Helzberg's I AM LOVED® campaign. The slogan survives today as an integral part of the company's corporate identity.

Barnett Helzberg Jr. and one of his brothers outside the Country Club Plaza store in Kansas City in the early 1940s

Helzbergs announces the

button

The age old problem hasn't changed. She still wants to know she's loved. And you still wonder how to tell her.
Now Helzbergs is first to offer you a choice of methods:

(1) Give her a Certified Perfect diamond solitaire. The eloquent one. ($50 to $5000. Exclusively at Helzbergs.)

(2) Give her an "I AM LOVED" button. It says a lot, too. (No charge, of course. Also exclusively at Helzbergs.)

Of course, the "I AM LOVED" button will never replace the Helzbergs Certified Perfect diamond. But, while you're stalling, at least you've told her how you feel!

Helzberg's
Middle West's Largest Jewelers

Every Helzberg Certified Perfect Diamond is certified and guaranteed by us to be of fine color, perfect in cut and proportion, and free from imperfection of any kind.

CELEBRATING GREATER KANSAS CITY

1916	BLACKWELL SANDERS PEPER MARTIN LLP	1945	FIKE CORPORATION
1916	THE UNIVERSITY OF HEALTH SCIENCES	1945	GENERAL MOTORS CORP./ MLCG FAIRFAX ASSEMBLY PLANT
1917	FOGEL ANDERSON CONSTRUCTION CO.	1946	HARMON INDUSTRIES, INC.
1918	CAMP FIRE BOYS AND GIRLS	1946	THE LARKIN GROUP, INC.
1919	HAVENS STEEL	1947	MARK ONE ELECTRIC CO., INC.
1919	UNION BANK	1948	DiCARLO CONSTRUCTION COMPANY
1920	AMC ENTERTAINMENT INC.	1948	LEWIS, RICE & FINGERSH, L.C.
1922	MARLEY COOLING TOWER COMPANY	1948	THE ZIMMER COMPANIES
1924	J.E. DUNN CONSTRUCTION COMPANY	1949	ALLIEDSIGNAL FEDERAL MANUFACTURING & TECHNOLOGIES
1924	YELLOW CORPORATION	1949	IBT, INC.
1928	UNION SECURITIES	1950	HOECHST MARION ROUSSEL, INC.
1929	BOARD OF PUBLIC UTILITIES	1951	JAMES B. NUTTER & CO.
1929	FARMLAND INDUSTRIES, INC.	1951	SPENCER FANE BRITT & BROWNE LLP
1932	THE RIVAL® COMPANY	1953	KCTV5
1932	UNITOG COMPANY	1953	MANPOWER, INC.
1933	UNIVERSITY OF MISSOURI-KANSAS CITY	1955	H&R BLOCK, INC.
1936	HOTZ BUSINESS SYSTEMS	1958	AMERICAN CENTURY INVESTMENTS
1938	EXECUTIVE BEECHCRAFT, INC.	1958	NORTH KANSAS CITY HOSPITAL
1943	IBM CORP.		
1944	THE SALVAJOR COMPANY		

REVITALIZATION: IN FACILITIES, IN SPIRIT, AND IN curriculum. That's where The University of Health Sciences has positioned itself for the new millennium. After more than 80 years of educating some of the finest osteopathic physicians in the country, The University of Health

Sciences (UHS) is experiencing a wholehearted revitalization. UHS is enthusiastically unveiling a new face to Kansas City and continuing to be a major player in the field of medical education. While revamping curriculum to meet the challenges of the 21st century, UHS is also becoming one of Kansas City's most civic-minded organizations.

Located northeast of downtown on a beautiful, 10-acre campus, UHS is the oldest—and the only private—medical school among the three based in Kansas City. The school offers a treasury of resources and opportunities to the nearly 800 students enrolled in its four-year academic program. With 21 applicants for each of the 225 first-year seats available, it is little wonder that UHS turns heads. To date, UHS has graduated more than 6,500 physicians, who have gone on to practice in high-tech, prestigious medical centers around the country, as well as to serve in rural communities as traditional family doctors.

UHS is not only a leader among the 18 osteopathic medical schools across the United States, but also among major allopathic (conventional) medical schools with the same rigorous, four-year curriculum and preparation for the same licensing exams in each state.

Primary Care Focus

More than half of UHS graduates—after completing two years of on-campus lectures and labs, and two years of

clinical training in hospitals and ambulatory settings in Kansas City or rural and urban settings throughout the country—have chosen to pursue a career in primary care. Due to the gatekeeper role that primary care physicians play in the managed care climate, primary care has experienced exceptional growth. In fact, UHS is one of the most highly sophisticated medical schools in the country in terms of teaching equipment and facilities, while it is one of a handful of medical colleges leading the way in a renewed emphasis on "high-touch" medicine.

"Stressing care with a humane, holistic, and compassionate focus is not only a practiced philosophy at UHS, it is also a 100-year-old tradition dating back to the inception of osteopathic medicine," said Karen L. Pletz, the school's president and CEO. "That emphasis truly underlies all that we do here."

Totally refurbished in recent years, the University of Health Sciences Administration Building was originally Children's Mercy Hospital (below).

Students pause outside the University of Health Sciences Educational Pavilion, a 96,000-square-foot, $10 million addition to the campus in 1996 (right).

Medical Roots

The Kansas City College of Osteopathy and Surgery was founded in 1916. Five years later, the school moved to its present location on Independence Boulevard. It was a time of great growth and prosperity in the region: J.C. Nichols was transforming 10 acres of wasteland in the south into the Country Club Plaza district and helping create Kansas City as the City of Fountains.

At the same time, George J. Conley, D.O., the school's first president, was building a virtual fountain of knowledge in the northeast: the city's first medical school. In 1971, the UHS Alumni Association purchased 8.5 acres of ground and a building—once the original Children's Mercy Hospital—to serve as the administration building. The school was renamed The University of Health Sciences College of Osteopathic Medicine in 1980.

Today, the UHS campus, now the largest medical school in Missouri, has never sparkled so brightly. The stately buildings of yesteryear, with their limestone bases and red brick exteriors, are reminiscent of a rich history and proud tradition. Beautifully landscaped grounds provide a welcoming environment for students and faculty. The picturesque, historic campus has been artfully blended with architecturally compatible new facilities that belie the state-of-the-art medical teaching facilities housed within. All in all, UHS has become an oasis of learning

in the Kansas City urban core, a section of the city that the school has made a commitment to revitalize.

The UHS Educational Pavilion, for example, is a $10 million structure built in 1996, that houses a plethora of resources under one roof. Inside its 96,000 square feet, students and faculty have easy access to a sports medicine center, a two-story library with the latest in electronic resources, lecture halls, and labs equipped with cutting-edge technological advancements. UHS' contribution to the local economy garnered the pavilion a Cornerstone Award by the Kansas City Economic Development Council.

Emphasis on People

But the vitality and pride emanating from UHS stem from much more than bricks and mortar. Students, faculty, and administration all take a proud and active role in advancing the mission of the school—a mission that promises the preparation of exceptionally competent physicians who practice with compassion and care.

To emphasize this purpose, UHS was recently one of 40 medical schools in the nation, and the first in Kansas City, to conduct

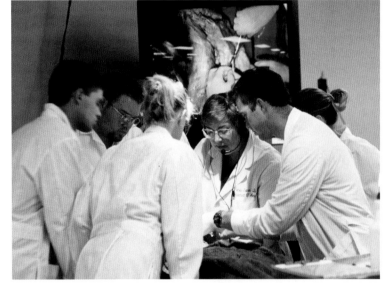

a distinctive ceremony marking the beginning of a medical student's career. "The White Coating Ceremony is more than just a special occasion," says Pletz, who foresees that the ceremony will become an annual, time-honored event at UHS. "It represents a meaningful and lasting commitment to the profession and what it really means to be the arbiter of human life," Pletz adds.

As 2000 approaches, UHS stands on the leading edge as high-tech medical education again reaches back to its roots of stressing high-touch medicine and a humane, compassionate, caring emphasis on patient care.

Clockwise from top:
The University of Health Sciences' Educational Pavilion houses labs and classrooms, faculty offices, a cafeteria, a two-story library, a sports medicine facility, and various meeting spaces.

Sophisticated cameras and monitors allow students in the anatomy lab an up close view, via a screen, of the professor's work.

A student takes advantage of a quiet spot on the rooftop terrace of the administration building to study.

N 1916, SEVEN YOUNG ATTORNEYS FORMED A KANSAS CITY LAW practice called McCune Caldwell & Downing, specializing in general corporate and banking matters. The practice expanded its focus to meet the changing needs of its clients, and soon became Blackwell Sanders Matheny Weary & Lombardi LLP. ■ In 1941, Peper, Martin, Jensen,

Maichel & Hetlage was founded in St. Louis, and grew to 82 attorneys. In 1997, the firm expanded its intellectual property practice by merging with the St. Louis law firm of Kalish and Gilster. Peper, Martin's clients included A.G. Edwards & Sons Inc., Monsanto Co., The Boeing Co., Ameritech, Planet Hollywood, St. Louis University, Bunzl Distribution USA, and the St. Louis Art Museum.

In mid-1998, Blackwell Sanders merged with Peper, Martin, creating one of the largest law firms in the region. With 312 attorneys

in six midwestern cities and London, England, the firm can serve its clients' needs across the central Midwest. Blackwell Sanders Peper Martin LLP offers clients unparalleled strength in a number of areas, including corporate and securities, mergers and acquisitions, labor and employment, education, real estate, environmental law, tax, litigation, and intellectual property.

Blackwell Sanders Peper Martin is Kansas City's second-largest legal practice. *The National Law Journal* recently ranked it as one of the top 20 fastest-growing firms in the nation over a three-year period. With attorneys in 32 practice areas, the firm has offices in Kansas City; St. Louis; Overland Park; Omaha; Springfield, Missouri; Belleville, Illinois; and London.

But even with its rapid growth, Blackwell Sanders Peper Martin still offers services custom-tailored to its clients' needs. "We like to be known as the law firm that thinks like a business partner," says John Phillips, a member of the firm's executive committee. "We offer our clients what we believe is the best value in the region."

Practice Makes Perfect

Over the years, Blackwell Sanders Peper Martin's client list has become an impressive roster of noteworthy concerns. The firm is general or securities counsel to dozens of public companies, including eight listed on the New York Stock Exchange. In addition, the firm has represented the Kansas City, Missouri School District since its founding, and has maintained a variety of other long-standing clientele, including Commerce Bancshares, Black & Veatch LLP, UtiliCorp United, Payless Cashways, Hallmark Cards Incorporated, Mutual of Omaha, and the J.C. Nichols Company.

The firm's expertise is nationally well respected, in large part because of its attorneys, 19 of whom were named to the *Best Lawyers in America* 1997-1998. Those so recognized include Stephen T. Adams, Donald A. Culp, David A. Fenley, Ernest M. Fleischer, James D.Griffin, George R. Haydon Jr., Richard A. Hetlage, Robert O. Hetlage, Melanie Gurley Keeney, Larry L. McMullen, John R. Phillips, William A. Richter, William Sanders Sr., John R. Short, James M. Warden, Daniel C. Weary, Mark D. Welker, David L. West, and Ralph G. Wrobley.

With an office in London and cooperative relationships in China, Spain, and Mexico, Blackwell Sanders Peper Martin can serve clients who are expanding their operations across the region, as well as nationally and internationally. "Many of our nationally and internationally based clients are increasingly seeking the opportunity to work with one firm that is willing to go where their business takes them," says Phillips. "Our firm is prepared to do just that."

Kansas City Executive Committee members of Blackwell Sanders Peper Martin LLP sit in the Blackwell Sanders Room at the Nelson-Atkins Museum of Art after its recent dedication (top).

Partner Tim Triplett (right) takes the time to learn about his clients' industries so he can address their needs with business solutions (bottom).

N ITS EARLY DAYS, THE NOW COEDUCATIONAL ORGANIZATION OF Camp Fire Boys and Girls was a character-building group dedicated to developing interests in community service and self-betterment for girls. Established in Vermont in 1910, the association, founded as Camp Fire Girls, organized young women of all races, creeds, and economic

backgrounds into clubs that were focused on building positive qualities in work, health, and love.

These days, the organization's ideals are much the same, but the methods have changed with the times. Now called Camp Fire Boys and Girls—having recognized boys' formal participation since 1975—this nationwide organization unites all youth, up to 21 years of age, in programs that cultivate personal life skills, social responsibility, healthy lifestyles, and leadership.

From its national headquarters in Kansas City, where it has been a strong local council presence since 1918, the organization strives to live by its vision statement, which asserts, in part, "Camp Fire Boys and Girls strives to be a contemporary, inclusive coeducational youth-development agency providing programs for children and youth that develop personal life skills, social responsibility, healthy lifestyles, and leadership."

The Business of Youth

We've evolved as an organization and are committed to positive development

for all youth," says Stewart Smith, Camp Fire's national executive director. "We still develop assets with small-group programming—long-term friendships, progressive learning, and commitment to community. Camp Fire is, however, also very market driven."

If that sounds like business-speak, it's because Camp Fire Boys and Girls is a business—one that concentrates on youth development as its chief product. Each year, Camp Fire equips some 670,000 participants with skills for life, providing them with positive experiences that help make their formative years both valuable and meaningful. The organization's 127 councils carefully assess their communities' needs and tailor their programs for local children and youth. No matter what their specific programs, the Camp Fire motto, Give Service, resonates throughout the organization.

One thing many communities need is reliable and accessible child care. To that end, Camp Fire is piloting *Building on Sesame Street* in partnership with the Children's Television Workshop (CTW). The program

Lifelong friends are made in Camp Fire Boys and Girls.

improves the quality of family child care by providing training, support, and materials to providers.

To reach all children, Camp Fire Boys and Girls created Absolutely Incredible Kid Day. Significant in Camp Fire's purpose statement is a commitment ". . . to seek to improve those conditions in society which affect youth." Absolutely Incredible Kid Day illustrates that pledge and encourages adults to convey their appreciation of children by writing letters to children on the third Thursday in March.

Another program, A Gift of Giving, sends volunteers into classrooms, child care centers, and other environments to help children explore how they can make a difference in their own backyards—then embark on projects to do just that.

"Our in-school self-reliance programs serve a quarter-million kids a year, teaching them how to learn, grow, and give back to their communities," says Smith. "Like all our programs, they follow our core mission: To help young people on their journey from birth to adulthood—from dependence, to independence, to interdependence."

The wonder of the great outdoors is reinforced at Camp Fire Boys and Girls.

FOGEL ANDERSON CONSTRUCTION CO.

IT IS DIFFICULT TO DRIVE THROUGH THE KANSAS CITY METROPOLITAN area without seeing the work of Fogel Anderson Construction Co. The fifth-oldest construction firm in the region, Fogel Anderson has built countless retail centers, grocery stores, office buildings, schools, and hotels throughout Kansas City and the Midwest. With billings averag-

ing between $27 million and $31 million a year, Fogel Anderson consistently ranks in the top 10 among the area's largest construction firms, according to the *Kansas City Business Journal.*

At Fogel Anderson, which is located in the heart of the Paseo West Industrial area, high-profile projects have included Manor Square in Westport, Dickinson Theatre's Great Mall Cinema 16 in Olathe, and the Regency Park Shopping Center in Overland Park. Fogel Anderson has also generated an impressive list of repeat clients, including Wal-Mart, a customer the firm has worked with on some 60 projects since 1977; Kansas City Power & Light Company, which has called

on the company for more than 50 years for hundreds of projects, including a recent, $25 million expansion program of two new service centers and eight new buildings; and Schnuck's Markets, for which Fogel Anderson has built 10 grocery stores.

"We rarely build one unit for anyone," says Phillip Bartolotta, president and chief operations officer, who's been in the construction industry for more than two decades. "Customers always want us to do more. Our strong emphasis on customer service, cost control, and keeping quality levels high mean that customers are satisfied with the immediate project and interested in working with us again in the future."

Building a Foundation

A decidedly family-owned and -operated company, Fogel Anderson was incorporated in January 1917 by Martin Fogel and his son, Paul, as Fogel Construction, a general contractor. Another of Martin's sons, Lyle, joined the firm later that year and, by 1922, O.T. Anderson signed on to help run the growing concern. In 1940, Lyle's son, John Fogel, entered the business his father, uncle, and O.T. Anderson had made successful during the previous two decades.

In 1942, the company became a partnership called Fogel Contracting Co., and in 1946, the name was again changed, this time to Fogel Contractors

Clockwise from top:
The Moreland Ridge Middle School, built in Blue Springs by Fogel Anderson Construction Co., features sectional pods for grades six, seven, and eight.

The Exchange National Bank in Shawnee, Kansas, has a large banking lobby and a six-lane customer service drive-through, with an ATM lane.

The Hampton Inn, Shawnee, Kansas, is a 128-room hotel with indoor pool and conference center.

VLEISIDES PHOTO STUDIO

VLEISIDES PHOTO STUDIO ▶

DAVE ROCHÉ/SKY FOTO ▶

Inc. In 1953, O.T. Anderson's son, Ted, joined the firm. Later that year, the company purchased Paul Fogel's interest and changed its name to Fogel Anderson Construction Co. Ted Anderson introduced metal building sales in the mid-1960s—for which he was perceived as a renegade in the industry—and diversified the company's client base. Today, Ted Anderson still leads the company as its chief executive officer. Phillip Bartolotta, Ted Anderson's son, joined the company in 1975, and is Fogel Anderson's president and chief operations officer.

"Our success is mostly due to the fact that we've been a family-owned business that's always operated with honesty and integrity," says Bartolotta. "Our employees have always been a strong asset, and for the most part, we don't have the high turnover that some companies do. People here are like family, and many have been with us for years and years."

Team Tactics

Like families that work well together, Fogel Anderson believes in a team approach. Starting with one of the most crucial elements of any company, Fogel Anderson stresses that all 65 employees are part of the sales team, all responsible for keeping their eyes and ears open to potential projects through which the company could shine. As part of normal, day-to-day operations, the estimating department puts together bids for negotiated and open-bid projects, while project managers and their assistants oversee work from start to finish. The accounting department maintains all financial records for each project, a crucial component for every construction company.

Together, the firm's employees have created an organization set apart by its integrity, longevity, financial stability, competitive edge, and ability to handle large projects in a primarily four-state region that includes Kansas, Missouri, Oklahoma, and Iowa.

Perhaps the most important aspect of Fogel Anderson's working philosophy, however, stems from its mission statement, which reads: "From our field construction laborers to our senior management, we all agree that we are committed to unsurpassed service for our customers. We pledge to provide the best quality construction, competitive cost control, and on-time completion, and to maintain that service edge to create overall customer satisfaction and valued long-term customer relationships."

High-Quality Future

Any company that's been in business for more than eight decades can reasonably expect to continue its forward momentum. At Fogel Anderson, that's certainly the case, as the company has always focused on building lasting relationships with clients who continue to look to them for their next site improvement, remodeling, design services, or start-to-finish construction. In addition, the family-owned firm has ensured that the same values that have been at the heart of its history will continue far into the future.

"We've been in the same building for more than 50 years and with the Builders' Association since 1917," says Bartolotta. "These point to the fact that we're proven and will be there for the customer. Down the road, we see some growth and we see the younger generation taking over the company with the same focus on customer relations and satisfaction that has ensured our success for all these years."

Clockwise from top left: The Dickinson Theatre Northrock is a 14-screen megaplex with stadium seating.

The Hen House in Lee's Summit offers drive-up grocery pickup, a child care area, and specialty food items.

The Wal-Mart Supercenter in Lebanon, Missouri, includes a grocery, garden center, and tire and lube express.

W HAT DO THESE HIGH-PROFILE BUILDINGS HAVE IN common: Coors Field in Denver; the Pyramid in Memphis, Tennessee; and the International Terminal at Chicago's O'Hare airport? All were created with steel that was fabricated, managed, and erected by

Clockwise from top:
Havens Steel designed, fabricated, and erected the structural steel for three buildings at the 1.7 million-square-foot steel finishing plant for AK Steel in Rockport, Indiana.

Havens is working with JY Design Planning Inc. on Phase I of the Dong Hai Plaza in Shanghai. This 53-story office tower is the cornerstone of the 1.5 million-square-foot plaza.

Coors Field in Denver was fabricated and erected by Havens Steel.

Kansas City-based Havens Steel. And that's just a sampling of the many projects that have contributed to the employee-owned company's $200 million in annual revenues.

Founded in 1919, Havens Steel has evolved into one of the world's leading structural steel contractors. Havens' employees have a vested interest in making their customers happy. The company started an employee stock ownership plan (ESOP) in the mid-1970s and became 100 percent employee owned in 1987. "Being employee owned has been a big motivating factor," says President and CEO Ken McCullough. "It makes everyone go the extra mile to perform for our customers."

Construction Quality

H avens is committed to providing a high-quality product, delivered on time and within budget. The company specializes in steel structures

for automotive factories, power plants, public assembly venues, industrial and commercial buildings, and long-span structures. Havens' design/build capabilities provide turnkey development services for building owners and investors.

Havens' two domestic fabricating plants—in Ottawa, Kansas, and in Kansas City—combine state-of-the-art equipment with experienced steelworkers to create cost-effective steel structures. Havens SPI, a wholly owned subsidiary, provides clients with the latest electronic data inter-

COURTESY THORNEY LIBERMAN, BOULDER, COLORADO

change technical experience to assist in drafting operations.

"Customers come to us because of our reputation for being on time," says McCullough, "as well as for the quality of our work and our competitive numbers. Our project management is something special: It provides more flexibility to the customer because of the way we plan jobs, and because we're right there to make any changes they may need."

Going Global

In fact, customers come to Havens Steel from farther and farther away these days. The company is active in Russia, where Havens has been performing projects since 1991. The company also has a presence in China, where it maintains a joint venture facility, United Steel Structures Ltd., in Guangzhou.

"Our international push began in 1991 with a large bank building in Russia that was a multi-million-dollar project," says McCullough. "Recently, we became the first U.S. steel fabricator to earn the coveted ISO 9002 rating, the set of quality-measuring standards long popular in Europe, which we're hoping will give us an edge over the competition."

Power Partner

One component of Havens' formula for success has been its association with Wilmington, Delaware-based E.I. du Pont de Nemours & Co. Since 1993, Havens has been DuPont's alliance partner. DuPont, a $43.8 billion-a-year company, operates 78 manufacturing facilities in the United States and numerous plants worldwide.

Havens has completed projects for DuPont in locations ranging from Ireland to Singapore to Mexico. "Our China plant is capable of shipping steel throughout the world," says McCullough.

Internationally, Havens is also considering other joint ventures, according to McCullough. "We're the kind of people who don't like the status quo," he says. "We like to grow. We're not afraid to try new things."

Clockwise from top:
First Bank Place in Minneapolis was built for IBM Corporation using materials from Havens Steel.

Havens supplied 16,000 tons of steel to Terminal 5 Venture for the construction of the International Terminal at Chicago's O'Hare airport.

Havens Steel supplied materials to Huber Hunt & Nichols for the construction of the Pyramid arena in Memphis, Tennessee.

COURTESY CITY OF CHICAGO

I N TODAY'S AGGRESSIVE BANKING ENVIRONMENT, ONE KANSAS CITY bank stands out from the crowd. Union Bank is one of the few independently owned local banks that has avoided the consolidation trend. According to Executive Vice President and CFO Carl Eichenberger, "Bigger isn't always better." And for nearly 80 years,

Union Bank's main office is located in the heart of downtown Kansas City at the corner of 12th and Wyandotte streets (left).

Union Bank is headed by (from left) Chairman Jerry Green; Executive Vice President and CFO Carl Eichenberger; President-Southern Region Jim Greene; and President and CEO Robert Stratton (right).

Union Bank has been offering the same high-quality banking services as national bank chains, but with the personal touch only a smaller bank can provide.

It all started in 1919, a decade before the depression. The bank opened its doors at the corner of 31st Street and Prospect Avenue under the name Cornflower Exchange. From the very beginning, the bank focused on providing special attention for its customers, both big and small. And aside from the name, the heart of the bank hasn't changed much since that first day. The

original location is still in operation. The bank is still independently owned. Most important, the bank is still dedicated to providing personal service for clients throughout Missouri.

A few things have changed over the years, though. Union Bank now has six locations in the area, and another will soon open in North Kansas City. In 1998, the bank experienced $12 million worth of growth, and it currently has $150 million in assets. The bank's services have also expanded according to the needs of its customers, which include various small to midsize businesses and individuals. "We're small enough to listen to individual requests," says Eichenberger. The bank even offers some tailor-made programs to fit specific client needs. According to Eichenberger, "We know how our clients do business in Kansas City."

The people at Union Bank also know how to do business with their clients. The bank is headed by Chairman Jerry Green; President and CEO Robert Stratton; Eichenberger; and President-Southern Region Jim Greene. All four are actively involved with the bank's day-to-day activities. They personally meet with many of the bank's clients, and they're all involved in various community activities.

"We have the ability and resources to remain committed to the communities we serve," says Eichenberger. This commitment will only grow stronger. The bank plans to expand into the Kansas City community not just with new locations, but also by increasing the number of services available to customers. However, this expansion will never overshadow the importance Union Bank places on staying in touch with each and every customer.

WHAT STARTED AS A SMALL, LOCAL CAR DEALERSHIP back in 1928 is now one of the largest companies in the area. In fact, this year Union Securities had more than $130 million in gross revenues and was ranked by the *Kansas City Business Journal* as the metro

area's 36th-largest privately held company.

Union Securities owes its success primarily to good timing. Under the leadership of Chairman and President Jerry Green, the company now invests in a wide variety of businesses across the country. Green, a third-generation Kansas Citian, inherited Union Chevrolet from his father and transformed it into a holding company in 1960. One of the company's first investments was a Budget Rent-A-Car franchise in St. Louis. It currently operates three other Budget Rent-A-Car franchises in Kansas City, Memphis, and Wichita.

Although Green sold Union Chevrolet in 1969, the company today owns and operates Greenleigh Farm, Inc., a 10-acre farm in Stilwell, Kansas, that raises and sells show horses. More recently, Union Securities purchased KCTE-AM, a sports radio station in Kansas City. Other sizable investments include Union Bancshares in Kansas City, City National Bank of Beverly Hills, Union Planters Bank in Memphis, and Grey Advertising of New York, the world's seventh-largest advertising agency.

Union Securities is currently located in downtown Kansas City in the Union Bank Building. The company has 200 employees in Kansas City and more than 420 employees in 15 other locations companywide. Union Securities still relies on good timing and solid investments to fuel its growth—a practice that promises continued success for the company. According to Green, "We will continue to look for promising investments and business opportunities, both in Kansas City and elsewhere."

Union Securities is located in the Union Bank Building at the corner of 12th and Wyandotte streets in downtown Kansas City.

Union Securities Chairman and President Jerry Green, along with Corporate Secretary Stacey Hurst

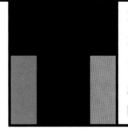

THESE DAYS, IT SEEMS NORMAL TO GO TO THE MOVIES AND CHOOSE from among eight, 10, or even 20 different shows. But it was Kansas City's AMC Entertainment Inc. that created the megaplex concept, giving moviegoers options the likes of which they had never seen. ■ AMC was founded in 1920 by Edward Durwood, who originally

Clockwise from top:
Stanley H. Durwood, cochairman and chief executive officer of AMC Entertainment Inc., revolutionized the movie exhibition industry with his many innovations—forever changing the way the world sees movies.

The Power & Light District— a unique, urban entertainment center—will transform a decaying, 12-block area of downtown Kansas City into a thriving, exciting destination for thousands of residents and visitors to the American Heartland.

Each year, AMC screens bring the splendor of Hollywood to life for more than 100 million moviegoers around the world. New theatres feature stadium-style seating, providing an unobstructed view of the screen. AMC's exclusive LoveSeat— plush, cushioned, high-backed seats with double-wide, retractable cup-holder armrests that lift—allows moviegoers to "cozy up."

built single-screen theatres. But by 1963, Stanley Durwood, Edward's son, decided the world was ready for its first multiplex, a two-screen theatre at Ward Parkway Shopping Center. AMC debuted the first four-plex in 1966 and the first six-plex three years later. The concept caught on quickly, revolutionizing the industry and forever changing the way film fans go to the movies.

"It was like jumping up and down in the middle of the living room floor. Your foot goes through, and oil gushes out," says Stanley Durwood, remembering his excitement at discovering the potential in side-by-side theatres.

Leading the Way

Although nearly all other motion picture exhibition companies have followed AMC's megaplex lead, the company has

remained among the most aggressive in locating large theatre complexes in booming metropolitan areas. Huge attendance and revenue levels generated by AMC megaplexes confirm that the company's growth strategy is on target, firmly positioning the company as a leading exhibitor in the United States, and one with a growing international presence. Today, AMC owns and operates more than 2,300 screens in 225 theatres in 22 states, the District of Columbia, Japan, and Portugal.

In addition, part of AMC's commitment to its customers involves leading the industry in innovation. AMC has been the driving force behind virtually every improvement in the movie exhibition trade, from computer-aided theatre designs to computerized box offices, automated projection booths, and advance credit card ticket purchasing. AMC also developed the Movie-Watcher program, the premier frequent moviegoer reward plan in the industry.

"We believe in making sure that everyone who comes to an AMC theatre will have a more enjoyable experience," says Durwood. "It's been natural

for us to introduce innovations into the mix because that's just part of the way we think about our customers' total moviegoing experience."

The Power & Light District

AMC's newest project involves a concept to build an urban entertainment district in downtown Kansas City. Durwood expects the development to transform a decaying, 12-block area into one of the city's feature attractions. The $454 million complex would cover 25 acres adjacent to Bartle Hall Convention Center. The complex will be known as the Power & Light District, and will include a 30-screen megaplex theatre, themed restaurants, live concert and theatre venues, dance clubs, interactive educational displays, and a variety of ongoing seasonal special events. The plan would also combine approximately 100 retail shops with new office buildings, residential units, and hotels.

"The heart of the city has been losing people," says Durwood of his passion for the project. "This is where I live, this is where I was born. I love this city, and I want to help take it into the future."

POWER GENERATION, INDUSTRIAL MACHINERY, REFRIGERATION, and heating/ventilating/air-conditioning (HVAC) equipment all rely on external cooling systems to stay properly cooled and functioning. Cooling towers utilize the remarkable cooling efficiency of water to draw heat from equipment. By con-

stantly recycling the water, heat dissipates and the water is returned to the cooling system to continue the process. Marley Cooling Tower Company, a Kansas City firm, designs, markets, and manufactures water cooling towers for these industries, and more.

Leon T. Mart and Chester E. Smiley founded the company in 1922 to take advantage of America's industrialization boom, combining their last names to give the fledgling business its name. Mart and Smiley knew that steam plants then being built for power generation required extensive cooling, so they established their company by designing spray ponds to cool the massive steam power generators.

A post-World War II manufacturing boom gave the company a major sales surge. In the 1950s and 1960s, companies began clamoring for massive air-conditioning units, for which Marley provided the cooling towers. During the 1970s, power generation—from fossil-fired to nuclear power plants—became an important component of the cooling tower business. Today, increased industrialization in overseas locations has given Marley a presence in Europe, Australia, and Asia.

"We've been a market leader in new products and systems, in part, because there's always been a strong engineering content in everything we produce," says Dick Landon, company president. "Our market coverage is broad, and we are a very high-quality supplier."

Industrial Innovator

Since its earliest days, Marley has led the cooling tower industry through numerous technical innovations. Its engineers have been awarded more than 122 patents, for innovations from

the spray pond to the Aquatower® to the QuadraFlow®. Marley is the only full-service manufacturer that offers standard products that vary from 10-ton, factory-assembled units to multiple-fan, concrete towers and hyperbolic natural draft towers for large-utility use. Additionally, Marley applies its expertise on industrial towers to factory-assembled equipment for light industrial or HVAC duty. That way, customers can purchase the same degree of dependability and consistent quality, no matter the size of their business.

A subsidiary since 1993 of United Dominion Industries of Charlotte, Marley stands behind every product the company makes, regardless of its age. An impressively loyal staff means that engineers with long track records are available to devise solutions to customer problems, even if a

tower was constructed 20 or 30 years ago.

This combination of high-quality products and exemplary service has helped Marley land contracts around the globe. Recent major clients have ranged from Eastman Kodak in Rochester, New York, to China Steel Corp. in Kaohsiung, Taiwan; and from Phillips Petroleum in Bartlesville, Oklahoma, to Technipetrol in Rome, Italy.

"It's our intent to be the world leader in our industry while delivering a balanced return to our primary stakeholders, which include our customers, our owner, and our employees," says Landon. "We've accomplished a great deal in the last 75 years, and we have the right to be proud. But we must renew our commitment to our stakeholders every day and forge the global future together."

Clockwise from top:
Marley Class F400 fiberglass composite cooling towers are normally used in large HVAC, heavy industrial, chemical processing and refining, and power generation applications.

From the Marley Cooling Tower world headquarters in Overland Park, a staff of 300 directs the operations of the entire company.

Marley NC® Modular Cooling Towers are assembled in the company's factories in Louisville, Kentucky, or Eloy, Arizona.

WHEN JOHN ERNEST DUNN LAUNCHED HIS CONSTRUCTION company in 1924, he wanted to do more than erect buildings. The onetime professional baseball pitcher yearned to build relationships, too. So Dunn founded his company with strong values at its core, both human and economic. Whether he dealt with customers or craftsmen, he intended for all to be treated fairly and with respect. And, Dunn believed that a prosperous company would then owe something to the community in which it built its accomplishments.

Dunn's plan more than succeeded. Today, J.E. Dunn Construction Company has grown to include more than 1,000 employees, and is one of the oldest and most successful family-owned construction firms in the Midwest. Recently, the firm celebrated 75 years of operation under the leadership of the Dunn family. It is the largest commercial contractor in the Kansas City area, based on total billings and contracts awarded with revenues exceeding $550 million a year.

As the company grew, the Dunn family created a holding company, Dunn Industries Inc., in 1981. Dunn Industries Inc., through acquisition and development, now owns five construction units operating under the name Dunn Construction Group. J.E. Dunn Construction Company is the largest of the five companies. Reporting as Dunn Construction Group, the company consistently appears in *Engineering News-Record*'s annual Top 400 contractors survey. In 1997, it ranked 39th overall, and 17th in the general contractors category. Although J.E. Dunn works primarily in the Midwest, the companies comprising Dunn Construction Group allow it to extend its expertise across the country. Those companies are Witcher Construction Co. in Minneapolis; Drake Construction Co. in Portland, Oregon; Dunn Industrial Group in Kansas City; and CE Ward Constructors in Houston.

"We thrive on long-term relationships built on trust and performance," says Terry Dunn, who, as president and CEO, represents the third generation to lead the construction company founded by his grandfather. "We give 100 percent to the client, and when in doubt, the client is always right."

Creative Construction

Of course, it takes more than good relationships to get the job done. At J.E. Dunn, creativity and innovation make the difference. From preconstruction services to construction management to design/build, J.E. Dunn focuses on producing cost-effective, quality-oriented work that more than serves the client's needs.

Through the years, J.E. Dunn projects have included everything from banks to apartment buildings, office complexes to hotels.

The Sprint World Headquarters campus in Overland Park, built by J.E. Dunn Construction Company, consists of a 240-acre site with office space for more than 14,000 employees.

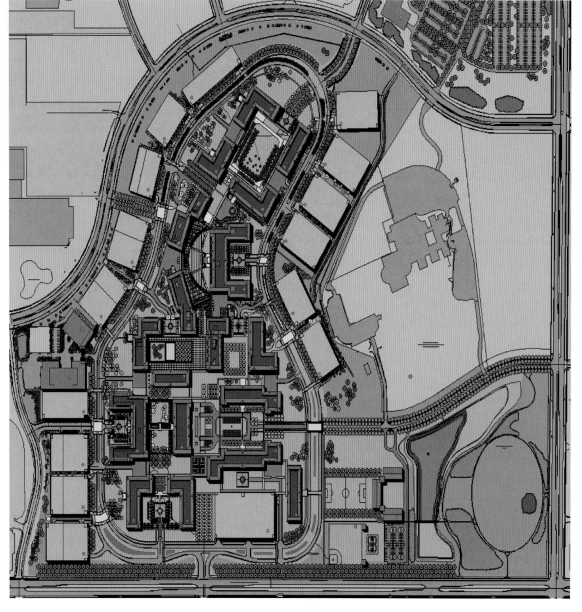

The company, for example, is responsible for the dramatic spire that tops the Reorganized Church of Jesus Christ of Latter-day Saints temple in Independence; the Sprint World Headquarters campus in Overland Park; the Shawnee Mission Medical Center in Overland Park; and the Joint Institute for Laboratory Astrophysics at the University of Colorado in Boulder. Moreover, the firm created the striking Flamingo Hilton Riverboat Casino in Kansas City; Johnson County Community College's stylish Cultural Education Center; and Kansas City's contemporary Kemper Art Museum.

The impressive list of completed projects goes on and on. The company was responsible for the historic renovation of the New York Life Building for UtiliCorp United's world headquarters in Kansas City, as well as for building the new U.S. Federal Courthouse in downtown Kansas City. J.E. Dunn also built the innovative Saint Luke's Medical Campus in Overland Park and the American Century Towers I and II, as well as data

centers, schools, hospitals, prisons, industrial facilities, garages, and renovation projects.

"We are constantly asking ourselves, 'How can we do this better than anyone in the industry?'" says Terry Dunn, whose father, Bill Dunn Sr., serves as chairman. "That's how we benchmark ourselves against the competition, and how we market ourselves."

Giving Back

At J.E. Dunn, the commitment to values extends beyond the immediate company and clients. Since John Ernest founded the company in 1924, it has been important to the Dunn family that it gives back to the community.

During the past several years, for example, J.E. Dunn employees have been among the highest per capita givers to the Heart of America United Way. In addition, organizations such as the American Cancer Society, Boy Scouts, Crittenton Center, Junior Achievement, Kansas City Neighborhood Alliance, Learning Exchange, Ronald McDonald House, and

Women's Employment Network—among many others—have benefited from J.E. Dunn's belief in community involvement.

"Businesses have a moral obligation to give back to the communities that have supported them," says Terry Dunn. "This means showing a commitment that goes beyond the checkbook. We need to show that business cares."

J.E. Dunn's long reign as Kansas City's construction leader can be traced back to its founder's belief in business- and community-relationship building, coupled with a strong respect for the people who have helped the company succeed. "My grandfather believed that employees, suppliers, owners, and designers should be treated in the same fashion that we would like to be treated," says Terry Dunn. "We've carried on his legacy in the past and expect to continue it into the future. As we approach the year 2000, we believe we'll keep growing in size and expertise. There really are no limits for a company that bases its business on the right values."

The world headquarters for the Reorganized Church of Jesus Christ of Latter-day Saints includes an 1,800-seat temple sanctuary and a 110,000-square-foot administration and classroom building (left).

J.E. Dunn Construction Company completed an award-winning, historic renovation of the 100-year-old New York Life Building for UtiliCorp United's world headquarters in Kansas City (right).

TRAWBERRIES IN JANUARY, FURNITURE FROM BALI, THE LATEST designer clothing—thanks to Yellow Corporation, which owns and operates the largest less-than-truckload system in the country, products like these have become widely accessible across the United States and around the world. With a transportation network that

spans North America, Europe, Asia, the Pacific Rim, and Central and South America, Yellow Corporation has helped to shrink the globe considerably.

It hasn't always been so easy. A few years ago, Yellow Corporation was losing money as deregulation, increased competition, and internal uncertainty took their toll on the transportation industry as a whole. But the

company instituted drastic measures, launching new technological systems, focusing on new market initiatives, and paring unnecessary costs. Today, Yellow boasts a leaner, meaner operation with revenues of more than $3 billion and net income well in the black.

"We've taken $180 million in expenses out of the company," says A. Maurice Myers, Yellow's

chairman, president, and CEO, whose hiring in 1996 was the start of the company's profit-oriented restructuring. "We've also changed the corporate culture to one that's not as bureaucratic, and become more entrepreneurial. We get ideas from everyone and encourage more communication from within."

Going to Kansas City

Yellow landed in Kansas City in 1952 after it was rescued from receivership by George E. Powell Sr., his son George Powell Jr., and Roy Fruehauf, owner of the Fruehauf Trailer Company. The enterprise had its roots in Oklahoma City as the Yellow Cab Transit Company, founded in 1924. By the time Yellow Cab founder A.J. Harrell sold the freight-hauling portion of his business to a New York-based investment group 20 years later, he had established a strong route

Clockwise from top left:
A. Maurice Myers is chairman, president, and chief executive officer of Yellow Corporation.

William D. Zollars is president of Yellow Freight System, one of four subsidiaries making up Yellow Corporation.

The company's transportation network reaches the entire continental United States, and recently expanded overseas.

system in Texas, Kansas, Missouri, Illinois, and Indiana.

But the New York group was inexperienced, had little interest in a midwestern trucking line, and, during the next eight years, made a series of ill-fated moves. That was when George Powell Sr., a former banker who had spent five years as president of Riss and Company trucking line, raised $750,000 to buy the bankrupt company, then known as Yellow Transit Freight Lines.

Throughout the following decades, the Powells acquired several other carriers and freight forwarders as part of their strategy to build a less-than-truckload freight company with true national coverage. Yellow Corporation helped pioneer the concept of consolidating small freight shipments into trailer loads for interstate transport, deconsolidation, and distribution. In 1957, George Powell Jr. became president and CEO; his son, George Powell III, succeeded him in 1987. By 1996, however, the Powells—although still shareholders—had removed themselves entirely from managing the company.

Competitive Edge

Yellow's done a good job over the years," says Myers, "but we have to keep changing to remain competitive."

In fact, Yellow Corporation has taken the competitive bulls by the horns. The company's subsidiaries—Yellow Freight System, Saia Motor Freight Line, WestEx, and YCS International—have all adjusted to meet a variety of new transportation realities. From dealing with lower-cost, nonunion competition to forging international transportation opportunities to reconsidering rail utilization, Yellow has stepped up its own pace of change. "One thing is certain about the freight transportation business," says Myers. "We have entered a new era of dramatic change. Competition continues to increase from all quarters and will continue to be unrelenting."

One area that's been especially key for the Overland Park company has come from rethinking

the technology it uses to serve customers. Recently, Yellow spent about $70 million to install a system that would emulate a customer service center approach in receiving and transmitting orders between terminals and customers. It's been an innovative addition for a trucking company.

"Customers are demanding more, such as state-of-the-art tracking systems and time-definite shipping," says Myers. "They want the same from us as they get from expedited services, such as UPS and FedEx. We're the first trucking company to institute this sort of system, and it allows us to differentiate ourselves from the competition."

Yellow also expects that growth will swell in the international arena. The company launched service in Europe in 1992 with its partnership agreement with Royal Frans Maas Group of the Netherlands. Soon after, the company announced similar agreements in Hong Kong, Singapore, Thailand, Australia, New Zealand, and South and Central America. In 1997, Yellow's international business brought in some $100 million in revenues;

the company expects $200 million by 2000.

"We see our international markets growing three to four times faster than our domestic markets," says Myers. "So we're looking at how to leverage what we've accomplished so far into growing internationally in the future."

No matter where they find themselves operating, Yellow Corporation staff and management say they will rely on their core belief in doing good business. "We try to offer superior service at a competitive price," says Myers. "It all boils down to value."

Yellow subsidiaries Saia Motor Freight Line and WestEx have adjusted to meet a variety of new transportation realities.

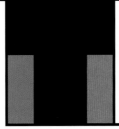

TODAY, NEARLY EVERYONE IN AMERICA TAKES AUTOMATIC AND unlimited supplies of electricity and water for granted. Flip a switch, turn on the tap, and light and liquid are supplied. At the beginning of the 20th century, however, such reliability was practically unknown. Heating and lighting were provided by natural gas, and indoor plumbing was still an unheard-of extravagance for most.

This was certainly the case when the Board of Public Utilities (BPU) of Kansas City, Kansas, was founded in 1929. The city's water service had begun some 20 years earlier, but electricity to run municipal water pumps was undependable. City leaders decided it was time to band together and form a utility company that would reliably provide both water and electricity to its citizens, at an affordable rate.

"Even today, we are a municipal utility that has never forgotten its roots," says Leon Daggett, BPU general manager, from the organization's office in downtown Kansas City, Kansas. "BPU continues to deliver the services traditionally provided by an electric and water utility, but we also have become a premium provider set apart from most conventional public utilities."

An Entrepreneurial Utility

For more than a decade, industries ranging from airlines to banks have begun to deregulate their businesses. Although utilities are still governed by a regulatory body, some forward-thinking companies are approaching the market more competitively. BPU, for example, has worked with the Kansas state legislature to draft new rules and regulations that will encourage change in the utilities industry.

Daggett himself took the lead in looking out for smaller utilities by suggesting the now famous "opt out or in" clause, which became a key component in the state of Kansas' new regulations. The clause allows small utilities to make some of their own decisions about how to compete successfully in the changing environment within their own communities.

"Within BPU, decisions are being made today to operate as if we were in a deregulated market," says Daggett. "One of the goals for our staff of 725 employees is to think and act like owners of a business. We empower each and every one of them to look for opportunities to focus on competitive products and services that will further differentiate us from our competitors."

Setting Themselves Apart

One way the BPU differentiated itself was to create a family of brand names to identify its products and services. The EnergySmart℠ brand provides customers with a portfolio of electric products that includes everything from energy use advice to satellite television services and accent lighting. The WaterSmart℠ brand offers similar services for those who turn to BPU for water. BusinessSmart℠ is the brand BPU uses for its communication systems with commercial customers, while CustomerSmart℠ is its public relations brand name.

Through all of its Smart brands, BPU has enhanced its dedication to furnishing lower-cost, high-quality services to business and household consumers. In addition, part of BPU's success with the strategy comes

A Board of Public Utilities (BPU) worker obtains a water sample at secondary basins at Quindaro Water Treatment Plant.

A BPU control room operator adjusts a fly ash panel at Quindaro Power Plant.

All photos courtesy of BPU

from its caring employees who can provide a quick response to customer concerns.

"Our employees are a key asset at BPU, which is why we offer educational training and assistance for employees who want to continue their education," says Daggett. "BPU employees understand that we must maintain high-quality service at a reasonable cost as a key to our future competitiveness."

In addition to new branding, marketing, and a commitment to employee empowerment, BPU also continues to update its facilities to make sure customers find the best products and services. Decades of expertise in power generation and service delivery have helped the company become a national leader among the nation's 2,200 municipal utilities, as will a new, state-of-the-art water processing plant at the utility's Nearman Creek location. The new plant joins another water processing plant at Quindaro, as well as two electric generating stations at the Nearman Creek and Quindaro power plants.

Industry and Community Leader

BPU has done more than work on its own competitiveness. The utility began and nurtured the American Public Power Association (APPA), based in Washington, D.C., that now serves as an industry representative for the nation's municipal utilities. In fact, many of BPU's employees have served on APPA boards and committees. Likewise, BPU has been instrumental in the American Water Works Association and has frequently won awards from that group.

In addition to its leadership among municipal utilities, the BPU is also active in its own community. The organization has become one of the best supporters of Kansas City, Kansas's United Way, and its employees annually raise money for children's services through an annual golf tournament, among other avenues. Moreover, BPU's economic development efforts have helped to create new jobs throughout the community by helping to attract Fortune 500 businesses

such as General Motors, Owens-Corning, CertainTeed, and the University of Kansas Medical Center.

"Yes, we are a leader in the industry," concludes Daggett, "but we believe our mission is to be a supplier of premium products and services for our customers. We remain a municipal utility with the community in our minds and in our hearts, providing electricity and water at an exceptional value."

A BPU lineman make repairs to utility lines.

At Nearman Power Station, a BPU control room operator verifies unit operating parameters.

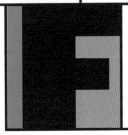

ARMING CALLS FOR PATIENCE, BUT EVEN FARMERS CAN ONLY TAKE so much. In 1929, frustrated by the high prices they were forced to pay for transportation, supplies, and interest—and the low prices they, in turn, received for their products—six farmer-owned cooperatives formed a petroleum products brokerage called Union

Oil Company. Grouped together, the mavericks figured they could at least control the perennial cost-price squeeze they constantly faced for fuel.

Nearly 70 years later, this powerful group—still owned by the farmers it serves—has moved out of its original home in a two-car garage into an impressive world headquarters in Kansas City. With 1997 sales totaling $9.1 billion, Farmland Industries, Inc. is now the largest farmer-owned cooperative in North America, doing business in all 50 states and more than 80 countries.

"Throughout our history, we've had an unwavering focus on generating economic benefits for our independent producer-owners," says Farmland President and CEO H.D. "Harry" Cleberg. "But we've also succeeded because we've paid attention to our customer base. We make sure that the food and agricultural products we produce and market consistently satisfy our customers' expectations for quality and value."

Expansive Business

Part of the reason for Farmland's success lies in its diversity. After forming the oil brokerage months before the stock market crash of 1929, the group launched an extended line of products that started with paint and twine, then reached 200 components by 1936. Before long, the group founded a transportation department, built a petroleum refinery, established an animal feed business, and acquired a fertilizer plant. In the 1960s, Farmland purchased a pork processing plant, initiated a grain processing operation, and extended its processing to beef.

But the farmers weren't finished. In the 1970s and 1980s, the cooperative consolidated its insurance services and extended its feed mill network until finally, in the 1990s, the organization had diversified into 10 core businesses with a single mission: To be a producer-driven, customer-focused, and profitable agricultural-supply-to-consumer-foods cooperative system. The diversity in core businesses also has allowed Farmland to more readily cope with farming's cyclical nature.

More recently, Farmland has concentrated on widening its reach even further by establishing relationships with a variety of farm-oriented companies. "In the last six or seven years, we've embarked on forming ventures to increase the size, efficiency, and technical know-how of what we do," says Cleberg. "Farmland now has more than 60 ventures and alliances with customers, overseas entities, and other agribusinesses."

In fact, the international aspect of Farmland's business has grown to include members in Mexico and Canada, as well as offices in Switzerland, Argentina, France, Germany, England, Russia, the Ukraine, Korea, and Kazakhstan. In addition, Farmland products—from grains

Clockwise from top: Farmland Industries, Inc. provides a ready market for member-grown grain and adds value to its member-owners' livestock by producing wholesome food products and marketing them under the Farmland® "Proud to be farmer owned"® brand.

Nora Burtnett sorts feeder pigs at a Farmland production facility in Oregon, Missouri.

With 1997 sales totaling $9.1 billion, Farmland is now the largest farmer-owned cooperative in North America, doing business in all 50 states and more than 80 countries.

to meats—are developed, marketed, and distributed in countries from Japan to Italy.

"Whether it's a co-packing arrangement with a meat processor in Mexico, a distribution agreement with a customer in Japan, or the joint design of a product to serve a market niche in Moscow, Farmland is expanding its strategic business alliances around the globe to satisfy more customers and to generate greater returns for its owners," says Cleberg. "In fact, we are doing more business internationally now than we did entirely in 1990. The future for American agriculture will be bright indeed if we continue to open access to world trade."

Powerful Representation

Over the years, Farmland's ownership has expanded, too. Since the first six cooperatives formed the company in 1929, Farmland has grown to include 26 midwestern states as well as Mexico and Canada. The 600,000 farmers represented as Farmland owners by 1,500 farmer-cooperative associations account for some 80 percent of U.S. grain and livestock production.

Farmland provides these members the crop production and protection products that help them use their land efficiently to grow crops used around the world. The company's petroleum products fuel and lubricate farm equipment, keep farm families and their livestock warm,

and provide additional revenue by selling petroleum products outside the cooperative system. Nutritionally sound animal feeds help produce quality animals, from cattle and swine to horses and elk. At the other end of the food chain, Farmland provides a ready market for member-grown grain and adds value to its member-owners' livestock by producing wholesome food products and marketing them under the Farmland® "Proud to be farmer owned"® brand.

Establishing a knowledge-based farming cooperative has been paramount to Farmland's success. The company's farmer-owners stay involved in learning the latest farming technologies, but also maintain a close relationship with their communities. In fact, many believe that combining the rural nature of farming with a new global perspective will successfully take agriculture into the next century.

"Agriculture has been the leader in producing exports for the country, and the future can be very exciting," says Cleberg. "But our communities are going to have to help our leaders in Washington understand the importance of free trade to the future of agriculture. The American farmers depend on it."

Clockwise from top:
As the sun burns away the morning fog near Red Oak, Iowa, the Farmland day begins.

At Elevator Y in Enid, a Farmland Grain scaleman bins grain arriving from a local co-op.

In 1929, frustrated by the high prices they were forced to pay for transportation, supplies, and interest—and the low prices they, in turn, received for their products—six farmer-owned cooperatives formed a petroleum products brokerage called Union Oil Company.

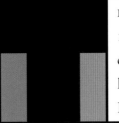

HE RIVAL® COMPANY MAKES LIFE AT HOME EASIER. AND SINCE 1932, when the company introduced its first product, a manual citrus squeezer called the Juice-O-Mat®, Rival's success has gone hand in hand with consumers who have needed help in the kitchen. From food slicers to can openers to its landmark Crock-Pot® slow

cooker—the number one item registered for by today's brides—Rival has led the way in providing quality products that make life at home more comfortable.

Today, Rival has expanded far beyond the kitchen. Primarily through an aggressive acquisitions plan initiated in the early 1990s, the Kansas City-headquartered company now manufactures products under six brand names: the Rival® brand of small kitchen appliances; the White Mountain® brand of high-quality ice cream makers; the Pollenex® brand of personal care products—primarily shower heads and electric massagers; the Simer® brand of utility and sump pumps; the Patton® brand of consumer and industrial fans, heaters, and home ventilation; and the Bionaire® brand of high-quality air purifiers and humidifiers.

"We have grown through internal development and outside acquisitions," Tom Manning, chairman and CEO, says. "We have added 15 new product lines in the past five years through acquisition. These companies did not have a particular strength in product development or marketing, so we have been able to add those disciplines. In addition,

we have been able to control the expense side of manufacturing and administration costs."

Rival's acquisition strategy has also allowed it to strengthen its distribution base. "Our recent growth has come not only from existing customers, but new presence in other channels. Hardware and home centers are now our second-largest type of customer after mass merchant. Industrial supply channels will contribute 10 percent of our volume and, although international is now 10 percent as well, we envision it growing to 20 percent," Manning adds.

Cooking Up Success

How well has this home appliance designer, manufacturer, and marketer earned its keep? In 1986, The Rival Company reported $95 million in revenues. That same year, the company went through a leveraged buyout, making private the organization that had originally gone public in 1964. The new owners immediately put in place an aggressive strategy to increase sales.

By 1992, Rival reported $165 million in sales and was in a position to reenter public owner-

ship. The tremendous increase in sales proved that the company's growth strategies were working, and by sharing ownership publicly, Rival could expand even further. By 1997, the company's revenues approached $400 million.

"We have gone category by category, specifically identifying where we could improve our product offerings," Manning says. "We want to develop innovative products that dominate their market categories. We believe that we can do that by focusing on consumer needs and wants."

Once only suppliers of small kitchen appliances, Rival now divides its business into four units to provide even greater concentration of its efforts. The largest division is Kitchen Appliances. The Home Environment division includes fans, space heaters, shower heads, air purifiers, and humidifiers. Industrial/Building Supply provides electrical and industrial wholesale distributors with products such as bathroom and kitchen ventilation, chimes, ceiling fans, and industrial-duty heaters and fans. The International division concentrates on expanding The

Once a small kitchen appliance manufacturer focused on the U.S. market, The Rival® Company has become an international marketer of a broad range of electric products.

Rival Company into Canada, Central and South America, and Europe.

Expanding Outward

Although its headquarters is in Kansas City, The Rival Company has a much broader presence. Of its 2,500 employees, some 70 percent work in Missouri. In addition to its headquarters, Rival operates manufacturing plants in Clinton, Sedalia, Warrensburg, and Sweet Springs. The other 30 percent of its employees are in plants in Indiana, North Carolina, and Mississippi, as well as in offices in Toronto, Hong Kong, and the Netherlands.

Today, Rival's international business is concentrated in Canada and Europe. New opportunities, however, are emerging in Central and South America as major U.S.-based multinational retailers, who already stock Rival products, begin to open stores south of the border.

"We have to approach our international business diligently," Manning says. "In addition to understanding the different cultures, we have additional issues, given the nature of our electricity-based products. Electric appliances are not as simple to translate as other products. There are a lot of standards to meet in each country. Every item has to be evaluated and modified to match a particular market."

As The Rival Company continues to expand its reach around the world, the onetime maker of the Juice-O-Mat and the current manufacturer of the Crock-Pot slow cooker will continue to emphasize consumer-driven product development. "Improving our existing lines is vital," Manning says, "as we continue to search for acquirable companies with products that expand our scope."

The Bionaire® brand is The Rival Company's entry into the high-quality air cleaner and humidifier categories. Retailers such as Sears carry a complete range of Bionaire products.

Marketed under Rival® and Rival Select® brands, the company offers small kitchen appliances in 23 different categories. The most famous Rival product is the Crock-Pot® slow cooker.

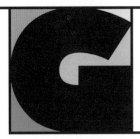

GIVING CUSTOMERS WHAT THEY WANT IS A UNIVERSAL RULE IN business. At Unitog Company, that familiar maxim has led to explosive growth. Founded in 1932, the Kansas City-based uniform manufacturing and garment rental giant has set annual revenue records for more than 40 consecutive years. In 1997, the publicly traded organization reached $261.7 million in gross revenues, an astonishing 22 percent increase over the previous year.

Unitog provides high-quality uniform rental services to a variety of industries and sells custom-designed uniforms to national companies in connection with their corporate image programs. The company manufactures virtually all of the uniforms it rents or sells, and claims the largest number of national accounts in the industry.

"We look at the marketplace and what our customers' needs are," says Randolph K. Rolf, Unitog's chairman, president, and CEO. "Then we respond to those needs."

International Service and Value

Since the company went public in 1989, Unitog has embarked on an aggressive acquisition program. Since 1991, the company has completed 28 acquisitions, including industrial uniform routes, production facilities, and uniform rental companies across the United States and Canada. Together, these acquisitions have accounted for nearly $110 million in annualized revenue. "Many of our U.S. customers also have Canadian operations," says Rolf. "We are pleased that we now have the ability to provide rental services to these accounts."

Throughout the company's evolution, Unitog has maintained the core philosophy established by founder A.D. Brookfield. "We operate at the high end of our marketplace," says Rolf. "Our customers like value in terms of materials, design, and customer service. We want to project their image to their customers, and that can't be done effectively with a low-end product." Unitog, noted for the superior-quality products and services it delivers, ranks among the top five companies nationwide in the rental garment industry.

Today, Unitog's client list includes oil companies, breweries, and automotive concerns—as well as thousands of small businesses. The country's largest supplier of postal uniforms, the company derives about 80 percent of its revenues from uniform rentals.

People Power

Rolf has assembled a dynamic group of executives and personnel who are focused on moving Unitog into the next century. "Our people are superb," he says. "For a company to grow, it takes good people and we've got them."

Certainly, the benefits of Unitog's aggressive growth program have been substantial, and Rolf sees no end in sight. "We provide an excellent-value, no-hassle apparel program for our customers," he maintains. "Growth and new challenges are a definite part of our future."

Unitog provides high-quality uniform rental services to a variety of industries and sells custom-designed uniforms to national companies in connection with their corporate image programs.

T'S SAID THAT GREAT CITIES NEED STRONG UNIVERSITIES AS PARTNERS in progress. In Kansas City, the University of Missouri-Kansas City (UMKC) has been putting its intellectual powers and research expertise to work for more than 65 years. Today, UMKC is the city's leading source of advanced graduate and professional study. ■ UMKC is

counted among the top 150 public colleges and universities in the United States. With such exceptional programs as its master of fine arts in theater, ranked as one of the nation's best, UMKC stands out among America's urban universities. Moreover, UMKC is home of a debate team currently ranked seventh nationally.

"UMKC is essential to Kansas City's economic future," says Chancellor Eleanor Brantley Schwartz. "As a center for graduate and professional education and research, the university is an incubator for the scientists, doctors, nurses, pharmacists, dentists, biologists, engineers, economists, lawyers, teachers, business leaders, musicians, writers, and artists who will respond to the social and economic challenges of the 21st century."

A Proud Past

UMKC was chartered in 1929, when the Kansas City Chamber of Commerce and local church leaders pooled their resources and influence to create what was then called the University of Kansas City. In 1963, the private institution became part of the University of Missouri system and was renamed the University of Missouri-Kansas City. From the beginning, UMKC has dedicated itself to building community partnerships.

Community Connections

During her tenure, Schwartz has expanded UMKC's partnerships. For example, to help the area build quality elementary and high school programs, UMKC has established more than 40 outreach programs that help both at-risk and exceptional students reach their potential.

Kansas City is a regional health center in a state with an aging population. UMKC is a founding member of the innovative Scientific Education Partnership, along with the University of Kansas and Hoechst Marion Roussel (formerly Marion Merrell Dow), developed to study the aging process and diseases of the aged.

UMKC is the University of Missouri's campus for urban affairs, health sciences, and the performing arts. The school has teamed with the Nelson-Atkins Museum of Art, Kansas City Symphony, Theater League of Kansas City, and Starlight Theater, among others, to enhance the community's cultural life. As a result, students in UMKC's visual and performing arts programs have a communitywide learning laboratory. UMKC also is home to the Missouri Repertory Theater and KCUR-FM, the city's only public radio station.

As broad in scope as UMKC's partnerships are, they are still only part of what the university is doing to reach the standards of excellence set forth in its Strategic Plan for 2005 and beyond.

"UMKC faculty and students are engaged in programs and research important to the city's need for future 'knowledge workers,' " says Schwartz. "UMKC touches everyone. At the same time, UMKC's programs are dynamic because of the energy that comes from campus connections with city locations and people. It is a partnership that will only get better in the years ahead."

**Clockwise from top:
The University of Missouri-Kansas City is a comprehensive, public university offering undergraduate, graduate, and professional programs. UMKC has been called the prettiest urban campus in the United States.**

UMKC competes in NCAA Division I sports. There are 16 sports for men and women, from basketball to softball, tennis, rifle, and volleyball.

UMKC's Henry W. Bloch School of Business and Public Administration is nationally accredited by the American Assembly of Collegiate Schools of Business and the National Association of Schools of Public Affairs and Administration—one of a small percentage of business schools to earn both.

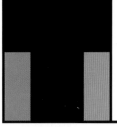

HE NIGHT R.D. KERLEY GRADUATED FROM A SMALL-TOWN Arkansas high school, he boarded a train for the bright lights of Kansas City. Kerley landed a job with the B.J. Hotz office supply business as a delivery boy and quickly moved into sales. By 1964, only five years later, the confident 23-year-old had managed to

purchase the company with his wife, Jo Ann.

When the Kerleys took over, the business had been around for nearly three decades under the leadership of founder B.J. Hotz. It boasted three employees who worked primarily in carbon paper and typewriter ribbon distribution from a location in downtown Kansas City. After buying the company, later renamed Hotz Business Systems, the Kerleys formed a corporation, shifted

the product focus to copiers, and began expanding from that base. It was the right move: Annual revenues have increased to a current total of $12 million, employees now number nearly 100, and the company maintains five office/showroom locations in the region.

"We can give the customer more attention than larger companies because we're concerned about quality, not quantity," says R.D. Kerley, president and CEO. "We offer our customers service, support, and innovative products that keep up with technology."

Embracing the Information Age

Hotz has witnessed a technological explosion during the decades it has been in business. Now a premier copy dealership, the company has introduced digital color, black-and-white copiers/printers, and facsimile systems to local businesses looking for state-of-the-art office management solutions. As the exclusive Minolta dealership in the metropolitan area, Hotz has put Minolta's CS Pro Series technology to work for Kansas City companies. In addition, Xerox engineering copiers and scanners, Autodesk Software, and Hewlett Packard network copiers, as well as Sharp and Muratec facsimile systems, afford Hotz customers a wide range of cutting-edge products.

Changing technologies are what make the business so challenging, say Hotz executives, who include Jo Ann Kerley as vice president; daughter Cindy Kerley, operations manager; son Russ Kerley, who manages the customer service department; and several others who have been with the company many

years. As copiers evolve from analog to digital, color reproduction will gradually replace black-and-white in the workplace. Hotz also believes that companies will increasingly deal with networking and connectivity issues, an area the Kerleys and their able staff are more than ready to address. Hotz recently acquired a photo lab to add another dimension to the company's image reproduction capabilities.

"We train all our service personnel and administrative people to know our products so that anyone here can help solve your problems," says R.D. Kerley. "The next generation of family, along with our employees, will lead us into the digital world, and we'll continue to be independent leaders in this industry and in this market."

Focus on Today

Despite its position at the forefront of changing technologies, Hotz has always succeeded by taking good care of its customers. The company's reputation has been built on its abilities to provide a complete source for equipment, services, and attention to the customers' unique needs.

Hotz's customer focus has paid off on many levels, including recognition by a number of industry experts. The company was selected as one of the few office equipment dealers in the nation to receive the Elite award from *Office Dealer* magazine. The Hotz service department has been awarded Minolta's Inner Circle for service excellence, and has received the Minolta Pro Tech Award every year since the award's inception in 1989. In addition, the company's Xerox marketing staff consistently ranks among the top 10 percent in

R.D. Kerley, president of Hotz Business Systems, leads a company that prides itself on national recognition. Kerley stands in front of some of the 22 Honor Council awards that his company has earned (top).

As a family-owned business, the Kerleys are proud of the family atmosphere that helps make Hotz a cohesive and successful organization. Shown here are Cindy, Russ, Jo Ann, and R.D. Kerley (bottom).

the region. Twice, Xerox has awarded its Service Excellence Award to the engineering division of Hotz Reprographics.

"We really listen to what customers are asking for," says R.D. Kerley. "A lot of suppliers are pushing products they want to sell. We offer solutions to what the customers want. In fact, our motto is 'Customer Relations through Customer Care.' We still have our first copier customer, which says that we're doing something right."

Caring Extended

At Hotz Business Systems, concern for customers extends into the community as well. The company believes in supporting a variety of causes, including the Cancer Fund, Mayor's Christmas Tree Fund, March of Dimes, Ronald McDonald House, and many others.

"We work with Hope House and Little League and participate in many different chambers of commerce," says R.D. Kerley,

who also believes in rewarding his employees with fair and equitable wages and excellent benefits. "Being part of the community means you put things back into it. We believe in reinvesting in Kansas City."

A portion of that reinvestment came to fruition when the company needed to expand in 1995. Hotz renovated space at 1617 Baltimore in a historic building just a few blocks from where the firm had been head-

quartered for more than 20 years. Says Kerley, "It is imperative that our location has quick access to major freeways to respond to our citywide customers."

Kerley's unwavering customer orientation is typical of the attitude that pervades Hotz Business Systems. "After all is said and done," he adds, "we're a partner with our customers, both existing and potential. We make it easy for our customers to do business with us."

N THE SKIES ABOVE VIRTUALLY EVERY COUNTRY ON EARTH, COMPANY executives pursue business on the wings of corporate aircraft. That phenomenon is due, in part, to the efforts of Executive Beechcraft, Inc., a Kansas City company familiar to business aviators worldwide. ■ For 59 years this family-owned and -operated company has led the way

in the booming business aviation field. Providing aircraft sales and related services from four locations in the Kansas-Missouri area, Executive Beechcraft claims the leading network of fixed-base operations in the heartland.

"From aircraft sales and service to charters and flight training, our dedication to excellence has earned us a reputation as the place where business comes to fly," says Dan Meisinger Jr., president of the company his father founded.

The Early Days
In 1938, Dan Meisinger Sr. was a young aviator and entrepreneur who saw the airplane's exciting potential as a business tool. He recognized that the speed and efficiency of a corporate airplane could extend the

reach of business to unlimited horizons. By conquering the obstacles of time and distance, executives could gain the competitive edge of face-to-face communication.

Strong in his convictions and totally dedicated to flying, Meisinger founded the Topeka Aircraft Sales & Service Company to offer a full array of modern aircraft and support services. That same year, Meisinger also began his family's long association with Beechcraft, maker of some of the world's best-loved airplanes—including the famous Model 17 Staggerwing biplane.

World events, however, shifted the young company's priorities from serving business to supporting the country's war effort. America needed bomber and fighter pilots, and Topeka

Aircraft spent the next several years turning hundreds of raw recruits into skilled airmen.

By war's end, exciting new commercial and civilian aircraft were rolling off production lines, with Americans taking to the air in ever growing numbers. Meisinger and his company geared up to meet the challenge.

A Tradition of Excellence
In the early 1950s, Meisinger expanded by opening a facility at Kansas City's Fairfax Airport. In 1967, he acquired an aviation company called Executive Beechcraft, a name his family would later raise to prominence in the aviation world.

Dedicated to quality aircraft, meticulous maintenance, expert technicians, and attentive customer service, Meisinger built a tradition of excellence that twice won him Man of the Year honors for top achievements in Beechcraft sales and service. Now in its second generation of family ownership, Executive Beechcraft is keeping the elder Meisinger's tradition uncompromised.

Executive Beechcraft Today
When Meisinger acquired Executive Beechcraft and changed his own company's name, he also moved into new office and aircraft maintenance space at Kansas City's Downtown Airport, increasing the convenience and accessibility offered to traveling executives. Over the years, that facility has grown remarkably in size and capability, and currently includes more than 10 acres of hangar space.

Today, Executive Beechcraft and its staff of more than 200 professionals support business aviation from four state-of-the-art flight centers: Kansas City's

Executive Beechcraft's Kansas City Downtown Airport facility is only minutes from the heart of Kansas City.

Downtown Airport, New Century Air Center in Olathe, Spirit of St. Louis Airport, and Kansas City International Airport. These centers offer a range of services from fueling and ground support to maintenance, sales and leasing, 24-hour international executive charter, parts sales, flight instruction, and total aircraft management.

When it comes to aircraft sales, Executive Beechcraft offers an extensive line of piston, turboprop, and jet airplanes. Representing lines such as Bonanza, Baron, and King Air, the company's extensive inventory includes new and pre-owned planes. Executive Beechcraft also brokers aircraft for an international market. The company's Executive Sales Group, made up of highly skilled pilots who understand every aspect of aircraft ownership, helps clients acquire the new or resale model that meets their specific needs.

A vital part of Executive Beechcraft's customer service is total aircraft maintenance—a demanding specialty for which the company has earned wide acclaim. Perfection is a constant goal, and Executive Beechcraft's factory-trained and licensed technicians employ the most advanced equipment, tools, and materials to assure operators the highest standards of aircraft reliability. Technicians are certified to service most models, including

Beechcraft, Citation, Learjet, and Sabreliner planes.

The company's capability to inventory and deliver essential parts and components provides critical customer support. Fast, efficient response and 24-hour availability keep aircraft downtime to a minimum, thereby maximizing value for operators.

Executive Beechcraft is equally proud of its ground support services. Over the course of a year, thousands of arriving flights are greeted by Executive Beechcraft's courteous, safety-minded line crews who know how to take care of aircraft and passengers.

"Many companies count on Executive Beechcraft's Ready Aircraft Management Program to keep their planes prepared for duty at a moment's notice," says Dan Meisinger Jr. "Services cover everything from hangar space and total maintenance to dedicated pilots and crews."

Rounding out the company's offerings are 24-hour charter service and professional flight instruction. Executive Charter's seasoned pilots and crews have flown millions of miles carrying passengers to domestic and international destinations, while the Executive Flight department has helped thousands of pilots earn their wings and update their training with individualized instruction.

"As we guide Executive Beechcraft toward a new millennium, we're committed to maintaining our well-deserved position," says Dan Meisinger Jr. "Executive Beechcraft has made a name for itself among business leaders, and that reputation will continue well into the next century and beyond."

N A WORLD DRIVEN BY HIGH-TECH INDUSTRIES, IBM CORP. HAS BEEN leading the way for most of the 20th century. Soon after Thomas J. Watson Sr. joined the Computing-Tabulating-Recording Company as general manager, he realized that increasingly sophisticated office machines would change the way the world did business. In 1924, he

changed the company's name to International Business Machines Corp. (later, IBM) to reflect that philosophy.

The following year, IBM established a Kansas City presence to take advantage of the growing influence of this centrally located commercial hub. Since then, the Kansas City office has worked with clients to provide information and communication solutions. From hardware to software, and from system integration to support services, IBM's 300 local employees have helped launch both local and national businesses into the computer age. In addition, the company's Global Integrative Services organization serves a 10-state region from its Kansas City headquarters.

"We're really a solution-based organization, helping companies run their business better," says Randall Ferguson Jr., senior location executive in Kansas City. "The better we can understand our customers' needs and match those with IBM products, the more successful we are."

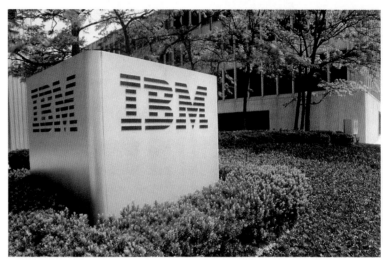

Rapid Change

It's hard to imagine an industry where change has occurred more rapidly than in the computer field. Not long ago, storing data called for enormous mainframe machines that only the most prosperous companies could afford. Today, desktop personal computers are standard fare, and new options are introduced on an almost minute-by-minute basis.

The popularity of computers means plenty of change in the ways products are marketed, which has kept IBM's Kansas City office busy. The midwestern sales, marketing, and service hub has battled increased competition and rapidly changing technology by improving customer service, becoming more solution oriented, and employing new sales techniques.

"We've become more flexible to meet the way our clients do business," says Ferguson. "We've got to deliver the same high quality we've always been known for, but in new and different ways."

In addition, the burgeoning Internet market has given IBM's Kansas City office a whole new technology arena to address. "The challenge customers have is that technology is changing

so fast that it's hard for them to keep up," says Ferguson. "That's where we come in."

Solid Corporate Citizen

For nearly 75 years, IBM has been a compassionate citizen of Greater Kansas City. As an employer, the company values the area's midwestern work ethic and customer-service-oriented employees.

IBM also takes seriously the supportive role it plays in the community. The company has donated money, equipment, and employee time to such organizations as the Kansas City Full Employment Council, the Kansas City Zoo, the Learning Exchange, Junior Achievement, and the Negro Leagues Baseball Museum. "IBMers as a whole are community minded," says Ferguson. "But those in Kansas City are even more so."

IBM's consistent level of care and concern is one reason Ferguson believes the company has been so successful in Kansas City. "IBM has found that the work ethic and values in America's heartland, as well as the diverse industries in the region, have contributed to the success of IBM and our customers in Kansas City," Ferguson says.

IBM Corp.'s Global Integrative Services organization serves a 10-state region from its Kansas City headquarters (top).

(From left) IBM Senior Location Executive Randall Ferguson Jr. meets with David Simms, services executive, PSS, and Scott Ferber, director of marketing, SMB WW Global Services (bottom).

DURING THE EARLY 1940S, GEORGE C. HOHL WANTED TO START a company that would make waste handling systems for the food service industry. But the world was at war, and steel was nearly unobtainable. After months of knocking on doors, Hohl finally went to Washington, D.C., where he

met with the War Production Board to see if they would approve a steel allotment.

Hohl's presentation was a roaring success. The young entrepreneur was able to prove that his machine, the Salvajor Senior, could save thousands of dollars worth of flatware that was being destroyed in inferior waste disposal systems throughout the nation's military camps. The board not only allocated the necessary steel for Hohl to make his machine, but also recommended the product to the Department of the Army.

In turn, the army gave Hohl his first order in 1944, requisitioning 600 units of the newly developed stainless steel waste-collecting system, which firmly launched his business. More than a half century later, The Salvajor Company remains a privately held, Kansas City-based manufacturer of commercial waste disposers and waste handling systems for the food service industry.

Branching Out

Salvajor's next step was to introduce its product in 1946 at what is now the National Restaurant Association Restaurant Hotel-Motel Show in Chicago. One of the first pre-flushing, scrapping, and food-waste-collecting systems in the industry, the Salvajor Senior was quickly accepted and soon found its way into the nation's restaurant, hotel, hospital, factory, and university kitchens.

The company continued to attract recognition. In 1964, Salvajor was honored with an invitation to attend the International Trade Exhibition in London. This opportunity gave the company the chance to establish its earliest overseas marketing representation.

It was also in the 1960s that Salvajor engineers began design-

ing new products in earnest—products that would help make Salvajor the leader in its field. Then headed by the late George O. Sherman as director of engineering, the firm developed five new products over the next 10 years.

When the founder's son, George C. Hohl Jr., took the reins of the company as president and CEO in 1970, research and development remained a top priority. In 1971, Salvajor introduced a new waste disposer that incorporated the first real improvements to disposer design in 50 years. As the company grew, it expanded its product line by attaching its waste disposer to other newly developed Salvajor systems. The ScrapMaster and TroughVeyor, for example, were two products designed to increase the speed and efficiency of scrapping.

Looking Ahead

Major factors in Salvajor's industry leadership have included its new-product development and its strategy to manufacture as many of its own components as possible. In addition, using computerized machinery maintains efficiency and accuracy for the company. Overall, Salvajor's devotion to quality products, reliable service, and cost-effectiveness has been the hallmark of its success and has prepared it well for the future.

"We are committed to the values that are important to us and the food service industry," says George Hohl Jr. "We will continue to be a leader in the market we serve."

Clockwise from top:
The Salvajor Company leadership includes (seated, from left) Don Misenhelter, vice president operations; George Hohl Jr., president and CEO; Caryl Applegate, chief financial officer; (standing, from left) Greg Wait, vice president sales; Chris Hohl, executive vice president; Gregg Hohl, service coordinator; and Marty Applegate, national service manager.

Salvajor warehouses an extensive inventory at its Kansas City facility.

New Salvajor disposers complete their test run before being boxed.

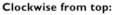
BOB GREENSPAN

WOLF PHOTOGRAPHY

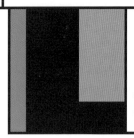

ESTER L. FIKE SR. HAD ALWAYS DREAMED OF OWNING HIS OWN business. A skilled machinist with an impressive reputation as shop foreman for a Kansas City manufacturer of rupture discs, he purchased the Carpenter Machine Shop in Independence in 1945. World War II had just ended, and his tiny operation, renamed

L.L. Fike Metal Products Company, was busy with tool and die work. However, at the urging of some of his previous employer's customers, Fike soon began designing and manufacturing rupture discs himself.

The rupture disc, a pressure relief device that protects personnel, equipment, and the environment against overpressure in pressurized systems, became Fike's most important product. Even today, this safety device generates some 30 percent of the company's revenues from clients such as Union Carbide, Monsanto, and Dow Chemical. Over the years, the Fike Corporation, renamed in 1985, has expanded applications for the rupture disc, and the versatile product is now used in space exploration for rockets, space shuttles, and astronauts' packs.

"Over the years, what's made us successful is believing we can do anything," says Max Jewell, Fike's president and chief operating officer. "Customers come to us with problems because we can do whatever's necessary to solve them."

Expansion Management

Today, the company's worldwide operations employ more than 500 people who apply their skills and expertise to a variety of Fike innovations. While the Metal Products Division still produces plenty of rupture discs, it also offers explosion protection products and services that include testing, venting, suppression, and isolation systems. Fike's Noble Alloy Valve Division, located in Houston, manufactures corrosion-resistant valves for its target industries using a patented pro-

cess that heat-treats zirconium and other exotic alloys to produce an extremely hard surface.

Fike Protection Systems is a division that specializes in custom-made automatic fire suppression systems that can detect and extinguish fires quickly and cleanly. Instead of water, the systems use an odorless, colorless, and people-safe gas to smother flames, making them the preferred fire control method for high-tech customers such as Sprint and MCI, as well as a number of museums and libraries throughout the world. The company's software-based fire detection system employs advanced sensor technology that also gives Fike an edge in this market segment.

The company's research and development efforts are a cornerstone of its business. In addition to ongoing research in Kansas

Fike Corporation's world headquarters is in Blue Springs (right).

Service valves are exposed to a high-temperature Nobelizing™ process (below).

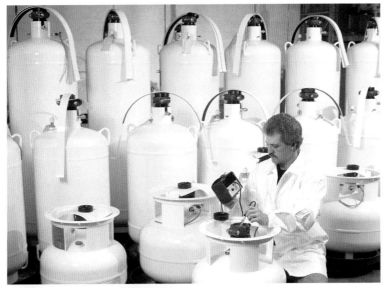

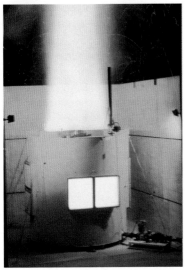

City, Fike maintains a laboratory facility in Orlando. The company's 10-cubic-meter, spherical vessel, the largest explosion testing device in North America, located in Blue Springs, gives Fike ample opportunities to analyze its explosion detection and suppression systems. As a result of its dedication to finding new and improved solutions to process safety, explosion management, detection, and suppression problems, the company currently holds more than 60 U.S. and foreign patents. Nationwide, all of Fike's divisions are leaders in their markets.

Going Global

Although Fike had been an active international exporter for many years, the company established its international operations in 1980. The company's first overseas joint venture was in Japan, where Fike is now the market leader

in sales of rupture discs. Today, Fike Japan offers a wide range of pressure relief products to the Japanese chemical, petrochemical, and defense industries.

"Our international operations continue to expand," says Jewell. "They now represent almost 40 percent of our overall business, and we're looking at new opportunities in new parts of the world."

Fike's manufacturing facility in Belgium is responsible for design, manufacturing, and sales in Europe, Africa, and the Middle East. Sales offices in France, the United Kingdom, Germany, Spain, Italy, and Russia assist in the company's European marketing efforts. Fike Canada handles both the pressure relief and fire suppression markets in that country, while Fike Southeast Asia serves China, as well as all member countries of the Association of Southeast Asian Nations.

"As the world becomes more safety conscious, that helps what

we do," says Jewell. "We continuously try to help bring safety systems to a new level for everyone."

A Family-Oriented Business

Despite its international reach, Fike Corporation remains a family-oriented operation. Lester Fike Jr. is now chairman and CEO of the company built by his father and mother, Rose Ann. Many current employees have spent their entire careers at Fike. "This is a family business, and we treat all employees as part of that family," says Jewell. "Our employees are loyal to us, and the company is loyal to them."

Fike employees have taken responsibility for maintaining the company's quality assurance program, and they prove their dedication by serving on boards of industry associations, governmental task forces, and other professional groups involved with establishing newer and better standards to meet worldwide safety and environmental needs. A sense of teamwork and dedication to common goals proliferates at Fike locations throughout the world.

"The principle of quality exists everywhere in business today," says Jewell. "But in our company, we're committed to the principle of exciting quality, the concept of exceeding the criteria perceived by our customers as both critical and necessary. That's how we've gotten ahead, and that's how we intend to stay there."

Clockwise from top left: Clean agent fire suppression systems using FM-200 are checked by a Fike employee.

Fike rupture discs are used as pressure relief mechanisms in the chemical, petrochemical, and defense industries.

Venting Fike Poly-SD rupture disc

Fike products are tested rigorously. Here, a large-scale explosion test takes place inside a 29-cubic-meter vessel.

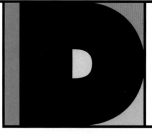

RESSED IN A COLORFUL HAWAIIAN PRINT SHIRT, A YOUNG Polynesian explains how his father long ago pioneered the wide surfboard for safety and handling ease in the rough Hawaiian waves. Now building big boards to capitalize on his dad's discovery, the narrator sagely concludes, "Wider is better."

The newly redesigned Grand Prix, with its sporty, wide-track look, is built exclusively at General Motors Corp.'s Fairfax facility. Since the improved model's debut, the car has received kudos from auto critics, and the buying public has taken note, as well.

This surfboard entrepreneur was only one of the characters featured in General Motors' highly visible television ads in 1996 and 1997 that equated the universal "wider is better" philosophy to the expanded wheelbase of the redesigned Pontiac Grand Prix. Thanks to memorable images, including kilt-clad Scotsmen wielding wider golf clubs and a tightrope artist whose family business fell off due to the use of narrow cable, the "wider

is better" mantra has reached a vast audience of consumers.

For General Motors' Fairfax Assembly plant in Kansas City, the clever advertising exposure provided a well-deserved nod to its manufacturing operation. The newly redesigned Grand Prix, with its sporty, wide-track look, is built exclusively at the Fairfax facility. Since the improved model's debut in late 1996, the car has received kudos from auto critics, and the buying

public has taken note, as well. In fact, according to General Motors Corp., Grand Prix sales have been up sharply ever since the first reporting period of its model year.

"Our mission is to build great automobiles that provide superior value for our customers," says Paul Marr, Fairfax plant manager. "We're always striving to improve on what we do. Around here, our motto is, 'The status quo is a plan to fail.'"

A Half Century of Success

General Motors (GM) launched its Kansas City operation in early 1945, after negotiating a lease with the federal government for the manufacturing facilities of what had been North American Aviation. In its heyday, North American produced the B-25 Billy Mitchell bomber used in World War II, so it took some remodeling for GM to begin manufacturing Buick, Oldsmobile, and Pontiac car lines there. The facility's first automobile, a black Pontiac two-door sedan, rolled off the assembly line on June 3, 1946.

Only five years later, the company again felt the effects of armed conflict when it was selected to manufacture the F84F Thunderstreak fighter plane for the Korean War. Not willing to give up its booming car business, Fairfax became the first plant in U.S. history to operate a dual-purpose facility when it began producing aircraft and automobiles side by side in the same building. In 1955, still assembling both cars and planes, GM impressively completed its aircraft production contract three months ahead of schedule. By 1960, the Detroit-based company was firmly entrenched in the Kansas City area; GM purchased the plant from the government for $4 million and embarked upon a $17 million modernization program.

The plant continued to manufacture automobiles at the renovated plant for the next quarter century. But in 1985, the company announced it would replace the aging facility with a modern complex of some 2.3 million square feet. In addition, GM planned to introduce a new midsize, front-wheel-drive car: the Pontiac Grand Prix. Within two years, Fairfax also announced that it would discontinue production of the Chevrolet Caprice, Buick LeSabre, and Pontiac Parisienne. During the facility's lifetime, more than 7 million cars had rolled off the line, including more than 2 million Buicks, 2 million Pontiacs, and 2 million Oldsmobiles, as well as nearly 500,000 Chevrolets.

"We have one of the most state-of-the-art assembly plants in the country," says Marr, whose operation maintains an annual payroll in excess of $234 million. "We have a lot of flexibility here to be able to build two different architectures and up to six body styles and subassemblies. That fact works to our advantage, and most importantly, to the customers', by enabling GM to respond much quicker to their needs."

Teamwork at Its Best

While cars continued to roll out of the original Fairfax facility during the two-year plant construction phase, GM negotiated a new agreement with its United Auto Workers Local 31 employees. The cornerstone of the company's popular mission statement was the Team Concept, because GM believed that teamwork is necessary to produce world-class quality products at a competitive cost. Although Fairfax employees had shown remarkable togetherness—such as massive cleanup efforts after the old building's roof blew off in 1979—the newly built plant would allow the company to enhance its teamwork concept. Before construction, the plant leadership agreed to install 51 team rooms throughout the facility, initiate joint departmental meetings and special events, and build state-of-the-art work areas that would ergonomically dovetail with other critical processes in the plant.

In 1997, when the newly installed flexible body shop was operational, GM's tradition of outstanding teamwork was demonstrated when the plant produced vehicles at its fullest capacity and flexibility. The plant built the 1996 and 1997 Oldsmobile Cutlass Supreme and the 1996 and 1997 Pontiac Grand Prix while preparing for the introduction of the 1998 Oldsmobile Intrigue. The Intrigue,

described as an elegant driver's car, was expected to compete with midsize imports—such as the Nissan Maxima and Toyota Camry. The entire launch effort was successfully executed and even set an industry benchmark with the Intrigue.

"We've long recognized that we can only be successful through our people," says Marr. "We need all employees to be enthusiastic about our business, and the only way to do that is through engaging employees in the process.

"That process begins with the Plan to Win, which is the master plan for all General Motors North America operations, focusing on employee enthusiasm, customer enthusiasm, and shareholder enthusiasm. If you can achieve all three, you can be successful. So that's what we try to do every shift, every day, every year."

General Motors has been a part of Kansas City since the company launched its local operation in early 1945.

The Fairfax plant built the 1996 and 1997 Oldsmobile Cutlass Supreme and the 1996 and 1997 Pontiac Grand Prix while preparing for the introduction of the 1998 Oldsmobile Intrigue, an elegant driver's car that competes with midsize imports.

In 1996, the company hosted an Employee Appreciation Day in connection with the 50th anniversary of GM's presence at Fairfax. Teamwork is such an integral part of the success of the Fairfax plant that the commemorative booklet welcoming employees and their families to the 50th anniversary celebration and open house emphasized the concept on its first page. "This look back at our first 50 years reinforces the principle that 'teamwork is the key to organizational success,'" it reads. "At every critical juncture in our history—be it the simultaneous manufacturing of cars and planes, quickly recovering from natural disasters, or developing and implementing a new agreement—teamwork made the difference. Teamwork has resulted in the successful day-to-day operation of assembling quality automobiles and will continue to assure a successful future for the Fairfax plant."

Wide Appeal

Thus far, GM's focus on teamwork has resulted in popularity in the marketplace, too. Only a few months after the Fairfax plant began making its newly designed Grand Prix, the J.D. Power and Associates 1997 APEAL (Automotive Performance, Execution, and Layout) Study ranked the car as one of its top automotive choices. The APEAL ranking measures what owners like and dislike about their new cars and trucks. For 1997, the organization awarded highest honors to GM cars and trucks in five out of 12 categories—more than any other automobile manufacturer.

GM is heavily advertising the sportier look of the redesigned Grand Prix, capitalizing on the model's style and essence from its 1960s heyday. Besides the expanded wheelbase, the Grand Prix's roof also has been lowered to accentuate its race car appeal.

These modifications have contributed to impressive sales jumps.

About 95 percent of 1997 Grand Prix sales were to individuals through dealers, rather than to leasing companies. With previous versions of the Grand Prix, about 30 to 35 percent of total sales were to fleets. In addition, the Grand Prix's sales performance proved particularly exciting because it took place in the midsize car market, which has struggled in recent years. The typical Grand Prix buyer is 40 years old and has a household income of $60,000. The car appeals to a varied cross section of the population.

The redesigned Grand Prix's popularity has helped raise employment at the Fairfax factory to its highest level in years. The plant's two shifts currently employ more than 3,500 people, who produce the more than 200,000 cars a year that roll off the Fairfax plant's assembly lines.

"We're fortunate that we can provide two high-demand products," says Marr, whose operation consistently ranks as the number one midsize and luxury group plant in GM's production program performance. "As long as we continue to keep our quality levels up and continue to reduce operating costs, we'll have a good future."

Bigger Is Better

Any facility that encompasses 572 acres—and was built with 27,000 tons of structural steel, 130,000 cubic yards of concrete, and 570 miles of electrical cable—should grab the attention of all who live and work nearby. But the Fairfax plant, which represents the highest single investment made in the state of Kansas for a manufacturing facility, operates quietly and beyond the view of most Kansas City-area residents.

Yet the plant workers' philanthropic accomplishments are felt throughout the region. GM's Fairfax operation, for example, pledges nearly $500,000 a year to United Way, making it the single largest United Way supporter in Wyandotte County. The company also gives generously to the Kansas City, Kansas Chamber of Commerce; the Red Cross; and scores of other organizations that benefit the plant's neighbors. In addition, Fairfax employees spend countless hours volunteering throughout the community.

"Part of our commitment to recognizing our employees includes backing their community involvement in any way we can," says Tony Costa, director of human resources at Fairfax. "Working together as a team, we have made, and can continue to make, a significant contribution to our company and the Kansas City region. We have the opportunity to be the best, and that's what we're constantly striving to do."

In fact, the future for General Motor's Fairfax Assembly Plant looks bright indeed. The Grand Prix leads its automotive field, continuously winning acclaim for its "wider is better" build. The Oldsmobile Intrigue has made a stunningly sought-after entrance into the car-buying arena. Times could hardly be better for the people and the company that produce two such desirable vehicles.

The Fairfax Assembly Plant is in a great position, and one that Marr expects is secure. "This plant has been here a long time, literally through storms and prosperity," he says, alluding to the days in 1951 when the Fairfax facility was inundated with nine feet of flood water, as well as to the success it currently enjoys with the exclusive manufacturing of the Grand Prix. "I'm especially proud of all the people who, throughout the years, have contributed to our great success, and I know that we have many more good times ahead."

J.D. Power and Associates has named the newly designed Grand Prix one of its top automotive choices, according to its APEAL (Automotive Performance, Execution, and Layout) ranking.

NYONE WHO BELIEVES THAT RAILROADS BELONG TO THE past and not to the future should take a closer look at Harmon Industries, Inc., an acclaimed Kansas City company that has provided train-oriented technology for more than half a century. With revenues increasing by double

digits each year and global productivity expanding, the publicly held company could easily be dubbed the "brains behind trains."

In fact, Harmon Industries has become a leading supplier of state-of-the-art signal and train control products to freight and rail transit systems worldwide. Through innovative technological solutions and corporate acquisitions, the company has become an engineering powerhouse that is at the forefront of the rail industry. From signal lights to computerized communications equipment, Harmon has set new standards in forging the future of safe and efficient rail transportation.

There are three fundamental factors for Harmon's success and leadership position: a heritage of innovation, exceptional customer service, and a superb and dedicated workforce.

A Heritage of Railroad Innovations

In 1946, Robert C. Harmon found himself unemployed when the company he was then working for went out of business. Harmon, an engineer, arranged to complete a contract his employer had started, which involved a communication system for

Kansas City Southern Railroad. He set up shop behind a small upholstery firm in Independence, and went to work. Harmon's initiative quickly paid off. That first product was technological innovation at its finest: it allowed continuous voice contact between moving trains and railroad staff along the track.

Soon, the company developed other technological landmarks, first improving the science of detecting trains approaching rail-highway grade crossings, and later expanding to electronic solutions for controlling the actual railroad switches and signals to keep trains moving safely. Harmon's Electro Code track circuits and Vital Harmon Logic Controller have become industry standards for controlling the signals and switches that keep trains moving efficiently and safely. The Ultra Cab II, combined with its unique antenna design that rejects electrical interference from locomotive power systems, has become a virtual standard for those freight railroads using onboard cab signals.

In addition, Harmon's broad-based microprocessor technology, developed initially for domestic

freight railroads, has been adapted for the transit market and is rapidly being embraced by rail transit authorities throughout the world. Harmon recently achieved a major technology advance by securing an exclusive license for a proprietary communications-based train control system called Advanced Automatic Train Control (AATC), which is based on adapted military technology. Its use enables transit authorities to significantly increase their capacity at much lower cost than building additional infrastructure while greatly enhancing safety.

Clockwise from top right: Harmon Industries, Inc.'s largest source of revenue comes from the North American freight rail system. Class I railroads rely on Harmon's innovative and dependable service to help maintain safety and efficiency.

With strategic locations throughout the country, Harmon's asset management business provides a single-source, convenient resource for a wide variety of commonly used parts.

Blue Springs is home to Harmon's new corporate headquarters.

Such innovations, as well as attentive customer service and project management services, have consistently led to recognition from Harmon's railroad customers in the form of working partnerships and specific awards, including top quality performance awards from Union Pacific, Burlington Northern, and Conrail.

Transportation Technology Worldwide

In recent years, many changes have occurred in the United States as railroads have continued their merger trends. Pursuing greater profitability and efficiency in the process, they have sought partners that could evolve with them. Harmon has met the challenge, providing solutions that have proved instrumental to the success of both Class I and short line railroads. Moreover, the company continues to add service offices near railroad customers to better serve them and to create a better sense of teamwork.

Harmon continues to provide railroad expertise worldwide, including Australia, China, the United Kingdom, and Brazil. The international portion of the company's business is experiencing phenomenal growth. While the firm has operated internationally for many years, Harmon products and the world's railroads have recently come together in terms of both privatization and technological compatibility.

The recent ISO 9000 certification of all Harmon plants supports future international growth. ISO publishes standards designed to increase quality and consistency and to ensure continuous improvements in manufacturing, production, and service. ISO certification is an essential part of Harmon's growth plans, enabling the company to do business in the international marketplace.

Harmon maintains its preeminent position on the cutting edge of railroad technology by keeping its customers' needs and wishes uppermost in mind. Harmon consistently invests

nearly 5 percent of its annual sales on research and development for new products and systems. This places Harmon in elite company on a national basis, regardless of the industry, as a company committed to developing new and better solutions to managing rail operations.

In spite of its global business and its multimillion-dollar annual revenues, Harmon takes a local approach at its Missouri headquarters. The 1,000-plus Harmon employees based near Kansas City are encouraged to

extend their family-style corporate culture into the community by volunteering and participating in charitable events. In addition, the Harmon Industries/ Education Partnership has been recognized by local and national organizations for its leadership role in working with educational institutions. The company also supports dozens of social service and cultural arts organizations.

A global leader in the rail supply industry and a corporate leader, Harmon Industries is committed to the Kansas City community.

Clockwise from top: The People's Republic of China is just one of the international rail markets in which Harmon has a growing presence. Harmon technology has also been implemented in many other countries, including Australia, Brazil, the United Kingdom, the former Soviet Union, and India.

The expanding domestic rail transit market continues to offer the company extended opportunities for growth. The train control system provided on Chicago Transit Authority's Green Line is an example of Harmon's innovative solutions to signal and train control.

In an industry focused on service and reliability, Harmon has maintained a position as an industry leader by employing state-of-the-art technology to meet high customer demand for quality and flexibility.

"IF YOU BUILD IT THEY WILL COME" IS A PHRASE THAT WAS MADE famous by a Hollywood movie about a magical midwestern baseball diamond. But the motto also describes the simple premise behind The Larkin Group, Inc., a consulting engineering practice with more than half a century of experience in satisfying the infrastructure requirements

Clockwise from top right: The Larkin Group, Inc. designed zero-depth entry, spray fountains, raised seating, and two waterslides to make the Flora Park Pool in Dubuque, Iowa, an attractive summer recreation alternative for residents and the surrounding communities.

Working closely with the Kansas Department of Transportation and Kansas City, Kansas, Larkin developed a plan for substantial improvements to the Interstate 70 interchange between Seventh Street and the Lewis and Clark Viaduct.

Since 1966, Larkin engineers have worked closely with the city of Prairie Village, Kansas, to study and manage the community's storm drainage problems. Larkin's original 1966 study has been updated periodically since then, and the firm continues to work with the city to provide creative solutions.

that draw residents to successful communities.

This multidisciplined firm provides municipal engineering services to towns and cities throughout the country. The firm's more than 120 engineers and support professionals design intelligent solutions that not only meet civic needs, but enhance the quality of life for those most directly affected.

"In everything we do, we're trying to give customers value and cost-effective service that meets their own goals and objectives," says M. Clark Thompson, P.E., president. "Our people bring a strong work ethic and an open mind to their projects. That's proven to be a combination that serves our customers well."

From the Ground Floor

That philosophy began more than 50 years ago, when Kenneth Larkin quit working for one of Kansas City's largest engineering firms to launch his own structural engineering practice from his basement in 1946. Equal amounts of talent, hard work, and salesmanship, as well as an eye for business opportunities, eventually led the practice into full municipal engineering services.

Today, Larkin's design work includes transportation planning and engineering, storm water

management, site development, dams and reservoirs, wastewater facilities, and waterworks. And those are just the beginning. The company's engineers have also designed award-winning swimming pools, and applied their nuts-and-bolts know-how to Kansas City's signature fountains, such as the Children's, Spirit of Freedom, and Firefighters fountains. And they even moved an entire town: Pattonsburg, Missouri, following disastrous 1993 flooding.

"There are very few things that our team of professionals cannot handle," says Thompson. "Our dedication to client service and our total commitment to everything we do have paved the way to our success over the years."

Bigger and Better

That future should prove particularly bright as the company continues to realize competitive advantages that were created in 1996 with The Larkin Group's formation. The parent organization includes Kansas City's Larkin Associates Consulting Engineers Inc., which also has a branch office in Springfield, Missouri; Andrews, Asbury & Robert, Inc., based in Albuquerque, with an office in Las Cruces, New

Mexico; and Larkin Southern, Inc., operating from Russellville, Arkansas.

Despite the company's expanding reach, Kansas City will continue to benefit from the firm's headquarters location. Through the years, Larkin staff members have taken community involvement to heart, raising funds for groups such as the United Way, March of Dimes, and Christmas in October; donating time and talent to the Multiple Sclerosis Society; and assisting in special events such as the Easter Seals' KC Hoops.

"We help build cities every day, but we recognize that volunteerism and concern for others is at the heart of all great communities," Thompson says. "Our people shine in both creating municipal improvements and improving the communities in which they live."

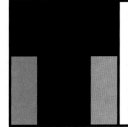

HE RENOVATION OF THE HISTORIC NEW YORK LIFE BUILDING seemed a romantic notion when Hugh Zimmer first expressed interest in Kansas City's oldest skyscraper. The 1888 structure had been empty for years, and it looked as though it would eventually fall to the wrecking ball. But in 1994, Zimmer—chairman of The Zimmer

Companies—told the Kansas City Land Clearance Redevelopment Authority that he was willing to spend the time and money necessary to assess renovation possibilities. He was given the go-ahead.

Today, the New York Life Building has become the success story of the Kansas City skyline. Only a year into its renovation—a $35 million project that would gut and rebuild the brick and marble jewel into a state-of-the-art technological wonder—UtiliCorp United signed on as the structure's sole tenant. Even better, the international utility company wanted additional, energy-saving innovations blended into the historic architecture. It was a developer's dream come true.

"The work not only restored a Kansas City landmark, but it established a lightning rod for people's feelings about the downtown area," says Zimmer, who in the early 1950s joined his father, Albert W. Zimmer, in the firm he had started in 1948. "The project gave us the satisfaction of doing something unique—at which others had failed—and it reemphasized our capabilities throughout the area for this type of innovative project."

Major Mark

In its 50-year history, Zimmer has had many success stories such as this one, and has become one of the most active commercial real estate developers in the Kansas City area. The company's activities in the commercial real estate field have made a significant impact upon the Kansas City skyline and its economic base. In addition to the award-winning New York Life Building, The Zimmer Companies has been responsible for the de-

velopment of more than 2,000 acres of business parks throughout the area, more than 21.5 million square feet of office and industrial buildings, and the current management of more than 4 million square feet of space.

Among Zimmer's high-profile projects have been the 260-acre Lenexa Industrial Park, the 300-acre Southlake Technology Park in Johnson County, the 240-acre Heartland Meadows in Liberty, the 330-acre AirWorld Center near Kansas City International Airport, the 80-acre Corporate Meadows Office Park in Topeka, the 80-acre Rollins Meadows Office Park in Lee's Summit, and the 340-acre Mitchell Woods Business Park in St. Joseph.

But Zimmer does much more than develop land and buildings. The company also specializes in

real estate sales, leasing, property management, project management, and consultation. Representing the third generation in the family-owned firm are Hugh Zimmer's son and daughter, President David J. Zimmer and Vice President Ellen Z. Darling.

"We try to provide the most comprehensive services tailored to the needs of our clients," says Hugh Zimmer, who has been honored as Realtor of the Year and Developer of the Year. "We help clients determine whether to buy, lease, hold, sell, or develop properties. We have always been quality minded rather than quantity minded. Our track record and our reputation mean there's never any question of integrity or commitment. We've proved for 50 years that we can get the job done."

The Zimmer Companies redeveloped and leased the venerable New York Life Building, which had survived as a Kansas City landmark.

Zimmer's own corporate headquarters is on Washington Street in Kansas City.

Zimmer developed this office building in Southlake Technology Park in Lenexa for Mobil Oil Credit Corporation.

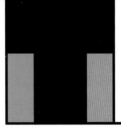

HE MARK OF ELECTRICAL EXCELLENCE IS NOT AN EMPTY PROMISE. It's the vision statement of Mark One Electric, a company proud of what it has accomplished in the last 25 years. Having built a reputation for hard work and dependability, Mark One currently ranks number three among the Kansas City area's top 25

electrical contractors. The company's ability to get the job done right the first time has led to Mark One's involvement in several of the area's most ambitious building projects, including Station Casino Kansas City, one of the largest casinos in the nation.

Making Its Mark

The company's founder, Carl "Red" Privitera, raised during the depression and no stranger to hard work, started out in 1950 as an electrician working for Monarch Electric, the business he would eventually own. Over the course of the next 24 years, Red rose through the ranks to the position of vice president. When the opportunity to purchase the business presented itself in 1974, Red took it. He renamed the business Mark One Electric and refocused its vision. Not content with the small-scale commercial jobs that were Monarch's bread and butter, Mark One went after challenging, large-scale, industrial projects.

Red's desire to work the big jobs did not go long unfulfilled. General Motors was building a new automobile plant in Fairfax, Kansas, and Mark One was

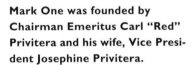

Mark One was founded by Chairman Emeritus Carl "Red" Privitera and his wife, Vice President Josephine Privitera.

The company's leadership today includes (from left) Richard A. Sheldrake, Carl Privitera II, Joe Privitera, Tony Privitera, and Rosana Privitera Biondo.

called in to work in the plant's paint shop. The company's skillful handling of this major job led to its involvement in several more GM projects over the years, including the construction of the new Saturn plant in Spring Hill, Tennessee. The company has also enjoyed a long relationship with the Ford Motor Company, and in 1998, added Kansas City newcomer Harley-Davidson to its list of clients.

And that list of clients is a long one. Mark One has been, or is now, involved in many of Kansas City's high-profile projects. The company has provided electrical services for the Argosy and Station casinos, Kansas City's new communications facility, the U.S. Bureau of the Census computer facility, the remodeling of the Oak Park JCPenney department store, Alliance Data's new customer service center, Rozzelle Court at the Nelson-Atkins Museum of Art, the new Kemper Museum of Modern Art, the Wyndham Garden Hotel, and the recently completed, $18 million annex to the Jackson County Detention Center.

Current projects include United Missouri Bank's Technology Center; the new Valencia Place project at the Country Club Plaza; expansions at Pembroke Hill Day School; ongoing renovations at the Westin Crown Center; the new Corporate Woods office of Shook, Hardy & Bacon; John Deere's new offices; and work at Sprint's world headquarters campus in Overland Park.

Bigger Business

The way business was done in the past is gone," says current company President Rosana Privitera Biondo. "The contracting industry has sped up. Companies need to market themselves a lot more. We're a very strong company that wants to grow. That's definitely where we're headed in the future."

Today, Mark One employs more than 100 field electricians with whom the company works closely to create innovative approaches to new projects. The firm's field supervision team boasts an average of 20 years of service in the electrical industry. This hardworking group of

electricians is supported by a management team determined to be the best and led by the Privitera family.

Red's daughter, Rosana, succeeded him when he became chairman emeritus in 1994. She is joined in the business by her mother, Josephine Privitera, who serves as a vice president, as well as her brothers Joseph A. Privitera, vice president of operations; Carl J. Privitera II, vice president of engineering; and Anthony L. Privitera, vice president of sales and marketing. Through numerous professional affiliations (International Brotherhood of Electrical Workers, National Electrical Contractors Association, Alliance of Professional and Specialty Contractors, Builders Association, and Kansas City Area Development Council) and specialized training (total quality management and ISO 9000), the management team is working hard to expand its networking contacts and Mark One's business.

Rosana Square

The company's most successful expansion project is now one of Johnson County's better-known shopping complexes, Rosana Square. Throughout his career, Red had the foresight to purchase land throughout the city, then resell the land to developers. Such was the plan for the 55-acre site at the corner of 119th Street and Metcalf Avenue until the original developers declared bankruptcy.

The Privitera family decided to forge ahead with the development of the tract, but tackled the project themselves, forming the Rosana Square Partnership. Signing 10 anchor tenants instead of the usual one or two created a new destination shopping center. The drawing power of big names such as Price Chopper, Parts America, Hobby Lobby, and Cinemark Movies, combined with the careful attention paid to traffic patterns and business hours, guarantees each of

Rosana Square's 45 shop owners a steady flow of customers morning, noon, and night.

Getting the Job Done Right

Mark One Electric and the Rosana Square Partnership have come a long way in the last few years, bringing a commitment to building long-term relationships and meeting the needs of their customers in everything they do. They work hard to live up to the high standards they've set for themselves. It is a team effort in which all employees of Mark One have dedicated themselves to the ideas of "The Mark of Electrical Excellence" and getting the job done right.

And getting the job done right the first time is what it's all about.

Mark One has done work for a number of big-name local companies, including Kansas City newcomer Harley-Davidson's motorcycle plant in 1997 (left).

Rosana Square, the company's most successful expansion project to date, is now one of Johnson County's better-known shopping complexes (right).

The company has completed high-profile work for Kansas City's Station (left) and Argosy (right) casinos.

SINCE 1948, PRIDE IN A JOB WELL DONE HAS BEEN THE cornerstone of DiCarlo Construction Company. When people throughout the company are asked what separates the firm from other general contractors, they point to the quality of projects it has completed. DiCarlo's consistent quality is evident whether the job

is a signature institutional project such as United Missouri Bank's headquarters, or a complex industrial facility such as the recently completed expansion of the water treatment facilities for Johnson County, Kansas. The firm has built everything from the monumental Hoch Auditorium at the University of Kansas to Gateway 2000's new technology center. DiCarlo's Kansas City contributions range from downtown's signature Barney Allis Plaza to the newly opened 18th and Vine Historic District, where museums, a visitors center, and entertainment spots have created a renaissance for the area.

All told, DiCarlo's consistent growth has earned it a position among Kansas City's top three general contractors, according to the *Kansas City Business Journal.* "No matter what we're working on or who we're working with, we aim for the highest levels of quality in construction and customer service," says company President Mitch DiCarlo.

DiCarlo provides a full range of preconstruction and construction services, and is at the forefront of design-build—a growing trend in the construction industry. Under the design-build method, DiCarlo assumes single-source

United Missouri Bank's headquarters is just one of the projects to which DiCarlo Construction Company has lent its design-build expertise.

DiCarlo Construction Company built Budig Hall (formerly Hoch Auditorium), located on the campus of the University of Kansas.

responsibility for every phase of a project, providing complete design and construction services from conceptual studies to the final move-in. Combining the best elements of general construction and construction management, the company monitors and controls the design and construction of each project, providing more value for a client's building dollar.

DiCarlo Construction is also a leader in the field of construction management, working with owners, architects, and other project consultants from the inception of a project through completion of construction. As the project team's construction authority, DiCarlo's expertise in construction techniques, scheduling, and costing is applied to the separate phases of a project. These services provide benefits not typically available when hiring a construction company under more traditional contracting methods. The result of the company's perfected methods, coupled with nationally experienced personnel, has been millions of dollars in savings to its clients.

"When performing traditional general construction contracts, we set ourselves apart by doing much of the work ourselves, in-

stead of just serving as brokers," says DiCarlo. "We can handle everything from excavation, concrete work, and masonry to carpentry, millwork, and precast erection. We're as complete a general contractor as you'll find in this area, or any other."

From Masonry to Majesty

It was only three years after World War II when Vincent DiCarlo decided to launch his own company. The son of Italian immigrants, the 22-year-old took out a small bank loan and founded his new venture, calling it V.S. DiCarlo Masonry Construction Company. Six years later, the young father had earned such success that he was able to build his own new company headquarters at 50th and Prospect streets.

By 1967, DiCarlo's firm had become one of the largest masonry contractors in the Midwest, and the entrepreneur decided to expand into the general contracting arena, changing the company name to V.S. DiCarlo General Contractors Inc. in 1968. DiCarlo also figured that his market expansion efforts would serve as a hedge against the growing influx of new materials. Masonry building elements were increasingly being

replaced with drywall, curtain wall, and other alternative materials. After sons Mitch and Mark joined the company in the early 1980s, the operation's name again changed, this time to DiCarlo Construction Company. Vincent DiCarlo died in 1995.

"My father's business philosophy was to treat his employees and customers with honesty and integrity, and to deliver the highest-quality project that he possibly could," says DiCarlo, whose brother, Mark, now serves the company as executive vice president of business development. "Those are standards that we continue to value to this day, along with making sure that we have at least one company principal involved in each project. Like our father, we are entrepreneurs at heart."

Quality without Compromise

Whether they're building hospitals, office buildings, manufacturing plants, hotels, parking structures, municipal facilities, or water treatment plants, the

300 employees at DiCarlo Construction concentrate on achieving both superior quality and cost efficiency. From project managers to superintendents, from foremen to skilled craftsmen, everyone at DiCarlo embraces the company's mission statement: "To provide the best construction services available, thereby enhancing our leadership in the community," it states in part. "We will perform beyond our clients' expectations, resulting in repeat business and stronger relationships."

The company's dedication to quality was especially evident in its work on the 18th and Vine Historic District. DiCarlo Construction played a major role as construction manager in conjunction with Courtney Day Construction Company. The two companies transformed the dilapidated former jazz mecca just east of downtown into an exciting tourist attraction that now includes the Negro Leagues Baseball Museum, the Kansas City Jazz Museum, the 18th and Vine Visitors Center, the Gem

Theatre, and the Blue Room, a reproduction of a 1930s jazz club. As *Modern Builder* magazine writes, "No city in America possesses a neighborhood of African-American culture that is as widely visited and enjoyed by a region's population and tourists—18th and Vine represents Kansas City's most significant 'bridge opportunity' in the last 50 years."

DiCarlo Construction Company remains committed to its role as facilitator, helping clients assess their construction needs, then carrying out the work with a precise attention to detail. "It's presumed that any selected method of construction can produce a building," says Mark DiCarlo. "But it's the integrity, ability, and skill of the committed individuals within our company that ensure superior quality and success in each project we undertake. Professionalism and dedication to excellence have been our hallmarks for many years, and they will continue to rule our actions in the future."

Two Pershing Square is a class A office building and corporate headquarters of Payless Cashways, Inc. (left).

The high interior finish and fast track construction of Sam's Town Casino is just one example of DiCarlo Construction Company's commitment to completing quality projects on time (right).

N 1998, THE KANSAS CITY OFFICES OF LEWIS, RICE & FINGERSH (LRF) celebrated the 50th anniversary of its founding. Started by Jack Brown and Joe Koralchik in 1948 as a two-lawyer general practice, the firm has grown to include more than 40 lawyers in Kansas City, and through its merger with Lewis & Rice of St. Louis in 1989, LRF now has offices

The real estate department of Lewis, Rice & Fingersh, L.C. has earned a national reputation for creative work backed by strong negotiating skills. Its efforts have helped clients reshape the landscape and change the work and shopping patterns for communities in Kansas City and around the world.

in Missouri, Kansas, and Illinois, with more than 160 lawyers providing the full range of legal services necessary to effectively support today's complex business needs.

From the early days of Brown & Koralchik, the hallmark of LRF has always been the astute and timely delivery of the highest-quality legal services. The firm has steadfastly sought and retained top-notch lawyers—those who listen to clients and understand their needs; who quickly

get to the heart of issues; and whose paperwork and trial skills evidence the required attention to detail to help clients realize their objectives.

The driving mission at LRF is to serve clients with a savvy, results-oriented team of legal professionals. Bill Carr, managing member of the Kansas City office says, "Over the years, we've worked with dynamic and creative entrepreneurs and businesspersons. We understand that our role as lawyers is to facilitate and not impede a transaction— to raise issues and recognize problems with a view to solving them in an intelligent, practical manner—and to vigorously litigate disputes in an economical manner with a watchful eye toward settlement when that will serve the best interests of our clients."

Nationally Recognized Real Estate Practice

Nowhere is the firm's commitment to results more visible than in its mainstay prac-

tice—real estate. The firm's real estate department has developed a national reputation for creative and thorough work, coupled with strong negotiating skills. Indeed, the efforts of LRF have helped the firm's many real estate clients literally reshape the landscape and permanently change work and shopping patterns for communities in Kansas City, around the country, and around the world.

From the development of Missouri's first enclosed shopping center in St. Joseph, LRF has built a real estate practice that has provided legal services in connection with literally hundreds of shopping centers, including Oak Park Mall and Metro North Shopping Center in the Kansas City area, and Westminster Mall, the largest shopping center in Colorado. LRF attorneys have worked on projects in virtually every state in the United States, as well as in Europe and Asia.

LRF has played a principal role in the revitalization of downtown Kansas City, including the development of One Kansas City Place, the city's largest office building; the Town Pavilion; other important office buildings; and the redevelopment of downtown's

◄ ARCHITECTURAL FOTOGRAPHICS

signature hotel, the Kansas City Marriott Downtown Hotel (formerly known as the Muehlebach and Allis Plaza hotels). In the Kansas City suburbs, evidence of LRF's services are literally everywhere, from Hallbrook Farms, the metropolitan area's most upscale new single-family residential development, to the Executive Hills Office Parks to apartment projects containing thousands of units.

"Real estate development has become increasingly complex," according to Charles Miller, head of LRF's Real Estate Department in Kansas City. "In addition to representation involving joint ventures, leasing, financing, operating and easement agreements, sales and purchases, and other real estate matters, our clients look increasingly to us as serving a vital role in helping them obtain the cooperation and support of local governments in their search for favorable zoning and incentives such as tax increment financing and tax abatements and credits. Such work may often be the difference between whether a project gets off the ground or dies on the drawing board."

Effective Tax Analysis and Business Planning

LRF has developed a large tax and general business practice, with particular emphasis on the issues facing pass-through entities, such as general partnerships, limited partnerships, and limited liability companies.

LRF's approach to business transactions involves "multifactored planning," according to Tony Luppino, head of the firm's Business and Tax Planning Department in Kansas City. "We consider primary economic goals, balancing of risks, income tax considerations, and estate planning in order to accomplish our clients' objectives in the most tax-efficient manner," Luppino says.

In the course of structuring large and complex real estate and other business transactions, the firm's business and tax lawyers have become proficient at finding creative solutions to problems in highly technical areas such as tax-deferred like-kind exchanges, organization of multitiered entities, restructuring of debt, partnership tax allocations, and corporate reorganizations.

Where Litigation Is a Business Decision

Indeed, litigation is now the firm's fastest-growing practice area. Its litigators have been involved in a wide range of areas, including commercial, employment, business, environmental, zoning, securities, banking, municipal, construction, taxation, real estate, and personal injury litigation, among others. The challenges are numerous and the results impressive. "Over the last year, we've experienced tremendous growth in our litigation department, and we expect more growth as we continue to offer a broad range of litigation and dispute resolution services," says Beth Nay, department head. "Unlike law firms that go to the mat with every litigation case regardless of the situation, we've distinguished ourselves by not overstaffing and staying cognizant of the key issues at every point in the process with an eye toward settlement if possible, and if not, a successful trial."

"I've always been proud of the quality of the firm's work," says senior member Jack Fingersh. Carr concludes, "We are a unique law firm, offering the personal attention of a smaller office in Kansas City, with the resources of our St. Louis office making us one of the broadest and largest practices in the region. Our focus is, and will continue to be, to render sophisticated, efficient, and economical service that a client has the right to demand and expect."

Some of the development projects in Kansas City for which Lewis, Rice & Fingersh has provided legal services include the Town Pavilion (center), One Kansas City Place, the Plaza Steppes office building, and the Renaissance Office Park I (bottom) and II (top) in Overland Park.

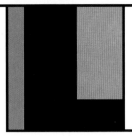

OCATED IN THE BANNISTER FEDERAL COMPLEX, ALLIEDSIGNAL Federal Manufacturing & Technologies (FM&T) has created a technology titan, employing more than 3,000 people at its Kansas City site. Precision products such as microcircuits, radars, and arming devices have become the company's specialty. In addition,

FM&T supports 80 advanced technologies, including failure analysis, machining, optics, laminates, and software engineering.

FM&T is a prime contractor for the U.S. Department of Energy (DOE), producing high-quality electrical, mechanical, and engineered materials for weapons production. Although the company has been working for the federal government since 1949, the plant dates back even further. Originally built by the U.S. Navy during World War II to assemble engines for fighter planes, the facility was transformed after the war by the Atomic Energy Commission (now the DOE), which contracted the Bendix Corporation to manufacture nonnuclear components for the nation's nuclear weapons defense system. In 1982, the Allied Corporation acquired Bendix, and later merged with the Signal Companies, creating AlliedSignal Inc.

After the cold war ended in the 1990s, the DOE consolidated its objectives. Because of its state-of-the-art capabilities and quality performance, FM&T continues to be the U.S. government's primary manufacturer of nonnuclear components for nuclear weapons.

A Commitment to Quality

FM&T's success depends on its commitment to continuous improvement through total quality (TQ) and six sigma principles. The nature of the company's work demands exacting precision to ensure the safety of the public and the U.S. weapons stockpile. The controls FM&T has in place are unparalleled.

In fact, the company has been honored for its outstanding performance and successful processes. FM&T was the first

DOE contractor to receive ISO 9001 certification, the most prestigious quality standard in the world. In September 1996, the company received the Missouri Quality Award for excellence in leadership, information and analysis, strategic planning, human resources, process management, business results, and customer satisfaction. That same month, it received the DOE Quality Achievement Award—the highest quality honor DOE has awarded to date.

FM&T has received additional awards for excellence in safety and health programs. The company was the first DOE contractor and the first AlliedSignal facility to become ISO 14001 certified, a designation given to organizations that effectively complete rigorous auditing of their environmental management systems.

Community Partner

FM&T associates are committed to the community. More than half of the company's senior managers hold community leadership positions, and its associates are longtime champions of organizations such as the United Way, Habitat for Humanity, Harvesters, and Christmas in October. FM&T is also widely recognized for its deep commitment to local science, math, and technological education.

"For nearly five decades, AlliedSignal has partnered with our community to make Kansas City the best place to live, work, and play," says Karen Clegg, FM&T president. "We are a vital member of the local business community, and we have the technology, talent, and commitment to carry us through the next half century."

Clockwise from top: AlliedSignal Federal Manufacturing & Technologies' Kansas City facility is part of the Department of Energy's network of national laboratories and production facilities across the nation that have developed unique, sophisticated, and state-of-the-art technologies.

Forces generated through centrifuge testing in FM&T's products test laboratory help determine if components are adequately constructed to withstand stresses caused by linear acceleration.

High-velocity shock and impact tests are performed on components and assemblies using an 18-inch bore, high-thrust actuator, which accelerates test specimen carriages down an 80-foot track system.

ACK IN 1949, IT WAS A RADICAL CONCEPT. UNTIL FORREST L. Cloud and his wife, Bonnie, established Industrial Bearing and Transmission, no one had offered the industrial community a one-stop resource for both bearings and power transmission products. From their modest storefront on Grand Avenue in

downtown Kansas City, the Clouds launched what has become a major distribution powerhouse in the Midwest.

Some 50 years later, their sons Forrest R. and Stephen R. Cloud run the $120 million company, now called IBT, Inc. The Cloud brothers—Forrest as chairman and Stephen as president—direct the operations of nearly 50 branch service centers and more than 400 employees from a 125,000-square-foot facility in Merriam, Kansas. IBT's product offerings have been expanded from bearings and power transmission components to include industrial rubber belting and hose products; industrial drives and controls; and conveying and warehouse equipment and supplies. The Automation Division at IBT offers a host of industrial automation products and engineering services to bring the power of rapidly advancing technology to the American workplace.

The IBT corporate distribution center maintains a massive central inventory of products, while the stock at each of the company's branch service centers is tailored to meet the needs of the industries in its service area.

IBT's radical thinking has also taken the company in another unique direction. "We have always recognized the importance of training our employees and customers," says Forrest Cloud. "We now spend more time, money, and effort in advanced training than anyone in our industry. Today, our fully equipped video department not only produces IBT's corporate and customer training programs, but has grown into one of the most powerful industrial video production resources in the country."

Looking Ahead

Superior products and exemplary customer service have always been the standard at IBT, but planning ahead has always kept the company in the forefront of its field. "We started the company selling bearings and power transmission products, and then rapidly expanded our lines to include a wider selection of the products our customers said they

wanted and needed," says Stephen Cloud. "The net result is that IBT now offers the broadest range of products in the industrial marketplace."

Responding positively to customer needs and employee issues will keep the company moving forward, say the Clouds. IBT typically opens between one and three new branch service centers each year in response to the growing Midwest industrial community. As technology evolves and businesses change and grow, IBT will continue to expand its offering of products and services to help keep its customers strong and competitive. Customers can learn more about IBT by visiting www.ibtinc.com. "Geographic growth and evolution in our product lines is to be expected: We've never stopped growing since we first opened our doors in 1949," says Stephen Cloud.

With an aggressive attitude and a steadfast commitment to quality and service, IBT is poised for continued success into the next century.

Clockwise from top: IBT's product offerings include everything from bearings and power transmission components to industrial rubber belting and hose products; industrial drives and controls; and conveying and warehouse equipment and supplies.

IBT offers the industrial community a one-stop resource for both bearings and power transmission products. Today, the company is a major distribution powerhouse in the Midwest, and can be found on the Internet at www.ibtinc.com.

IBT is led by Chairman of the Board Forrest R. Cloud (left) and President/CEO Stephen R. Cloud.

WING MARION KAUFFMAN FOUNDED MARION LABORATORIES Incorporated in 1950 as a one-man company operating out of the basement of his home in Kansas City. Among his early contributions to pharmacology were the Os-Cal® calcium supplement line; the cerebral vasodilator Pavabid®; and

Nitro-Bid®, a coronary vasodilator. Marion Laboratories merged in 1989 with Merrell Dow Pharmaceuticals to become pharmaceutical giant Marion Merrell Dow. Before Kauffman's death in 1993, his company had developed revolutionary health care products, including the first nonsedating antihistamine and one of the broadest lines of cardiovascular products, which are among the most widely prescribed heart medications in the United States today.

In 1995, Hoechst AG, the German chemical giant, acquired Marion Merrell Dow to form Hoechst Marion Roussel. Hoechst already owned a majority share of Roussel-Uclaf, and in 1997, acquired the remaining interest in the dynamic French pharmaceutical firm. With more than $8 billion in annual sales, the international powerhouse is one of the leading pharmaceutical companies in the world, and a leader in pharmaceutical-based health care.

"Hoechst Marion Roussel doesn't rest on tradition," says Gerald Belle, president of Hoechst Marion Roussel North America. "Each year, we commit more than $1 billion globally to re-

search and development, and we participate in partnerships with other companies to broaden the therapies we offer our customers even further. No matter what else we accomplish, we're dedicated to discovering and delivering prescription products that meet unmet medical needs."

An International Heritage of Pharmacology

Based in Frankfurt, Germany, Hoechst AG entered the pharmaceutical business in 1883 after discovering the first safe and effective analgesic-antifever drug. The former dye-making company followed with other early breakthroughs, includ-

ing the first safe local anesthetic, the first effective treatment for syphilis, and the first insulin produced in Europe.

Roussel-Uclaf was founded by Dr. Gaston Roussel, who introduced an early antianemic product called Hemostyl in 1911. The company was also responsible for the development and manufacture of synthetic hormones and the most widely used antibiotics. Roussel foresaw the importance of an international presence in the pharmaceuticals industry in the early 1920s, and began acquiring subsidiaries throughout Europe.

When the merger with Marion Merrell Dow was completed,

Clockwise from top:
The Hoechst Marion Roussel North American headquarters is located in Marion Business Park in southeast Kansas City.

Pharmaceutical products manufactured and packaged in Kansas City are shipped to patients around the world.

Hoechst Marion Roussel invests $3.5 million a day in research and development in an effort to find new therapies to address unmet medical needs.

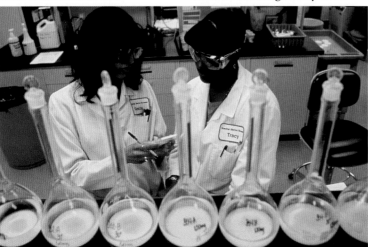

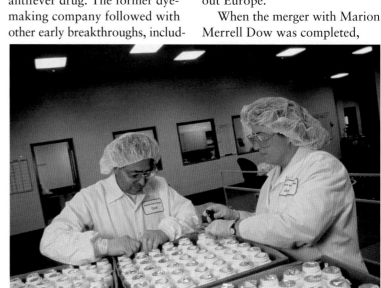

Hoechst Marion Roussel named Kansas City as its North American headquarters. Here, more than 2,200 people are employed at the facility anchoring South Kansas City's Marion Business Park. The 165-acre campus houses drug development, manufacturing, commercial, and administrative operations for the company. The Hoechst Marion Roussel Visitors Center is a popular attraction, offering hands-on exhibits that illustrate the company's dedication to extending and enhancing human life through the discovery, development, manufacture, and sale of prescription drugs.

As health care and competition have evolved, so has Hoechst Marion Roussel's commitment to developing medical solutions. Currently, the company is working on new and better treatments for complicated health issues such as respiratory and cardiovascular conditions, oncology, and infectious diseases. From hypertension to multiple sclerosis to rheumatoid arthritis, Hoechst Marion Roussel has aggressively pursued the world's most important medical quandaries.

In addition to developing medical products, Hoechst produces a variety of printed and electronic materials that assist physicians, health care providers, and patients with up-to-date information and advice. "There is more to patient care than just drug therapy. So, we are committed to going beyond medicine to health," says Belle. "Our patient education programs provide comprehensive but understandable information on a range of medical issues. And our programs directed toward health care professionals help put the latest information into the hands of the people who deliver patient care." Two of the company's best-known publications include *CardiSense®*, an award-winning newsletter that focuses on good health for adults over 55 who suffer from high blood pressure or angina, and *AllerDays Information Network*, a Web site, electronic newsletter, and series of mailings that

help patients learn to live with allergies.

A Prescription for the Community

Affectionately known as "Mr. K," Kauffman was a stalwart of the Kansas City community, generous philanthropist, and owner of the Kansas City Royals major league baseball team. Although Hoechst Marion Roussel is now an international pharmaceutical giant, the company keeps Kauffman's spirit alive on a local level. Just as Mr. K so fondly gave back to his community, so too does the enterprise that carries on his legacy. Through the company's Community Affairs department and the Hoechst Marion Roussel Foundation, funding and leadership are provided for programs such as Science Wise/Whys; Exchange City, a partnership with Junior Achievement Inc. and the Learning Exchange; and Science Pioneers, as well as many other local initiatives.

In addition, Hoechst Marion Roussel employees volunteer in essential areas throughout the community, especially supporting teachers, students, parents, and administrators within the local school districts. Through

the company's relationship with the University of Kansas and the University of Missouri-Kansas City, the Scientific Education Partnership supports biological and biomedical research related to human growth, development, and aging.

"We also support a myriad of educational and civic initiatives, sponsoring everything from museum exhibits to community development projects to charitable activities that benefit the entire community," says Belle. "Our work in pharmaceuticals takes us all over the world, but we've never forgotten the community that's always supported us and our efforts."

Guests to the Hoechst Marion Roussel Visitors Center enjoy a three-dimensional video demonstrating how an antihistamine fights allergies (top).

A clown troupe made up of Hoechst Marion Roussel employees and family members volunteers its time to put smiles on faces all over the Kansas City metro area (bottom).

TS CUSTOMERS LIVE IN EVERY STATE IN THE UNION, FROM THE row houses of Washington, D.C., to the sprawling suburbs of the Southwest. But James B. Nutter & Co. holds firm to its roots in the tree-lined Kansas City neighborhood where the company got its start in 1951. ■ "It is a wonderful and proud feeling to be able to go

Both James B. Nutters—Senior and Junior—take pride in the role their mortgage banking firm plays in building and strengthening Kansas City neighborhoods (left).

The familiar James B. Nutter & Co. logo has marked the road to the American dream for home owners nationwide. Pictured are a few of the 300-plus staff members who make it happen (right).

almost anywhere in the U.S. and encounter people who say, 'I've had my home loan with James B. Nutter & Co. for years,' " noted Jim Nutter Jr. "We derive a lot of satisfaction from having helped three generations of folks achieve the American dream."

Indeed, James B. Nutter & Co. has evolved into one of the largest privately owned and operated mortgage banking firms in the country, with a staff of more than 300 and a portfolio of industry firsts. As it has for almost five decades, the company still specializes in government-backed loans, and is continually looking for new ways to use FHA, VA, and conventional loans to assist the modern home buyer.

"A lot of our customers are middle-income, hardworking people," explains Jim Nutter Sr., who founded the company during the postwar housing boom

that changed the face of American cities. "Our niche is serving old-fashioned working people, and that has been the key to our longevity."

A Heartland Approach to Service

As James B. Nutter & Co. has grown and expanded, it has earned national recognition for willingness to try new and better approaches to customer service. Nutter & Co. was the first company in the United States to close an FHA Senior Citizen Reverse Mortgage, enabling the borrower—a Kansas City woman—to receive a monthly payment backed by the equity in her home.

For many years, the company has supported urban housing programs, and in 1995, James B. Nutter & Co. became only the third lender in the country

to sign a HUD Best Practices Agreement. The agreement formally recognized the company's efforts to promote home ownership among historically underserved borrowers with safe, sound mortgage-lending principles.

"You can't just pick the choicest cherries and expect the trees to grow stronger," says Jim Nutter Sr. "American cities are like orchards; you need to cultivate them and nurture them, because at some point the sprawl will stop and, when that happens, the center must be strong."

Helping America Grow

The senior Nutter was just entering the Kansas City real estate market when the historic post-World War II migration began. In 1951, the generation that fought the war was transforming America by starting families and spreading out

Habitat for Humanity is just one of the civic causes supported by the company (left).

The people who work in this midtown Kansas City neighborhood, the headquarters of James B. Nutter & Co., call it Nutterville (right).

from cities into new suburbs. A young Jim Nutter found himself in a position to assist former schoolmates purchase homes.

Nutter's first job after graduating from the University of Missouri (thanks to the GI bill) had been processing loans and doing construction inspections for a local mortgage company. This gave him a firsthand understanding of the housing business. While building a few small houses of his own on speculation, Nutter was introduced to the new home loan program for veterans.

"I had some VA money, which nobody else in town had at the time," Nutter recalls. "Young couples came to us and, before I knew it, we had sold 25 houses in the first two months."

Nutter's boyhood friend Bob Evans joined the budding firm to help handle the demand. Nutter's mother and father came out of retirement to answer phones and field sales calls. Steady growth

continued through the 1950s and into the 1960s.

Family and Friends

In 1983, Nutter's daughter, Nancy Moore, joined the company. In 1984, son Jim Jr. followed suit. And during this time, the company and the mortgage banking industry were facing new rules, volatile interest rates, and new opportunities.

"We went national in the late 1980s," Jim Jr. remembers. "The ups and downs of the marketplace were dizzying, exhilarating, and stressful. But we worked hard, found a lot of great people to join us, and it has paid off. We're a bigger, stronger, better company than ever before. And we have maintained an incredible level of customer loyalty along the way."

The elder Nutter and Evans scrambled to make 10 or 15 loans a month in the early 1950s. "At our peak in 1993 [during a boom in home refinancing brought on

by plummeting interest rates], we were doing that many every hour," says the younger Nutter.

A Kansas City Company First

Today, James B. Nutter & Co. is still headquartered in midtown Kansas City, in a carefully restored area of historic Westport affectionately referred to as Nutterville. The houses in Nutterville have been refurbished and painted every color of the rainbow ("I believe in a bright outlook," says the senior Nutter). In the summertime, impatiens line the sidewalks, and Nutter customer service associates hurry from building to building.

"I grew up here. This is who we are, this is what we're all about," explains Jim Nutter Sr., a devoted Democrat in a Republican-dominated industry. As a young man, the elder Nutter was influenced and encouraged by the legendary Kansas City-area statesman Harry S. Truman. The Nutter family remains active in civic and community affairs, supporting the Harry S. Truman Library, Children's Mercy Hospital, and Habitat for Humanity, among other causes.

"We've visited other cities and we do business all over the United States," adds Jim Jr., "but Kansas City's our home. Our roots are here, with these people, in these neighborhoods. We've been here since 1951, and 47 years from now, James B. Nutter & Co. will very likely still be here, in the heart of the city."

N LEGAL CIRCLES, THE WORD "PARTNER" OFTEN DESIGNATES ATTORNEYS in a law firm. But at Spencer Fane Britt & Browne, attorneys form partnerships with their clients so they can assist them with more than just the challenge at hand. ■ "One reason people come to us is because we work from their point of view," says Teresa Woody, a partner at Spencer Fane, which has offices in downtown Kansas City, Overland Park, and Washington, D.C. "We're one of the few firms in the area to conduct client audits, asking them 'How did we do?' and 'How can we help you do better?' It's not a marketing strategy, but a way to improve our services by dedicating ourselves to helping our clients do their business better," Woody says.

At Spencer Fane, the attorneys and support staff also work together as partners. "Throughout the firm, we have a sense of teamwork and respect for each other's abilities," says Woody. "That's not just among the attorneys, but from top to bottom."

The Practice

Spencer Fane was formed in 1951 when two smaller firms—one of which was founded before 1900—merged. Since then, growth has been held to a moderate pace, so that the firm could consistently adhere to its core values: integrity, quality, and teamwork. Such a commitment to prudent expansion plans has meant that Spencer Fane can be selective in the attorneys it hires, so that some 30 law schools are now represented. Most of the team are members of Phi Beta Kappa and Order of the Coif, and have received their degrees with honors. In addition, many have held judicial clerkships and governmental legal positions.

Over the years, Spencer Fane has developed a number of key specialty areas, now subdivided into 12 practice areas. Of these specialty groups, litigation is the largest. These attorneys work predominantly in the areas of business litigation, handling everything from antitrust to security litigation to the protection of intellectual property and trade secrets. Attorneys practice before federal and state courts at all levels, and represent clients before a variety of administrative agencies.

Since the early 1960s, Spencer Fane's labor and employment group has developed into a highly respected and well-recognized national practice in both traditional labor law and employment litigation. The firm is national or regional labor counsel for a number of Fortune 500 and New York Stock Exchange companies, whose major industries include everything from retailing to media to heavy construction.

Spencer Fane is recognized in a number of specialized areas. The firm's real estate group represents developers, lending institutions, and individuals involved in everything from financing to leasing to zoning. Spencer Fane's health care group provides services to hospitals and other health care providers, as well as to state and local hospital associations. The firm has the most comprehensive employee benefits group in the area, serving regional clients in this highly technical area of the law.

Spencer Fane has developed a strong client base in new areas, such as intellectual property, telecommunications, and international business. The firm represents a wide range of hardware and software developers, composers, writers, and motion pic-

Spencer Fane Britt & Browne was formed in 1951 when two smaller firms—one of which was founded before 1900—merged. Since then, the firm has consistently adhered to its core values: integrity, quality, and teamwork.

The attorneys at Spencer Fane recognize that their profession will grow more complex as the world does the same—and that great attorneys stay ahead of changes in their field.

ture producers, as well as large cable operators, the nation's largest cellular telephone company, and domestic companies wanting to invest abroad. Spencer Fane has a unique exchange program with corporate counsel and private lawyers in Japan, which allows lawyers from both countries to develop a better understanding of law and business at home and abroad.

One of the fastest-growing areas at Spencer Fane has been in the environmental law group, as exemplified by its representation of Fortune 500 companies in complex environmental matters throughout the country. The firm has served as key defense counsel in two of the nation's largest Superfund hazardous waste cleanup cases.

Spencer Fane's financial services group is experienced in every area of financial service. The firm's lawyers are savvy business advisers and know the

banking industry, as well as insurance, mutual funds, brokerage, securities, thrifts, mortgage banking, and fiduciary and other trust services.

"We can bring a select team of lawyers to a number of specialties, ranging from intellectual property to environmental law to securities litigation to labor issues," says Woody. "People think of Spencer Fane when they have sophisticated issues to address in their business."

Moreover, the attorneys at Spencer Fane recognize that their profession will grow more complex as the world does the same—and that great attorneys stay ahead of changes in their field. "All law will become more specialized because society and business are going in that direction," Woody says. "There are more and more laws to comply with and more regulations coming down the pike. Our goal is to continue a cutting-edge legal

practice in these areas in order to help our clients meet these challenges in their businesses."

When it comes to creating partnerships, Spencer Fane attorneys and staff also include their community, supporting a wide variety of local agencies, services, and charities. The firm has joined with groups like the Boys & Girls Clubs, Young Audiences, and the Don Bosco Center.

"We've always had the theory and practice of being very involved in the community," says Woody. "The firm is not limited in its perspective or dedication to the community. We're people with a broad base of interests, and that's reflected in the services and charities we support. The key component to making Spencer Fane work is the respect and camaraderie people have for each other here—and that emanates into the community in a very unique and special way."

OR NEARLY A HALF CENTURY, ONE KANSAS CITY TELEVISION STATION has dedicated itself to serving the local community. KCTV's stable yet dynamically forward-thinking ownership and management has created quality news and community affairs programming delivered by an experienced on-air staff. Kansas City residents trust

KCTV to offer the most up-to-date news, weather, sports, and community coverage. The station's commitment to reliable and interesting programming has made it a market leader and a regional broadcasting powerhouse.

Each week, Kansas Citians faithfully depend on news features such as "Call For Action." An investigative team led by consumer advocate Stan Cramer, "Call For Action" swoops in on scammers and con artists. Airing often-fascinating video footage each day on KCTV newscasts, "Call For Action" helps resolve an average of 300 viewer problems each month. Then there are other KCTV special news elements, such as Betty Sexton's "Crimestoppers" and Anne Peterson's "Family Health," as well as popular news anchors like Tracy Townsend, Gary Amble, William Jackson, and Wendall Anschutz, who has been with

KCTV for more than 30 years. All contribute to KCTV's strong image in the market as a news and community affairs leader.

"We've set high standards," says John Rose, vice president and general manager at Channel 5. "The consistency of our reporters and of everyone in the newsroom has really gone a long way toward establishing our credibility and our outstanding reputation."

Sending Strong Signals

CBS affiliate KCTV began broadcasting in 1953 from studios at 31st Street and Grand Avenue, just south of downtown Kansas City. Then known as KCMO-TV, the station erected its 1,000-foot tower there and it remains in use today despite Channel 5's studio relocation in 1978. In fact, the Kansas City landmark, illuminated each night, remains one of the tallest self-supported structures in the world.

Channel 5 continues to operate from studios in Fairway, just across the state line from the Country Club Plaza. When the station's owner, Meredith Corporation, sold its Kansas City radio stations KCMO-AM and KCEZ-FM, KCMO-TV's call letters were changed in 1984 to KCTV.

"Throughout the years, our goal has been to offer high-quality news, information, and entertainment," says Rose, "while providing customer service to both our advertisers and our audience."

Cutting-Edge Technology

Since its earliest days, KCTV has been a proven leader in new technology. In 1976, for example, the station became the first in Kansas City—and one of the first television stations in country—to eliminate film in favor of all-tape news gathering.

KCTV's primary anchor team consists of (from left) meteorologist Gary Amble, Tracy Townsend, Wendall Anschutz, and sportscaster William Jackson.

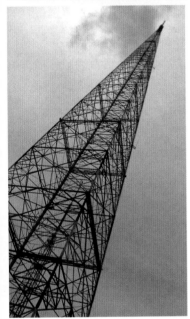

In 1982, Channel 5 installed a computerized newsroom that enabled it to become the first commercial television station in the country to offer closed captioning of local newscasts for hearing-impaired viewers.

Two years later, KCTV became the second television station in the nation to install a remote-controlled camera on its transmitting tower. That move launched a CityCam Network that now includes live city views from 12 sites. In 1993, KCTV established a Neighborhood Weather Network that allows station meteorologists to continuously monitor current and changing weather conditions at some 25 sites throughout the station's viewing area.

Weather technology remains a priority for KCTV. Its Web site (http://www.kctv.com) includes photos from the CityCam

Network, as well as constant neighborhood weather reports and links to other weather-related information from local to national to global sites. The Web site also includes news, anchor interviews, and programming information. In early 1998, the station installed a new Doppler radar system that is significantly more powerful than any other in use at this time. KCTV enhanced this acquisition by making the radar available to emergency management agencies in major surrounding counties.

"We now have 250,000 watts of power and street-level mapping that gets us down to less than a square mile," says Rose. "We're able to provide truly live reports of severe weather conditions as they happen."

Strong Network Affiliation

Part of KCTV's solid image in the community comes from its affiliation with CBS. Award-winning shows such as *60 Minutes*, *Chicago Hope*, and *Touched by an Angel* have given KCTV a loyal audience that tunes in on a frequent and regular basis. Syndicated shows such as *Wheel of Fortune* and *Jeopardy!* also attract an enormous following.

But KCTV's connection to the community comes with shows that hit close to home, too. In early 1998, CBS bid for—and was awarded—the rights to broadcast American Football Conference (AFC) games for the National Football League, which includes most Kansas City Chiefs games. This means that most Sundays between late August and early January, Kansas Citians will be turning their dials to KCTV to watch the Chiefs battle other NFL teams.

"We're happy we will be able to provide Chiefs' fans with coverage of their favorite team," says Rose. "Throughout the years, we've established our commitment to Kansas City through programs like 'PhoneFriend,' 'Crimestoppers,' and 'Call For Action.' Being able to broadcast AFC games will allow us to give our friends, neighbors, and customers even more in the way of high-quality news and entertainment."

From top:
Anne Peterson and Wendall Anschutz prepare for their 5 p.m. newscast. First paired in 1979, they are believed to be the nation's longest-running anchor team.

Lighted at night, the landmark **KCTV tower** can be seen from 30 miles away.

Meteorologist Katie Horner delivers a weather forecast using **Kansas City's most powerful Doppler radar system.**

WHEN COMPANIES NEED TEMPORARY HELP, THEY OFTEN turn to Manpower, Inc., the world's largest provider of staffing services. In Kansas City, hundreds of leading businesses call on Manpower for skilled workers to help them meet production peaks, staff

special projects, and launch new products.

In the Kansas City area, seven Manpower offices provide companies with staffing services that *Fortune* magazine has called "one of the world's best products and services." Manpower has also appeared on *Fortune*'s list of America's Most Admired Companies, and has been ranked first on the magazine's list of most admired staffing firms.

The company, which opened its first Kansas City office in 1953, was founded in 1948 in Milwaukee. Manpower networks across the country provide businesses with workers who have production, office, customer service, technical, and professional skills. Whether a business needs workers for assembling small parts, staffing a call center, supplying quality control in a laboratory, or administering a computer network, Manpower can provide people with the right skills and abilities.

"Kansas City is a great place for us to do business because the workforce here is so stable," says Bill Yarberry, general manager of Manpower's Kansas City op-

Founded in 1948 in Milwaukee, Manpower networks across the country provide businesses with workers who have production, office, customer service, technical, and professional skills.

erations. "We are very confident about the quality of the employees we send out to perform work at customer sites."

Tools of the Trade

Through the years, Manpower has developed a unique set of tools to deliver a quality product to its customers. In 1994, the company's headquarters first attained its ISO 9000 rating, the international standard for service quality. "When the Kansas City offices registered in 1997, we had to smile at some of the questions asked by the

auditors who reviewed our quality system," says Yarberry. "For example, there were questions about how we store, handle, and package our products. Obviously, the creators of the standard thought of 'products' as inanimate objects, not living, breathing individuals.

"However, once we began to think of our service as a product, we realized that our employees do go through a quality control process, just as manufactured goods do," continues Yarberry. "The people who come to us for employment opportunities are our raw materials. We use interviews and skills assessments to evaluate their abilities. We provide training that enhances their value by equipping them with new skills. Then, we match them to the work opportunities that can best use their unique combinations of skills and interests."

The training Manpower offers is one of the major reasons why people work for the company and why businesses seek its services. Manpower has become one of the world's largest corporate training organizations, having prepared more than 2 million workers worldwide in information technology, quality

Whether a business needs workers for assembling small parts, staffing a call center, supplying quality control in a laboratory, or administering a computer network, Manpower can provide people with the right skills and abilities.

service, and office computing skills.

Training for information technology (IT) professionals has been the newest addition to Manpower's spectrum of training services. In fact, the IT area is the fastest-growing part of Manpower's technical business. The need for qualified IT professionals, from application developers to systems implementation specialists, is booming. To meet the demand, the company developed TechTrack, an ever growing library of more than 400 courses in the latest networking and Internet technologies, including Novell NetWare, Windows NT, SAP, and many others.

Like all of Manpower's training programs, TechTrack is available to the company's employees free of charge and is accessible to the company's customers, as well, for use in training their own employees. In fact, 90 percent of Fortune 100 companies have received training for their permanent employees from Manpower. "Delivering corporate training services is another way we can ensure that our customers have the skilled workers they need," says Yarberry.

But technical skills alone don't make staffers successful on the job. "Workers need both technical skills and the skills to do their jobs in a way that pleases customers and exceeds expectations," says Yarberry. "Employers want workers who have what we call 'employability' skills: taking initiative, problem solving, asking questions, treating co-workers like customers, and going the extra mile to ensure customer satisfaction."

Manpower's training program for employability skills, called Putting Quality to Work, is designed to teach quality service skills to workers ranging from production employees to software engineers. Trainees learn phone skills, listening skills, and other basics of providing quality service to customers and coworkers.

Manpower also continues to expand its vast library of Skillware training for office computing skills. Skillware has equipped workers worldwide with the skills to use word processing, spreadsheet, database, desktop publishing, and presentation graphics software. For personnel going into clean manufacturing environments, such as food and chemical processing, Manpower provides Good Manufacturing Practices training. And to help alleviate the shortage of skilled soldering technicians, Manpower has developed training in soldering techniques.

"The goal of our training effort has always been to keep one step ahead of employers' skill needs," says Yarberry. "We're committed to anticipating those needs and developing training for the skills employers and workers will need most."

The company also develops new services to meet businesses' needs. Manpower's original role as a provider of short-term workers has evolved into a more sophisticated human resources function. In response to customer demand for a broader, more comprehensive set of services, Manpower often acts as an extension of a customer's human resources and training department.

Looking toward the future, Yarberry foresees a continued effort to provide the staffing and training services that Manpower customers need in order to stay competitive in their own industries. "We'll always be here to provide Kansas City businesses with their most essential resource: a well-trained, motivated workforce."

Manpower's Skillware equips workers worldwide with the skills to use word processing, spreadsheet, database, desktop publishing, and presentation graphics software.

Manpower provides Good Manufacturing Practices training for personnel needed for clean manufacturing environments, such as food and chemical processing.

H&R BLOCK, INC.

N 1946, AS RECENT BUSINESS-SCHOOL GRADUATES, BROTHERS HENRY and Richard Bloch launched United Business Company in Kansas City to offer bookkeeping, management, and collection services for small companies. With increasing frequency, however, clients asked the Blochs to help them prepare their taxes. In fact, tax preparation was

in such demand that the two men were soon working around the clock.

In January 1955, realizing the enormous consumer need for professional tax assistance, the Blochs inaugurated their new tax return preparation company as H&R Block, Inc., changing their surname's spelling to make pronunciation of their company name clearer. Their first season was so promising that Henry and Richard opened seven offices in New York during the next year alone. By 1960, the company had blanketed the Midwest, and by 1969, it had more than 3,000 offices throughout the United States, Canada, and Puerto Rico.

"We just filled a niche," says Henry Bloch, now chairman of the board. "When we started,

the company fulfilled an unmet need to help people prepare their taxes. Back then, wealthier people went to accountants, but others had few places to turn to. At the same time, taxes were becoming more complicated and costly; in other words, calculating taxes accurately was more important to people because of the effect on their income."

Finding a Need

H&R Block has been a classic example of finding a need and filling it. Now, with more than 10,000 offices in the United States, Canada, Australia, and the United Kingdom, the company has a sure hold on its market. In 1998, the company served 18.2 million tax customers and handled 51 percent of all electronic returns

filed with the Internal Revenue Service.

Astonishingly, Block has no large-scale competition. When the company entered the market in 1955, tax returns were prepared by accountants or taxpayers themselves. That fact still holds true today. "Our biggest competitor is the person who does his or her own taxes," says Henry Bloch. "But we've always tried to give people more than they expected, and because we've got offices nearly everywhere, we've made it easy to come back year after year."

One way Block has dominated the market has been through its educational system. In the early days, the Bloch brothers realized they needed a reliable source of trained tax preparers, so they created the H&R Block Income

Set near the site of H&R Block's original location, the company's newly constructed, 93,000-square-foot building was linked with a 44,000-square-foot structure that Block completed in 1982. The pair of buildings, joined by their contemporary architecture and amenities, overlook the Country Club Plaza to the west.

Tax Schools. By 1996, approximately 100,000 people were enrolled in one of the company's numerous tax courses. In addition to the basic course, which involves 66 hours of classroom instruction, the company offers four advanced sections covering individual, partnership, corporation, and fiduciary returns. Although many new students enroll each year, a large number of Block employees take the advanced courses to stay current with changes in tax legislation and rulings.

Expansion Plans

In 1986, H&R Block was one of the first companies to offer electronic tax return filing to its clients. Known as Rapid Refund, electronic filing significantly reduces the amount of time required for taxpayers to receive their refunds. During Rapid Refund's first year, Block filed 22,000 returns electronically from two test areas: Cincinnati and Phoenix. A decade later,

the company filed more than 6 million returns electronically in the United States alone.

Block's personal tax preparation software, Kiplinger TaxCut®, has gained kudos from critics and users alike. In 1998, TaxCut more than tripled its stake in the market and now claims a market share in excess of 30 percent. Block publishes information about its services—as well as quarterly shareholder information—on its Web site at www.hrblock.com. In addition, Block is moving into other financial areas, such as financial planning, insurance, and home mortgages. The company purchased Option One Mortgage Corporation, which boasts a network of more than 5,000 mortgage brokers in 46 states. In all cases, H&R Block has stuck by the maxim that has made its tax preparation services so popular: Always be dependable and affordable.

H&R Block is committed to Kansas City, and demonstrated that commitment in 1996 with

the debut of its new world headquarters. Set near the site of Block's original location, the newly constructed, 93,000-square-foot building was linked with a 44,000-square-foot structure that Block completed in 1982. The pair of buildings, joined by their contemporary architecture and amenities, overlook the Country Club Plaza to the west. The company supports the community in other ways also: H&R Block, together with the H&R Block Foundation, gave more than $2.2 million in charitable donations in 1997, primarily to organizations in Kansas City.

"Regardless of what we undertake, we've always been a company dedicated to growth, exceeding customer expectations, and improving shareholder value," says Henry Bloch. "We also believe that it's important to give back to the community that has supported us all these years. We want to be reliable to everyone who knows and works with us."

From its Kansas City headquarters, H&R Block stands firm by the maxim that has made its tax preparation services so popular: Always be dependable and affordable.

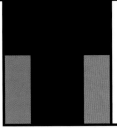

WELVE THOUSAND PHONE CALLS ANSWERED, 75,000 TRANS-actions processed, 12,000 letters opened and scanned, and another 115,000 letters mailed are all in a day's work for American Century Investments' 2,500 employees. Based in two Country Club Plaza towers and four other Kansas City locations, the company serves

nearly 2 million shareholders who have entrusted more than $75 billion to American Century.

Back in 1958, this daily scene would have been unimaginable to a sales representative named James E. Stowers, who launched his first two fledgling mutual funds with a $10,000 personal stake. Stowers' venture was hardly an overnight sensation, spending years in an unobtrusive office beneath a bank in Kansas City's Country Club Plaza. "Some days were pretty bleak," admits Lin Lundgaard, a member of the American Century board of directors. "In fact, the first 15 to 18 years were tough."

Formula for Success

American Century has since grown into one of the country's largest no-load fund complexes, with major offices in Kansas City; Denver; and Mountain View, California.

The company's two flagship growth funds—Growth Investors and Select Investors—are among the industry's top funds for long-term performance, and they now lead a successful family of nearly 70 funds. Almost 2 million investors—along with a who's who of U.S. corporations, institutions, universities, and hospitals—look to 4500 Main Street in Kansas City for investment leadership.

"Even though we've earned recognition on Wall Street, we plan to stay right here on Main Street," Stowers says. "While many mutual fund companies are based on the East Coast, we've always felt we can do our job as well, if not better, right here in our hometown."

Growth Connections

In 1995, Twentieth Century and the Benham Group—a mutual fund company known

for fixed-income and money market funds—joined forces to offer a full spectrum of funds. In 1997, the company changed its name to American Century, yet retained the Twentieth Century and Benham monikers. Twentieth Century offers growth, aggressive growth, and international funds; Benham consists of corporate and government bond funds, tax-free funds, and money markets; and American Century offers income and growth, balanced, and specialty funds.

American Century's next major step came in January 1998 when one of the world's leading financial institutions, J.P. Morgan & Co. Incorporated, purchased a 45 percent economic interest in American Century. The initial focus of the business partnership is to market full-service capabilities to corporate sponsors of defined contribution plans.

An Industry Pacesetter

In an industry that boasts more funds than the number of stocks on the New York and American stock exchanges combined, American Century stands out for more than investment results. In the early 1970s, Stowers unveiled a common-stock investment philosophy that is still synonymous with his name. The best way to make money for his investors, he decided, was to follow the axiom "money follows earnings"—investors gravitate to strong, growing companies.

The firm has long been a pacesetter in high technology, having virtually pioneered the use of computers in investment management more than 20 years ago. After spending long hours on the phone each day searching for growth companies, Stowers bought an IBM computer and

American Century's main office is located at 4500 Main Street near the Country Club Plaza.

a self-help programming book, hoping to create a system that would flag fast-growing companies. His programs still form the cornerstone of a system used by American Century's investment teams to monitor the progress of more than 11,000 companies around the world.

The company's technological farsightedness extends past investment management, including state-of-the-art, companywide computer workstations and a high-speed, automated mailing center. American Century has also demonstrated its commitment to technological innovation in its pioneering of digital imaging. More than 15,000 documents are scanned daily into the company's computer system, enabling account service representatives, who execute more than 700,000 transactions per month, to work from electronic records. The system also allows 400 customer service representatives to provide prompt answers for the thousands of shareholders who call each day.

Building Wealth

Stowers has never forgotten that he, too, started out as a small investor. As an aid to thousands of first-time investors, he shared the secrets of successful mutual fund investing in his 1992 book, *Yes, You Can . . . Achieve Financial Independence*.

In addition, American Century remains a fund complex that strives to meet the needs of a wide range of investors. "We want to be our investors' primary financial institution, and we have the investment options and services we need to fulfill that role," says James E. Stowers III, the founder's son and American Century's CEO.

American Century's investment success has paid dividends for Kansas City as well. American Century has long supported civic activities in Kansas City and continues to invest in the future of the metropolitan area. The company sponsors the annual Plaza Lighting Ceremony and the American Century Duck

Derby—both family-oriented events for the people of Kansas City.

As one of Kansas City's top employers, American Century is widely viewed as a progressive, enthusiastic, people-oriented company, having won an Employer of the Year Award presented by the Kansas City chapter of the Personnel Management Association in 1989 and again in 1995 for the quality of its training and benefits programs. "I've always wanted to help people improve their financial positions and,

more important, their lives," says the elder Stowers. "I've always believed that if I help people become successful, they, in turn, will help me become successful.

"We're known as a company that searches for the best people," Stowers continues. "It might be more accurate to say that we seek people who are talented, resourceful, and dedicated, and then provide an environment where they can excel. We're fortunate—the best people are right here in Kansas City."

James E. Stowers Jr. (right) founded American Century Investments in 1958 with two mutual funds based on a $10,000 personal stake. Today, he serves as company chairman. James E. Stowers III is the chief executive officer.

American Century virtually pioneered the use of computers in investment management more than 20 years ago.

N THE 1950S, COMMUNITY LEADERS AND RESIDENTS TOOK DECISIVE action to bring a health care facility to the Northland. By March 1958, five years after the North Kansas City Chamber of Commerce kicked off a fund-raising campaign with a two-day chili affair, North Kansas City Hospital (NKCH) treated its first patient. Today, the

city-owned hospital offers more than 550 physicians representing 45 medical specialties. With more than 1,900 employees, NKCH is one of the Northland's largest employers and contributors to the local economy.

Conveniently located near Interstate 35 and Armour Road East, NKCH strives to meet the health care needs of residents in Northwest Missouri's 19 counties, including Clay, Platte, and Ray counties. A modern, acute care facility, the hospital offers a broad range of sophisticated services, including a Level II trauma center, maternity unit, neonatal intensive care, open-heart surgery, radiation therapy, chemotherapy, rehabilitation services, skilled nursing, home health, dialysis, Workers' Rehab Center, behavioral health, and community education classes. Additionally, NKCH participates in a joint venture to own and operate Creekwood Surgery Center, an outpatient surgery facility. The hospital also works with Grand

North Kansas City Hospital is one of the area's most modern acute care facilities.

River Health System to lease and manage Hedrick Medical Center and its medical office building in Chillicothe, Missouri.

Building for the Future

During the past 40 years, NKCH has grown with the community. The original 80-bed facility has expanded into a 350-bed hospital situated on a 72-acre campus with three other buildings. Medical Plaza North and Professional Building North

house physician offices, and Health Center North accommodates a behavioral health unit and other services.

The hospital continues to grow to keep up with rising health care needs. In fall 1997, NKCH broke ground on a six-story, 290,000-square-foot tower addition—at a cost of $94.8 million. The facility, scheduled for completion in 2000, is designed for outpatient services such as cardiac treatment, outpatient imaging, a gastrointestinal lab, physical and occupational therapy, speech pathology, and ambulatory surgery. Physician offices will be located on two of the floors, and a new, 560-car parking garage will be constructed near the tower.

"Outpatient services have grown phenomenally during the past several years, and our projections indicate that they will continue to grow," says Interim President Nettie Agnew. "Our current facility is bursting at the seams, and we simply need more space to provide patients with the level of care they need."

Cardiac Care

A prime focus of NKCH is treating people with heart disease and other cardiac problems. The hospital is home

The hospital's Home Health Services program enables area residents to receive expert care in the comfort of their own home, where the surroundings are familiar and family members can provide support.

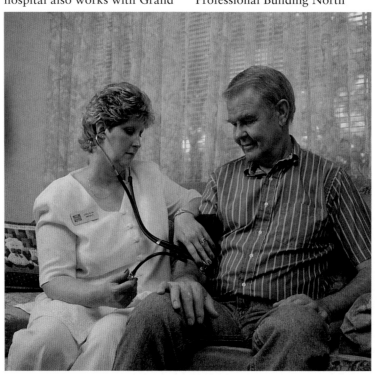

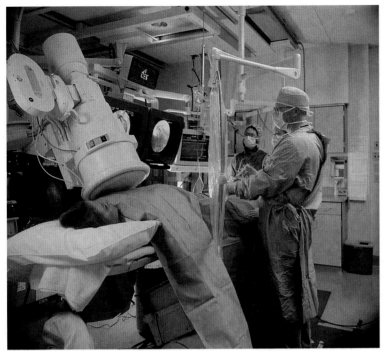

to the Chest Pain Center, Kansas City's first such facility devoted to treating chest pain on an emergency basis. Through state-of-the-art diagnostic testing, the hospital staff can easily determine whether pain is caused by a heart attack or other disorder.

NKCH is one of fewer than 100 hospitals nationwide to offer minimally invasive direct coronary artery bypass (MIDCAB) grafting. During the MIDCAB procedure, a surgeon uses a five-inch incision to perform open-heart surgery instead of the traditional method of dividing the breastbone to reach the heart. Recovery time is reduced to weeks instead of months, and a heart-lung machine is not required during surgery. This keyhole procedure also can be used on some patients to repair an atrial septal defect.

In addition, the hospital offers directional coronary atherectomy, a nonsurgical method for treating coronary artery disease. This procedure involves the use of a specially equipped catheter inserted into the blocked artery to remove plaque and open the impeded vessel.

Echocardiography, a type of ultrasound, is used at NKCH to better diagnose heart blockages and ensure more accurate results. Open-heart surgery, critical care rooms with the latest in monitoring emergency equipment, and a three-phase cardiac rehabilitation program are also a regular part of the hospital's cardiac care program.

Oncology

According to Agnew, a key to NKCH's success is the high quality of its employees, such as the caring professionals who make up the oncology staff. Offering both inpatient and outpatient care for cancer, the team also helps administer chemotherapy and radiation. Staff members educate patients and families, encouraging them to actively participate in care and treatment.

NKCH is the first hospital in Kansas City, and one of only a few in Missouri, to offer a revolutionary outpatient treatment for prostate cancer called radioactive seed implant. "A urologist implants radioactive seeds into the prostate gland," Agnew explains. "The seeds give off low-energy X rays, which kill the cancer but do not affect the rest of the body."

A multidisciplinary team meets weekly to discuss patients' care plans, ensuring that they receive individualized treatment. The team members include a social worker, dietitian, pharmacist, radiation therapy nurse, respiratory therapist, occupational therapist, physical therapist, chaplain, hospice representative, and nursing staff.

Members of the community can take advantage of the hospital's cancer support groups, cancer screenings, and free education classes. Women who participate in the free breast cancer awareness class receive a coupon for a reduced-fee mammogram.

Serving the Community

Vision and leadership from area residents made NKCH a reality in 1958. Now, the hospital is an active participant in the community through school partnerships, service projects, wellness programs, and education classes. "The focus of health care is to try to keep people out of the hospital," says Agnew. "We continue to develop outreach programs and work with community groups, providers, and insurance carriers to keep people healthy."

Through its dedicated staff and service, and its community outreach programs, North Kansas City Hospital is working to ensure a healthier future for Kansas City.

The NKCH Maternity Care Unit is an all-inclusive facility that features labor, delivery, recovery, and postpartum rooms where all the birthing events happen (above).

The Cardiac Care Unit at NKCH has become a leader in providing patients and their families with the most advanced technology and treatment methods available (left).

CELEBRATING GREATER KANSAS CITY

1959 - 1998

1964	VARIFORM, INC.	1987	APPLEBEE'S INTERNATIONAL
1966	TranSystems Corporation	1987	Kansas City Marriott Downtown
1968	ASAI Architecture	1987	Peripheral Vision Infosystems, Inc.
1968	Entercom		
1969	ITRAVEL	1988	Bioff Singer and Finucane
1971	La Petite Academy	1988	Turner Construction Company
1972	LabOne, Inc.		
1972	Pfizer Animal Health Group	1989	Advantage Health Systems
1972	Polsinelli, White, Vardeman & Shalton, P.C.	1989	Andersen Consulting
1973	Devine deFlon Yaeger Architects, Inc.	1989	Executive Teleconferencing Services
1973	Worlds of Fun and Oceans of Fun	1989	Historic Suites of America
1974	Gould Evans Goodman Associates	1990	Accommodations by Apple
1974	Ingram's Magazine	1990	CCP
1975	Corporate Woods	1990	ESOT Resources, Inc.
1975	Fortis Benefits Insurance Company	1990	Spencer Reed Group
1976	Kansas City Area Development Council	1991	Eveans, Bash, Magrino & Klein, Inc.
1978	Greater Kansas City Community Foundation	1992	Best Computer Consultants, Inc.
1978	Stewart Title of Kansas City	1993	CyDex, Inc.
1979	Clinical Reference Laboratory	1993	GST Steel Company
1980	Haldex Brake Products Corp.	1994	Gateway
1981	Right Management Consultants	1994	Realty Executives/ Metro One
1982	Kansas City Business Journal	1994	Transamerica Life Companies
1983	IKON Technology Services Kansas City	1995	Fort Dodge Animal Health
1985	Walton Construction Company Inc.	1997	Doubletree Hotel Kansas City

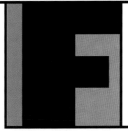

OR MANY HOME OWNERS, VINYL SIDING HAS BECOME THE COVERing of choice for home building and renovating. Thanks to the efforts of Variform, Inc.—one of the fastest-growing vinyl siding companies in North America—product improvements have created a market that is now clamoring for the ease, durability,

and good looks of high-quality siding.

Based in Kearney, Missouri, just north of Kansas City, Variform is one of the largest manufacturers of vinyl siding, soffit, skirting,

Variform is one of the largest manufacturers of vinyl siding, soffit, skirting, and accessories for residential and commercial applications. The company has expanded into international markets, added several new facilities, and pioneered the creation of siding that resembles the natural appearance of wood.

and accessories for residential and commercial applications. During more than three decades of business, Variform has expanded into international markets, added several new facilities, and pioneered the creation of siding that resembles the natural appearance of wood. Such activity resulted in double-digit growth during every year in the decade between 1987 and 1997.

"We're the largest single supplier to the retail segment of the industry," says Lee Meyer, Variform's president. "Siding has experienced a renaissance over the past 20 years as home owners have discovered how durable and easy it is to maintain. People are also busier and simply don't have the time or inclination to paint their houses every couple of years."

One Word: Plastics

Founder and Chairman of the Board Ralph Ayers established his company in 1964 in a leased, 5,000-square-foot space in North Kansas City. He named the operation Variform because plastic and other incorporated materials can take various forms. Within two years, Ayers had expanded his extruded terminal-block shield product line to include custom profile extrusion and fabricated Plexiglas products in the company's line of see-through display holders. Variform outgrew its location by 1969 and moved to a larger facility.

Two years later, Ayers began producing accessories for other manufacturers of vinyl siding. Eventually, he began making his own siding and accessories, such as corner posts and trim. By 1979, Variform was operating out of seven locations before it finally consolidated into a new building in Kearney. In 1997, Variform spent $750,000 on an expansion that received an award from the Clay County Economic Development Council for contributing to the area's economic growth. "Today, we're a very efficient company that's not burdened by significant overhead," says Meyer.

Bigger and Better

In 1986, Variform became a wholly owned subsidiary of Ply Gem Industries, one of the nation's leading residential construction suppliers. Following the ownership change, Variform established additional manufacturing facilities in West Virginia and Tennessee, and created a strategic alliance with building products giant Georgia-Pacific.

Based in New York, Ply Gem has 11 operating subsidiaries that offer a broad line of high-quality building products. In turn, Ply Gem was acquired by Nortek, Inc.—a Rhode Island-based heating, ventilation, and plumbing concern—in 1997. The association has been beneficial, giving Variform access to additional customers and a broader base of corporate capabilities. International business now accounts for about 1 percent of Variform's annual $200 million in revenues, but the company expects that activity to increase to 20 percent of revenues by 2003. In addition, Variform has begun developing its presence among wholesalers, a market niche the company has left largely untapped.

"The acquisition has been a great experience," says Meyer. "Because of Nortek's capabilities and customers throughout the construction industry, we believe we'll find new synergies and opportunities inside our own parent company."

Solid Foundation

Some of Variform's best moves, however, were initiated long before such far-reaching growth. Customer service, for example, has been a crucial priority at Variform since its earliest days. The company's professional and technical workers are rewarded for thinking like entrepreneurs, and are encouraged to make on-the-spot decisions when it comes to customer satisfaction.

"Our customers rave about our customer-service people because they're always looking out for the customers' interests," says Ken Logue, vice president of sales and marketing. "Every area here, from sales to manufacturing to human resources, constantly makes sure that both our internal and external customers are being served. That attitude has always been present in the company, but in recent years, we've really worked to make this happen through everything we do."

Another backbone of Variform's success has been its product innovations. Once shunned because of its shiny appearance,

Vinyl siding now comes in a variety of sizes, textures, shapes, and colors. Variform has led the way, creating the Timber Oak line to replace stained natural wood siding. The company's Varigrain line resembles painted wood, without the upkeep and deterioration of wood.

vinyl siding now comes in a variety of sizes, textures, shapes, and colors. Variform has been at the leading edge of such progress, creating the Timber Oak line to replace stained natural wood siding. Timber Oak comes in grains ranging from red oak to weathered cedar to cherry wood, its multitoned colors falling into a naturally random pattern. The company's Varigrain line resembles painted wood, "minus, of course, the paint and wood," notes its brochure. Variform

offers sidings that capture ornate Victorian detailing and others that are reminiscent of early New England craftsmanship.

"We've been able to develop products that have the look and feel of wood, retain color, and weather naturally," says Logue. "But what we really offer customers is leisure time. Our vinyl siding is a durable and colorfast product that requires little maintenance. That gives people more time to enjoy what's really important in their lives."

HAT IS THE SHORTEST DISTANCE BETWEEN TWO POINTS? TranSystems Corporation, a national transportation consulting firm headquartered in Kansas City, is sure to know the answer—whether the points connect highways, ports, or railroads. With more than 500

employees and 20 offices, TranSystems helps clients plan, design, build, and manage transportation facilities and infrastructure across the globe. According to Brian Larson, P.E., CEO of the firm, "At every turn, our primary goal is to add value to our clients by converting transportation challenges into economic benefit. To consistently accomplish this, we are students of the business environment in which our clients operate—we listen to their needs and objectives, and we commit to them a solution-oriented team with profound industry experience."

The firm began its roots in Kansas City in 1966 as JBM Engineers and Planners, and originally concentrated on highway, bridge, and municipality work. A merger in 1995 with Boyd Brown Stude & Cambern and Vickerman•Zachary•Miller combined the talents of three

TranSystems Corporation serves air shippers and airport authorities. Clients in this market sector include U.S. commercial airports and developers of airport facilities, such as the Trans World Airlines Overhaul and Maintenance Facility at the Kansas City International Airport.

highly respected companies to bring together a total of 80 years of collective transportation experience. The merger also expanded the capabilities of the firm to new markets that include rail, maritime, energy, air, warehousing, trucking, and transit.

By carving out an engineering and design niche in the transportation industry, TranSystems has created an entire company dedicated to the needs of moving people and freight in the most efficient manner.

"One of the main reasons that clients come to us is because we focus on the transportation industry," says Ed Mulcahy, P.E., TranSystems principal and Midwest regional vice president. "Transportation is a broad sector with many unique challenges to each service facet, and we serve them all. We have the ability to deliver service capabilities for a project from start to finish and

therefore can take a project from conceptualization to completion."

Market Specialization

Although the company merged under the TranSystems name in 1995, the three firms had been affiliated for three decades. During that time, the groups had experienced particular success in eight market sectors, a specialization that TranSystems continues as a single entity.

Among the market sectors served by the company are railroad companies that provide both passenger and freight transportation. TranSystems specializes in survey, design, and construction-related services for Class I railroads, short-line railroads, off-dock port facilities, and passenger rail. A recent project in Kansas City involved the Kansas City Terminal Flyover. This mainline "flyover" bridge for the third-busiest railroad intersection in the United States alleviates lengthy delays for the Burlington Northern Santa Fe, Union Pacific, and Kansas City Southern railroads. With rail capacity expected to increase substantially over the next several years, this project will result in significant improvements to rail operations in the Midwest.

TranSystems enjoys a close working relationship with many state departments of transportation, toll authorities, and municipalities. The company has successfully completed the planning, design, and construction of major highways, roads, bridges, and other transportation infrastructure facilities. This sector represents the largest portion of work for the company, which includes the design of roads, utilities, storm sewers, traffic signals, and street lighting, as well as the completion of feasibility

TREY CAMBERN

TREY CAMBERN

TREY CAMBERN

and traffic impact studies and the performance of construction management studies. In addition, TranSystems provides assistance to municipalities in acquiring transportation funding for projects.

Another group served by the company consists of air shippers and airport authorities. Clients in this market sector include U.S. commercial airports and developers of airport facilities, sponsored by both the public and the private sectors.

In addition, many trucking companies throughout the United States rely on the highway system to transport commodities, materials, and merchandise—such as TranSystems' work on the NYK Terminals, a 130-acre facility in Los Angeles. TranSystems also serves retail/wholesale/developer companies that construct warehouse and distribution centers, and need a reliable means to move their goods from point to point.

Other industries that rely on TranSystems include marine shippers and port authorities, from public and private ports to marine terminals and shipping lines; and energy and communications companies, from energy producers and distributors to those that deal in the telecommunications industry. Divisions of the federal government also depend on Tran-Systems, including the Department of Defense, the National Park Service, the Army Corps of Engineers, and the Federal Highway Administration. Combined, TranSystems helps a wide variety

of companies and agencies to cover the continent with transportation options.

Although nearly half of its annual revenues come from its Midwest region, TranSystems' Texas, Rocky Mountain, Pacific, Great Lakes, and Southeast regions have grown substantially. In addition, TranSystems has completed projects in Europe, Asia, Australia, and South America.

"We see tremendous growth opportunities, both within the United States and throughout the world," says Ted Cambern, principal of TranSystems. "We expect to be an integral part of transportation in the 21st century, and international business is certainly an area that we will pursue."

TranSystems Corporation has earned a solid reputation in the consulting business, due largely to its dedication to quality and thorough understanding of its clients' needs. With the growth that TranSystems has experienced in the past few years, it would be easy to overlook the main reason

for its continued achievements— its people. TranSystems works extremely hard to ensure that its employees find their work challenging and personally fulfilling. The company has a formalized training program for all of its project managers, encourages employees to pursue education through tuition reimbursement programs, provides a weekly communication forum through its internal newsletter, and advocates community activity through participating in charitable events such as Harvesters, United Way, and Christmas in October.

Overall growth is on the horizon at TranSystems, a unique company with architectural and engineering solutions for those on the move. Changes in transportation mean there are additional opportunities to provide movement solutions for people and goods. TranSystems gives quality service in a timely manner at a competitive price, which will continue to be the key to the company's success.

Clockwise from top left: TranSystems enjoys a close working relationship with many state departments of transportation, toll authorities, and municipalities.

Among the market sectors served by TranSystems are railroad companies that provide both passenger and freight transportation.

With the increasing popularity of hiking and biking trails, TranSystems has become sensitive to the unique requirements of integrating these routes into the natural environment.

TranSystems also provides full-service civil and structural engineering capabilities for a variety of building projects.

T WAS EARLY 1997, AND KANSAS CITY WAS AT THE DAWN OF A NEW radio age. That was the year Philadelphia-based Entercom entered the local market by acquiring four radio stations: KCMO-AM, KCMO-FM, KLTH-FM, and KMBZ-AM. A few months later, the company added two more local stations, WDAF-AM and KUDL-FM.

With these and other acquisitions made across the country, Entercom quickly became the nation's largest privately held company devoted exclusively to radio broadcasting. Entercom, founded in 1968, today owns or operates 38 stations in eight markets, has more than 1,000 employees, and enjoys more than $100 million in revenues annually.

Such growth is especially impressive in light of the current competitive conditions in radio broadcasting. In Kansas City alone, for example, stations have changed hands multiple times during the past several years. But Entercom's presence in the market has signaled a new era for the company's portfolio of stations, which feature innovative programming and have achieved improved profitability.

"We've got six stations now and have made significant moves to reduce program overlapping," says Bob Zuroweste, Entercom Radio Center market manager and general manager for KCMO-FM Oldies 95, KCMO-AM TalkRadio 710, KMBZ-AM

KCMO-FM Oldies 95 is one of six stations owned and operated in the Kansas City market by Entercom.

Newsradio 980, and 99.7KY Kansas City's Home of Rock-N-Roll (formerly KLTH). "We still have the personalities and a strong focus on music direction, but we've really tried to create niches that will do their best within their market segments."

Broadcast News

One of the most significant changes made by Entercom Kansas City involved the revival of Kansas City's classic rock and roll station, KYYS. In September 1997, KY102 ceased broadcasting. Entercom decided to take up the rock mantle, changing the identity of KLTH (then a light rock format) to the new 99.7KY and picking up the abandoned KYYS call letters. Studies have shown that people interested in 1970s through 1990s classic rock comprise some 29 percent of the total metropolitan area listenership. In addition to music, 99.7KY now features Max, Tanna & Moffitt in the mornings and great rock and roll all day long.

In addition, Entercom agreed to exchange the transmission fa-

cilities of KCMO-AM TalkRadio for the transmission facilities of WHB-AM. Both Kansas City stations retained their respective programming formats and call letters, while swapping broadcast frequencies. KCMO-AM now broadcasts at 710 kHz and features the legendary *Mike Murphy Show* on weekdays from 9 a.m. to noon, as well as programs hosted by Mike Reagan, Brian Wilson, and Dr. Laura Schlessinger, among others.

"Even with our two talk-oriented stations, we've avoided duplication in that each attracts a different audience," says Zuroweste. "KMBZ is focused more on the male listener, while KCMO is more female-based in its programming. All our stations target the 25-year-old-and-over crowd, so we're basically adult-oriented."

All About Programming

It's easy to see why Zuroweste believes that KMBZ attracts a predominantly male audience. With KMBZ Sports Play-By-Play, listeners can tune in to the Kan-

sas City Royals, college football and basketball games, and *Monday Night Football*. In addition, the Newsradio 980 format features *Sportsline* with Don Fortune, *Sportsnite* with Dan Clinkscale, and *Sports Byline USA* with Ron Bar and David Brody. Moreover, *Rush Limbaugh*; Toby Tobin's *Over the Back Fence* home advice show; and *Talk Back*, which pits liberal against conservative, all have loyal followings.

Among its mix of radio stations, Entercom also owns WDAF-AM 61 Country. This popular station has played country-western music to faithful Kansas City listeners for more than two decades, using its tag line, "We were country when country wasn't cool." In addition to tunes by the likes of Clint Black, Trisha Yearwood, and Brooks & Dunn, WDAF offers personalities ranging from David Lawrence in the morning to Dan Roberts in the afternoon slot.

Over at KCMO-FM Oldies 95, Entercom runs the only station in Kansas City that plays Top 40 music from the late 1950s to the early 1970s. Tunes from artists such as the Beatles, the Four Tops, and the Supremes are played 12 in a row, with limited

commercial breaks, which consistently helps to rank the station among the top 10 for reaching large numbers of listeners. Oldies 95 specializes in live remotes, special events, and retailer-driven programs, which help promote its theme: "Good times and great oldies."

KUDL-FM (pronounced "cuddle") is the only adult-contemporary station in Kansas City, playing light-rock favorites from the past and present, such as Elton John, Celine Dion, and James Taylor. KUDL has enviable demographics: primarily female, KUDL's market boasts an average family income of more than $50,000 per year. Two-thirds have some college edu-

cation, while one-third work in the professional/technical fields or as a proprietor/manager. More than half are married. Like KCMO-FM, KUDL gets out into the community with cash giveaways, shopping sprees, and other promotions. It also has one of the most popular morning shows, *Dan, Glo, and Darcie*.

"We want to give our listeners the most entertaining programming combinations that we possibly can," says Zuroweste. "And we want to work with our advertisers to develop marketing plans that will make them successful. It's not our goal to be the biggest in Kansas City, but to be the best."

Entercom today owns or operates 38 stations in eight markets, has more than 1,000 employees, and enjoys more than $100 million in revenues annually (left).

In addition to news and community forums, KMBZ-98 provides coverage of the Kansas City Royals baseball team (right).

Entercom's stations maintain a high profile in the community through paticipation in numerous community events and local appearances of personalities.

ASAI ARCHITECTURE (FORMERLY ABEND SINGLETON ASSOCIATES, INC.)

N DOWNTOWN KANSAS CITY ON A TRACT ONCE NOTED FOR ITS BLIGHTED structures, a dramatic stone and glass building began to take shape during 1997. The gleaming crescent rising on the bluffs south of the Missouri River soon became the new, $93 million federal courthouse, and its presence there has sparked a regeneration of the civic center, inspiring

additional redevelopment, new business move-ins, and grand plans from the community at large.

This creative revival has occurred in part because of the efforts of ASAI Architecture, formerly Abend Singleton Associates, Inc., the architectural firm that designed the Charles Evans Whittaker U.S. Courthouse. Many of the firm's projects are Kansas City landmarks—the Liberty Memorial and Museum, United Missouri Bank headquarters, the State of Missouri Court of Appeals, the Episcopal Diocesan Center at the Grace and Holy Trinity Cathedral, Westport House, Swinney Recreation Center at the University of Missouri Kansas City campus, and the upcoming Robert Dole Institute of Public Policy—all are projects by ASAI.

Celebrating its 30th anniversary, ASAI is well known throughout the Midwest for highly distinguished work, such as the recently completed State of Kansas Center for Historical Research near the capitol in Topeka, Clay County's Government Center in historic Liberty, and the Milo Bail Student Center at the University of Nebraska—projects that have received local, regional, and na-

tional honors. But those kudos are merely the most recent in a long line of awards the firm has accumulated since it was founded in 1968.

"Our firm has become known for architecture that's tailored to the unique needs of our clients," says Steve Abend, principal in charge of architectural design. "Because of our ability to produce appropriate, functional, cost-effective projects that exceed people's expectations, our clients' projects have received more than 150 major awards for architecture, interior design, planning, landscape design, and historic preservation."

Focus on Clients

At ASAI, clients are of paramount importance. Instead of offering only certain types of architecture, this firm adjusts to fit clients' demands. In fact, the principals at ASAI emphasize the importance they place on clients who are willing to commit themselves to an intimate dialogue with their architects in the mutual development of a project's particular features. According to the principals, each commission constitutes a professional trust, which, in turn,

stimulates an all-out drive for excellence.

The ASAI team starts by analyzing a client's alternatives. Needs assessment and accurate cost projections are essential to this process, so the firm uses the most comprehensive data. In this way, clients have a complete picture of the economic, as well as the architectural, realities of the project they have in mind.

Such an approach gives ASAI the ability to develop entirely new environments, incorporating everything from broadly based planning to all aspects of project design and construction administration. That well-rounded competency has been evident in the recently completed $10 million Lebanon Civic Center, St. Luke's Hospital's $15 million medical office building and parking garage, a $60 million casino and entertainment complex, and the $18 million Jackson County Jail. It can also be seen at the Yellow Freight corporate headquarters, Leawood City Hall, Hillcrest Bank, Jeanne Jugan Nursing Center, and numerous schools throughout the community, such as Broken Arrow, Knotts, George Washington Carver, and Spring Hill.

ASAI's diverse projects include (clockwise from top left) the Charles Evans Whittaker United States Courthouse, United Missouri Bank headquarters, St. Paul's Episcopal Day School, University of Nebraska Milo Bail Student Center, and ASAI's office.

such as security, acoustics, and technologically complex systems.

ASAI's management team includes five principals whose average experience exceeds 25 years and 15 years' tenure with the firm. Founding principal Steve Abend, FAIA, has more than three decades of experience, as well as advanced degrees and certifications in architecture and landscape. He has been advanced to the College of Fellows of the American Institute of Architects in the design category, one of the two highest honors given for exceptional design achievement.

Byron Emas, AIA, another partner, directs multidisciplinary teams in broad-based problem solving assignments, completing complex projects for corporations and governmental agencies within tight time frames and budget constraints. Steve Evans, AIA, directs the Construction Services Group at ASAI. A principal with three decades of expe-

rience in construction, Evans handles a range of responsibilities from bid solicitation and quality control to construction assistance. Principals Christopher Ross, AIA, and Greg Schultz, AIA, also tackle specialized areas of expertise—from academic and recreation buildings to interior design and analytical needs assessment—in order to fully serve each individual client.

"Our goal is to create architecture that communicates— every project must have qualities that make it distinctive, unique, stimulating, and always with the appropriate sense of propriety," says Abend. "We work hard to produce projects that will please our clients and the communities they live in, by creating cost-effective environments that are both valuable and enhance people's well-being."

Among the firm's other projects are (clockwise from top left) the State of Missouri Court of Appeals, Episcopal Diocesan Center & Grace and Holy Trinity Cathedral, Deloitte & Touche, Liberty Memorial and Museum, Hillcrest Bank, Kansas Center for Historical Research, and University of Missouri Swinney Recreation Center.

"Our projects have an impact on how communities are perceived," says Abend. "When clients are seeking excellence within their budget, when they want the project to stand out in the marketplace, when they want the community to sense pride and feel the project is of great value, they come to us."

Teamwork

ocated in the historic Bonfils Building in downtown Kansas City, ASAI relies on the talents of its multidisciplinary staff of architects, interior designers, landscape architects, planners, and construction specialists. The firm also involves specialists for unique program requirements,

BY THE TIME IT WAS SOLD IN MID-1997, ITRAVEL, THEN CALLED International Tours and Cruises, was a thriving, $65 million-a-year travel agency. In the company's 28-year history, founders Lillian and Rex Hoy had successfully weathered a barrage of changes in the travel industry, from airline deregulation and its

resulting bargain carriers, cut-rate fares, and agency commission caps, to computerization and the revolution in scheduling, ticketing, and invoicing. Along the way, International Tours had pioneered significant industry trends and consistently ranked as one of the top 100 among the nation's 32,000 travel agencies.

The new ownership team, comprised of five locally based executives, was drawn to this Kansas City success story for obvious reasons, but the partners also wanted to capitalize on some of the changes now affecting the industry. Soon after purchasing the company, they set in motion plans to increase efficiency, install new technology, and enhance flourishing specializations. As they put it, they were ready to take International Tours and Cruises to the next level, which included renaming the company ITRAVEL in January 1998.

"The success of International Tours and Cruises during its first 28 years was the result of the creativity of its owners in a changing industry," says new co-owner and CEO David O'Toole. "We took over a company that was recognized nationally through its 50 offices around the country, and revamped it by consolidating our branches and using a reservations center that handles most of our corporate business under one roof. We've completely changed the model, and we hope that, 28 years from now, we will have enjoyed the same kind of success."

Improvements and Innovations

Among ITRAVEL's many innovations is a new travel management system. Already the leading system in Europe, the integrated software is being tested domestically through ITRAVEL's U.S. offices. In addition, the company launched its ITRAVEL Service Guarantee, which promises to unconditionally refund any agency fees generated in booking travel whenever the customer is unsatisfied. These innovations, combined with the pooling of resources into the reservation-center environment, serve to set ITRAVEL apart as trailblazers in a constantly evolving industry.

As the Internet continues to affect the travel industry, ITRAVEL has sought ways to combine the convenience of on-line booking with its expertise, giving clients cost savings, knowledge, and efficiency. To serve clients who find it easier to book through one company, ITRAVEL has linked up with major corporations that already have their own intranets. The agency is also developing an on-line booking product so any company can book through ITRAVEL via the Internet.

Despite all the changes, ITRAVEL recognizes that, in a customer-oriented business, employees are critical. The agency has worked hard to retain its staff members, many of whom are longtime travel consultants. As a result, ITRAVEL consultants average 10 years of experience, which means they are reliable sources for information on destinations as well as travel details.

"Our vision for this company is to move both business and leisure customers around the world with a high degree of efficiency," says O'Toole. "Our plan is to be one of the survivors in a rapidly changing industry."

ITRAVEL is recognized nationally through its many offices around the country. By consolidating its branches and using a reservations center that handles most of its corporate business under one roof, the company expects to continue as a travel industry leader.

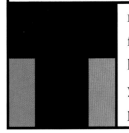

THE MOST IMPORTANT TIME OF LIFE OCCURS IN THOSE formative childhood years when children grow, explore, and learn. That's why parents across the country entrust their youngsters to La Petite Academy, the nation's second-largest preschool and child care organization. From infant to after-school

programs, La Petite has maintained a strong commitment to each and every parent and child it serves.

For more than 25 years, La Petite has offered quality care and education to more than 2 million children. La Petite's exclusive Journey® curriculum program is specially designed to be appropriate for each child's age and level of development. With the help of the well-trained early childhood staff, La Petite helps children develop confidence in their abilities to create, discover, explore, and realize a lifetime love of learning.

La Petite Journey is comprised of different interest areas, providing activities that integrate all elements of a child's total development—physical, emotional, social, language, and cognitive. The program provides a balance of individual play and teacher-directed activities.

"Through our Journey program, learning happens naturally because it allows the teachers to be sensitive to each child's need and their rate of development," says James Kahl, president and CEO. "We know that children learn best by doing, with opportunities for choice, experimentation, and problem solving. That's what our program is all about."

While La Petite's utmost priority is children, it also recognizes the pressures and time constraints busy parents face. That's why La Petite prides itself in being The Parent's Partner®. It proves this commitment by offering a special plan exclusive to parents called the Parent's Partner Plan. This plan includes guaranteed parent communications, six free holidays, two weeks' worth of absences per year, and free extended hours during the holidays. These benefits are offered based on each child's age and schedule.

Growing Up

Founded in 1969 in Illinois, La Petite expanded two years later to Houston and Kansas City, where the company has

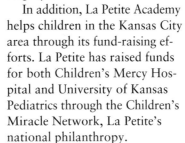

been headquartered since 1971. Today, La Petite has grown to include 750 residential, corporate, and Montessori schools in 35 states and the District of Columbia. All La Petite Academy locations are owned by the company.

La Petite currently operates 32 corporate care sites, providing its program and services within companies. La Petite also owns 20 Montessori schools under the name Montessori Unlimited, located in Texas, Georgia, and Florida.

Local Presence

La Petite has 27 locations in the Kansas City metro area, offering a variety of education and care options for infants, toddlers, and preschoolers, and an after-school program for school-age children. With La Petite's open-door policy, parents can drop in unannounced at any time, including the option to stop by on their lunch hour.

In addition, La Petite Academy helps children in the Kansas City area through its fund-raising efforts. La Petite has raised funds for both Children's Mercy Hospital and University of Kansas Pediatrics through the Children's Miracle Network, La Petite's national philanthropy.

La Petite has 27 locations in the Kansas City area, offering education and care options for infants, toddlers, and preschoolers, and after-school programs for older children.

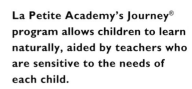

La Petite Academy's Journey® program allows children to learn naturally, aided by teachers who are sensitive to the needs of each child.

WHEN IT COMES TO REFERENCE LABORATORIES, THE LabOne name says it all. Celebrating a quarter century of business in 1997, the firm has become the nation's leading provider of risk assessment testing for insurance companies, an innovator in clinical testing by marketing directly to health care payers, and a growing force in the substance abuse testing industry.

With approximately 715 employees as of mid-1998, the Lenexa-based company—publicly traded on Nasdaq under the symbol LABS—tests more than 25,000 specimens daily from all over the world. But at LabOne, it's more than a numbers game. The accuracy of test results is the company's top priority. Fully accredited and certified, the laboratory undergoes the most stringent quality assurance programs in the industry. In fact, LabOne received no deficiencies on its last two inspections from the College of American Pathologists (CAP). Only 3 to 5 percent of accredited laboratories in the country receive no deficiencies on any one CAP inspection.

"Our centralized and efficient laboratory means our clients can count on value, consistently high-quality results, uniform billing, and responsive client services," says W. Thomas Grant, LabOne's chairman, president, and CEO. "Our centralization, combined with our advanced information systems, has also made us the leader in providing sophisticated statistics and results analysis, which has increasingly become a point of differentiation for LabOne."

Diversity of Testing Services

The foundation of LabOne's business is risk assessment testing for U.S. and Canadian life insurance companies. The insurance division has held the largest market share in the industry since 1972 and is currently experiencing renewed growth as insurance companies begin testing a higher percentage of their applicants.

In 1993, LabOne diversified into clinical and substance abuse testing. Clinical outpatient laboratory testing in the United States is estimated to be a $15 billion industry that comprises 4 to 5 percent of the country's health care spending. LabOne became a unique player in this field by marketing directly to health care payers, such as PPOs and HMOs, and through its Lab Card® Program. The Lab Card Program saves self-insured groups and insurance companies approximately 50 percent on their out-patient laboratory testing while providing their plan participants with free testing.

LabOne also markets substance abuse testing to *Fortune* 1,000 companies, third-party administrators, and occupational health providers. This division has been growing steadily and has added a number of high-profile clients. LabOne's quick turnaround times, reliable service, and advanced database capabilities have helped to differentiate the company in this competitive market.

Because of its impressive growth, LabOne plans to expand and consolidate its three metro-area facilities. A new complex in Lenexa, scheduled for completion sometime in 1999, will double the company's testing capacity.

"We have spent the past 25 years building a reputation based on a strong commitment to our clients, a dedication to the highest-quality testing, and a company spirit that fosters innovation and service," says Grant. "This strong foundation has provided us with many opportunities for growth. We are excited about the future of LabOne."

Clockwise from top right: LabOne owns and operates one centralized laboratory for three lines of business.

From cutting-edge networking systems, to advanced testing equipment, LabOne is quick to adopt new technologies in and out of the laboratory.

LabOne scientists maintain the most accurate and efficient testing protocols in the industry.

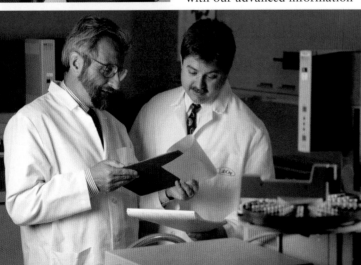

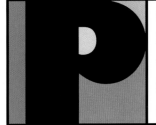

FIZER ANIMAL HEALTH GROUP THINKS BIG. A WORLD leader in the animal health industry, Pfizer Animal Health—with its Greater Kansas City manufacturing center—sums up its market in Pfizer Inc.'s 1996 annual report: "Today, it is estimated that there are more than one billion cattle . . .

750 million pigs, 850 million sheep, 500 million turkeys, and 30 million horses worldwide, as well as 115 million pet dogs and 118 million pet cats in developed countries. More than 30 billion broiler chickens are processed every year worldwide. Pfizer expects to be well positioned to meet the medical needs of these and other animal species in increasingly important world markets."

As part of Pfizer Inc., an $11 billion global health care company, Pfizer Animal Health launched its local operation in 1972. Situated on a 104-acre site in Lee's Summit, the plant employs more than 200 people dedicated to manufacturing and distributing leading animal pharmaceutical and medicated premix products.

"We have some of the best people you could find anywhere," says Frank LaPietra, director of operations for the Lee's Summit plant and a 40-year Pfizer veteran. "In addition, Pfizer has invested so heavily in state-of-the-art facilities that we're ready to begin manufacturing new products as soon as they come out of development. That only points to more optimism for our operation here."

Think Global, Act Local

Although Pfizer Inc. serves more than 150 countries around the world, the local enterprise finds that a significant majority of its livestock customers are situated within a 500-mile radius of Kansas City. In fact, this strategic location in the midst of the country's primary agricultural region was one reason Pfizer originally chose the site. Pfizer Animal Health's role in a giant, research-oriented com-

pany has paid off in a big way for all Pfizer Animal Health customers, no matter where they are.

"Pfizer as a corporation has always had a passion for high quality," says LaPietra, "not just in our products, but in our customer service and everything else we do. We're part of a big, research-based organization, but there's a lot of synergy among all the divisions, whether we're working on animal or human health care."

As a corporation, Pfizer spent an impressive 15 percent of its 1996 revenues on research. For Pfizer customers, this research has paid benefits in the delivery of innovative, value-added products. For the Lee's Summit operation, this investment has also meant new facilities, such as the $12 million sterile liquid filling and packaging system and the $13 million renovation of the pharmaceutical compounding area, both in 1995; and most recently, in 1996, the $9 million

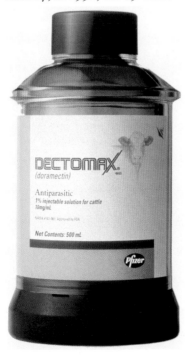

nonsterile liquid filling system. All improvements are aimed at enhancing Pfizer Animal Health's ability to manufacture products such as Dectomax, a parasite control product used for cattle and swine; Stafac, an anti-infective that promotes feed efficiency and weight gain in swine and poultry; and Aviax, a product that controls coccidiosis, a serious parasitic infection in poultry.

"I think we'll continue to be optimistic about continued growth here in Lee's Summit because of a healthy new product pipeline within Pfizer, and our ability to begin manufacturing and distribution immediately," says LaPietra. "We'll become more of an international supplier from here, too, because the Food and Drug Administration has revised export restrictions affording us new, worldwide opportunities and because we've made investments in developing products of interest to an international marketplace. We are starting to play a more critical role in Pfizer's global strategy."

Pfizer Animal Health Group is a world leader in the animal health industry.

Pfizer has invested millions of dollars in improvements to enhance its ability to manufacture products such as Dectomax, a parasite control product used for cattle and swine.

POLSINELLI, WHITE, VARDEMAN & SHALTON, P.C.

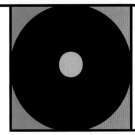

NLY SUPREMELY SELF-ASSURED LAWYERS, COMFORTABLE WITH who they are and what their firm represents, would willingly hop on a motorcycle or pose with a black-and-white cow for ads congratulating clients Harley-Davidson and Gateway for choosing to move to Kansas City. ■ "Clients come to us because we're

Members of Polsinelli, White, Vardeman & Shalton include (from left) Frank Ross, Business Department chair; Mike White, vice chair of the Real Estate/ Public Law Department; Russ Welsh, managing partner; Jeff Rosen, Litigation Department chair; and Lonnie Shalton, Real Estate/Public Law Department chair.

known for being experienced, aggressive advocates, willing to be innovative in solving their legal challenges," says Polsinelli, White, Vardeman & Shalton Managing Partner Russ Welsh. "Our independent, entrepreneurial zeal also helps set us apart."

Polsinelli White is one of the largest law firms in Kansas City, but it still recalls how things were when it started as one of the smallest in 1972. It was entrepreneurial then, and the firm has tried to retain that culture, even though it now has about 100 lawyers in offices in Kansas City, St. Louis, and Jefferson City, Missouri, and in Overland Park and Topeka, Kansas.

The firm has 26 practice areas—including litigation, public law, securities and corporate finance, health care, employee benefits, bankruptcy, and real estate and development—that attract national and international clients.

Polsinelli White's lawyers bring a great amount of legal experience to the table. Among the firm's partners is the lawyer who wrote the definitive college text on land use law in Missouri; the nation's preeminent legal mind in the field of not-for-profit associations; former chief counsels to governors and a U.S. senator; and the former chairman of the American Bar Association's Products Liability Committee.

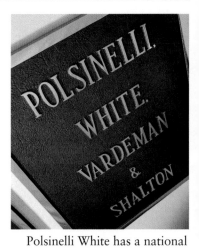

Polsinelli White has a national reputation in many practice areas, including product liability. Welsh, who was chairman of the Litigation Practice Group, has been regional or national counsel in product liability cases for Bristol-Myers Squibb Co.; Owens-Illinois, Inc.; and Ford Motor Co.

The firm's Real Estate/Public Law Department, dedicated to solving the complex issues facing expanding and relocating companies, has been involved materially in virtually all of the Kansas City area's major real estate developments in the past 15 years. Polsinelli White's experience in commercial real estate and lending has resulted in a client list that includes national and regional real estate developers, resident and foreign real estate investors, institutional lenders, major property tax consultants, and Fortune 500 companies locating new facilities in Missouri. Current projects include the Times Square Redevelopment/ Planet Hollywood Hotel in New York City.

The firm's Governmental Affairs Group is a vital segment of the Real Estate/Public Law Department. It has its own long record of success in issues involving administrative and regulatory law, legislative affairs, real

estate and land use, tax increment financing, health policy, energy, public utilities, telecommunications, and banking.

The Corporate Finance Group complements the other practice areas with its blend of experience. Over the last three years, this group has been directly involved in billions of dollars worth of financial deals, including initial and secondary public offerings of equity, debt- and asset-backed securities, small-business offerings, private placements, tender offers, exchange offers, offshore offerings, negotiated acquisitions and exchange offers, hostile takeovers, and bankruptcy reorganizations.

Polsinelli White's team approach to law creates efficiencies that provide clients the benefit of the entire firm's knowledge, skill, and experience, while giving them a lead attorney who is responsible for communicating their wishes to the team members and assuring that their needs are met.

A key element in the firm's success has been its effective integration of technology. When a Polsinelli White lawyer opens his briefcase, it's likely to be a notebook computer that comes out, to connect him with national databases, colleagues, and the firm's state-of-the-art computer system. Polsinelli White's remote research network enables team members working in another city or state to tune in to its database, which brings them up to speed on the latest developments and helps them formulate strongly supported arguments in a matter of hours.

"Our mission has always been, and will continue to be, focused on providing clients with the best possible legal services," Welsh says. "A sign that we are achieving our goal is that many new clients are referred to us by other clients. We believe that is a testament to our way of doing things. As a firm, Polsinelli White is innovative, independent, and thinking. Those three words

spell success to us. And if I had to add a fourth word, probably it would be 'fun.'"

That addition seems to be a fitting choice for a firm that takes a "family photo" with a black-and-white cow.

ANYONE WHO TRAVELS TO SYDNEY, AUSTRALIA, FOR THE 2000 Summer Olympic Games will find him- or herself in the company of Kansas City architectural firm Devine deFlon Yaeger. That's because Devine deFlon Yaeger Architects, Inc. (DdY) designed the new arena, in

Clockwise from top:
The North Patrol Police Head-quarters, designed by Devine deFlon Yaeger Architects, Inc., represents an intense effort to portray a new image and working relationship with the general public by representing a revitalized organization and an awareness of public needs.

The 30,000-square-foot addition to the Harry S. Truman Presidential Library in Independence includes administrative offices, conference rooms, and multimedia facilities consisting of seminar rooms and auditoriums.

Winwood Apartments were constructed in a Des Moines suburb as an extension of the community parkway system.

association with the Sydney firm of Cox Richardson Architects, that will serve as the gateway venue to the Olympic competition. Inside the 20,000-seat facility, gymnasts and basketball players will battle for athletic dominance.

The road to this internationally acclaimed project has taken a quarter of a century. DdY is celebrating its 25th anniversary, and throughout those 25 years, it has contributed to the architectural landscape of Kansas City, as well as throughout the United States and various points internationally.

DdY has built a reputation based on a devotion to providing top-notch client service, award-winning design, and close attention to clients' budgets. Project construction costs have ranged from thousands of dollars to more than $200 million—and all receive the same close attention to client goals, needs, and dollars available.

Over the course of its 25-year history, DdY has designed virtually all types of buildings. The firm takes pride in the fact that buildings it designed 20 years ago are still in use and functioning well. Significant examples include the North Patrol Police

Headquarters, a major addition to the Harry S. Truman Presidential Library, and Booth Manor, a high-rise complex for the elderly. DdY has designed more than 4,000 units of multifamily apartments, town houses, and condos, of which one project—the Winwood Complex for the J.C. Nichols Company—received the Best in American Living award for excellence in design from the National Association of Home Builders.

The firm enjoys contributing to the environmental fabric of Kansas City and actively pursues area projects. High-profile projects such as the Sydney Olympic Arena are terrific, but the real

soul of DdY's practice exists in its own backyard. DdY has long-time professional relationships with such community-service organizations as the Jackson County Board of Services, the Kansas City Public Library, and Catholic Charities. These projects contribute to the quality of life for residents of the Kansas City area.

DdY's consistently dedicated work has brought the firm to the attention of local and national leaders involved with high-profile projects. In addition, DdY has attracted dedicated professional staff who believe in the firm. The firm employs a diverse group of professionals from

across the country who enjoy working on a wide range of interesting projects.

DdY is a full-service firm that provides planning, architecture, interior design, space planning, site planning, landscape architecture, and graphic design. It has the very latest in computer equipment and software with all the bells and whistles, as well as good old-fashioned rendering artists and model builders. The firm is completely networked and utilizes the latest computer-aided design and drafting (CADD) software along with 3-D software capable of producing finished renderings as well as videotaped computer animation.

Because of its reputation, DdY has recently been the recipient of such commissions as the new Sprint World Headquarters campus (with the Hillier Group and two other Kansas City architectural firms, BNIM and RAI)—a $500 mil-

lion project that includes more than 3 million square feet of office space and rates its own zip code; a major entertainment complex addition to Six Flags Great America (outside of Chicago) that includes a water theme park, an events center, multiple hotels, and an entertainment complex; and a new Plaza branch library—located on Kansas City's historic Country Club Plaza that includes a 200-plus unit residential tower with day care and retail facilities.

The principals of DdY— Tom Devine, Rick deFlon, Carl Yaeger, and Michael Brady— have a solid grip on the firm's direction. As a firm, they decided not to set a goal to be the biggest firm in the city, the state, the country, or the world, but to grow naturally and never be in a situation where they compromise their ability to do a great job for their clients. The partners want to maintain a firm large enough to produce any

size project, while retaining the ability to be extremely flexible and responsive to all projects— big or small.

With DdY, clients can be assured they will receive principal-level attention, close attention to budget and schedule, and the most creative design imaginable. DdY enjoys its work, and it wants its clients to thoroughly enjoy the experience right along with the firm.

Clockwise from top: Devine deFlon Yaeger Architects, in association with HWA, provided complete architectural services—including full-time site representation—for the comprehensive restoration of the historic Raffles Hotel in Singapore City, Singapore.

Trinity Lutheran Church in Shawnee Mission grew from the initial worship space constructed in the 1950s, and Devine deFlon Yaeger worked to create a much-needed, identifiable entry space.

The Plaza Library Development centers around a new branch library for the Kansas City Public Library system. The plans also include a residential section, sculpture garden, storybook garden, reading gazebos, gourmet coffee shop, restaurant, gift shop, and day care center.

Devine deFlon Yaeger Architects, as part of the Millennium Consortium, is designing a new arena for the 2000 Olympics in Sydney, Australia. DdY served as sports architect to the consortium, working in conjunction with the Sydney firm of Cox Richardson Architects.

N THE SPRING OF 1998, MAMBA SLITHERED INTO KANSAS CITY AND became the newest attraction at Worlds of Fun, which, along with Oceans of Fun, comprises one of the largest amusement park complexes in the Midwest. ■ The thrilling new scream machine—named for one of the most feared snakes in Africa, the mamba—is the park's biggest

expansion in its 26-year history. In fact, MAMBA is one of the tallest, longest, and fastest roller coasters in the world. More than a mile long, it has two monstrous hills, including a 205-foot drop; hits speeds of 75 miles per hour; and reaches 3.5 g's.

"We've introduced new attractions each year, so that there's a good variety for everyone," says Daniel R. Keller, vice president and general manager. "Adding MAMBA to Worlds of Fun's diverse lineup of rides and attractions gives Kansas City and the Midwest an opportunity to experience a world-class roller coaster."

A History of Fun

Launched in 1973, as an internationally themed park, Worlds of Fun features 175 acres of rides, shows, and attractions, including Timber Wolf, a top-ranked wooden roller coaster, and Detonator, a gravity-defying twin tower ride. Open from spring to late autumn, the family-oriented park celebrated its 25th season in 1997 by introducing Berenstain Bear Country and the Summer Spectacular Laser Light Show.

Next door, Oceans of Fun offers water attractions on 60 acres, including a million-gallon wave pool, children's play areas, giant water slides, and an adults-only pool with a swim-up cabana serving tropical libations. Opened in 1982, Oceans of Fun is the Midwest's largest tropically themed water park.

"When people come to Worlds of Fun and Oceans of Fun, they're

looking for that special day," says Keller. "They want to step outside their normal worlds. As employees, we provide that fantasy world for guests, and we do it in a safe environment."

Consummate Thrill Seekers

In 1995, the two Kansas City amusement parks were acquired by Cedar Fair, L.P. of Sandusky, Ohio, a company that specializes in the amusement park business and boasts more than a century of experience. Cedar Fair, L.P. owns and operates its flagship park, Cedar Point in Sandusky as well as Valleyfair in Shakopee, Minnesota; Dorney Park & Wildwater Kingdom in Allentown, Pennsylvania; and Knott's Berry Farm in Buena Park, California.

Since Cedar Fair's acquisition of the parks, Worlds of Fun and Oceans of Fun have experienced significant growth and development. "We try to use cutting-edge technology to deliver the best guest experience," says Keller. "We really believe that Worlds of Fun and Oceans of Fun are wonderful attractions and will continue to deliver more of the same excitement for years to come."

DAN FEICHT

**Clockwise from top:
The Berenstain Bears are part of Worlds of Fun's family-oriented attractions.**

MAMBA—a major attraction at Worlds of Fun—is one of the tallest, longest, and fastest roller coasters in the world.

Worlds of Fun, which opened in 1973, covers 175 acres and features rides, shows, and attractions. Next door, Oceans of Fun offers 60 acres of water attractions.

BUILDING PARTNERSHIPS WITH CLIENTS AND SEEKING PROJECT diversity have been key ingredients to the growing success of Gould Evans Goodman Associates over the years. ■ A mix of services including architecture, interior design, community planning, urban design, landscape architecture, graphic

design, and construction services has fueled the firm's growth to the largest architectural practice in Kansas City.

"We make a strong effort to develop long-term relationships," says Bob Gould, founding principal of the national and international design firm. "We will continue working on small, unique projects. But doing a series of projects for a client, rather than just a onetime job, has allowed us to build a successful practice," says Gould. "Our interactive approach involves the client with a design team," he continues. That approach, coupled with the firm's project diversity, resulted in an average business increase of 30 percent or higher during each year over the past decade. Repeat clients include AMC Theatres; the City of Kansas City, Missouri; the Johnson County Library System; the National Weather Service; Northwest Missouri State University; and Butler Manufacturing.

In the 1980s, the firm made the deliberate decision to maintain project diversity. And the decision has paid off. In *World Architecture*'s 1998 World Survey of the Top 500, the firm ranked as one of the fastest-growing architectural firms nationally and internationally.

"Good architecture is created within the community. We therefore developed a network of affiliates that operate in the local environment," Gould says. "So far, we have opened offices in Tampa, Philadelphia, Phoenix, Denver, Toronto, Vancouver, and Overland Park. We link all affiliates electronically so we can support each other and ride the waves of the local and national economies."

In keeping with its commitment to preserving the urban core

of Kansas City, Gould Evans Goodman Associates relocated to its high-tech office in the historic Westport area. Local and national features in magazines, newspapers, and on television highlighted the company's adaptive reuse of a vacant retail space into a highly functional, flexible, and mobile office. Desks and other equipment are on wheels so associates can easily form new teams as projects evolve. (Employees are called "associates," and that is how management relates to them.)

The firm's recent high-profile projects in Kansas City include several new AMC Theatres, the Historic 18th & Vine District, the Unitog Company Corporate Headquarters, the Congregation Beth Torah Synagogue, the Francis Child Development Institute at Penn Valley Community College, the Johnson County Central

Resource Library, the W. Jack Sanders Justice Center, and the FOCUS Kansas City Plan.

The company's associates have contributed substantially to its success. "In our business, the people are absolutely the key asset," says Gould. The company provides an extensive benefits package, creates a friendly work environment, and rewards entrepreneurialism. Outdoor courtyards can be used for meetings or relaxation. A children's play area helps to entertain associates' children while the parents are at work. An art gallery displays the work of local artists.

Looking ahead, the company is optimistic that it can sustain double-digit growth by strengthening affiliate relationships with architectural firms in other cities and eventually establishing additional satellite offices.

The Francis Child Development Institute at Penn Valley Community College in Kansas City, Missouri (left), and the Johnson County Central Resource Library in Overland Park (right) are just two of the recent high-profile projects completed by Gould Evans Goodman Associates.

The firm was the lead architect of the Historic 18th & Vine District (left).

Gould Evans Goodman Associates' Kansas City office (right)

VERY DAY IN OVERLAND PARK, SOME 6,000 PEOPLE GO TO WORK in the woods. But these workers aren't forest rangers or conservationists. Rather, they're the employees of companies that are part of the comprehensive office park known as Corporate Woods. With 23 buildings for offices, retail shops, a bank, and a Doubletree Hotel set on nearly 300 tree-covered acres, Corporate Woods combines the seriousness of business with the quiet serenity of nature.

Opened for business in 1975, Corporate Woods was a joint venture between a group of Jones & Co. investors and Metropolitan Life. Developers such as Tom Congleton, Dick Wagstaff Jr., Whitney Kerr, Phillip Lyman, Russell Jones, and Charles Sayres envisioned a unique suburban complex that would appeal both to small local companies as well as large national concerns. In 1973, the group signed its first option contract, then spent two years building its first structure. In 1975, 23 Corporate Woods opened with Farmer's Export as its first tenant.

Nearly 25 years ago, the vision for Corporate Woods was one of buildings nestled within a natural and inviting landscape. It was a vision of excellence, and the vision became real.

Business with a View

Located adjacent to the I-435 beltway and College Boulevard, Corporate Woods today houses approximately 250 companies. Tree-lined lanes wind through the complex, connecting the buildings and giving tenants ample opportunities to enjoy the outdoors. Some 30 varieties of trees cover the property, including oak, hickory, pine, and sycamore. Additionally, animals such as beaver, deer, fox, and owls have been spotted in Corporate Woods' groves. In all, some 201 of its 294 acres remain open to nature and those who enjoy it.

The complex emphasizes this link to the natural world in a variety of ways. The 50-acre Corporate Woods Park features picnic tables, jogging trails, an exercise course, a winding woodland stream, and breathtaking beauty throughout the seasons. Annual events also provide a way for the community to enjoy Corporate Woods, as the complex sponsors everything from races to the Corporate Woods Jazz Festival to a juried show called Art in the Woods. And, each summer, Corporate Woods hosts the Overland Park Fourth of July fireworks display.

By its size, Corporate Woods is a thriving center of commerce that's busy with ideas and innovation. By its feel, however, the Woods is a vast and sprawling landscape, which daily absorbs the intense pace of its occupants and yet remains unmistakably true to its original, serene vision. Corporate Woods is a special place that's simply unrivaled in Kansas City.

Clockwise from top left:
The 50-acre Corporate Woods Park features picnic tables, jogging trails, an exercise course, a winding woodland stream, and breathtaking beauty throughout the seasons.

Some 30 varieties of trees cover the property, including oak, hickory, pine, and sycamore. Additionally, animals such as beaver, deer, fox, and owls have been spotted in Corporate Woods' groves.

Annual events provide a way for the community to enjoy Corporate Woods, as the complex sponsors everything from races to the Corporate Woods Jazz Festival to a juried show called Art in the Woods.

Located adjacent to the I-435 beltway and College Boulevard, Corporate Woods today houses approximately 260 companies. Tree-lined lanes wind through the complex, connecting the buildings and giving tenants ample opportunities to enjoy the outdoors.

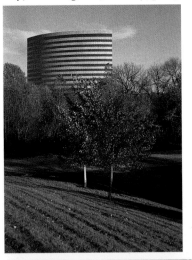

APPLICATION OF THE SIMPLEST CONCEPTS OFTEN LEADS TO THE best results. Such is the case with *Ingram's*, Kansas City's business magazine. The golden rule: Treat others as you would like to be treated. The result: Respect by the business community, a loyal readership, and strong advertising support.

Since 1974, *Ingram's* has focused on providing accurate, timely, and decisive coverage of the area business community. And through this commitment to quality editorial, *Ingram's* has developed into the authority on commerce in Kansas City.

Ingram's has long-established ties with the region's business leaders, which has led to many important partnerships that are reflected on the award-winning publication's pages. Features in *Ingram's* explore the businesses, organizations, and people within the region that make the community work so well together. *Ingram's* Regional Publications showcase the surrounding cities and counties of the Greater Kansas City area and economic development regions throughout Missouri and Kansas.

Ingram's magazine has earned the respect of journalist peers and readers throughout the area and across America. In 1998, the Association of Area Business Publications awarded *Ingram's* the Best Overall Magazine Design, the Best Feature Layout, and the Best Front Cover of business magazines in North America.

The staff was delighted to see *Ingram's* recognized as one of America's more respected business publications. Their work ethic was rewarded for its example as being committed to the journalism profession.

As much as *Ingram's* is committed to commerce, it is also strongly committed to community. Staff members believe philanthropy is good business. They have pledged their resources and commitment to make a positive difference in the lives of all Kansas Citians. They know positive messages about the people in

▶ V. CRAIG SANDS

Kansas City make it a better, more caring community.

Many of *Ingram's* business and professional relationships evolve around working with and helping not-for-profit agencies and the companies that support them to assist in satisfying the philanthropic needs of the community. *Ingram's* has been a leader in Kansas City's Promise: The Alliance for Youth. *Ingram's* has also initiated efforts with business publications throughout the country to support America's Promise.

Kansas City is truly the heart of America and it's not because of its location. It's a well-documented fact that Kansas City is among the most giving cities in America. Businesses have discovered the more they give to the community, the better the climate is for business. *Ingram's* endorses that concept

here in Kansas City and supports those efforts throughout the pages of the magazine.

Still following the golden rule, *Ingram's* celebrates its silver anniversary in 1999. The year 2000 represents the sesquicentennial of Kansas City.

The future of Kansas City and the communities that make up the region looks very bright. This is truly a city on the verge of aggressive, healthy growth and strategically planned economic development. *Ingram's* is proud to be a part of this city's past and strives to make a significant contribution to its future.

Ingram's magazine looks forward to continuing to showcase the business community and to being an active part in building a greater Kansas City.

(From left) Vice President of Finance Jim Ryan, Senior Vice President Michelle Sweeney, Publisher Joe Sweeney, and Editor Pat Lowry

WHEN IT COMES TO ATTRACTING A TOP-NOTCH STAFF, salary decisions are often the easy part. Choosing from among the vast array of employee benefits, however, can be an increasingly complicated endeavor. That's why Fortis Benefits Insurance Company has become such a critical component in the human resources field. Through comprehensive surveys, innovative programs, and trend forecasting, the Kansas City-based company has defined the future in employee benefits.

Licensed in 49 states and the District of Columbia, Fortis Benefits is a customer-driven, service-oriented organization continually examining its work processes and its approach to the marketplace. The company regularly enhances its existing products and continually introduces new services based on close customer contact and vigorous research. Such strategies have helped Fortis Benefits claim its place in the industry. In fact, in terms of master contracts in force, the company is ranked second in long-term disability

and life insurance and fourth in dental insurance nationwide.

"We continue to see a lot of changes in the employee benefits area and have positioned ourselves to deal with them," says Robert B. Pollock, Fortis Benefits' president and CEO. "To be successful, you've got to go out and demonstrate to employers how to add value—and that's what we've done."

Vast Resources

Fortis Benefits arrived in Kansas City in 1991 after purchasing the group insurance operations of Mutual Benefit Life Insurance Company and combining it with the group division of the former St. Paul, Minnesota-based Western Life Insurance. Fortis Benefits is a division of Fortis, Inc., a financial services company headquartered in New York. That entity is in turn part of Fortis, an international insurance, banking, and investments group that is jointly owned by Fortis AMEV of the Netherlands and Fortis AG of Belgium.

"We chose Kansas City for its good labor pool, midwestern work ethic, and central location," says Pollock. "When it came time to put the two companies together, Kansas City was the logical place to stay." But the international powerhouse behind Fortis Benefits brings a global perspective to the company as well. Not content to be a follower, the company routinely searches for the next important issue, the next area of concern, the next product that will best serve its clients.

Recently, Fortis Benefits wondered why some individuals return to work faster than others after an injury or illness. So the company joined forces with the Gallup Organization and the Menninger Return to Work Centers to conduct groundbreaking studies showing that both demographic and attitudinal factors play key roles in claimant behavior.

Robert B. Pollock is president and CEO of Fortis Benefits Insurance Company (top).

The home office of Fortis Benefits is in Kansas City (bottom).

Fortis Benefits used this new information to create an innovative approach to the problems of disability. The company's Managed Disability Solutions® go beyond income replacement by putting experienced clinical and vocational rehabilitation staff to work for both employee and employer. Fortis Benefits' new way of looking at an old problem helps everyone: Claimants restore their quality of life faster, employers enjoy lower costs and the speedier return of valued employees, and Fortis Benefits earns the success and industry recognition that come with breaking the mold.

Likewise, the company saw that dental care was heading toward a managed care model and that the way to deliver the best program was by working more closely with the providers themselves. So Fortis Benefits put together a partnership with Dental Health Alliance to create a plan that would attract a wider, and therefore better, pool of dentists. The company also introduced provider excess insurance, a stop-loss program that covers providers for catastrophic losses above a certain level.

More recently, health care trends have been heading toward creating benefits menus for employees, allowing them to choose what they want in the way of employment extras. Again, Fortis Benefits has been at the forefront of this new movement. "People want more of a sense of controlled destiny in what they're being provided," says Pollock. "It's become a fundamental issue of allowing more choice to employees, while transferring more of the costs from employers."

Giving Back

Although Fortis Benefits is in the business of providing benefits to employees and employers, it also believes in community benefits. That's why the company gives its 1,200 home office employees time off for volunteer work with a variety of local organizations. Two key programs are the Milton

Fortis Benefits employees participate in Model Block, a program designed to improve inner-city neighborhoods.

Moore Spanish Magnet School tutoring project and the Model Block program. But employees also volunteer their time to Goodwill, Boys Club, Girl Scouts, and numerous other organizations. If an employee becomes a board member for a community charity or agency, Fortis Benefits makes a corporate financial donation as well. "Being a good corporate citizen means giving back to your community," says Pollock. "But getting people out into a different environment makes them more creative and better problem solvers, too."

With a focus on helping people, Fortis Benefits remains committed to its vision as it enters the 21st century: to be the recognized leader in providing bold, innovative, and affordable solutions for employee benefits.

N TODAY'S INFORMATION AGE, CORPORATIONS CAN LOCATE VIRTUALLY anywhere in the country. But one choice offers an exceptional workforce, advanced telecommunications infrastructure, low business costs, and central U.S. location: the Kansas City area, promoted as America's SmartCities®. That's the message the Kansas City Area Development

Council (KCADC) delivers daily, and judging by the overwhelmingly positive response, companies large and small are convinced.

America's SmartCities (www.smartkc.com) represents a unique partnership among business and community leaders dedicated to marketing and making the 14-county Kansas City metropolitan area the single best place in the nation to do business electronically.

"The SmartCities initiative is positioning our area as a leading location for firms relying on information technology," says KCADC president Bob Marcusse. "By giving the Kansas City metro area a brand identity, our message is getting the attention of key business leaders worldwide."

The Kansas City Area Development Council's Web site, www.smartkc.com, provides a detailed economic profile of the Kansas City region, and links to more than 170 major corporations and 35 communities in the area.

America's SmartCities: Workforce, Technology, Value, Location

The trademarked SmartCities initiative is built around the Kansas City area's greatest strengths for attracting business. Recent national surveys have ranked the area's SmartWorkforce® near the top in areas such

Harley-Davidson Motor Company recently roared past 20 cities in 12 states to choose Kansas City for its $82 million plant—the company's first new manufacturing facility in 25 years.

as productivity, health, education, and computer literacy. The metro's strong work ethic is underscored by a recent National Center for Health Statistics study, which noted that Kansas City workers take the fewest sick days of any major metro area.

Providing the tools for those workers is Kansas City's SmartTechnology®. With the world headquarters presence of Sprint and hundreds of other telecommunications-intensive corporations, the Kansas City area provides businesses with a solid information infrastructure and direct access to cost-efficient, state-of-the-art communications services.

The area also offers SmartValue®, for both business and living expenses. City comparison studies consistently rate Kansas City's labor, taxes, transportation, and other costs among the lowest in the nation. And the area has been designated the most affordable housing market among major U.S. metro areas.

The area's SmartLocation®, near the country's true geographic

and population centers, makes Kansas City the most geocentral major U.S. market. That means businesses can capitalize on the central time zone, considerably lower distribution costs, and timely access to both coasts.

America's Best Place for Electronic Business

Companies are recognizing that because of our strong information infrastructure, they can conduct global business very effectively from Kansas City. Plus, Kansas City offers a perfect blend of big-city amenities and small-town livability," says Marcusse.

Such positive attributes have drawn numerous companies to the Kansas City area in the past few years, including Gateway, EDS, Alliance Data Systems,

SITEL Corporation, FedEx, and ADT. In 1997, Harley-Davidson Motor Company roared past 20 cities in 12 states to choose Kansas City for its $82 million plant—the company's first new manufacturing facility in 25 years.

Not all these corporations are viewed as traditionally high-tech, but all rely on the area's strong information infrastructure to conduct business. "Even manufacturing companies conduct business electronically today," says Marcusse.

As the new American headquarters city, Kansas City recently attracted the home offices of AlliedSignal Aerospace and Fort Dodge Animal Health, as well as divisional operations for Transamerica Life and John Deere. Hundreds of start-up companies continue to set up shop in Kansas City, while home-grown organizations—including Yellow Freight, Hallmark, H&R Block, and Sprint—increasingly utilize superior technology to conduct business.

Bridging Kansas and Missouri: The Bistate SmartCities Partnership

The KCADC, supported by more than 170 corporations and 35 communities, works to attract job-creating investment to the 14-county, bistate Kansas City metro area of nearly 2 million people. The council's professional staff acts as the central focus for economic development groups throughout the region, coordinating efforts and providing companies with the clearest picture of what's available in the area.

"We're like matchmakers," says KCADC Cochairman Bob Green. "We work hard to understand a company's culture, needs, and parameters; then we match those with our area communities, looking for the best fit."

The process works, in large part, because KCADC has developed a deep trust among its partners in both states. "We work to position the Kansas City area competitively against other major cities to ensure that we're a final contender for top

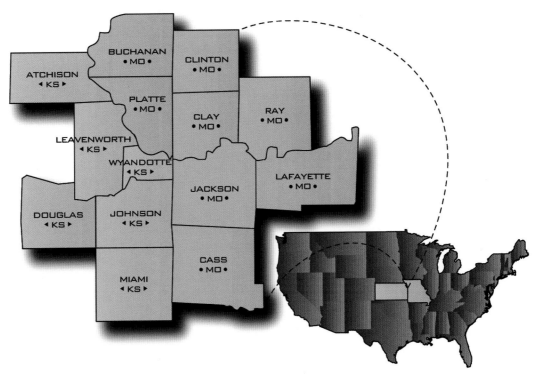

projects," says Green. "We remain neutral once a company narrows its search to sites within the metro area."

While development councils are common, those faced with the challenge of promoting two states at once are rare. More unusual still are organizations like KCADC that can turn bistate competitiveness into an advantage. When a company like Swift Transportation considers building a multimillion-dollar terminal in the area, or an operation

like Fort Dodge Animal Health wants to relocate its headquarters, both Kansas and Missouri become viable options.

"The KCADC has turned what would often be considered a divisive state line into a marketing asset," Green says. "Because we are a bistate organization, we are able to offer business prospects far greater options than most metro areas with regard to tax structures, incentives, regulations, and labor considerations."

As the metro area's umbrella economic development organization, KCADC partners with 35 communities and 14 counties in Kansas and Missouri.

Businesses are drawn to Kansas City's blend of big-city amenities and small-town livability. The Country Club Plaza, for example, offers more than 200 shops and restaurants, and a bordering river walk.

REATER KANSAS CITY HAS A WELL-ESTABLISHED TRADITION OF caring and giving. One of the most visible expressions of this spirit of philanthropy has been the tremendous growth of the Greater Kansas City Community Foundation and its capacity to help improve the region's quality of life. ■ The Community

Foundation is a collection of people, families, and companies that care about their community. They have established more than 750 funds that help them invest their resources in bettering the quality of life in the Kansas City region and beyond.

Today, the organization is one of America's fastest-growing community foundations and one of its youngest. When its founders passed the hat in 1978 to collect the original $219 in seed money, no one imagined that less than 20 years later, the Community Foundation would rank in the top 10 foundations nationally in assets. More importantly, grants paid out each year regularly exceed those of community foundations in cities with larger population bases like Chicago or Cleveland. Since 1986, the foundation has awarded more than $250 million in grants to combat homelessness, improve educational opportunities, nurture the arts, and increase immunization availability, as well as contributing to a broad range of other charitable interests.

"Our growth is an outstanding tribute to the generosity of

Clockwise from top:
People donate all types of assets to the Greater Kansas City Community Foundation, from cash to stocks to property. In 1993, Ewing M. Kauffman donated the Kansas City Royals baseball team.

One program initiated by the Community Foundation, YouthFriends, connects caring adults with young people in 13 school districts in the Kansas City area.

New attractions within the 18th and Vine Historical District received important assistance from grants from Community Foundation donors.

the Kansas City community," says Richard Green, chairman and CEO of UtiliCorp United, Inc. and chairman of the Community Foundation's board of directors. "We believe the community's strong commitment to growing local philanthropy will produce even greater results in the future."

In-depth knowledge of complex community issues enables the Community Foundation to establish connections between its numerous donors and the charitable work those donors want to accomplish. "Connecting donors to what they care about is our main goal," says Janice Kreamer, Community Foundation president. "When donors see the measurable impact of their donations, they often do even more."

National recognition—combined with effective fiscal management and widespread endorsement from the community, business, and civic leaders who serve as board members—increases the foundation's local support. A prominent example of this support is Ewing Kauffman's decision to entrust ownership of the Kansas City Royals to the Community Foundation. The donor-advised funds established from proceeds of the sale will

benefit local charitable causes for generations.

"Donations of all sizes play an important role in addressing community needs in this era of government downsizing," Green says. "We work to make charitable giving easier and more effective for the donors who increasingly provide Greater Kansas City with the resources it needs to maintain and improve citizens' quality of life."

The foundation has made great strides in addressing community needs since that humble hat was passed more than 20 years ago. With the continued support of area residents, the organization will continue to address the essential needs of Greater Kansas City for years to come.

This page was made possible by a grant from UtiliCorp United, Inc.

BUYING A HOME RANKS AMONG THE MOST IMPORTANT investments a person can make. More than just a financial decision, acquiring a house represents an enormous emotional judgment that is also firmly tied to the future. That's why it is so critical that the dream of home ownership is not dashed

on the rocks of an unclear title.

Stewart Title of Kansas City has written title insurance policies in the area since 1978, including nearly 10,000 policies in 1997, to ensure residents that no one will be able to declare any liens, claims, or encumbrances against their home, other than those already set forth and agreed to in their mortgage. In addition, Stewart Title makes the process easier for lenders, who can remain assured that their own investments have involved a reputable title insurance company that provides state-of-the-art technology to deliver its products. Stewart Title is the only title insurance company in the nation to increase its reserves and statutory surplus for 22 consecutive years. Customers have come to recognize Stewart's commitment to continuous growth in the assets backing its title insurance policies.

"We are part of a strong national network, which now includes more than 1,000 independent agents issuing title insurance policies of Stewart Title Guaranty Company," says Bud Whisler, president and CEO of Stewart Title of Kansas City and senior vice president and mid-central division manager for Stewart Title Guaranty Company. "We believe that technology is the future, and we are spending our time and money coming up with new ways to work faster and better in the real estate community."

Service-Oriented from the Start

Stewart Title was founded in 1893 when Maco Lee Stewart purchased his first abstract company in Galveston. Some 15 years later, he incorporated his booming venture as Stewart Title Guaranty Company. From

its earliest days, Stewart Title was instrumental in the evolution of the title insurance industry, writing the first policy in Texas and helping the government develop regulations for the industry.

As title insurance became standard practice in real estate transactions, Stewart Title opened offices statewide, then nationwide. Today, still run by Stewart family descendants, the company has diversified into numerous real estate information services, including mapping, surveying, mortgage services, flood compliance, appraisal services, mortgage document preparation, real estate tax reporting, credit reporting, and a golf course real estate listings service.

Even though the firm was among the first in the title insurance industry, Stewart Title now

operates in a crowded field. To set itself apart from its competitors, the company focuses intently on customer service. Everyone at the company follows its vision statement—"Magnificent Service by Inspired Professionals"— working as a team to achieve the highest levels of customer satisfaction. All associates go through a two-day quality training program, and every office reports on its success each quarter.

"We are building a company with associates for the future who care about the type of service that goes out our door. They understand that our product is not only the title insurance policy, but service as well," says Whisler. "They understand that customers come first. If we don't take care of our customers, someone else will."

Stewart Title has diversified since its early days into numerous real estate information services, including mapping, surveying, mortgage services, flood compliance, appraisal services, mortgage document preparation, real estate tax reporting, credit reporting, and a golf course real estate listings service.

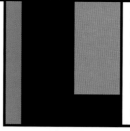

IKE THE MEDICAL COMMUNITY IT SERVES, CLINICAL REFERENCE Laboratory (CRL) prizes confidentiality. Multinational clients—who work in everything from telecommunications and aviation to trucking, retailing, and biotechnology—call on the Lenexa-based facility to handle their substance abuse, corporate wellness,

insurance, and pharmaceutical testing. And through it all, Clinical Reference Lab handles each with the utmost skill and privacy.

"Integrity is very critical to all that we do," says Timothy Sotos, the firm's chairman and CEO. "Clinical Reference Lab's strategy has always been to provide our clients with a competitive advantage in the marketplace. To that end, we have emphasized the importance of highly personalized service, rapid turnaround of test results, state-of-the-art technology, and continuous reinvestment in research and development."

Multinational clients—who work in everything from telecommunications and aviation to trucking, retailing, and biotechnology—call on Lenexa-based Clinical Reference Laboratory to handle their substance abuse, corporate wellness, insurance, and pharmaceutical testing.

Testing, Testing

Clinical Reference Lab opened in 1979 with a handful of visionary technicians, led by Dr. Robert L. Stout, who is now president of the company. These visionaries saw a growing need for fast and reliable testing capabilities. In the 1980s, their belief was borne out when the U.S. government passed mandatory workplace drug testing legislation. In addition, an aging population more concerned with health and wellness—and the emergence of diseases such as AIDS—has fueled the company's growth.

"Society is under intense pressure to treat ailments, and every pharmaceutical company in the country has spent billions," says Sotos. "Our company has not only been in the right place at the right time, but we've had the right skills, right people, and right corporate culture. It's been an evolution for us."

Today, CRL has grown into a dynamic, respected reference laboratory that employs more than 300 people. Not only is its client base international, but it's also part of a global network of affiliated laboratories located in Europe, Asia, Africa, and Australia. Moreover, since 1988, CRL has been one of the top three national laboratories that provide testing services to the life and health insurance industry. Sophisticated management information systems and the latest in laboratory equipment have enabled CRL to meet the exacting, time-sensitive needs of some of the largest insurers in the world.

Into the 21st Century

As a relatively new company, Clinical Reference Lab has positioned itself to be a leading worldwide provider of high-quality laboratory testing services well into the 21st century. Several qualities have made the company successful, notes Sotos, and will continue to guide it for the future.

"First, we are keenly aware of our technical and business strengths, and we're concentrating our resources in these areas," Sotos says. "Second, we've bucked the industry trend and remained privately held. This has given us a greater ability to respond to client needs without delay or conflicting interests, and a way to maintain a long-term business perspective. Third, we're dedicated to reasonable profitability. And fourth, we strive to attract employees with spirit, enthusiasm, and a good work ethic. In return, we promise a collegial environment, challenging work, stability, and competitive compensation.

"The 21st century will open a whole new world," Sotos continues. "If you're positioned with the right technology and the right people, then you're going to be successful. That's our mission."

HE *Kansas City Business Journal* WAS THE FIRST NEWSPAPER IN the metropolitan region devoted entirely to news of interest to the local business community. Established in 1982, the *Business Journal* provides thorough coverage of business news in a community with a vibrant mix of commercial activity. ■ "The

Business Journal is the primary source of information on the local business scene for influential executives and rising small-business entrepreneurs who must stay informed about their city and industry to remain competitive," says Publisher Joyce Hayhow. "It affords a prime vehicle for advertisers and salespeople who want to reach the local business market."

In addition to reporting breaking business news each week, the *Kansas City Business Journal*'s staff of professional editors and writers presents lively, in-depth coverage of important trends and issues affecting a variety of industries and professions, including law, health care, manufacturing, telecommunications, hospitality, advertising, banking, retail, and real estate development. The publication reaches more than 85,000 readers every week.

A Network of Business Coverage

The *Kansas City Business Journal* was founded by Mike Russell and William "Doc" Worley, two Kansas City-area businessmen who, along with editor Don Keough, realized that the local business community did not receive adequate coverage from existing press sources. The newspaper's parent company, American City Business Journals Inc., expanded the idea to other cities. The fledgling chain was subsequently purchased by Ray Shaw, former president of Dow Jones & Company Inc., who took over as chairman and moved the headquarters to Charlotte.

In 1995, American City was purchased by New York-based Advance Publications Inc., one of the world's largest privately held media companies. Advance is owned by Newhouse Newspapers, one of the nation's premier news and magazine publishers. Shaw remains as chairman of American City, which is continuing its expansion efforts.

The *Kansas City Business Journal* and its staff of 35 employees now belong to a family of 47 American City publications located in major cities across the country. Besides its comprehensive coverage of news, the *Business Journal* each week provides profiles on businesses and their executives, and reports on successful business strategies.

Staying on Top

Each year, the *Business Journal* produces nearly two dozen special publications that target a specific need or market. The valuable *Book of Lists*, for example, compiles an entire year's worth of weekly business reference material on the city's top companies and organizations. In addition, *Space* offers quarterly snapshots and insights concerning the city's retail and office real

estate market, while the *Health Care Resource Guide* provides a mixture of topical stories, lists, and directories aimed at health care professionals.

"After 16 years of serving the business community, the *Journal* remains fresh, innovative, and responsive to the needs of its readers and advertisers," says Hayhow. "In the past year, the *Business Journal* added coverage from Washington, D.C., and introduced an Internet Web page, which is linked to its sister business newspapers. This kind of growth is indicative of how the publication continues to evolve."

Clockwise from top left:
The *Kansas City Business Journal* produces nearly two dozen special publications each year, including *The Book of Lists*, *Space*, and the *Health Care Resource Guide*.

The *Business Journal* was the first newspaper in the metropolitan region devoted entirely to news of interest to the local business community.

The *Business Journal*'s professional editors and writers reach more than 85,000 readers each week with lively, in-depth coverage of important trends and issues affecting a variety of industries and professions.

URE, PRICE IS IMPORTANT. BUT MORE THAN ENOUGH CONSUMERS will pay a little more for a superior product and attentive salespeople. That's the rationale at Haldex Brake Products Corp., the Blue Springs-based manufacturer of automatic brake adjusters for heavy-duty commercial vehicles. ■ A look at the company's

impressive numbers makes it clear the strategy has worked. Haldex commands some 50 percent of the world market for automatic brake adjusters and is the market share leader in North America—even though its prices are higher than the competition's. Moreover, Haldex Brake Products is the world leader in the manufacture and sale of several other brake system components for heavy-duty trucks, buses, and trailers.

"There's a tendency for many companies to think customers are only concerned about the initial purchase price," says Charles Kleinhagen, Haldex Brake Products president. "But customers can find value beyond price if you present it properly and deliver what you say you will. At Haldex, we have a strong reputation for the performance of our products and for serving the

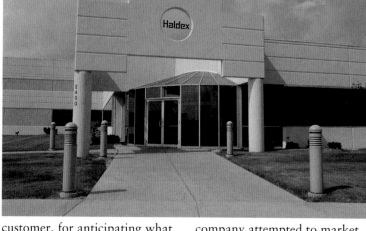

Haldex Brake Products Corp.'s modern office and manufacturing complex opened in Blue Springs in 1994 (top).

Haldex provides superior products for braking systems for the global trucking industry (bottom left and right).

customer, for anticipating what the customer will need and supplying it before he needs it. The fact that we're the world leader tells us we're doing something right."

Explosive Growth

A subsidiary of Haldex AB in Sweden, Haldex started making and selling automatic brake adjusters in Europe in 1968. The superior engineering immediately saved fleet owners and drivers time by reducing their need to manually manipulate their brakes. In the 1970s, the

company attempted to market its product in North America through a licensee, but the effort failed. Undaunted, Haldex established its U.S. plant in Blue Springs in 1981 to manufacture, market, and distribute its revolutionary product to truck manufacturers and end users. As truckers discovered the engineered-in reliability of Haldex's automatic adjusters, demand rose quickly. Of course, imitators also cropped up, attempting to chip away at the company's sales.

But Haldex prevailed, largely with its refined European engineer-

ing and responsive, innovative staff. Between its manufacturing plants in Blue Springs and Landskrona, Sweden, the company has produced nearly 25 million automatic brake adjusters in its history, some 60 percent of them in the last seven years. The firm expanded its U.S. facilities twice and now operates from a 70,000-square-foot plant in the Adams Dairy Parkway Development in Blue Springs. In fact, the latest move resulted in a 30 percent growth in staff as well as a 25 percent increase in production.

In addition to its automatic brake adjusters, Haldex has also created a line of air dryers, air disc brakes, lining wear sensors, and limited-slip couplings for trucks, cars, and industrial vehicles with a special emphasis on performance and safety. The Haldex Brake Systems Division supplies brake products for heavy-duty vehicles; the Haldex Traction Systems Division supplies advanced four-wheel-drive systems for cars and trucks; the Haldex Barnes Hydraulics Division makes pumps and systems for power steering and lifting functions on industrial vehicles and trucks; and the Haldex Garphyttan Wire Division focuses on specialty steel-alloyed wire products, mainly for applications in combustion engines.

"We've tried to look for products that others aren't doing very well," says Kleinhagen, whose division achieved its ISO 9001 certification in 1997. "We're specializing in a niche where a lot of competitors are trying to be everything to everyone; we're specialists in a very narrow field. We want to keep our narrow focus, but within that area, we want to excel and be the dominant provider worldwide."

Out and About

From Haldex's European origins—setting the stage for its global perspective—the company continues to expand its product lines into new regions. When Kleinhagen became the first American to head the Brake Systems Division, he set goals to rapidly expand markets in Asia and Latin America. In addition, a corporate restructuring in 1997 prepared the company to make greater inroads into the passenger vehicle arena. "As a worldwide group, we're in the initial stages of 'doubling twice,' as our group CEO says," states Kleinhagen. "We've dramatically increased research and development spending to bring new products to market, and there are a lot of acquisitions in our field as well."

But an international focus hasn't kept Haldex from looking at the community that surrounds it. Since it was launched in 1981, the Blue Springs operation has been a civic leader in various organizations throughout Kansas City. Haldex participates in the Blue Springs School District Adopt-a-School Program, supports the Annual Swing for St. Mary's Golf Outing, sponsors the Missouri State Basketball Tournament for the Missouri Special Olympics, and became the first Heart of Gold corporate sponsor for the Rainbow Center.

"Kansas City has provided a great blend of having a relatively low cost of doing business and all the benefits of a major metropolitan environment," says Kleinhagen. "Also, our workforce is very involved, both in the community and in their jobs. Their commitment has been a major portion of our success." In addition, employees serve on numerous boards, including the Economic Development Commission of Blue Springs, Blue Springs School of Economics, Rainbow Center for communicative disorders, St. Mary's Hospital Auxiliary, and Eastern Jackson County Diabetes Council, among others.

Team members produce Haldex products to the highest quality standards in the industry (top left and right).

Haldex Automatic brake adjusters are subjected to rigorous, continuous testing (bottom).

A GENERATION AGO, EMPLOYEES HIRED ON WITH A COMPANY and stayed there until retirement. Now, however, the world has become faster-paced, with mobile careers, downsizing, and corporate reorganizations the norm. Changing business cultures have created an industry that is today

being successfully served by Right Management Consultants.

Founded in Philadelphia in 1980, the career transition and organizational consulting firm went public in 1986. Now, with 179 offices worldwide, Right has been named repeatedly to *Forbes'* 200 Best Small Companies in America and to *Business Week*'s list of the 100 Best Small Corporations. Moreover, the regional firm has been listed on *Ingram's* Corporate Report 100 roster of fastest-growing companies.

"The driver of our business is change," says Steve Carter, managing principal and CEO of the Overland Park office. Carter, along with his wife, Rosalind, executive vice president and CFO, purchased the Overland Park office in 1990. "As long as change continues to be the strong factor it is in today's business world, then career transition will be vital to a company's success," he says.

Managing Change

Initially, Carter's business focused primarily on advising companies on how to separate people from their jobs, voluntar-

ily or otherwise. Then called Right Associates, the firm evolved, adding consulting services in 1995 to help client companies manage organizational changes, define leadership qualities, provide employee coaching, and partner relocation assistance. From the Kansas City headquarters of Right Management's Heartland Region, offices in Omaha, Des Moines, and Wichita consult with Midwest-based companies on their organizational problems.

"We try to help companies and their employees go beyond their limitations and to see opportunities they may have overlooked

in the past," says Carter. "We're problem solvers; we help organizations more fully define themselves."

Such concentration has transformed the company into the largest of its kind. Systemwide, Right Management Consultants has worked with more than 80 percent of Fortune 500 companies, as well as a host of smaller organizations both locally and around the globe. "Clients get the best of all worlds," says Carter. "They get the network of 179 offices and the consistency in how we carry out our consulting practice. But because we're locally owned, we have an entrepreneurial spirit: We're dedicated to growing the business and investing in this community. It's a strong combination."

People Power

As a people-oriented business, Right Management Consultants knows the value of hiring the right staff. The 50-person Heartland Region includes top-notch counselors, technology experts, and human resources specialists. Among them, Right's personnel helped develop the region's state-of-the-art computer network system, which gives companies and individuals a differen-

"The driver of our business is change," says Steve Carter, Right Management Consultants' managing principal and CEO of its Overland Park office. Carter, along with his wife, Rosalind, purchased the Overland Park office in 1990.

Right has been named repeatedly to Forbes' *200 Best Small Companies in America and to* Business Week's *list of the 100 Best Small Corporations. The regional firm has also been listed on* Ingram's *Corporate Report 100 roster of fastest-growing companies.*

tial advantage in managing change, as well as finding creative employment opportunities. The region's depth and breadth of knowledge also help consultants to focus companies on what's needed in the way of business transformation, leadership development, coaching, and outplacement.

"The most unique feature of our company is that we're able to successfully attract and hire the brightest and most creative counselors in the industry," says Carter. "We can attract talented people because of our integrity and values, which truly reflect our organization as the leader in the industry."

Onward and Upward

At Right Management Consultants, the trend continues upward. The company has grown rapidly, and Carter expects it to continue. "Although corporate downsizing has lessened in the last two or three years, the need for organizational effectiveness is growing, so our consulting practice has grown tremendously," he says. "The rapidly changing metamorphosis that exists in the world today means that companies need new skills as never before, yet a lot of businesses today find that the person who was a stellar performer for years may not be able to change in the way a company needs them to."

Corporatewide, Right Management Consultants has also changed the way companies handle their human resources by adding a technology-based group called Marketplace Resources Service. For example, the firm has added a proprietary, Internet-based career search resource, called Right Associates JobBank, that is available exclusively to clients; launched Right Match®, designed to assist individual clients in the career transition process; and devised hundreds of databases in CD-ROM and Internet formats.

And in Carter's view, such internal improvements only demonstrate further that companies with people issues need Right Management Consultants. "If you're looking for a company with a passion for helping businesses and people," sums up Carter, "you can't do better than Right Management Consultants."

Clockwise from top: Systemwide, Right Management Consultants has worked with more than 80 percent of Fortune 500 companies, as well as a host of smaller organizations both locally and around the globe.

As a people-oriented business, Right Management Consultants knows the value of hiring the right staff. The 50-person Heartland Region includes top-notch counselors, technology experts, and human resources specialists.

The region's depth and breadth of knowledge also help consultants to focus companies on what's needed in the way of business transformation, leadership development, coaching, and outplacement.

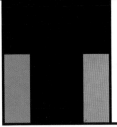

HESE DAYS, NEARLY EVERYONE TAKES PERSONAL COMPUTERS AND communication for granted. But when IKON Technology Services Kansas City was getting its start back in 1983, the concept was a complete novelty. That's when the Kansas City firm was founded as a modest consulting company to help clients set up PC networks

with a new network operating system called Novell NetWare. The company was named Executive Automation Consultants and incorporated four years later.

Known today as IKON Technology Services Kansas City, the local operation is part of a Fortune 500 industry giant with hundreds of offices worldwide and more than 40,000 employees. The largest supplier of office products in North America, IKON, based in Valley Forge, Pennsylvania, also maintains Technology Services offices in most major metropolitan areas throughout the United States and Canada that focus on network integration, project management, application development, technology consulting, and network training services.

"IKON's mission is to help our clients use automated solutions to solve business problems and give them a competitive edge," says Kevin Grawe, the company's local president. "We help them use information technology to support their business goals."

Local IKON President Kevin Grawe with the IKON Falcon, an award won for best of class among the company's Technology Services offices (top)

Clients in the entire Kansas City region are serviced from the IKON Technology Services office in Overland Park (bottom).

Plugged In

IKON fulfills its mission in many ways. As a consultant, the company provides comprehensive, vendor-neutral information that helps clients make informed technical decisions. When they need assistance with strategic planning, Internet/intranet services, network management solutions, or infrastructure designs, customers turn to IKON.

As a systems integrator, the company can link disparate hardware and software into seamless information delivery systems that conform to industry standards and allow for future growth and flexibility. Through IKON's in-house technology lab, engineers can simulate various network configurations and test them before actual implementation.

The company also is a service organization, offering comprehensive and customized support options that help clients manage their networks. Support plans often involve the use of IKON's Help Desk, which provides quick response to client inquiries. As an applications developer, IKON uses industry standard development tools from major manufacturers to build collaborative business applications. The firm also provides outsourcing services, furnishing supplemental staff on a part- or full-time basis.

IKON's technical staff is organized in a unique way. Consultants and engineers are teamed into Practice Areas. Each Practice Area concentrates on one particular technology, such as wide area networking, Internet security, or enterprise messaging systems. The purpose of forming these teams is to allow people to focus their efforts, become experts in their field, and provide even better services to IKON clients.

"There are no other companies in the Kansas City area that provide all of the products, services, and training programs available from IKON," says Grawe. "We know our clients would rather deal with fewer vendors—those who provide a wide range of services and with whom they can form closer partnerships. They get that benefit when they work with IKON."

Getting beyond the Learning Curve

With IKON, clients can do more than passively wait for computing answers. Back in 1989, the company established its Network Institute of America as an industry-authorized education center. Today, education remains an important part of what IKON offers. One of the nation's leading providers of networking education services, the company's Kansas City Education Center includes a wealth of instructors, training rooms outfitted with the latest equipment, student labs, workshops, and seminar rooms.

IKON's Education Center offers technical certification programs from today's leading manufacturers with unique program offerings, such as evening and accelerated curriculum classes.

IKON discovered it was uniquely positioned to help fill the need for trained technical people in the Kansas City area. Recently, a special program was developed to take a high school or college student all the way from basic PC training through industry certification and, finally, an internship at a local company. Upon completion of the program, the student has a résumé complete with experience and a reference.

"Sometimes, the greatest challenge to our success is just trying to stay ahead of what's going to be the next popular technology and the next big need in our marketplace," says Grawe. "Fortunately, we learned long ago how to be flexible, empower our people, and make changes rapidly." Grawe cites the growing need for Internet and intranet services as one of the most explosive areas the company has ever had to address. "We saw it as both a challenge and one of the greatest opportunities to ever come along," he says.

Being able to anticipate and quickly gear up to handle rapid marketplace changes, without sacrificing customer service, has led to a consistently high growth rate for the company—70 percent during 1997 alone. Future growth plans include expanding into secondary market areas in the four states surrounding Kansas City, by either opening offices or acquiring companies that are already established and making them part of the IKON team.

Roots in the Heartland

Although now part of an international company— one that is poised to be a $10 billion corporation by 2000— IKON Technology Services Kansas City maintains a solid connection with the communities it serves. Part of that closeness is due to the strong association the company maintains with the midwestern work ethic, and the enjoyment its employees gain from living in America's heartland.

"The people in our Kansas City office have been the key contributors to our success," says Grawe. "We believe in investing in their continued training and career development with technical and management education programs, providing interesting work and career paths, and creating a fun and exciting workplace. In turn, our employees work hard, keep our customer service standards high, and enjoy working for IKON."

IKON employees, shown here with the company's Hummer, work hard, maintain high customer service standards, and enjoy their work.

I N 1985, AFTER 16 YEARS OF WORKING IN THE CONSTRUCTION BUSINESS, Greg Walton was confident that he had gained the knowledge and expertise needed to start his own company. Within only six years, Walton Construction Company Inc. was recognized by *Inc.* magazine as one of the 100 fastest-growing companies in the United States,

and in 1995, Walton earned the Entrepreneur of the Year Award for Construction in Missouri and Kansas. Presently, his company is ranked as the second-largest general contractor in the Kansas City metro area, and has a host of projects to its credit.

In addition, Walton has gone national. Division offices in Atlanta, Phoenix, and Springfield, Missouri, handle a variety of projects, from suite hotels to grocery stores, banks, sports facilities, and shopping malls nationwide. Several of the company's most notable projects are located right in Kansas City: the $91 million Bartle Hall Exhibition and Conference Center in downtown Kansas City; the $35 million American Royal Arena in the West Bottoms; and Station Casino's $250 million Kansas City Station on the north bank of the Missouri River, with the fourth-largest gaming floor in the country.

Walton Construction Company Inc. has played a major role in creating some of Kansas City's most notable landmarks. Among them are (clockwise from top left) Station Casino, Bartle Hall Convention and Exhibition Center (exterior and interior), and American Royal Arena.

"When the City of Kansas City awarded Bartle Hall to us, it was the beginning of a new era in Kansas City's construction industry," says Walton. "Everyone at Walton feels the same way I do when they see those four pylons against the skyline of downtown. It's an extraordinary feeling."

Team Effort

A driven entrepreneur, Walton has not achieved success entirely on his own. In 1992, he supplemented his senior staff by forming a partnership with Ray Braswell, president of an international construction company. More recently, Braswell headed up the international construction division for Kansas City-based Butler Construction. A degreed architect, Braswell's emphasis on pre-construction services—including market research, site evaluation, rezoning, and utility availability—was an ideal match for Walton's expertise in site and construction management. Braswell is now president of Walton Construction, and Walton serves as chief executive officer.

In addition, a well-trained staff handles a spectrum of construction-related functions at Walton, including technology, engineering, sales and marketing, and project management. Together, they land and successfully complete projects for industries that range from hospitality and health care to office and shopping centers.

"Over the years, we have developed a solid base of experience and expertise in a wide variety of projects," says Walton. "This helps us work as a team to do the best job possible for each and every client." It is that expertise and teamwork that have enabled the company to grow, and that will keep Walton Construction Company in the forefront of its industry for many years to come.

LOCATION IS A MAJOR CONTRIBUTOR TO THE SUCCESS OF THE Kansas City Marriott Downtown. Connected by an underground tunnel to the Bartle Hall Convention Center and surrounded by downtown Kansas City's illustrious theater, government, and central business districts, the 1,000-room hotel offers not only

an ideal setting, but first class amenities as well.

Since it opened in 1987 as the Allis-Plaza, the Marriott has consistently provided state-of-the-art accommodations and first-class service—both for meeting attendees and leisure or business travelers. "We're big enough to draw large convention groups," says Carol Pecoraro, Marriott's general manager, "but we make sure that we always cater to individuals, too."

Beginning with the two-story waterfall that greets visitors in the hotel lobby, the Marriott makes every effort to welcome guests to one of the area's finest lodging experiences. At the Kansas City Marriott Downtown, the needs of its guests are taken care of within the hotel—from a choice of restaurants and bars to laundry and dry-cleaning services. For those attending meetings, the hotel provides a variety of meeting equipment, and for guests interested in recreation, the Marriott offers a health club complete with a sauna and an indoor lap pool.

Major Expansion

Recently, the Marriott made the front pages of national newspapers when it opened a sparkling tower, connected by an above-street walkway to the hotel proper, by expanding into the old Muehlebach Hotel. "We did extensive renovations on the Muehlebach Tower," says Pecoraro, "calling in artistic architectural experts and hiring craftsmen who returned the hotel to its original 1915 grandeur." The $73 million construction project included renovating space in the Muehlebach to create a grand lobby and meeting space on the first few floors of the original hotel.

The combined restoration and new construction added 400 rooms to the Marriott's existing 573-room inventory and provided a connection with the city's history. The famous Muehlebach opened in 1915, and claimed visitors that ranged from politicians to movie stars. Harry Truman used the Muehlebach as his summer home, and celebrities such as the Beatles, Clark Gable, Elvis Presley, and 13 U.S. American presidents stayed there before it closed in 1985.

In a Different League

In addition to the sense of history the Muehlebach adds to the property, the Marriott's recent expansion permits it to host larger convention groups,

a critical element in the downtown area surrounding Bartle Hall. Besides nearly doubling its room count, the hotel now has almost 100,000 square feet of public space, including two ballrooms. This enables the Marriott to host two 1,000-person functions at the same time.

The additional space makes the Kansas City Marriott Downtown the largest hotel not only in the city, but also in a five-state area. "The hotel's increased size gives Kansas City the opportunity to draw larger conventions in one-hotel groups as well as city-wide functions," says Pecoraro. "It puts us in a different league and brings us up to what we needed as a property."

Clockwise from top left: Since it opened in 1987, the Kansas City Marriott Downtown has consistently provided state-of-the-art accommodations and first-class service. A two-story waterfall greets visitors in the hotel lobby, as part of the Marriott's effort to welcome guests to one of the area's finest lodging experiences.

The Marriott recently opened a sparkling tower, connected by an above-street walkway to the hotel proper, by expanding into the old Muehlebach Hotel. Extensive renovations on the Muehlebach Tower included using artistic architectural experts and hiring craftsmen to return the hotel to its original 1915 grandeur.

The Marriott offers guests a choice of restaurants and bars, and other amenities including laundry and dry-cleaning services. The hotel provides a variety of meeting equipment, and for guests interested in recreation, the Marriott features a health club complete with a sauna and an indoor lap pool.

Whεn Bill and T.J. Palmer opened their humble Atlanta restaurant in 1980, they wanted T.J. Applebee's Edibles & Elixirs to serve consistently good food in a sit-down setting, with reasonable prices and high-quality service. In addition, they planned it

to be a neighborhood gathering place where customers could have fun and relax. Today, their dream has been fulfilled in the nore than 1,000 Applebee's Neighborhood Grill & Bar restaurants around the world.

Within three years of opening, the Palmers—who now own 21 Applebee's locations in Atanta—

had sold the business to W.R. Grace and Company. The operation was later sold to Kansas City franchisees Abe Gustin and John Hamra in 1988. The powerful duo took the company public in 1989, then began rapidly expanding the 54-restaurant chain. "In the future, I think we'll have an Applebee's in neighbor-

hoods throughout the world and on every continent," says President and CEO Lloyd Hill, pointing out that the company or its franchisees open a new Applebee's about every three days. "I think we will eventually become the McDonald's of casual dining."

Recently, the company has expanded into Canada, Germany, Sweden, Greece, and the Netherlands, an internationally oriented move favored by restaurant stock analysts. In 1997, Applebee's achieved a four-year compound annual growth rate of some 42 percent. Following the company's move into the global arena, analysts predicted a 20 percent growth in sales from 1997 to 1998. Closer to home, Applebee's has continued expansion of its newly acquired Tex-Mex chain, opening both company-operated and franchised Rio Bravo Cantinas.

Applebee's is committed to high-quality customer service. Each month, thousands of customers judge Applebee's in five key areas that make up the APPLE acronym: atmosphere, personality, performance, lightning speed, and excellent food (top).

Founded in Atlanta in 1980, Applebee's goal is to serve consistently good food in a relaxing, neighborhood-type atmosphere, with reasonable prices and high-quality service. Today, there are more than 1,000 Applebee's Neighborhood Grill & Bar restaurants around the world (bottom).

Quality Counts

Applebee's hasn't succeeded on numbers alone. The restaurant focuses on producing a consistently high-quality, casual dining experience, revising its 60-item menu twice each year. Designed to appeal to all tastes, the eclectic menu incorporates everything from burgers and sandwiches to soups, salads, appetizers, and desserts, plus signature items such as spicy riblets and Bourbon Street steak.

"In a study we conducted a few years ago, our customers told us that high-quality, tasty food is the single most important element of a satisfying dining experience," explains Hill. "Our food proposition says we'll take your order, prepare it with fresh ingredients, and get it to you within 15 minutes. We make sure that the quality, taste, variety, and presentation always ex-

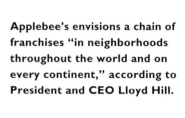

Applebee's envisions a chain of franchises "in neighborhoods throughout the world and on every continent," according to President and CEO Lloyd Hill.

ceed what our customers expect and what our competition can offer."

Applebee's also knows that service is critical. To ensure prompt, friendly service, the company launched a comprehensive program called Applebee's World-Class Service, which incorporates elements such as computerized order taking, shortening the time between ordering and delivery, and giving diners accurate wait times. Part of the company's ongoing commitment to service comes from a program called the Customer Satisfaction Index. Each month, thousands of customers judge Applebee's in five key areas that make up the APPLE acronym: atmosphere, personality, performance, lightning speed, and excellent food.

In addition, Applebee's concentrates on its more than 80,000 employees nationwide, giving priority to selection and training, as well as recognition and rewards. "When you look at the value equation of the dining experience, it used to be only price and quality," says Hill. "Now, in addition to those expectations, you have people who say, 'I want you to remove some of the stress from my life.' That's where our people come into play. We hire for attitude, then train our people in the skills we need."

People Power

Applebee's expects the total of its corporate-owned and franchised restaurants in the United States to eventually exceed 1,500, a likely scenario given its impressive momentum so far. But the company has always

known that a global organization relying on people could face challenges when it comes to creating corporate solidarity. So Applebee's staff and executives have developed a corporate culture dependent on respect, family values, and neighborhood camaraderie.

"About three or four years ago, we asked each other what we want to be when we grow up, and how we want to treat each other," says Hill. "Our culture is a result of that effort. We think outside the box, we get lots of input, and we're basically going to have respect for people until they show us otherwise. Core values—like integrity, trust, open communication, passion for service, and fun—guide all our decisions and actions."

Part of the Applebee's all-for-one corporate culture comes

into play each year when executives work in the front lines at a restaurant for a full day. In addition, part of the training for newly hired headquarters staff involves a week of rotating through every job in an Applebee's restaurant. Realizing that dissatisfied employees can't deliver superior service, the company instituted a variety of plans that make working more pleasurable, from flexible schedules to transferring hourly employees between regions when they need to move.

"We're trying to build a unique, 21st-century organization that engages people's minds," explains Hill. "We're people-dependent, and we'll grow and succeed based on our success in perpetuating that culture."

As part of the restaurant's focus on providing a consistently high-quality, casual dining experience, its 60-item menu is revised twice each year. Appealing to all tastes, the eclectic menu features everything from burgers and sandwiches to soups, salads, appetizers, and desserts.

WITH COMPUTER TECHNOLOGY EVOLVING AT THE SPEED of light, how do companies decide which combinations of hardware and software will best suit their needs now and in the future? Many call on Peripheral Vision InfoSystems, Inc. (PVI), a computing solutions integrator that helps its clients make sound investments in information technology (IT) by leveraging their existing technology while laying a solid foundation for the future.

PVI has been working in the fast-paced IT world since the company was founded in 1987. The firm originally acted as an independent sales representative that focused primarily on providing peripheral equipment in the ASCII marketplace. Within a few years, as times and technology evolved, so did PVI. The company began a quest for the best UNIX operating system on the market, with a solid symmetrical multiprocessing (SMP) CPU direction, and a tight distribution model that would allow the company to invest in a new architecture based on full-service integration, development, and installation of a minicomputer platform. The company chose Sun Microsystems as its primary platform, and then established key competencies with other well-respected technology partners such as Oracle, Netscape, Informix, and Cisco, among others. PVI gradually became an organization that provided business technology solutions rather than just shipping products.

"We realized early on that what's now called 'open systems computing' would be a real breakthrough in the future," says Scot Kane, PVI's founder and CEO. "But our success has also come from our integrity, our vision, and our competency. This business is about 30 percent technology and 70 percent understanding the impact of that technology on a client's business. The key to our success has been a commitment to the highest development of our people and their skills."

In addition to helping companies decide what combination of technological elements will best suit their business needs, PVI provides training, system integration and network management, network security consulting, and database development, among its many services. PVI holds a number of certifications and authorizations from its strategic partners, including being named Sun Microsystems' first Enterprise Elite partner.

In only a decade, PVI has become the recognized leader in open systems integration and consulting in the Midwest. Based in Overland Park, PVI now employs some 35 individuals in four locations and has estimated annual revenues of more than $25 million. In early 1998, the firm opened its first Sun Authorized Training Center and continued to expand its resource investment as new technologies attracted PVI's core client base. Clients include aerospace, finance, manufacturing, telecommunications, and wholesale distribution companies, as well as state and local governments.

"It isn't difficult to find an information technology partner who is technically astute and tuned into the latest developments," says Kane. "The challenge is in finding a partner that can grasp the dynamic relationship between the client company and its market, and visualize the role that information must play in managing and capitalizing on that relationship. At Peripheral Vision InfoSystems, we provide companies with just that sort of relationship."

In only a decade, Peripheral Vision InfoSystems, Inc. (PVI) has become the recognized leader in open systems integration and consulting in the Midwest. Based in Overland Park, PVI now employs some 35 individuals in four locations and has estimated annual revenues of more than $25 million (top).

In addition to helping companies decide what combination of technological elements will best suit their business needs, PVI provides training, system integration and network management, network security consulting, and database development, among its many services (bottom).

ORE THAN A DECADE AGO, ALLAN BIOFF, LEONARD Singer, and Brian Finucane comprised the labor and employment law department of a large Kansas City law firm. As their specialty evolved and grew, the three decided they could better serve their clients with a

boutique firm, which they opened in downtown Kansas City.

Today, Bioff Singer and Finucane has made a name for itself as Kansas City's only law firm exclusively devoted to representing management in labor and employment legal matters. Clients ranging from the telecommunications industry with Sprint to the bakery industry with Interstate Brands Corporation, along with a host of other national, regional, and local small businesses, now call on Bioff Singer and Finucane for advice on employment issues and litigation.

"Our field of expertise lends itself to a boutique-firm environment," says Finucane, one of four partners in the 10-attorney firm. "With what we bring to the table, our clients benefit from the expertise of a large firm combined with the focused efficiency that comes from a small organization that is supported by the latest in technology. Our mission is to provide the highest-quality legal services in an efficient manner that promotes the client's business interests."

Bioff, the firm's senior partner, has concentrated on labor and employment law for more than three decades, and has been recognized as one of the foremost management labor lawyers in the country. He has served as chair of the American Bar Association's Labor and Employment Law Section, which consists of 20,000 employment attorneys across the country. In addition, Bioff has served on the Section's Governing Council and was management coeditor of *Developing Labor Law*, the leading national treatise on the National Labor Relations Act.

Singer and Finucane have both practiced labor and employment

BOB BARRETT

law for more than 20 years, earning accolades in their field. Each has extensive employment litigation experience, and consults daily with clients who seek to avoid labor and employment problems before they materialize. J. Randall Coffey, who became a partner in January 1998, has added his comprehensive litigation background and previous staff work with the Justice Department in Washington, D.C., to the client-focused attorney skills at Bioff Singer and Finucane.

Bioff Singer and Finucane's attorneys are active in a variety of organizations that are vital to the Kansas City community, including the Spofford Home for Children, United Cerebral Palsy Association of Kansas

City, Multiple Sclerosis Society of Kansas City, Don Bosco Community Center, Kemper Museum of Contemporary Art and Design, and American Royal Livestock Horse Show & Rodeo.

"This is a field of law that continues to grow," says Finucane. "The rules are changing due to new laws, skilled lawyers representing employees, and an increasingly litigious environment in which juries decide the outcome of more and more employment disputes. Because of these changes, our practice has an expanding role in helping clients avoid the problems that lead to litigation. We expect to provide those services to our clients in Kansas City and nationwide for a long time to come."

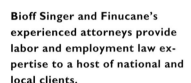

Bioff Singer and Finucane's experienced attorneys provide labor and employment law expertise to a host of national and local clients.

BOB BARRETT

Focused efficiency allows this boutique firm to flourish.

DURING WORLD WAR II, THE CONSTRUCTION INDUSTRY WAS booming. Men who didn't march off to war often spent their time erecting factories or banks or government buildings. In fact, it was during this time that Turner Construction Company initially entered the Kansas City market, when it was commissioned to

build the Pratt & Whitney Aircraft Corp. plant that would produce much-needed airplane engines.

The year was 1942, and Turner already had four decades of experience under its belt. Founded in 1902 by Henry C. Turner in New York City—where the corporate headquarters remains today—the company had earned its stripes while constructing everything from the Breakers Hotel in Palm Beach, Florida, to the James River Bridge in Virginia to Harvard University buildings to Municipal Stadium in Philadelphia. The Pratt & Whitney plant was a mammoth, 3.5 million-square-foot facility that would employ more than 24,000 people during its peak. Turner was more than up to the challenge.

Although the firm followed the aircraft plant with a few other projects in the four-state region, it wasn't until 1988 that

Turner opened a local office, after Marion Laboratories awarded the firm a $30 million project. Since then, Turner has grown into Kansas City's fourth-largest construction company, as ranked by the *Kansas City Business Journal*.

Projects completed by Turner have included construction-related services on the H. Roe Bartle Hall expansion, Menorah Medical Park, Hoechst Marion Roussel, Truman Medical Center-West, the Jackson County Detention Facility, Kemper Arena, Boehringer Ingelheim, and Bayer Corp., among many others. In fact, the $144 million expansion project at Bartle Hall, with Turner acting as consultant to Kansas City, was the largest public project ever undertaken by the city.

"We get a great deal of work through references from others," says Rod Michalka, Turner's vice president and manager of

the Kansas City office. "We're found to be a reliable ally during the preconstruction decision-making process and that, in turn, makes clients and potential clients realize the true benefit of our early involvement. We've become, in a sense, friends by helping clients with key global decisions before the construction phase ever starts."

A Solid Foundation

As the largest construction management firm in the country—with total revenues in excess of $3.1 billion in 1997—Turner Construction Company has diversified into a builder of everything from hospitals to hotels, and office complexes to educational facilities. In fact, *Modern Healthcare* magazine has named Turner the nation's leading health care builder for more than a dozen years running. In Kansas City, proximity to several of the oldest and largest sports architectural firms has helped give Turner an edge in building arenas, stadiums, and other recreationally oriented facilities, including the proposed speedway in Kansas City, Kansas.

Throughout its history, Turner has combined its enormous international resources with local networks and expertise. As a result, the company now has successful offices in South America, Europe, Asia, and the Middle East. Concurrently, Turner's offices have grown with the clients they serve in locations throughout the world. When it opened in Kansas City, Turner's office was staffed with only a handful of people. In the last five years, the local group has swelled to more than 65.

"We bring the experience and knowledge of a $3 billion company and apply it to a specific

Turner Construction Company acted as consultant to the City of Kansas City for the $144 million expansion project at H. Roe Bartle Hall, which was the largest public project ever undertaken by the city.

◄ DAVE BAHM

▲ MICHAEL SPILLERS

local or regional challenge," says Michalka. "We like to think that we set the bar a little higher every day, both for ourselves and for others."

Beginning to End

Not only has Turner diversified in the kinds of projects it offers, but the company has also expanded into all aspects of the construction business. From preconstruction consulting and design/build to new buildings and maintenance, Turner provides clients with a high degree of assistance and service.

"What sets us apart is that we bring good guidance based on experience that helps our clients before the prints are drawn," says Michalka. "Every building has to be analyzed on its own merits and according to the clients' needs. We pride ourselves in helping an owner make the right decisions based on accurate data; then, we let good information and serving the client pay its own dividends."

Like other Turner locations, the Kansas City office boasts an impressive 75 percent repeat rate among clients. In addition, says Michalka, the experience, reliability, and flexibility of the local office staff—which includes project executives, project managers, engineers, superintendents, estimators, cost-scheduling engineers, accountants, and sales/marketing/contract specialists—

have established a constantly growing account base. Among their recent projects are the University of Health Sciences; Lennox Industries in Marshalltown, Iowa; a new retail store for Sportsman's Outfitters & Marine in Lee's Summit; and a new medical office building for the Skiff Medical Center in Newton, Iowa.

"The biggest factors in our success have been client sensitivity, service, and honesty," says Michalka. "Many people have tried to come into this market and set up an office, but our thinking is that we'll be here for a very long time. We believe we have all the right qualities to make this company a success in Kansas City for many years to come."

Menorah Medical Park (left) and Hoechst Marion Roussel (right) are two of the major projects for which Turner Construction has provided construction services.

Proximity to several of the oldest and largest sports architectural firms has helped give Turner an edge in building arenas, stadiums, and other recreationally oriented facilities, including the recent expansion of Kemper Arena.

WHEN COMPANIES CALL ADVANTAGE HEALTH SYSTEMS, Inc., they are often frustrated. Many businesses, when hobbled by rising workers' compensation costs or befuddled by a rash of job-related injuries, turn to Advantage for answers. The workers' compensation consulting and employee education company founded by Anne Tramposh employs about 30 professionals—including physical therapists, occupational therapists, nurses, and exercise physiologists. The company has provided solutions for countless organizations across the country, from Fortune 500 firms to smaller companies looking for ways to eliminate or reduce costs associated with injuries.

"We've basically tried to focus on working with companies that want to do the right thing instead of those just concerned with government compliance," says Tramposh, who has a bachelor's degree in physical therapy and a master's degree in health service administration, both from the University of Kansas. "Our target market has been companies that have voluntarily chosen to take care of their employees and realize the positive impact this can have on their bottom line."

On a Mission

After several years in private practice, Tramposh founded Rehabilitation Professionals—a physical therapy and work-hardening center—in the mid-1980s. She soon merged the company with Work Assessment and Rehabilitation Center to form Wx: Work Capacities Inc. In 1989, Tramposh separated the consulting side of the business to create Advantage Health.

Since its founding, Advantage Health has been on the leading edge of programs that have proved successful in controlling workers' compensation costs. Tramposh herself has published books that include *Avoiding the Cracks: A Guide to the Workers' Compensation System* and *Arms, Hands, Fingers and Thumbs*, a guide to keeping extremities healthy in the work environment. Her numerous articles have included "On-Site Therapy Programs" in *The Source Book of Occupational Rehabilitation*, "Work Hardening" in *Work Injury Management and Prevention*, and "Job Simulation" in *Industrial Therapy*.

"Rising workers' comp costs are a real problem, but the solutions are not difficult to find, so for me it's almost like a crusade," says Tramposh. "Rather than be a consultant to companies, we work to enable companies to do it themselves."

Big Dollars

Tramposh's rationale may be too humble, especially if you look at the success experienced by Advantage Health Systems' clients, which have included companies in diverse industries, from apparel and food processing to manufacturing and office workers. One company cut its carpal tunnel syndrome complaints by 25 percent the first year it sought assistance from Advantage. Another firm implemented a preventive approach and saw annual lost workdays fall from more than 300 to none. Some have hired Advantage Health for its consulting abilities, while others have attended one of the firm's valuable seminars, which represent about 30 percent of the business.

"In the future, we're looking at broadening our services in order to focus on companies of about 100 to 1,000 employees, a market segment where there haven't been a lot of solutions available. We're looking at how we can partner with local rehab and therapy providers to better serve that market," says Tramposh. "Our mission says it all—'We're committed to an injury-free workplace, and that's better business.'"

Clockwise from top:
Workers' compensation claims in heavy industries such as construction can mean the difference between profit and loss.

Awkward hand positions can contribute to reduced employee productivity, dissatisfaction, and injuries, which can all affect a company's bottom line negatively.

Even light industries such as data processing or customer service can experience expensive workers' compensation claims. Appropriate workstation design and employee education can significantly reduce occurrence of injury.

NOT EVERY 22-YEAR-OLD FRESH OUT OF COLLEGE CAN successfully launch a business in a major U.S. metropolitan area. But Kierstin Higgins not only started Accommodations by Apple in 1990—the first temporary executive housing company in Kansas City—she has also built it into a $5

million-a-year business. Today, Accommodations by Apple leases more than 300 units and counts among its clients nearly all the biggest business names in town, including Sprint, Applebee's, and the Kansas City Chiefs.

"It was a new concept in the Midwest, which really gave us an edge," says Executive Director Higgins, a Dallas native who attended the University of Kansas. "The people who work here also have been very enthusiastic and willing to work hard. We've really tried to make it a five-star, concierge-type service."

The Ultimate Midwestern Hospitality

Providing executive accommodations can be a demanding business, in large part because satisfying high-powered people trying to do their jobs in the midst of a move can be challenging. But Higgins relishes her ability to work magic for newcomers. In fact, the company founder calls her brand of customer service, "the ultimate midwestern hospitality."

Higgins and her staff of 15 have been known to take executives grocery shopping, help them line up emergency dental appointments for their children, and act as general contractor for a client's custom-built dog kennel. "We want them to stay here and we want them to come back, so we do everything we can to make that happen," she says. "We're the first impression people have of the Kansas City area. We feel we have an obligation to make that a special experience."

Coming Home

Among its corporate lodgings, Accommodations by Apple features everything from

apartments to town homes to luxury, single-family retreats. Conveniently located throughout the greater metropolitan area, the hospitality company's properties include the special touches that make a house a home: from fully equipped kitchens to baths with all the plush necessities; from plenty of drawers and closet space to desks with ample work space. Each facility also features cable TV, housekeeping, and private phone lines with voice mail, allowing guests to remain connected to the rest of the world.

Accommodations by Apple also provides a home-away-from-home atmosphere with special touches such as a welcome basket brimming with treats, around-the-clock access to its service staff, and the knowledge that just about any reasonable request is possible. As its mission statement says, "At Accommodations by Apple, we work hard to make you forget you're not at home—by offering not just accommodations, but real homes for real people."

"We really think of it as people 'coming home,' even though they're away from cities they normally live in," says Higgins, whose company—due to its ex-

cellent customer service—was named a Greater Kansas City Chamber of Commerce Top 10 Small Business of the Year in 1997. Because of its outstanding service, Apple has also received other awards, including the Crystal Merit Award for best corporate housing, a place on Ingram's top 10 fastest growing companies, the Blue Chip Enterprise Award, and the Ernst & Young 1997 Entrepreneur of the Year. "We get to know our clients so well that they can call us like they would one of their neighbors," says Higgins. "This business can mean long hours, but you would do all this for your neighbors. We do it for our customers."

Clockwise from top: **Lovely decor and comfortable surroundings are an Accommodations by Apple trademark.**

The company specializes in creating a cozy home environment for its guests.

Guests enjoy all the comforts of home, plus everything they need to get down to business.

ANDERSEN CONSULTING OPERATES FROM A FUNDAMENTAL supposition: As markets, technologies, and competitors evolve, successful companies must continually change. Andersen Consulting, the world's largest management and technology consulting firm, excels in helping organizations

deal with this reality. "Our mission is simple," says Tim Jury, Andersen Consulting's Kansas City-based managing partner of the Communications Industry Group for the central United States and Canada. "We want to help our clients change to be more successful. That mission is reflected in everything we do, and it means that our success is derived from their success."

Serving clients in 47 countries, with 53,000 people around the world, Andersen Consulting is a truly global organization. The firm believes that serving clients globally requires more than having people and offices in many countries. The key to the firm's success in providing global service is its ability to share knowledge, expertise, the best management thinking, and resources seamlessly across geographic boundaries.

Working in virtually all industries, ranging from financial services to products to communications, Andersen Consulting is committed to delivering quantifiable value to its clients. What distinguishes the company from other consulting firms is its Business Integration Client Service Model. The firm can help clients with all the major components of their organizations, aligning technology, processes, and people in support of an organization's overall strategy.

A Commitment to Excellence

Since opening its Kansas City office in 1923, the Andersen Worldwide Organization has seen incredible growth and change. In 1954, it installed the first computer application for commercial use at General Electric, thus establishing its

leadership role in technology management. In 1989, Andersen Consulting became a separate business unit from its sister company, Arthur Andersen, and today, Andersen Consulting employs more than 700 of its 53,000 people in the Overland Park office. Applying a wide range of management strategy, change management skills, process design knowledge, and technology expertise, the company serves clients in the Kansas City area and throughout the world.

Andersen Consulting has had tremendous success with 20 to 26 percent growth annually for the past three years. Since 1988, the firm's revenues have grown 600 percent, jumping from just more than $1 billion to $6.6 billion in 1997. The firm works with more than three-quarters of *Fortune* magazine's global 200 largest public companies

The Center for Professional Education, a 151-acre campus facility located in St. Charles, Illinois, demonstrates Andersen Consulting's commitment to the continuous education and training of its consultants.

and all but one of *Fortune*'s 30 most profitable global public companies. It also serves many of the world's most innovative governments and private companies.

Andersen Consulting has developed a wide range of services that are targeted toward specific client needs. The firm understands the importance of a solid strategy as the essential beginning of any substantial change effort. It has demonstrated with clients all over the world the benefits of starting with a vision of far-reaching transformation, then having the commitment to see the change efforts through to completion. Andersen Consulting can also help develop companies' operational and business units, which might include improving marketing and sales effectiveness, research and development management, and information and technology management.

Numerous clients rely on Andersen Consulting to manage many of their business-critical operations, such as information technology, logistics, customer service, finance, and administration. This kind of outsourcing arrangement has become a strategically smart way for companies to reinvent and manage key processes without the constant upheaval of internal reengineering. Andersen Consulting's Business Process Management has the ability to offer clients a total solution, drawing upon a global network of firmwide resources that focus on relationships, service, and cost management.

Additionally, through Andersen Consulting's solid and systematic approach to shaping skills and day-to-day behavior, clients learn how to maximize human performance. The firm has developed, refined, and tested methods that are aimed at helping organizations create high-performance workforces that are nimble and adaptable to change.

"We have an enormous range of services that we provide, which offer our clients the best knowledge available from our global resources," says Jury. "That's

how we are able to apply what we call business integration to solve our clients' problems. And our methods have been extremely well received. Our business—both locally and around the world—continues to grow at a rate that exceeds the industry average."

Extraordinary Standards

Andersen Consulting continually explores new, creative ways for delivering value to clients. For example, its Business Integration Centers, each tailored for a particular industry, encourage out-of-the-box thinking and long-range planning. Its Centers for Strategic Technology in Palo Alto and in Sophia Antipolis, France, help translate research into results. Its Solution Centers provide a new design for creating valued, reusable answers to client needs and its Knowledge Xchange®

system enables its professionals to share information and ideas.

In addition to helping other businesses in the ways of change, Andersen Consulting continually shapes its own destiny through transformation. Guided by its vision for the consulting firm of the future, Andersen is constantly evolving to meet the needs of the marketplace through internal improvement and innovation. One of its guiding principles states: "We must continue to have enough pride in Andersen Consulting to have the courage to change it."

"Our reputation is one of being able to deliver what we say we will," says Jury. "This commitment to keeping our promises means that organizations rely on us to give them the very best. By having the best people armed with the right knowledge, and by partnering with our clients, we can deliver the value we promise."

Andersen Consulting brings together the skills, the expertise, and the best strategic management thinking of its 53,000 professionals, seamlessly, throughout the world.

INCE ITS EARLIEST DAYS, EXECUTIVE TELECONFERENCING SERVICES has built a solid reputation for its professional quality, exceptional service, and high level of application knowledge. Executive has established itself as the primary source for cost-effective solutions for business communication, utilizing everything from teleconferencing

to videoconferencing to broadcast fax. The company offers a comprehensive suite of services from audio, video, and document conferencing to broadcast fax and systems consulting.

Unlike industry giants that handle group communications services secondary to long distance, Executive focuses solely on the conferencing industry. The organization's success comes from providing exceptional services that satisfy every business customer's communications needs. Executive's Reservations Specialists skillfully handle every detail in the scheduling of a customer's event. Operations experts precisely execute events ranging from spur-of-the-moment crisis management sessions to highly sensitive board meetings, on time and without error. Services such as recording, transcription, and translation add to the lengthy roster of value-added services.

"We continue to effectively compete with telecommunication companies and increase our market share based purely on our superior service levels," says

Executive Teleconferencing Services' corporate headquarters is located on the front line of Kansas City's telecommunications network (top).

Committed to providing superior quality, Executive offers the latest in communications technology (bottom).

Ben Cascio, who launched the immediately successful venture when he was in his late twenties, and is now CEO of the firmly established company. "Today's teleconferencing business is a buyer's market. Our clients want to be treated like they are our only customer. Chances are, when dealing with one of the major telecommunication corporations, a typical user may never talk to the same person twice. While our larger competitors choose not to provide premium levels of service, Executive fills the gap by providing exceptional group-communications services."

A Foundation of Service

Cascio always knew that he would start his own company. Three generations of entrepreneurs preceded him in the grocery business. Cascio anticipated that he, too, would follow in the family tradition. The senior Cascio, however, advised his son that computers would be the wave of the future. After obtaining his bachelor's degree in political science and history from Rockhurst College, the younger Cascio worked for the next 11 years selling computers in the Kansas City

region for a leading Silicon Valley firm.

The young salesperson continued to dream of starting his own business. He was very cognizant of the rapidly changing technological environment and the numerous opportunities that it presented. Cascio recognized, and often discussed with colleagues, the multiple directions he could take in establishing a new business venture. One day, after experiencing a low-quality conference call, it became apparent that this was an industry in which he could call on his service-oriented background and technical knowledge to fill a niche. Cascio and a partner would establish a teleconferencing company that would actually exceed customer expectations.

Today, Executive's clients enjoy a wide range of choices in business resources that provide a means for timely communication with those outside their office. The conferencing division includes a tiered mix of premium audio, video, and data services. Each satisfies the various volume, rate, and application requirements of businesses of any size and budget. Custom broadcast fax and related document distribution methods offer alternatives to direct mail and manual mass faxing. These services work together to form a comprehensive crisis management program.

Executive also offers expert consulting services that stem from years of researching and exploring the ever changing technology for use in its operations. Consulting provides clients with non-biased solutions to the development and upgrade of their telecommunications systems.

Growing Strong

Executive started with three employees in the basement of an office complex in Overland Park. As the staff continued to expand, it became evident that Executive would need to relocate to a much larger facility. Although most clients never visit the company's office, Cascio believed it was important for his staff to work in the same type of professional environment as Executive's clients. To accommodate the employee expansion, advanced technical infrastructure, and high standard of professionalism expected of all employees, Executive purchased and renovated a sophisticated new facility in Olathe during March 1997.

Continuing its explosive growth, Executive plans to open nine national branch offices by 2000, to be followed by the creation of international divisions in Canada, Mexico, and Europe. As technology changes, Executive will continue to expand. Each expansion will add increasingly innovative products and systems that will be incorporated into the company's existing services.

Kansas City Commitment

Executive Teleconferencing Services was located in Kansas City for several reasons. Cascio knew that his company would connect clients around the country and world via telephone lines. Being a telecommunications hub, Kansas City's infrastructure was one of the best in the country. In addition, the central time zone would provide access to competitive long-

distance rates that would make it possible to offer a truly superior product at a fair price. Kansas City's midwestern work ethic was also appealing, as was its residents' fairly indistinguishable accent. In return, Executive actively supports such local organizations as the Don Bosco Center and the Kansas City Sports Commission.

Executive is a successful and innovative company. It is one of the few privately held teleconfer-

encing companies in the nation that has proved incrementally profitable and reliable when many competitors were unsuccessful. Since the beginning, Executive's determinate factors of success have been superior quality and service combined with the use of state-of-the-art technology. This founding principle is what has kept Executive moving ahead and will continue to propel the company forward for years to come.

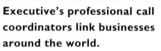

Executive's professional call coordinators link businesses around the world.

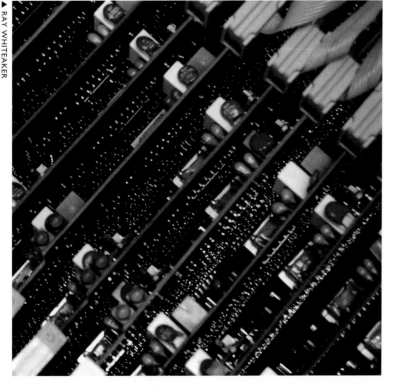

Standards-based videoconferencing technology allows for maximum interoperability.

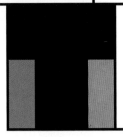

UCKED INTO THREE 19TH-CENTURY BRICK BUILDINGS IN DOWNTOWN Kansas City, Historic Suites of America is a distinctive, elegant hideaway. Guests lose themselves in luxurious period architecture and decor, enormous suites, upscale amenities, and the attention of a devoted, professional staff. Historic Suites is a calm,

Located in Kansas City's venerable Warehouse District, the flagship building of Historic Suites of America was erected in 1887 to house the Builders and Traders Exchange. The structure is a grand, five-story edifice of pressed brick, cast iron, and cut stone.

comfortable oasis of gentility amid the bustle of a major modern city.

Now listed on the National Register of Historic Places, the property has grown in popularity since opening nine years ago. During 1995 and 1996, revenues doubled as occupancy rates climbed. General Manager Carl Galbreath has added innovative marketing programs and hospitality events, and uses his extensive expertise in both operations and human resources to create a historic hotel that runs smoothly and satisfies guests.

"At Historic Suites, we've combined architectural treasures and contemporary comforts to present some of the finest suites in the hotel industry," says Galbreath. "People who stay here say they feel like they've found a home away from home."

Past Perfect

Today's Historic Suites offers visitors a refined and comfortable respite, but the hotel was originally a tribute to the skill and craftsmanship of a group of local contractors and architects. Located in Kansas City's venerable Warehouse

District, the hotel's flagship building was erected in 1887 to house the Builders and Traders Exchange.

Designed to be a statement of the creativity of the esteemed Builders and Traders group, the structure is a grand, five-story edifice of pressed brick, cast iron, and cut stone. Inside, a sunlit atrium is topped with a massive, glass-and-ironwork skylight, while a grand staircase with bronze posts and railings climbs to the upper floors. Today, the building represents a rare surviving example of high Victorian Italianate architecture in the Midwest.

The Exchange building, combined with the former Barton Brothers Shoe Factory and the Burnham-Munger-Root Dry Goods Co. building, is a reminder of days gone by, and an unmatched

Historic Suites offers a complimentary breakfast buffet and hospitality each day in the drawing room.

setting for a modern hotel. "You will not find another hotel in Kansas City—or, for that matter, the world—that contains the architectural attributes found at Historic Suites," says Galbreath. "We've taken three special buildings and forged a distinctive lodging experience within them."

Lodging Options

Historic Suites offers 100 beautifully appointed suites carved from the three handsome buildings. Guests can choose from 32 different floor plans that range from 550 to 1,200 square feet. Each suite boasts original architectural features, from skylights and Palladian windows to 12-foot ceilings and spiral staircases that lead to sleeping lofts.

Although the structures themselves are historic, all interior hotel amenities are strictly state of the art. Every suite contains a fully equipped kitchen so guests can dine on-site or entertain in their quarters. Social gatherings—from evening drinks and hors d'oeuvres to bountiful breakfast buffets—permit visitors to enjoy the hotel's public areas and mingle with other guests.

Fitness buffs can stay in shape while away from home in the on-site fitness facility that features a variety of exercise equipment, as well as a whirlpool, sauna, and outdoor swimming pool. Historic Suites also provides complimentary passes to Gold's Gym Family Fitness Center, located within blocks of the hotel.

In-room cable television and daily delivery of *USA Today* keep guests up to date on the world's news. One-day dry-cleaning service, on-site laundry, complimentary parking, and in-room iron and ironing board enhance Historic Suites' home-away-from-home atmosphere.

A Place for Meetings

Set within Kansas City's central business district, only a few blocks from the convention center's newly expanded H. Roe Bartle Hall and adjacent to the headquarters of several major corporations, Historic Suites is a favorite location for small board meetings, sales gatherings, and conference groups.

"Groups that come here for meetings all enjoy the richness of our surroundings and the ease with which we can accommodate them," says Beth Krizman, Historic Suites' director of sales. "From the moment we begin planning their event until they walk out our front doors, the people who meet here know that they've received our special attention."

The hotel's largest meeting space is the Conference Room, a 1,750-square-foot area that offers conference seating for 30 participants and theater seating for 45. The space includes public address, audiovisual, and overhead projection equipment. A built-in kitchenette is equipped with a refrigerator, ice maker, coffee service, and glassware.

Smaller groups often opt for the Carriage Room, located on the hotel's second level. This 775-square-foot area, roughly the size of a two-bedroom suite, is configured to provide conference-style seating for 30 participants. A bank of floor-to-ceiling windows floods the space with natural light. Meeting attendees also enjoy a casual seating area, a fully equipped kitchen, and built-in rest room facilities. A soundproof break-out room is attached.

Whether guests choose Historic Suites for their meetings, an extended business stay, or a romantic weekend getaway, the property provides a cozy, distinctive experience. "At Historic Suites, visitors continually discover a turn-of-the-century emphasis on service," Galbreath says, "and an up-to-the-minute focus on comfort and convenience."

Guests of Historic Suites are greeted in the historic atrium rotunda at the entrance of the hotel.

Historic Suites offers 100 beautifully appointed suites carved from its three handsome buildings. Guests can choose from 32 different floor plans, including this two-bedroom, loft-style suite with dining area.

FORMED IN 1990 THROUGH A JOINT VENTURE BETWEEN COOK PAINT and Varnish, and the chemicals division of TOTAL—a multibillion-dollar French petrochemical organization—CCP is the world's largest producer of polyester gel coats and the world's second-largest producer of polyester and coatings resins. The company's roots in

Kansas City date back to 1913, when Charles R. Cook established Cook Paint and Varnish. CCP's corporate headquarters and research laboratories are located in newly renovated buildings that have been a part of the Cook Paint and Varnish properties since 1916. Currently, 700 people are employed by CCP, 275 of whom are based in Kansas City.

The company's essential markets include the agricultural, automotive, coatings, construction, maintenance products, industrial, marine, recreation, sanitary, and transportation industries. TOTAL—which is the 35th-largest manufacturing company in the world, having more than 54,000 employees—has businesses in its chemicals division that produce rubber products, inks, paints, and adhe-

sives, as well as polyester and coatings resins. CCP enjoyed revenues exceeding $450 million in the company's 1997 fiscal year.

Diverse Products

CCP's Composites Division produces gel coats, casting resins, fiber enhancement products, hybrid resins, laminating resins, molding resins, and putties. Gel coats are used in boatbuilding, auto manufacturing, tank building, and furniture making. Unsaturated polyester resins are used by paint, furniture, and appliance manufacturers, as well as in the production of "sanitaryware," which includes cultured marble for sinks, tubs, and shower stalls. These resins are also marketed to automakers, tank builders, architectural and construction suppliers, marble suppliers, and distributors. CCP supports its customers with the second-largest composites distribution network in North America.

As a participant through TOTAL in the world polymers markets of the Americas, Europe, South Africa, and Southeast Asia, CCP's Polymers Division develops and manufactures synthetic resins and additives for coatings. Polymers products include acrylics, polyesters, alkyds, and silicones. CCP's aqueous emulsion polymers are marketed worldwide to maintenance products industries and for specialty applications. Maintenance products include surfactants, concentrates, emulsion polymers, and polyethylene waxes.

Technology, assistance with application, and waste disposal are basic elements of CCP's Industrial Products business. This division produces cleaners and

cleaning equipment designed for the fiberglass-reinforced plastic (FRP)/composite, industrial, and cultured marble/cast polymer industries.

Local Roots, Worldwide Reach

The company's products are made at 11 manufacturing facilities, which are located in North Kansas City; Arlington, Washington; Chatham, Virginia; Houston and Marshall, Texas; Lemont, Illinois; Orlando, Florida; Oxnard, California; Pennsaukcn, New Jersey; Sandusky, Ohio; and Saukville, Wisconsin, as well as two locations in Canada and one in Mexico.

D. Patrick Curran serves as chairman of the board of CCP and as president of the Curran Companies, the continuing joint-venture partner in the business arrangement with TOTAL. Chief executive officer is Charles Bennett, and vice presidents of the three main operating groups are Del Wilkinson (Composites), Craig Lampani (Polymers), and Sherwin Chasen (Emulsion Products).

Today, CCP's research facilities, analytical services, and technological resources have been expanded through networks that connect CCP with both similar and diversified associates of TOTAL. CCP customers are further assured of product quality through the company's implementation of the International Organization for Standardization's ISO 9002 standard for quality management and quality assurance, which encompasses all manufacturing sites. Through such dedication to quality and innovation, CCP will continue to be recognized as a worldwide leader among the industries it serves.

Clockwise from top left: CCP's central research facilities in North Kansas City are a state-of-the-art home for more than 50 chemists.

Significant capital investment has been made since 1994 to automate CCP's 13 manufacturing facilities.

CCP's corporate headquarters and research laboratories are located in newly renovated buildings that have been a part of the Cook Paint and Varnish properties since 1916.

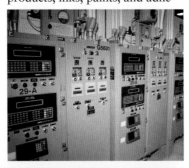

SOT Resources, Inc. is a consulting firm that considers itself to be a "financial architect" to CEOs of closely held corporations. The firm's primary mission is to help CEOs develop and implement corporate and personal strategies for capital financing, wealth preservation, business succession, and asset protection.

Over the past several years, the firm developed the FLPSOP℠ wealth preservation strategy. In November of 1997, the firm obtained a registered service mark from the U.S. Patent and Trademark Office and in August of 1998, the IRS issued a very favorable Private Letter Ruling (PLR 98103433) to one of the firm's clients that affirmed the general strategy involved with the FLPSOP℠ concept.

The FLPSOP℠ concept is a proprietary product of ESOT Resources and can be described as the strategic coordination of a Family Limited Partnership (FLP) and an Employee Stock Ownership Plan (ESOP). Additionally, the FLPSOP℠ is a state-of-the-art financial strategy for successful entrepreneurs who seek to maximize the value of their life's work and protect their hard-earned assets from being lost to capital gains taxes, estate taxes, and lawsuits.

ESOT Resources, Inc. is proud to have been closely associated with the establishment or enhancement of about 90 ESOPs that today cover about 23,000 employees and hold about $400 million in employer stock. Industry statistics indicate there are about 11,000 ESOP companies in the United States today.

Collectively, those 11,000 ESOPs cover about 15 million employees and hold about $120 billion of employer stock.

ESOT Resources, Inc. has helped clients structure an ESOP to finance working capital from the pre-tax earnings stream of the client's company. With an ESOP as a financial conduit, investments in capital assets effectively become tax deductible expenses when acquired and the company retains its full depreciation benefit. An ESOP presents the only opportunity for corporations to internally finance working capital in a manner that is deductible and depreciable.

By far, the most popular use of an ESOP is to create a controlled market for closely held stock to provide shareholder liquidity that is tax free to the selling shareholder. Most of the firm's clients have no intention of ever selling their company. They most often use their ESOP as a means to achieve a prudent level of tax free diversification of their personal net worth. It is common for clients of the firm to have 90 percent or more of their personal net worth concentrated in one investment—their closely held company. The ESOP tax free rollover allows entrepreneurs the opportunity to avoid

capital gains taxes and reinvest 100 percent of their equity in a portfolio of publicly traded, blue chip, income-producing securities.

The firm's typical client is a creative entrepreneur who owns a manufacturing, construction, or distribution company, and who started with about $1,000 in his garage 20 or 30 years ago, and who today may be worth $10 million or more. In a situation like this, the FLPSOP℠ strategy will save the client over $2 million of capital gains taxes during his lifetime. The FLPSOP℠ strategy will also save the client about $2.5 million in estate taxes, while shielding the client's personal assets from being seized by judgment creditors.

**Clockwise from top:
ESOT Resources' typical client is a creative entrepreneur who owns a manufacturing, construction, or distribution company.**

Industry statistics indicate there are about 11,000 ESOP companies in the United States today.

The FLPSOP℠ strategy can save the closely held business owner significant capital gains taxes during his lifetime.

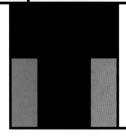

HE STAFFING INDUSTRY IS EXPERIENCING A BOOM LIKE IT'S NEVER seen before—and no one knows that better than Overland Park-based Spencer Reed Group. Founded in 1990, Spencer Reed provides staffing services for virtually any employer by concentrating on three areas: contract staffing and outsourcing, direct

placement, and temporary staffing solutions.

The consultants at Spencer Reed are specialists in the placement field. Consultants who recruit and place medical doctors only work with medical doctors. Consultants who recruit and place engineers only work with engineers. This practice means Spencer Reed employees are intimately familiar with the ins and outs of the industries in which their clients are involved.

SCOTT IRWIG

This understanding and respect for clients' work translates to long-term relationships and big-time revenues. Every year since Richard Plodzien founded the firm, Spencer Reed has doubled its sales. Other cities currently serviced include St. Louis, Phoenix, Salt Lake City, Denver, and San Antonio, along with most of Southern California. The firm counts Pepsico, Ford, General Motors, Black & Veatch, and Anheuser-Busch among its clients, 98 percent of which are repeat customers. In 1997, Spencer Reed rang up $30 million across 11 states in 27 offices.

Spencer Reed is made up of six divisions: Spencer Reed Executive Search, Spencer Reed Technical Group, Spencer Reed Medical Group, The Personnel Connection, The Law Connection, and Encore Staffing Services. Besides numerous direct placements, the company puts 1,300 people to work in temporary positions each week.

Spencer Reed has a far-reaching impact on the business economy of metropolitan Kansas City. In

1997, the company was responsible for a payroll of $23 million, ranging in positions from temporary to executive levels. By playing the matchmaker role, Spencer Reed contributes to its clients' livelihood. The company helps make it possible for parents to find flexible-hour and part-time jobs that allow them to spend more time with their children, and for career-driven executives to stay challenged, and thus happy, in their fields.

Spencer Reed Group gives its employees the opportunity to take their careers as far as they want them to go. An extensive library of training materials and up-to-date information on industry trends turn employees into virtual entrepreneurs.

Being proactive in retaining employees allows Spencer Reed to be on the cutting edge of the staffing services industry. The company's continuous, innovative solutions to rapidly changing staffing needs include an engineering design center and an architectural service, which supply outsourcing services to its clients. The management team plans to add other new services, including insurance and the gaming industry, direct placement, and contracting, as well as human resources outsourcing. And plans are in the works to take the company public. The initial public offering will help Spencer Reed maintain its growth record into the next century. Already, plans are on the table to open offices in Atlanta; Jacksonville, Florida; Orlando; Memphis; and Charlotte.

As Spencer Reed blossoms, so too do its clients and employees. By keeping a step ahead of the competition through specialized disciplines and innovative programming, the firm is definitely one to watch.

SCOTT IRWIG

Founded in 1990, Spencer Reed provides staffing services for virtually any employer by concentrating on three areas: contract staffing and outsourcing, direct placement, and temporary staffing solutions.

The consultants at Spencer Reed are specialists in the placement field. Consultants who recruit and place medical doctors only work with medical doctors. Consultants who recruit and place engineers only work with engineers. This practice means Spencer Reed employees are intimately familiar with the ins and outs of the industries in which their clients are involved.

ITH THE U.S. ECONOMY ON A RECORD UPSWING, MORE and more people are investing in the stock market. Reflecting this trend, legions of companies have materialized to help those investors manage their money. From mutual funds to discount brokers to on-line trading, investment strategies have proliferated wildly, leaving some people exposed to excessive risks.

Through the maelstrom, the firm of Eveans, Bash, Magrino & Klein (EBMK) has remained a stalwart adviser, dedicated to professional, fee-only money management with a distinct emphasis on maintaining personal relationships with its clients. The firm's value-oriented investing style means that its clients can realize competitive returns while maintaining significantly less risk than the broad market. That has made an enormous difference to the firm's clients, which range from some of the metro area's largest companies, foundations, and endowments to medical practices, high-net-worth families, and individuals.

"All of our clients have one of the four partners assigned to them, and they understand their concerns are important to us," says Tom Bash, one of the firm's four managing directors. "We consistently get very high marks for taking the complexities of the market and making them understandable to investors or their employees."

Growth Oriented

EBMK has experienced solid, but controlled growth since it was launched in 1991 by Mark Eveans, Bash, Frank Magrino, and Jim Klein after the four bought out the owners of a firm for which they had previously worked. That first year, EBMK managed $325 million for fewer than 100 clients. Today, the firm has tripled in size, with more than 300 clients and $900 million under management. Its sister company, Investors Services Trust (IST), acts as custodian or trustee to more than $500 million in assets.

From the beginning, the four partners built—and continue to develop—one distinct investment style. Because it is quantitatively based, disciplined, and detailed, the firm was able to secure a federal service mark on its Core Value® process, which favors lower-risk, high-quality investments. The process identifies and ranks investments that possess specific measures of value and growth, characteristics that are reflected in each of the company's client portfolios.

Eveans, Chartered Financial Analyst (CFA) and managing director, notes that "both firms are organized into functional teams that are focused importantly in the investment process, and also on technology, marketing, operations, personal trust, and retirement planning. This team focus is vital to giving each client tailored, personal service for their money."

Clients understand that their total investment needs can be handled in a highly professional, "one-stop shop" through the combination of EBMK managing the assets and IST providing safekeeping, custody, record keeping, and wealth transfer to their heirs via trusts.

"Because we have a trust company and truly professional advisers, our clients feel there is more than one person they can turn to," says Klein, CFA and managing director. "They don't feel like they are just a number, and they obviously like that. They also appreciate the notion that there is a real substance behind how investment decisions are made, and we obviously like that. It's a nice combination for everyone."

Eveans, Bash, Magrino & Klein, Inc. was founded in 1991 by (from left) Jim Klein, Mark Eveans, Frank Magrino, and Tom Bash.

The Eveans, Bash, Magrino & Klein team is made up of many professional disciplines who provide a broad range of talents to the clients of EMBK and IST.

GE HAS NEVER STOOD IN KANNAN SRINIVASAN'S WAY. Born to a mathematician and his wife in India, Srinivasan was only 28 when he launched Best Computer Consultants, Inc. from a College Boulevard office in Overland Park. Srinivasan had learned discipline from his father,

determination from his mother, and patience from dealing with nine older siblings. He figured that starting a business on his own terms in a new country would simply be another exciting challenge.

Lacking any financing, Srinivasan raised start-up capital of a mere $2,000. He didn't go full-time with the company for nearly a year after opening the doors in 1992 and, even then, the entrepreneur sometimes went without a salary so he could meet payroll. A hands-on manager, Srinivasan dealt personally with clients, building name recognition and traveling the globe to secure clients.

Best Computer Consultants, Inc. (BCC) now boasts more than 125 staff members working with clients across the United States from offices in Overland Park and Atlanta. In 1996, Srinivasan opened a subsidiary in Madras, India—where more than 125 employees work out of two offices—to provide offshore development facilities for U.S. companies. By 2000, Srinivasan expects BCC to be a $50 million company that will employ more than 500 people serving businesses all over the world.

"The need for trained information technology professionals was far surpassing the available labor pool," says Srinivasan, who hatched his idea over dinner one night with several fellow consultants. "As a company, we're still new to the market, but we're developing good relationships with clients that will sustain us far into the future."

A New Consulting Philosophy

As a consultant, the BCC founder and CEO knew that contract consultants, who traveled from company to company providing advice, felt disconnected from distant home offices that were often unsupportive. With his own company, Srinivasan decided to furnish attractive wages and benefits, keep the lines of communication open, and provide training that would be directly beneficial to both staff and clients.

"I set out to form a company that offered a full benefits package, job guarantees, and ways to build a sense of belonging and support for consultants," says Srinivasan, who stays in touch with employees through frequent job-site visits and invitations for dinner and Sunday cricket games. "Our people must have honesty and ethics, and treat people with dignity in everything they do. We have to remember that this is a people business and that we must treat

"I set out to form a company that offered a full benefits package, job guarantees, and ways to build a sense of belonging and support for consultants," says Best Computer Consultants founder and CEO Kannan Srinivasan, who stays in touch with employees through frequent job-site visits and invitations for dinner and Sunday cricket games.

people the way we want to be treated. That won't change, no matter how big we get."

First in Technology

In addition, Srinivasan wanted his company to provide top-notch technology consulting and software development to organizations around the globe. These days, BCC consultants are involved in many cutting-edge products, including the development of universal servers, parallel servers, and graphic user interface (GUI) development platforms, such as Power Builders, X-Windows, and others. Consultants also work on legacy and client server technologies, including ES9000, IBM 3090, IMS, CICS, Cobol, DB2, Oracle DBA, Sybase, Sybase DBA, Lotus Notes, ODBC calls, Datablade, Data Warehousing, Java, HTML, CGM, and CGI Perl, among others.

In the future, Srinivasan plans to acquire a 64-kilobyte-per-second satellite/fiber-optic connection between Kansas City and Madras so information can move even more quickly between company sites. In addition, BCC's first commercial product launched the company into a new business by offering customer-ready, pro-prietary software for sale in the United States and around the globe. Within the next several years, Srinivasan envisions opening offices in Europe and the Far East that will enhance considerably BCC's information technology consulting opportunities.

The company's attention to technological advancement has resulted in various awards for BCC. For several years, Best Computer Consultants, Inc. has been recognized as one of the top 10 minority-owned companies in Kansas City. Named the sixth-fastest-growing information technology company in the state of Kansas by the Kansas Department of Science and Technology, BCC also takes a leadership role in the Kansas City software consulting industry.

As a member of the Better Business Bureau, Greater Kansas City Chamber of Commerce, Kansas Chamber of Commerce and Industry, Silicon Prairie Technology Association, Kansas City Area Development Council and Information Technology Association of America, Best Computer Consultants, Inc. has supported local, state, and national business efforts to improve both business and legislative practices. Srinivasan also donates a significant amount of dollars to organizations such as the Special Olympics and Heart to Heart, an Olathe-based organization that airlifts medical supplies and food to Third World countries. In addition, Srinivasan contributed to the Nelson Gallery Foundation, St. Jude Children's Research Hospital, American Heart Association, and to the Chiefs/Arrowhead Stadium's 25th anniversary. As the first member of the National Association of Computer Consulting Businesses (NACCB) in Kansas City, BCC has embraced the concept of bringing ethics back into the consulting industry. The company has promoted membership and adherence to these business principles to other Kansas City-area computer consulting businesses.

"I believe that people who work here should feel like they're operating their own company," says Srinivasan. "That way, they can be satisfied with what they do and can make decisions that will beneficially affect all of our futures. All in all, we are growing in the best ways possible, both in terms of technology and relationships with each other and our clients."

BCC consultants are involved in many cutting-edge products, including the development of universal servers, parallel servers, graphic user interface development platforms, and also mainframe applications.

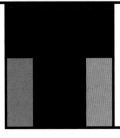

HE ADVANCES MADE BY THE MEDICAL AND PHARMACEUTICAL COMmunities in the past several decades are nothing short of astounding. Now, thanks to Overland Park-based CyDex, Inc., medicine is taking another quantum leap. ■ CyDex's major product, Captisol®, has the potential to initiate breakthroughs for medical compounds

that previously were not absorbable by the human body. Captisol, which is a patented cyclodextrin derivative, works by enhancing water solubility while remaining nontoxic to people. This means that researchers will be able to adapt disease-fighting drugs more quickly, efficiently, and cost effectively. Drug developers can take compounds that might advance the fight against everything from cancer to the common cold and improve the probability of using them to successfully battle these human ills.

"We are working with a wonderful technology that will prove to be of great assistance

CyDex, Inc.'s president, Peter Higuchi, is also founder and CEO of the company.

in the development of new pharmaceutical products that wouldn't otherwise be developed," says President Peter Higuchi, CyDex founder and CEO. "Of those new drugs, there will be many used in lifesaving situations. That makes it very motivating for us, to see technology applied in ways that will be so beneficial."

Fathers of Invention

CyDex was established in 1993 to license and market Captisol, the unique product developed and patented by Drs. Valentino Stella and Roger Rajewski, researchers at the University of Kansas (KU) in

Lawrence. In fact, CyDex was originally conceived based on discussions with KU's Higuchi Biosciences Center for Drug Delivery Research, where the product was developed. The center was named for Peter's father, the late Takeru Higuchi, who was a Regents Distinguished Professor of Pharmaceutical Chemistry, the author of more than 300 published pieces, and the holder of more than 50 patents.

Like his father, the younger Higuchi brought his own impressive history of scientific and business experience to the launch of CyDex. He had worked in the pharmaceutical industry for more than a decade, including positions at Touche Ross & Company and Marion Merrell Dow, Inc. In addition, Higuchi's law degree from Washburn University and a master's degree in international management from the American School of International Management have helped him take the cyclodextrin compounds from the private research sector to countless research-oriented pharmaceutical companies.

But Higuchi's experience alone has not propelled CyDex to its current success. "The people we've attracted to work with us here are very capable and loyal, sharing their efforts in building this company and the technology to its commercial potential," says Higuchi, who willingly shares credit with everyone who works at CyDex, including Vice President of Research and Development Dr. Diane Thompson. Thompson adds, "Pharmaceutical research is a very big-dollar environment, with companies making large bets in allocations of their resources. They're conservative companies,

"CyDex is marketing the product directly and expects it to do well because of new requirements by the Food and Drug Administration that chiral drugs be analyzed by other than optical methods," says Higuchi. "This should result in a growth in the use of new analytical methods."

In fact, Higuchi expects CyDex to grow so rapidly and significantly that he will be able to take his company public by 1999. "Our plate is much fuller than it was even a year ago, and we will be adding additional people soon," says Higuchi. "Also, we're probably going to be in a position to make an initial public offering within 24 months. Although we are currently focused on the development of this technology, it's within our growth plans to secure additional, complementary technologies. We're truly paving our own way."

The management team has an optimistic outlook for the future of CyDex, Inc. The team includes (from left) Vice President of Corporate Development Karl Strohmeier; Chief Financial Officer Ed Mehrer; and Vice President of Research and Development Dr. Diane Thompson.

so that challenge is not always easy."

Within five years of its start-up, however, CyDex has signed evaluation agreements with more than 100 companies. These agreements allow the company to test Captisol for use with its own pharmaceutical research. "Overall, Captisol has been a welcomed product," says Higuchi, "because much of the initial biotechnology research is being done on university campuses, rather than in businesses. In fact, the University of Kansas maintains part equity in the company through a university/private sector liaison that's becoming more common."

In the Future

Down the road, Higuchi sees CyDex continuing to look for companies that believe their research and products would be enhanced by Captisol. Since its beginning, CyDex has provided initial samples of research-grade Captisol—free of charge under confidentiality agreements—to potential research partners who wish to test the material in their formulations. In the future, Higuchi says he'd consider the possibility of building a manufacturing facility to create the company's product in bulk quantities.

In late 1996, CyDex introduced a new product. Like Captisol, Advasep is a cyclodextrin derivative. It acts as a resolving agent for chiral and

achiral separations performed via capillary electrophoresis, which means researchers can use it to analytically distinguish between compounds that are too similar to discern using other methods.

CyDex's major product, Captisol®, has the potential to initiate breakthroughs for medical compounds that previously were not absorbable by the human body.

WITHOUT EVEN KNOWING IT, MILLIONS OF PEOPLE around the world regularly come into contact with GST Steel Company. That's because the Kansas City mill—once a division of Armco, Inc.—produces high-carbon wire rod that is used in everything from pianos

GST Steel Company's Kansas City mill turns red-hot steel bars into wire rod products used in everything from piano wire to bedsprings to bridge cables (top).

GST's grinding balls and grinding rods, used to turn ore-rich rocks into a fine powder for separation, set the industry standard (bottom).

to bridges to brake pads. In fact, GST is one of the largest wire rod producers in the nation.

In addition, GST's grinding balls and grinding rods, used to turn ore-rich rocks into a fine powder for separation, set the industry standard. Made with top-quality alloying elements and heat treatment, these and other GST products are backed by extensive research and testing. Furthermore, for GST's parent

company, GS Industries, two production sites—its sister plant is located in South Carolina—help the company provide unique scheduling flexibility, economies of scale, and the ability to choose between different manufacturing methods to better meet customer requirements.

"Our goal every day is to produce the highest-quality product to meet the rigorous demands of our customers," says Bud Rossi, who in the spring of 1998 became a GS Industries vice president and general manager-operations of GST Steel Company. "We're now in the process of making organizational changes necessary to bring our quality, productivity, and customer service up to the higher standards required to do business in the global marketplace."

Growing Together

For two years, GST Steel Company was known as GS Technologies, after a management-led buyout of Armco Worldwide

Grinding Systems of Kansas City. But in 1995, the local company merged with Georgetown Industries of Charlotte, North Carolina, to form GS Industries, now based in Charlotte. Today, the new enterprise is one of the largest mini-mill steel producers in the United States, with net sales of approximately $1 billion a year and an annual raw steel-making capacity of more than 2 million tons.

As a global leader in special products, GSI manufactures more high-carbon wire rod than any other supplier in North America. The company is also the largest provider of grinding media products, including steel balls, rods, and abrasion-resistant liners for the world's mining industry. And GSI leads the market in the production of prestressed concrete strand and galvanized guy strand.

In Kansas City, the company continues to break new ground in the production of steel products. It is one of the few companies in the world to use a new material called Direct Reduced Iron (DRI) to augment conventional steel scrap—including cars, household products, and industrial cast-offs—in the steelmaking process. DRI, which is produced by another GSI sister company, improves the quality of the finished product and also allows for the use of lower-quality scrap.

In terms of end users, the largest portion of the company's business comes from the automotive, construction, furniture, and other industrial markets. GST has earned a commanding market share in these industries and many others by providing exceptional product quality and customer service.

"Our focus today must be on strengthening our leadership

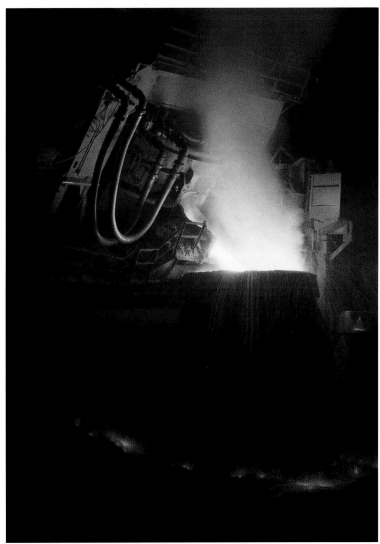
© 1998 MIKE FUGER

position, which we have earned by emphasizing our technical expertise, but which is now challenged by competitors domestically and overseas," says Rossi. "We've got a great reputation in every segment, but we face significant challenges today to maintain that reputation and that leadership position."

World Class

When GS Industries was formed, the newly created company immediately embarked upon a $35 million renovation of the Kansas City mill. Now, according to Rossi, the company is focused on ensuring that the state-of-the-art facility produces grinding balls up to its full potential.

Although Kansas City executives report to GSI headquarters in Charlotte, the centrally located facility was an important factor in the company's drive toward increased profitability. "Kansas City's central location is a big

factor in our success because it's a tremendous spot for obtaining raw material, mainly scrap," says Rossi. "And it's great from a distribution standpoint, too."

In addition to improving its facilities and equipment, the company has continued to focus on increasing its proprietary services and engineering systems to help customers optimize their manufacturing process when interacting with GST's products. From research and development to process control, GST adds value when and where it is needed.

In Demand

Steel is so ubiquitous that many people never give it a second thought. But imagine the combined amount of steel needed by the many companies that produce guitar strings, paper clips, shopping carts, elevator cable, bicycle spokes, nails, ball bearings, football helmet face masks, bedsprings, ballpoint pen springs, steering wheels, and

steel wool. GST supplies all of these markets and many others.

That worldwide pervasiveness is why the company believes that demand for high-quality wire rod and grinding media will grow—and why GST will be there to answer the call with cost-effective products, advanced technology, and superior service. Although the world marketplace is becoming increasingly complex and competitive, GST views the future with confidence and optimism.

"There are plenty of ways for us to grow in the future," says Rossi. "Enhanced global expansion, new markets, new inventions—all of them create new opportunities for GST Steel. However, all of us must work hard to capture these opportunities, because we're not the only ones reaching for them. By focusing on a philosophy of constant change and continuous improvement, we will strive to make our company even more influential in the future."

"Our goal every day is to produce the highest-quality product to meet the rigorous demands of our customers," says General Manager Bud Rossi. "We're now in the process of making organizational changes necessary to bring our quality, productivity, and customer service up to the higher standards required to do business in the global marketplace (left).

As a global leader in special products, GSI manufactures more high-carbon wire rod than any other supplier in North America (right).

WHEN GATEWAY ANNOUNCED PLANS TO OPEN A SALES and customer service center in Kansas City in 1993, local officials were delighted. A leading marketer of personal computers, Gateway would take advantage of the high-technology emphasis that had been

building in the region and add hundreds of jobs in the process. Ironically, the publicly held company chose to set up shop in a decidedly nonfuturistic location: a freshly renovated and expanded building in the heart of the former Kansas City stockyards.

"Gateway is fondly described as being 'born in a barn' on the Waitt family cattle ranch," says Sandra Lawrence, vice president of administration. "The West Bottoms, which was once a bustling livestock hub and home of the stockyards, is actually a natural fit."

Filling a Need

Gateway has experienced phenomenal revenue growth since it was launched in 1985 in Sioux City, Iowa. By the time it had moved to North Sioux City, South Dakota, in 1990, the company had achieved some $275 million in annual sales. By 1997, revenue had reached $6.3 billion.

In the beginning, founder Ted Waitt sold peripherals and software to owners of Texas In-

Gateway is based on founder Ted Waitt's theory that technically sophisticated customers would buy completely configured PCs sight unseen if they could get a good price. Since then, Gateway has expanded globally, and today, its products include the NS9000, Destination DMC, and Gateway G6-300XL.

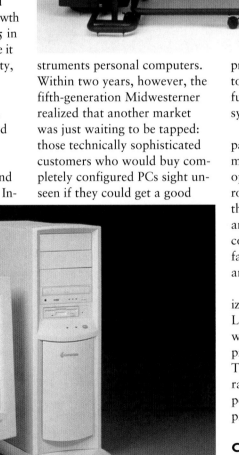

struments personal computers. Within two years, however, the fifth-generation Midwesterner realized that another market was just waiting to be tapped: those technically sophisticated customers who would buy completely configured PCs sight unseen if they could get a good

price. So, Waitt directed Gateway to design and assemble its own fully configured, PC-compatible systems.

Since then, Gateway has expanded globally, opening a direct marketing and manufacturing operation in Ireland and showrooms in France, Germany, Japan, the United Kingdom, Sweden, and Australia. In addition, the company has built new manufacturing facilities in Virginia and Malaysia.

"Gateway's vision is to humanize the digital revolution," says Lawrence. "Our strength lies with our people, our innovative products, and our business model. To sustain growth, we constantly raise the bar, setting higher expectations and goals for our products and our people."

Computer Specialization

Gateway is a leader in bringing new technology to market quickly and turning multimedia into an industry standard. *Dataquest* reported that

Gateway ranked ninth worldwide in total shipments of PCs in the third quarter of 1997. The company has been at the forefront of new technology with the introduction of Pentium®, Pentium® Pro, and Pentium® with MMX™ technology processors across its product lines. Gateway systems feature Intel processors ranging from Pentium® to Pentium® II, and boast top-quality components and high-value software packages. The company's portable products include the award-winning Gateway Solo™ notebook line, which offers modular design, industry-leading technology, and interchangeable parts. In 1996, Gateway introduced the Destination big screen PC/TV. As the first convergence product in the industry, the Destination quickly established a new category that combines the best elements of a state-of-the-art multimedia computer with the visual drama of a home theater system.

Also in 1996, the company's subsidiary, Gateway Country Stores, Inc., announced a pilot program to test its showroom expansion in the United States. Already, European stores have proved successful for customers who want to learn about Gateway products on a face-to-face basis before buying direct. Thirty-seven stores were in operation by the end of 1997.

"By concentrating primarily on the direct channel, the company has built a reputation for excellent values by consistently providing reliable products and outstanding customer service and support," says Lawrence. "Because we sell directly to end users, Gateway has developed and maintained a strong relationship with our customers. This closeness has enabled us to respond to customer requirements more rapidly than the competition."

A Lively Work Environment

To be sure, Waitt has customer satisfaction uppermost in his mind. But providing his more than 13,000 employees worldwide with a personally rewarding work experience ranks near the top, too. Waitt believes that if a company treats its people fairly, provides opportunities for professional growth, and creates a fun environment, then those people will generate profits for the company. As a result, he's given his staffers a direct stake in the success of the company, and provides opportunities for career advancement.

Employees also participate in Gateway's unique advertising programs. Created by the company's in-house advertising department, national ads feature employees in humorous skits that have defined the Gateway personality to customers around the world.

In addition to the rave reviews for its ads, Gateway has earned a variety of awards for its products. In 1997, the company was honored with 60 awards, including Aetna's Supplier of the Year for demonstration of excellent service and reasonable prices. Other awards in 1997 included the Best Buy awards from *Computer Shopper* for the professional and PC lines; the Editors' Choice awards from *PC Magazine* for the P5-200XL and G6-266M, and the solo 2200 and 9100 portables; and the World Class Award for best service and support from *PC World*.

"At its core, Gateway has eight guiding principles—respect, caring, teamwork, common sense, aggressiveness, honesty, efficiency, and fun," says Lawrence. "We uphold those values with our coworkers and our customers. When you couple our business principles with our great products, you have a formula for success."

Customer service is a priority for Gateway. Staff members field inquiries relating to sales and product operation from a huge customer service center located in Kansas City (top).

Gateway's sales, customer service, and support facility is located in Kansas City (bottom).

HEN TRANSAMERICA LIFE COMPANIES ANNOUNCED that it would move a 500-employee administrative operation from Los Angeles to the Kansas City area, many sat up and took notice. One of the largest corporate relocations in recent years, Transamerica's

1993 decision followed months of competition between Kansas City and several other prominent cities in the Midwest and Southeast.

"Everybody in the metroplex ought to celebrate the fact that we have a big fish that could grow bigger," Kansas City Mayor Emanuel Cleaver told the *Kansas City Star* after the announcement was made. Said Bill Nelson, cochairman of the Kansas City Area Development Council, "We worked hard to get them here. They're now a big part of the community."

From there, the excitement only grew. Although no one knew it at the time, Transamerica's move would become the first in a wave of high-profile relocations. After the life insurance company opened its office at downtown Kansas City's Town Pavilion, corporate giants such as Gateway, EDS, and Harley-Davidson declared that they would also transfer operations to the area. "I don't know if we had much to do with the wave," says Bill Scott, Transamerica's senior vice president and chief operations officer in Kansas City, "but one of the

Transamerica Life Companies' downtown skyscraper features the company's name in lights.

Visitors are greeted in the main reception area.

things that convinced us to come to Kansas City was the attitude of city and business leaders to welcome us here."

Significant Shift

Certainly, it was a coup for Kansas City to land the Transamerica Life division. Transamerica Life Companies is among the sixth-largest individual life insurers in North America based on life insurance in force, and is one of the top life reinsurers in the United States, based on new business and in-force volume. The companies had a combined $467.1 billion of life insurance in force at the end of 1997 and assets of $41.4 billion. The companies are subsidiaries of San Francisco-based Transamerica Corporation, one of the nation's largest financial services companies, with more than $51 billion in total assets.

Like many other insurance companies, Transamerica Life Companies, which is based in Los Angeles, was seeking to im-

prove its bottom line by moving its administrative operations to an area with a lower cost of doing business. A high quality of life was also a key consideration in selecting a city for the administrative operations. About a year before the Kansas City decision, company executives had considered moving the division to Charlotte, where it had recently relocated another group.

But Kansas City pulled out all the stops, with intense lobbying from local, state, and federal government officials and business leaders from both Missouri and Kansas. Moreover, there were business considerations that appealed to Transamerica. Kansas City offered a central time zone location, which gave the company a longer workday to communicate with other parts of the country. Flight times between Kansas City and the Los Angeles headquarters also were shorter compared with Charlotte.

In addition, Transamerica executives felt that Kansas City was a cosmopolitan city that had not

compromised its good quality of life. One major aspect they most admired was the midwestern work ethic. Studies have shown that Kansas City natives tend to work hard.

"We were able to relocate a core of our experienced people from Southern California, which was critical to the success of this operation," says Scott. "But we've also been very pleased with the quality and quantity of employees we've been able to find. Those who relocated like the quality of life and friendliness here."

Local Impact

The first group to move was Transamerica's insurance products division operations team, which included new business processing, billing, collecting, claims processing, systems support, and underwriting. Within two years, however, Transamerica moved two additional units to the company's Kansas City office, the downtown skyscraper that now features Transamerica's name in lights. The individual annuities operations group and long-term care insurance, a relatively new business unit, arrived in 1996.

"The experiences of that initial group had a tremendous effect on the decision to bring others here," says Scott, who points out that Transamerica employs some 700 people in Kansas City. "We've also set up a regional marketing center here, staffed with employees recruited from throughout the country."

In only a few years, Transamerica has had a likewise beneficial effect on Kansas City, as its community involvement has extended the company's reach through the metropolitan area. Transamerica's charitably oriented group, TLC Cares, has organized activities to raise funds for local endeavors such as the Mattie Rhodes Center, the Heart of America Boy Scouts, the Friends of Alvin Ailey, and Junior Achievement, among others. "We have a long history of encouraging our employees to be involved in the community," says Scott. "Our charitable gifts tend to follow our employees in their activities."

And, according to Scott, such a close relationship fits well with Transamerica's overall goal as a corporation. "As an insurance company, we're one of the most technologically advanced in the industry," he says. "That reputation is tied to our move to Kansas City, when we made this a paperless office using lots of image processing and other technological tools in our work. We're dedicated to supporting our customer base with quality service."

Clockwise from top left: Belinda Patton serves the company's customers from the Kansas City office.

Transamerica monitors and controls all of its Kansas City computer operations from a central command console.

Some of Transamerica Life Companies' senior executives are (sitting, from left) Frank LaRusso, Mary Spence, Bill Scott, (standing, from left) Dr. Paul Hankwitz, Jim Strand, Suzette Hoyt, Brian Hoyt, and Tom Dolan.

Karen Lauer-Moore is a research underwriting specialist.

FORT DODGE ANIMAL HEALTH

EVERY YEAR, RESPONSIBLE PET OWNERS TAKE THEIR DOGS AND cats to the veterinarian for their annual vaccinations. They know that keeping the pets current on their boosters means that faithful companions will live longer and healthier lives. What they may not realize, however, is how much work goes on behind the

Fort Dodge Animal Health, a division of American Home Products Corporation since 1946, employs 150 people at its Overland Park headquarters.

Fort Dodge Animal Health's mission is to research, develop, manufacture, and market innovative biologicals and pharmaceuticals to provide sound medical solutions for both pets and livestock.

scenes to make good animal health possible.

The mission at Fort Dodge Animal Health is to research, develop, manufacture, and market innovative biologicals and pharmaceuticals to provide sound medical solutions for both pets and livestock. Founded in 1912 in Fort Dodge, Iowa, Fort Dodge Animal Health ranks second in animal vaccines in North America, and is expanding rapidly in international biological and pharmaceutical markets.

"A big part of our success comes from our people, who work very hard in a very focused manner," says E. Thomas Corcoran, president of Fort Dodge. "From a technical viewpoint, we have made significant improvements in the area of biological and pharmaceutical manufacturing, and we're able to manufacture in a very cost-effective way."

Making a Move

In 1995, 83 years after its founding by Dr. E. Baughman to produce hog cholera virus and anti-hog-cholera serum, Fort Dodge Animal Health established a global headquarters in Overland Park. This move followed the acquisition of the American Cyanamid Company and Syntex

Animal Health businesses, and allowed the company to centralize its rapidly growing operations.

"Because of these acquisitions, we had a new company and we wanted a new culture, too," says Corcoran. "We also benefited in other ways. Once we moved to the Kansas City area, we found that we were able to have more frequent contact with customers than before, and nothing beats face-to-face meetings."

Operating as a global animal health business, Fort Dodge employs a staff of 150 at its Overland Park headquarters. The worldwide workforce numbers more than 3,700. In the United States, three important facilities keep Fort Dodge on the cutting edge of veterinary medicine. These include a production and biologicals research center in Fort Dodge; a biologicals production facility in Charles City, Iowa; and a pharmaceutical research and development operation located in Princeton, New Jersey. Veterinary biological and pharmaceutical products bearing the Fort Dodge label are marketed in more than 100 countries around the world.

Setting the Standard

Together, Fort Dodge employees have helped the company earn its place as a global leader in developing and producing a range of high-quality animal health products. Fort Dodge's history of breakthroughs in veterinary medicine and new product developments has earned the company a solid reputation for innovation among veterinary researchers around the world. Some of Fort Dodge's impressive firsts in the animal health industry include the first genetically cloned

feline leukemia vaccine, first modified live canine parvovirus vaccine, first modified live-virus hog cholera vaccine, first killed rabies vaccine in combination with feline rhinotracheitis-calici-panleukopenia, first complete line of equine vaccines, first killed rhinopneumonitis vaccine to prevent abortion in mares, first canine Lyme disease vaccine, first feline ringworm vaccine, and first complete line of killed-virus bovine vaccines.

Preparing for Tomorrow

The acquisition of the world-wide animal health business of the Belgian company Solvay S.A., in 1997, moved Fort Dodge into the top tier of global animal health companies, providing a significant presence in Europe and the Far East, and a strong entry into the global swine and poultry biological markets.

"We should see continued strong growth on the international front," says Corcoran. "But in every market we serve, whether it's domestic or international, we want to be recognized by our customer base as an innovative, responsive, and reliable animal health company. If we accomplish that, then it means our marketing, research, manufacturing, and everything else we're doing is working."

Fort Dodge Animal Health has been a division of American Home Products Corporation since 1946. American Home Products, one of the world's largest research-based pharmaceutical and health care products companies, is a leader in the discovery, development, manufacturing, and marketing of prescription drugs and over-the-counter medications. The company is also a global leader in vaccines, biotechnology, agricultural products, animal health care, and medical devices.

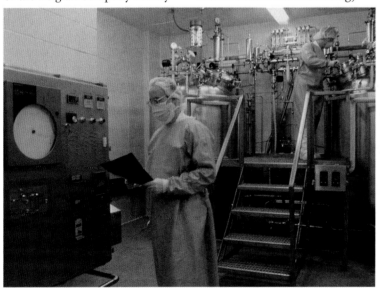

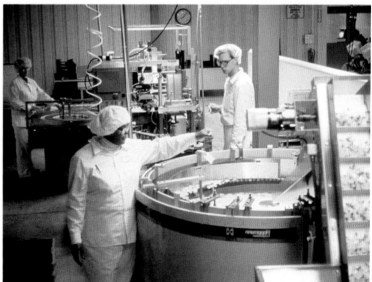

DOUBLETREE HOTEL KANSAS CITY

T WAS A DRAMATIC MOMENT IN LOCAL HISTORY WHEN THE DOUBLETREE Hotel Kansas City debuted in 1997. Once known as the Americana, the 1970s-era property had languished before finally closing its doors in 1994. About a year later, however, a visionary development group noticed the need for more hotel rooms in downtown Kansas City,

purchased the hotel, and announced a dramatic, $30 million renovation. As the newly transformed Doubletree, the 28-floor hotel has experienced an exciting rebirth and has added new life to the area.

"The Doubletree has quickly become a necessary ingredient in downtown Kansas City's hospitality mix," says General Manager Thomas Moriarty. "But it's also added a distinctive element with its look and its amenities." The hotel has quickly become one of Kansas City's premier places to stay, converting what had been a downtown eyesore into an upscale inn that attracts both business and leisure travelers. The renovation project, which some naysayers originally believed would prove an insurmountable challenge, has created a new ambience for downtown Kansas City.

The Doubletree Hotel Kansas City features 388 rooms and overlooks Barney Allis Plaza.

Upscale Accommodations

Decorated in a style dubbed "stately heartland," the hotel's 388 guest rooms include 99 suites and two club floors. These limited-access floors boast a private lounge, dedicated concierge attention, and food and beverage services specifically for club guests.

Throughout the hotel, rich wood detailing and mission-style furnishings with colorful touches in maroon, green, and taupe create a regal ambience that successfully combines old-world and new-world styles. The decor's triangle-and-diamond motif mirrors the design of the art-deco-style artwork atop nearby Bartle Hall, Kansas City's premier convention trade show facility. The main floor restaurant, Bistro 1301, has quickly become a popular dining venue, featuring grilled fare from the hotel's wood-fired ovens. Its casual elegance is reminiscent of an intimate European bistro.

Although stately inside, the hotel's exterior is lighted at night in tones of turquoise, providing an arresting and contemporary juxtaposition to its renowned art deco surroundings. "The Doubletree Hotel Kansas City

Doubletree's stately Heartland Lobby provides guests with a relaxing environment.

▲ MARK BOISCLAIR

Doubletree's Bistro 1301 is a popular gathering place for guests.

reflects the Midwest of today," says Moriarity, "rich in a history that's solid and simple, yet moving in a fast-paced world."

Room for Meetings

A lot has changed in the decades since the Doubletree Kansas City's facility was built. Originally, the Americana featured a circular, revolving bar at its summit. Now, however, the open space has become a ballroom and meeting area. The Doubletree's convention services department attracts many groups to the hotel, in part because of its location directly across from Bartle Hall. But the hotel's 12,000 square feet of meeting space also draws many more who simply want to surround their events with luxury.

Business travelers also find a state-of-the-art business center at the Doubletree, featuring the latest in electronic equipment, as well as secretarial and translation services, and pager and cell phone rentals. Guests who would rather work in their rooms can request a multiline telephone, order a computer, hook up their

▲ MARK BOISCLAIR

Doubletree's circular penthouse ballroom was previously a revolving bar.

own fax machines or modems, and use the hotel's voice mail system. To work off stress, the Doubletree offers an on-site fitness facility and an outdoor pool.

Something for Everyone

Of course, leisure travelers enjoy the Doubletree, too, with amenities such as a complimentary copy of *USA Today*, coffeemaker, in-room video entertainment, same-day laundry service, and hair dryers. Suites

in the hotel offer refrigerators, microwaves, two telephone lines, walk-in closets, double pullout sleeper sofas, and conference tables for four people.

"We believe the Doubletree will appeal to anyone who visits Kansas City and wants a truly one-of-a-kind experience," says Moriarty. "Of course, business travelers will be our most obvious market, but our hotel provides a comfortable and stylish experience. It truly offers something for everyone."

ORE THAN TWO DECADES AGO, NANCY KENWORTHY'S hobby was beginning to take over her life. She was working in the credit collections department for Mobil Oil in downtown Kansas City and acquiring investment property on the side. When she put her own home on

the market so she could buy another piece of real estate, an agent suggested she might want to officially get into the business. For Kenworthy, it was a brilliant idea. Today, she is a multimillion-dollar producer, co-owner, and associate broker of Realty Executives/Metro One in Lee's Summit and Independence.

"I love selling and have never been able to give it up," says Kenworthy, whose agency produced more than $100 million in sales in 1997. "We believe our mission is to bring our experience to the table so that what can be a very emotional event for people becomes as easy and fun as possible," she says.

Growth Mode

Although she's owned a local real estate firm since the 1980s, Kenworthy made the switch to a Realty Executives franchise in 1994. She was attracted by the company's approach to agents, which tends to lure more experienced and entrepreneurial salespeople. In only four years, the agency has grown from 22 to 60 agents, a team with an average of 10 years' experience in the field.

"What really makes this franchise unique is the 100 percent

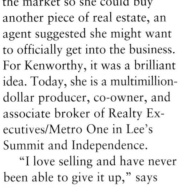

concept," says Kenworthy, whose co-owner, Doug Morris, is also the agency's broker. "That means the agents keep their entire commission, but pay a set cost each month for expenses. As a result, we tend to have bigger producers here with more experience. That's good for our clients," she says.

Sharing Success

Realty Executives/Metro One clients also benefit from the agency's belief in equity among agents. "At a traditional agency, prima donnas get fed the leads," says Kenworthy. "We don't do that here; leads are spread around. People know where they stand with Doug and me because we believe in always operating with integrity and honesty. We want our agents to be successful. It's an attitude that we instill in our people."

One way Realty Executives agents pursue success together is through their Internet site. There, each agent can include a profile that details his or her real estate achievements, as well as select properties he or she is currently listing. Some agents work with developers or commercial agents, rather than residential clients, so their marketing efforts are directed in other ways via the World Wide Web. In addition, covering the area with Realty Executive's signs helps build awareness throughout the agency's region.

"In the future, I see us continuing to grow and increase the market share we have, not just in the numbers of agents, but in the quality of agents here," Kenworthy says. "You either go forward or backward. There's only one of those directions that we like to go."

"I love selling and have never been able to give it up," says Nancy Kenworthy (top), whose agency produced more than $100 million in sales in 1997. In only four years, Realty Executives/ Metro One has grown from 22 to 60 agents, a team with an average of 10 years' experience in the field.

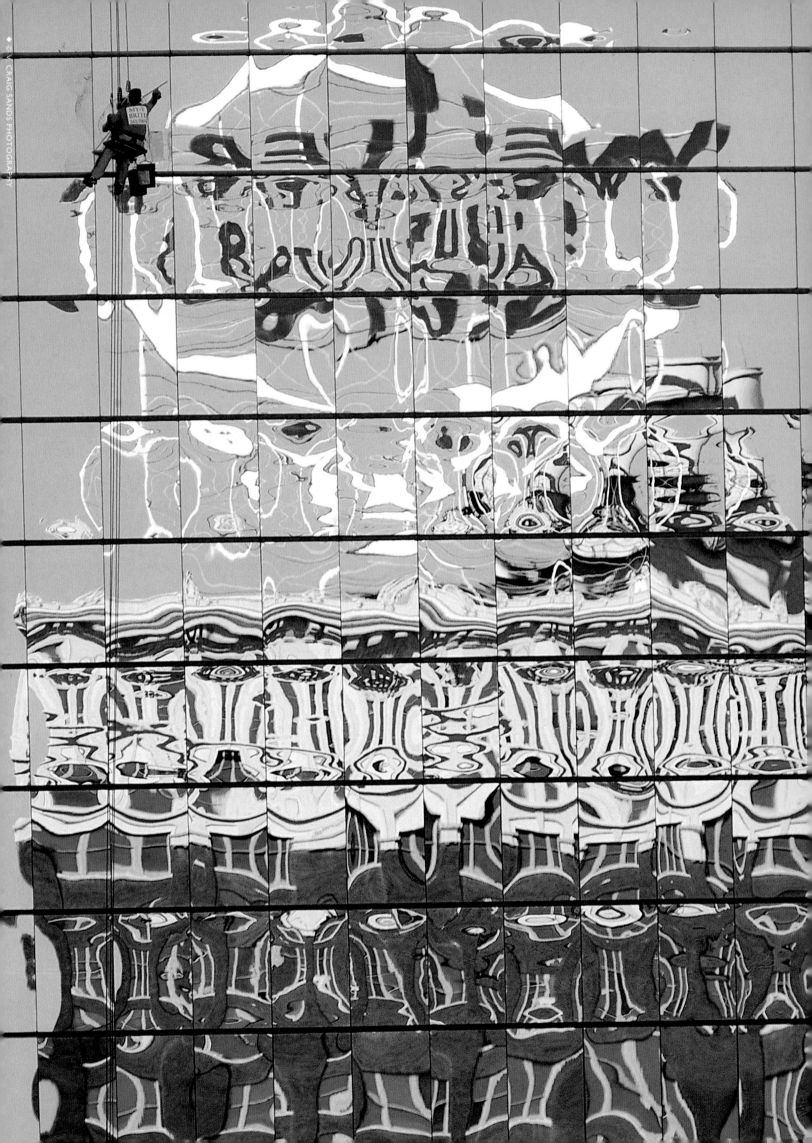

PHOTOGRAPHERS

JIM ARGO hails from Edmund, Oklahoma, where he is employed by the *Daily Oklahoman*, the state's largest newspaper. A graduate of Texas Tech University with a degree in journalism, Argo has had work published by Southwestern Bell and AT&T, in addition to *Newsweek*, *Time*, and *National Geographic*. He has covered the Oklahoma City federal building bombing, been awarded third place in the World Press Photo Foundation contest, and been inducted into the Oklahoma Journalism Hall of Fame. In his spare time, he enjoys camping with his wife, which allows him to capture the scenic side of his home state.

JOHN BAIRD, a native of Kansas City, specializes in 3-D abstract light painting. He describes this technique as "timed exposures using various self-made light sources to trace colors onto the film in three dimensions, creating two images shown through special viewers." Baird has had four one-man gallery shows exhibiting these creations. He has also been published in *Focus*

Kansas City, *Plaza*, and the *Kansas City Artist Coalition News*.

BOB BARRETT has operated Bob Barrett Photography Studio and Stock Photos since 1981. Originally from Newark, New Jersey, Barrett graduated from the University of Missouri in Kansas City with a bachelor of arts degree in psychology and sociology. He has done more than 100 covers for magazines, from *Architecture* to *Zoo-news*. His agency has provided stock photos to clients such as *Audubon*, *National Wildlife*, *National Geographic*, *Midwest Living*, and *Odyssey*. Barrett is affiliated with Liaison International's corporate photography network and speaks publicly on the various aspects of writing and photography.

HARRY BARTH graduated from the former Kansas City Junior College with a degree in photography. He specializes in commercial, portrait, and news images. Barth has photographed five presidents, including more extensive studies of President Harry S. Truman. The recipient of a

PPA national award and the Stern Award, he devotes most of his time to managing the Harry Barth Studio.

ERIC R. BERNDT, originally from Prairie Village, Kansas, is a self-taught professional photographer. After starting his own studio, Photo-technique, in 1973, Berndt focused on photographing heavy construction and industrial sites. He has been published in trade journals, books, and textbooks worldwide.

TIM BISCHOFF was an official photographer for the 1993 Paul McCartney tour. His duties included a photo session with the band members, and as a result, his images were included on the 1993 *Paul Is Live* album. His image of Eric Clapton was used for all tour promotions for the 1998 *Pilgrim* tour. Bischoff is the owner of Infinite Loop Digital Studios, specializing in commercial advertising, fashion, video production, multimedia, black-and-white infrared, and entertainment photography. His work has appeared in *USA Today*, *Rolling Stone*, *People*, and *Entertainment Weekly*.

REBECCA DOUGLAS, originally from St. Louis, moved to Kansas City in 1994. An avid traveler, she enjoys capturing everyday people in their environments. Douglas operates her own studio, Rebecca Douglas Photography, and concentrates on black-and-white portraiture, environmental photography, and black-and-white wedding images. Her photos have appeared in *Kansas City* and *Ingram's* magazines, and have been used by Big Brothers/Big Sisters, as well as by various local musicians.

DUSTY FANN, owner of Dusty Fann Photography, is a native of Lee's Summit, Missouri. He attended Longview Community College and the Kansas City Art Institute. His favorite photography subjects are sculptures and statues.

FRANK FARMWALD moved to the area from Goshen, Indiana, in 1995. He earned an associate's degree in commercial photography from Ivy Tech State College in Columbus, Indiana. Employed by *The Kansas*

▲ © COURTESY J. C. NICHOLS CO.

City Star, he focuses on wedding, commercial, tabletop, and digital photography. Farmwald worked as a freelance assistant for three years in Indianapolis, and is currently pursuing his interest in editorial photography.

REBECCA FRIEND received a bachelor of fine arts degree in painting from Central Missouri State University. She works for *The Kansas City Star* as an advertising photographer, specializing in portraiture and tabletop photography. Friend has also been published in *Taste*, *Prime*, and *Kansas City Weddings* magazines, and *Kansas City Clips*. Her spare time is devoted to perfecting her Polaroid emulsion transfer technique.

MIKE FUGER, owner of the Business of Photography, specializes in commercial work for manufacturing and business. His specialties include manufacturing operations, people at work, and micro/macro photography of small products for advertising. Fuger's clients include AT&T, American Hereford Association, Lockton Companies, Motorola, Progress Instruments, and United Way. He produced the Web sites www.photobiz.com and www.darkroom-on-line.com.

JACKIE GARVEY is a travel writer and photographer specializing in documenting indigenous tribes of third world countries. An employee of the Business of Photography, she is active in the Mid America Chapter of the American Society of Media Photographers. Her work has appeared in a number of publications, including a cover shot and feature article for *Transitions Abroad*. Additional selections of her photography can be viewed on the Internet at www.photobiz.com/cultures.

BOB GREENSPAN graduated from the University of Kansas with a bachelor of science degree in photojournalism. Through his studio, Bob Greenspan Photography, he specializes in architectural, small product, and stock images.

JAMES HOFFMAN graduated from the University of Kansas with a bachelor of science degree in journal-ism. He specializes in editorial illustration and is the owner of James Hoffman Photography. His clients include Yellow Freight Systems, Farmland Industries, Utilicorp United, the Learning Exchange, and the American Business Women's Association. Hoffman devotes his spare time to traveling, gourmet cooking, and raising his three children.

SCOTT R. INDERMAUR is a professional photographer who specializes in location, corporate, commercial, and editorial photography. He received a degree in photojournalism from Northern Arizona University and owns Scott R. Indermaur Photography. He moved to the area in 1993.

ROY INMAN was born and bred in Kansas, receiving a bachelor of science degree in journalism from the University of Kansas and a master's degree in photojournalism from the University of Missouri, Columbia. He has been published in the *New York Times*, *Better Homes & Gardens*, *Ebony*, the *Los Angeles Times*, and *Today's Home-owner*. He has contributed to or photographed exclusively six regional calendars and 10 regional books. His subjects have included the Goodyear Blimp (which he's also flown); the USS *Enterprise*; and Presidents Harry S. Truman, John F. Kennedy, Lyndon Johnson, and Richard Nixon.

KENNETH M. JOHNSON of Rush Studio, Inc. enjoys photographing everyday objects and situations and manipulating the composition in order to produce simplistic yet aesthetically pleasing images. Serving a client list that includes Sprint, Applebee's, Hallmark Cards, IBM, H&R Block, and Wal-Mart, Johnson has received a Mobius Award, a Cleveland ADDY, and several Omnis.

KIRK KIBLER is employed by Natural Reflections Photography. His fields of study include sports, action, and commercial photography. Kibler's clientele includes the Kansas City Blades hockey club, Kansas City Attack indoor soccer

© SUZANNE ROBINSON

team, International Hockey League, and Norman James International Corporation. Kibler is also an avid scuba diver and underwater photographer.

ED LALLO moved to Kansas City from Topeka in 1990. He attended the University of Kansas and counts among his specialties corporate, editorial, and location photography. His images have been used by DuPont, National Starch and Chemical Company, and *People* magazine.

ROBERT SCOTT MACINTOSH attended the University of Arizona, graduating with a bachelor of arts degree in creative writing. He is currently pursuing a master's degree in journalism at the University of Missouri. In his spare time, he enjoys traveling, learning about world cultures, music, and politics. Macintosh's coverage of Kansas City's jazz music has been published in *Down Beat*.

KATY MALLERY lives in Shawnee, Kansas. She earned a bachelor of science degree in photography from Central Missouri State University and currently devotes her time to the Katy Mallery Photography studio.

JOE MARTIN was named a Kansas PPA National Top Ten Photographer in 1997. A graduate of the Brooks Institute of Photography, he specializes in commercial and portrait images. His clients include Sprint, American Century, and Smith & Loveless, Inc.

BRUCE MATHEWS specializes in commercial photography, audiovisual and video production, and public relations. His images have been published in annual reports and industrial brochures, as well as publications such as *National Geographic Traveler* and *Audubon*. Mathews received a bachelor of science degree in business administration from Missouri Western State College.

MARK MCDONALD, originally from Kansas, moved to Kansas City in 1982. He received a bachelor of science degree in journalism from the University of Kansas. Through Mark McDonald Photography, he offers a variety of commercial photographs for marketing purposes,

and has worked for an assortment of publications.

MATTHEW L. MCFARLAND is a native Californian who relocated to Kansas City in 1994. He owns M Studios, which lists among its clients Architectural Details International, Ltd. and Hallmark Cards. McFarland graduated from Kansas City Art Institute, receiving a bachelor of fine arts degree. He credits the art institute with developing his conceptual and technical proficiency.

TERRY MCGRAW has lived in Kansas City for most of his life and graduated from Rockhurst College with a degree in economics. A self-taught photographer, McGraw specializes in architecture and architectural details. His images were included in the 1996 publication *Images of Kansas City*.

BEN EVERETT MERCER, a Kansas City native, graduated from Lincoln University with a bachelor's degree in education. He worked for the Kansas City Parks and Recreation Department for 30 years before retiring. A member of the Black Alliance of Artists and the Northeast Photographers Association, Mercer has had drawings and photographs displayed in shows throughout Kansas and Missouri. In 1993, he was honored by *Artist's Magazine* as a Top 200 Artist.

MIDWESTOCK, located in Kansas City, specializes in subjects that tend to epitomize the Midwest region and its people. The company's portfolio is constantly updated, and focuses on people, food, wildlife, agriculture, rural scenes, and nature/landscapes. Its images can be viewed on-line at www.midwestock.com.

MICHAEL MIHALEVICH has served as a photographer for Hallmark Cards, *The Kansas City Star*, and the U.S. Navy. He has been honored by the Advertising Club of New York Andy Awards, the Association of MultiImage Annual Awards, *Print Magazine* Annual Awards, and the Kansas City Advertising Club Omni Awards. A graduate of the University of Missouri, Mihalevich is also a commercially licensed pilot and a scoutmaster with the Boy Scouts of America.

M.J. HARDEN ASSOCIATES, INC. (MJH) has provided quality photogrammetric engineering services to Kansas City and the rest of the nation since 1956. Aerial photography by MJH provides the base for planimetric/topographic mapping and digital orthophotography. The company's extensive archives have been used by various businesses, including law offices, utility companies, real estate firms, and government agencies.

DALE MONAGHEN is currently employed by Lawrence Photographic. Originally from Dallas, he specializes in journalism, people, music events, and musicians. Monaghen has been published by Sipa Press, *Time*, and *Newsweek*.

DAVID MORRIS started his own business, David Morris Photography, in 1989. A 12-year veteran of the trade, Morris has amassed a clientele that includes Tyson, McDonald's, Cellular One, and the Bayer Corporation. His work has been featured in magazines, billboards, books, and galleries throughout the United States. Morris attributes his success to his philosophy of providing high quality, service, and value.

JOHN L. MUTRUX operates Mutrux & Associates/Photography, whose client list includes Exxon Corporation, Phillips Petroleum, Vectron International, and Holiday Inn. A graduate of Central Missouri State University with a bachelor of science degree in electronics technology, Mutrux specializes in advertising, conceptual/illustrative, and general commercial photography. His images can be viewed on-line at www.mutrux.com.

JULIE PARKS has been practicing photography since her childhood in New Orleans. After graduating from the University of Kansas with a bachelor's degree in photojournalism, Parks worked for a publishing company and a local photographer, honing her skills in fine-art Polaroid transfers and infrared imaging. Her favorite subjects are flowers, landscapes, and still lifes.

JOHN PERRYMAN, a native of Pratt, Kansas, has lived in the Kansas City area for 30 years. He received a bachelor of arts degree from the Brooks Institute of Photography, and has been employed by Hallmark Cards for 29 years.

SUSAN BARBARA PFANNMULLER is employed by Decisive Moments, where she specializes in photojournalism. She received a bachelor of science degree in elementary education from Kansas State University and is originally from Ohio.

ELI REICHMAN has been a freelance photographer for the past 10 years. His client list includes Anheuser-Busch, Ford Motor Company, Harley-Davidson, IBM, and Phillips 66. Reichman has been published in *Business Week*, *Forbes*, *Fortune*, *Sports Illustrated*, *Travel & Leisure*, and *Time Life*. A onetime staff photographer for the *Los Angeles Times*, *The Kansas City Star*, and the *Tulsa Tribune*, Reichman has won several silver and bronze Omni Awards through the Advertising Club of Kansas City.

JULIE FRAZIER ROBERTSON, originally from Malta Bend, Missouri, devotes much of her time to her company, Robertson Photography, where her client list represents a broad range of businesses from sportswear to pies, tractor trailer trucks to hospitals, security services to long-distance services, ball caps to jewelry, and engineering to packaging machines. Robertson enjoys traveling and meeting unique and interesting people, and finds inspiration and relaxation in small towns and rural communities.

TOM ROSTER resides in Mississippi, where he has lived and worked for more than 10 years. In addition to operating the Jackson, Mississippi-based Roster & Company Photography, Inc., he is represented by Black Star Photo Agency of New York. A freelance editorial and corporate photographer, he won the 1994 Photo of the Year Award from the Mississippi Press Association, which has honored him with some 20 other awards since 1982. Roster's clients include the *New York Times Magazine*, *USA Today*, *Inc.*, *London Sunday Times*, *Profil*, and *FDA Consumer*. His work can also be seen in Towery Publishing's *Jackson: The Good Life*.

V. CRAIG SANDS is a career photojournalist whose images have appeared in *National Geographic*, *Rolling Stone*, *Newsweek*, *Newsweek Japan*, the *New York Times*, the *London Times*, and *Kansas City* magazine. When not shooting, Sands can be found renovating his "money pit," gardening, and fine-tuning his skills on his mountain bike.

DEBBIE DOUGLASS SAUER received a bachelor of fine arts degree in photography from the University of Oregon. The Kansas City native enjoys photographing interesting people and places, and is in the process of publishing a book on her favorite subjects.

KEVIN SINK, a Kansas City native, received a bachelor's degree in psychology and a master's degree in physiology and cell biology from the University of Kansas. As the owner of Kevin Sink Photography, he focuses on large-format landscapes of the Midwest, the Pacific Northwest, and the Great Lakes region. Sink enjoys photographing locations uncontaminated by the presence of man.

MICHAEL SPILLERS was employed as a rehabilitation counselor before changing his occupation to photography. His studio, Photography for the Built Environment, focuses on architecture, interiors, lighting applications and design, and large-format landscapes. Spillers' clients include HKS architects, Hanrahan Meyers Architects, and Junk architects.

ROBERT D. STOUT enjoys photographing subjects ranging from buildings to people. His images have appeared in various books and brochures, and as the subject of several postcards. A freelance photographer, Stout is from Osawatomie, Kansas.

MARY S. WATKINS graduated from the University of Missouri with a bachelor's degree in education. Her photographs have appeared in publications for American Century, Country Club Plaza Merchants Association, Stenson Mag Law Firm, and Nelson-Atkins Museum of Art.

BEN WEDDLE, a graduate of the University of Missouri with a degree in photojournalism, serves a client list that includes Lee Jeans, GEAR for Sports, and Wal-Mart. Originally from St. Joseph, Missouri, Weddle moved to the Kansas City area in 1987.

DAN WHITE moved to the Kansas City area in 1981. Through White & Associates, he focuses on photographing people and places in black and white. A graduate of the University of Missouri, he received a bachelor's degree in journalism.

CHRIS WILBORN has followed in his father's footsteps through his work with Wilborn & Associates Photographers. Wilborn's company specializes in historic photographs of Kansas City, and has supplied these images for various projects around the world.

VIC WINTER owns and operates ICStars Astronomy, devoting his time to astrophotography. His images can be viewed on the ICStars Web site, located at www.icstars.com. Winter has won more than 70 awards from the National Press Photographers Association.

DONALD E. WOLF is the third generation of his family to live in the Kansas City area. He began his career as an aerial photographer in the navy. Wolf made seven trips to Croatia to photograph the Croatian and Serbian conflict, using the images to raise funds for Croatian orphanages.

HANK YOUNG established Young Company in Kansas City in 1971. He has photographed student life on the campuses of UCLA, Stanford, Princeton, and Harvard. Young also photographs corporate sponsorships and special customer events such as the Summer Olympics for AT&T, the Winter Olympics for Coca-Cola, and World Cup Soccer for Sprint. His images have appeared in *Newsweek*, *Sports Illustrated*, *Golf Digest*, and *Connoisseur*.

Other contributors to *Celebrating Greater Kansas City* include the Kansas City Art Institute, Kansas City Film Commission, J.C. Nichols Co., Lyric Opera of Kansas City, Missouri Repertory Theater, Kansas City Blades, and Kansas City Chiefs.